America Discovered

A Historical Atlas of North American Exploration

MAP 1.
This important summary of the state of geographical knowledge of North America was published in 1802 by London mapmaker Aaron Arrowsmith. It was the map that Meriwether Lewis and William Clark took with them when they embarked on their seminal trek across America to the Pacific, which they reached in 1805. The track of Alexander Mackenzie, who in 1793 became the first to reach the Pacific, is shown north of Vancouver Island. Arrowsmith, like others of his day, subscribed to the view that the Rocky Mountains were but a single chain with rivers whose headwaters were relatively close, thus providing an easy portage across them. Lewis and Clark were soon to be disabused of that concept.

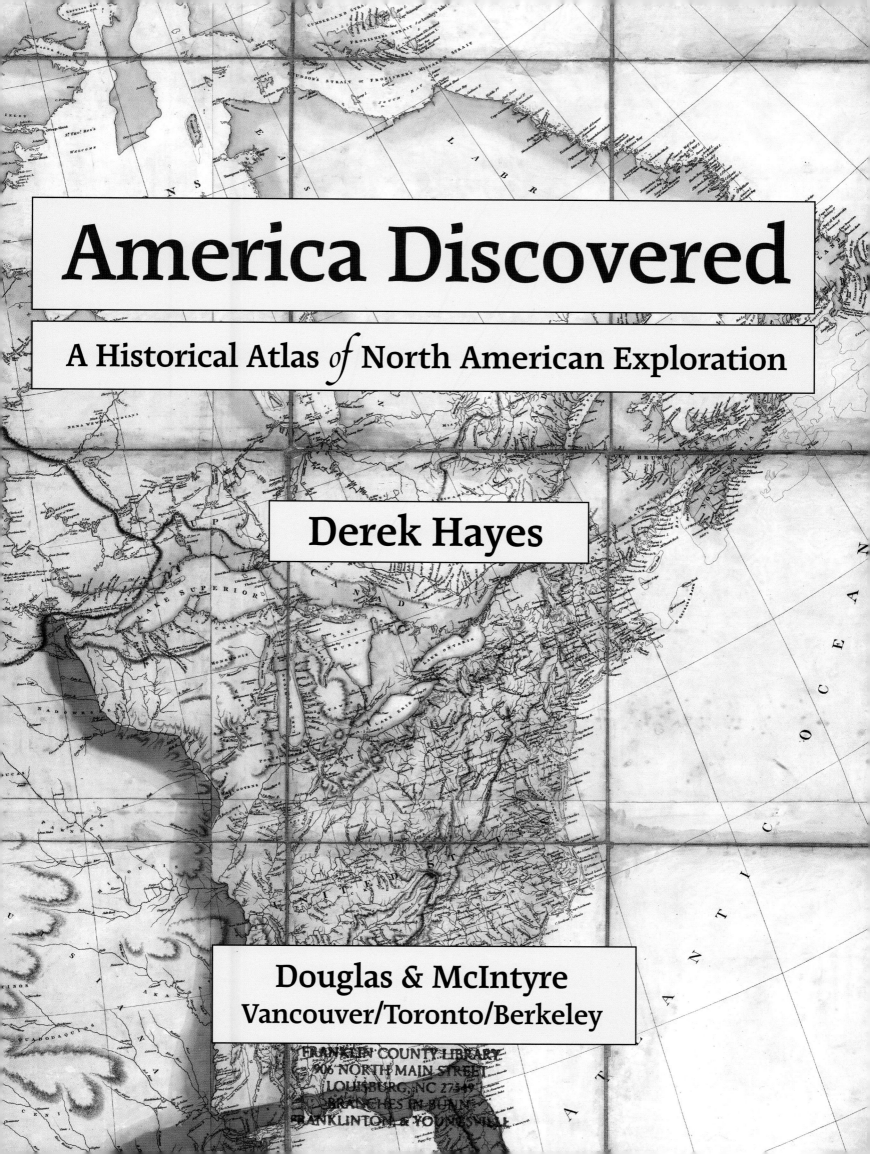

America Discovered

A Historical Atlas *of* North American Exploration

Derek Hayes

Douglas & McIntyre
Vancouver/Toronto/Berkeley

Douglas & McIntyre Ltd.
2323 Quebec Street, Suite 201
Vancouver, British Columbia, Canada V5T 4S7
www.douglas-mcintyre.com

**Library and Archives Canada
Cataloguing in Publication**

Hayes, Derek, 1947–
    America discovered : a historical atlas of
North American exploration / Derek Hayes.

Includes bibliographical references and index.
ISBN 1-55365-049-2

    1. United States—Discovery and explora-
tion—Maps. 2. America—Discovery and
exploration—Maps. 3. Canada—Discovery and
exploration—Maps. 4. United States—Historical geography—Maps. 5. Canada—Historical
geography—Maps. I. Title

G1106.S12H39 2004   911'.73   C2004-903290-9

Library of Congress information available
on request

Design and layout by Derek Hayes
Copyediting by Naomi Pauls
Jacket design by Peter Cocking
Printed and bound in China by C & C Offset
Printed on acid-free paper
Distributed in the United States by
Publishers Group West

We gratefully acknowledge the financial
support of the Canada Council for the Arts,
the British Columbia Arts Council, and the
Government of Canada through the Book
Publishing Industry Development Program
(BPIDP) for our publishing activities.

To contact the author:
www.derekhayes.ca
derek@derekhayes.ca

Image *right*: *The Grand Canyon*, by William
Holmes, from *Tertiary History of the Grand
Cañon District*, by Clarence Dutton, 1882.

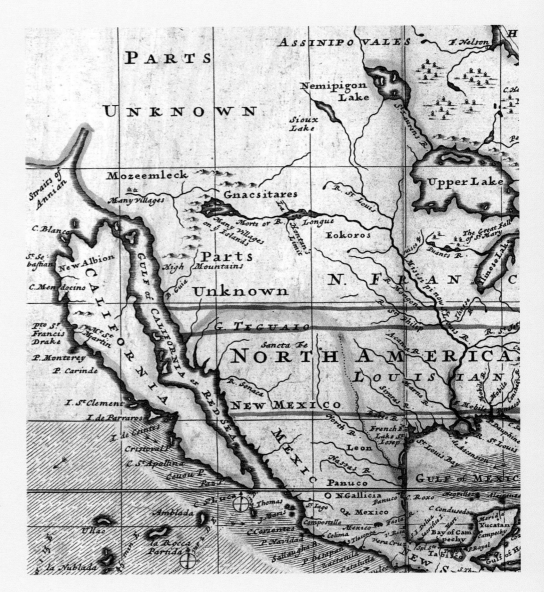

MAP 2.
Part of a map of North America published by British mapmaker Herman Moll in 1719. California is
still shown as the island it was thought to be until the explorations of Eusebio Kino in 1700–1702 (see
page 84) showed that Baja California was a mainland peninsula and Alta California also part of the
mainland. Much of the Northwest is shown as *Parts Unknown,* and the *Straits of Annian,* supposed
to be the western entrance to the Northwest Passage, are at top left. The red lines define the supposed western extensions of Virginia and Carolina. Their crown grants extended to the Pacific even
though no one knew where that was at the time.

Acknowledgments

A book such as this could not have been created without the assistance and cooperation of the
many institutions and individuals who hold the maps that have been reproduced. I should like to
thank Edward Redmond of the Geography and Map Division of the Library of Congress; Nicolas
Texier of the Service historique de la marine, Vincennes, France; Louis Cardinal and Jeffrey Murray
of the National Archives of Canada (Library and Archives of Canada); and also David Rumsey, of
Cartography Associates, for permission to use some of the maps in his collection. The following
other institutions provided maps: British Library; The National Archives (U.K.); the National Archives (U.S.); Hudson's Bay Company Archives, Winnipeg; Bibliothèque national de France; Archives
nationales, Centre des Archives d'Outre-Mer, Aix-en-Provence, France; New York Public Library;
Archives de la Compagnie de Jésus, Saint-Jérôme, Québec; British Museum; Archivo General des In-
dias, Seville, Spain; Museo Naval, Madrid; Hispanic Society of America, New York; Beinecke Library,
Yale University; American Philosophical Society, Philadelphia; Missouri Historical Society, St. Louis.
Thanks also to Naomi Pauls for her many corrections and suggestions for improvement.

Contents

A Continent Revealed

This book seeks to show and explain the way in which the continent of North America slowly appeared on the map of the world, using as illustrations contemporary maps made by explorers or by others to share this new knowledge. It necessarily focuses on those I have first referred to as Europeans, and later as Euro-Americans, as opposed to the indigenous peoples, who, while providing an invaluable contribution to geographical knowledge and most certainly being aware of the geography of their own backyard, rarely had the means to record their knowledge for posterity. The native maps that have survived are usually those that were copied onto paper by explorers or fur traders.

The line between explorer and trader, adventurer and gold-seeker is often somewhat blurred. But men had to have motivation for their explorations; although the desire to know what was over the next hill, beyond the next mountain range, or farther up the river was a motivator in a local sense, it was the desire to find wealth, expand trade, and find new routes for commerce that initiated their explorations, and drew others to invest in their venture in the hope of a return for their speculation. Without that investment, little exploration would have occurred.

There were several general types of explorer. There were those seeking their fortunes through discovery of a source of wealth—gold, or spices, or a passage to those riches, or merely land and perhaps people that could be exploited. Some were driven by a religious fervor to seek out the heathen and convert them to their true religion; some explored to find a place to colonize or settle, and then to supply such a settlement with food or raw materials to survive. There were those commanded in a military situation to investigate a threat or perceived threat and later those, often but not always also military, ordered to find routes for wagon roads and railroads, and to explore and record their explorations so others could follow them; these were the surveying explorers. There were

Map 3.
Part of a large map of North and South America drawn by Diego Gutiér-rez in 1562. The east coast of North America is imperfectly known, and the interior is covered by an allegorical Victoria to fill up space about which nothing was known. The Atlantic is full of imaginary creatures, and Neptune rides his carriage across the waves.

also a few pleasure explorers, those who explored for the sheer joy of discovery, or the scientific value in it.

But whatever their individual motivations, they all sought out the unknown—at least what to them was unknown—pointing their ships, their horses, their wagons, their canoes or even their feet bravely into a usually western wilderness.

Sometimes there are multiple roles, so we may sometimes find ourselves talking about those founding colonies or surveying a known region for a specific route for a railroad, for example. But they are all reaching into one unknown or another and adding geographical knowledge to the map; they were all thus explorers. Only the most significant explorations could be covered in a book of this scope; there were in the course of history probably thousands of individual explorations that passed unnoticed or unrecorded. When John Wesley Powell made his famous—and much recorded—journey down the Colorado in 1869, for instance, he found the name "D. Julien, 3 Mai, 1836" cut into the rock in an inaccessible canyon. So Powell was not the first past that spot for sure, yet we know nothing of poor Julien.

For the purposes of this book, North America is generally defined as the parts of the continent now covered by the United States and by Canada, with a few incursions into Mexico.

Apart from archives and libraries in the United States and Canada, the maps have been drawn from the countries that at one time or another had a colonizing interest in the continent: Spain, France, Britain, Russia, and, more fleetingly, Denmark, Portugal, and Norway. Of these countries, only France directly retains any territory on the continent today, and only small islands at that. Some of the French and British claims, some of the Spanish, and all of the Russian passed to the United States; the rest of the British and French claims passed to Canada, as did the never tested Norwegian claim; and the rest of New Spain became Mexico.

MAP 4.
A summary map of the routes of the "principal" explorers in the area that is now the contiguous United States, published in 1907. George Wheeler's 1873 summary map (MAP 258, page 196) is also useful for following the tracks of explorers.

MAP OF THE UNITED STATES
SHOWING
ROUTES OF THE PRINCIPAL EXPLORERS
FROM 1501 TO 1844
Whose work had an important bearing on the settlement of the country and the fixing of its successive boundaries
Copied from map prepared by
Frank Bond, of the General Land Office,
in 1907

Beginnings

The first explorers of the North American continent were those who migrated in search of new hunting grounds from Eastern Siberia. They came across the land bridge of the Bering Strait formed when so much water was locked into the ice sheets or perhaps, according to recent research, around the great curve of the continental coasts in short hops using skin-covered boats. By about 38,000 years ago North America was populated by humans as far south as Mexico. Then began a process of dispersion as individual groups looked for new hunting grounds and, later, a new place to plant their crops. These initial explorations by native peoples are easy to overlook, despite their significance, simply because there is no documentation other than that painstakingly extracted from the earth by archeologists.

Since this is a book about maps, we necessarily start with those that have survived, but we should remember that they do not represent a true beginning but merely the start of surviving documentation.

Chinese and Japanese sailors likely arrived on the west coast of North America as long ago as 200 B.C., but they were there involuntarily, victims of shipwreck, and so cannot be considered explorers in the sense normally meant. Possibly the celebrated Irish monk Saint Brendan made it to the shores of America in a skin-clad boat in the sixth century, but it is much more likely that his Terra Repromissionis Sanctorum—the "Land Promised to the Saints"—was no farther west than Iceland.

This unlikely scene is from a twelfth-century rendering of the Saint Brendan saga and shows the saint celebrating Mass on the back of a cooperative whale in mid-Atlantic. In 1976–77 Tim Severin sailed from Ireland to Newfoundland in a skin-covered boat such as Brendan might have used and made it—just. But, of course, the fact that something is possible does not mean it actually occurred.

The first archeologically proven European explorers of the New World were the Norse—Viking warriors in open boats sailing from settlements in Greenland. A Norse settlement was established at the beginning of the eleventh century at L'Anse aux Meadows, at the tip of the Northern Peninsula of Newfoundland. The sagas tell us of Leif Eiriksson (often spelled Ericsson), who about 1001 retraced a voyage by Bjarni Herjolfsson, who in 985 or 986 had been blown westwards by a storm to a forested land, generally thought to have been the coast of Labrador, then a forest. Eiriksson then continued southwards to a land he named Vinland. Where exactly this might have been is unknown, but it is likely somewhere in Newfoundland, perhaps even L'Anse aux Meadows. Whether "Vin" meant grapes or not has been discussed heatedly by historians, but we do know that Jacques Cartier found grapes on the shores of the St. Lawrence five hundred years later and so it is possible that their range was extended at that time. Or L'Anse aux Meadows could have been a collecting place. At any rate, the Norse settlement ultimately proved unviable, lasting only a few years at most.

After the Norse, but before Columbus, there are several claims that explorers came to North America from Europe, none of which have ever been proven. Nicholas of Lynn, another monk, was said to have sailed to Labrador and Nova Scotia about 1360. This voyage apparently was documented at one time, in a book Nicholas wrote, *De Inventio Fortunata*, "The Discovery of the Fortunate Isles," a copy of which was presented to the English king, Edward III. A map copied from this work by a Flemish author named Jacob Cnoyen eventually was used by the famous mapmaker Gerard Mercator as the basis for a map of the Arctic. Nevertheless, the geography shown on that map could have been derived from Aristotle.

Other apocryphal voyages include that of Prince Henry Sinclair in 1380, to Nova Scotia, and the second discovery of America has been attributed by some to a Polish mariner named Johannes Scolvus Polonus, in 1476. João Vaz Corte-Real, father of Gaspar and Michael

MAP 5 (*left*) and MAP 6 (*right, top*). These two maps were made in the early seventeenth century when the Danish king sent out several expeditions to west Greenland to determine whether any of his subjects still survived in that harsh land and, incidentally, to search for silver and gold and reassert Danish sovereignty. Interestingly enough he employed English sailors for the task, since, following the English voyages to Davis Strait in the late sixteenth century, they were the only ones with the navigational knowledge required. The maps are said to be copies of earlier Norse maps, an unlikely claim since the Norse are known not to have made maps, using landmarks on coasts to sail by. Nevertheless the maps were probably drawn from written accounts, and they do display the Norse conception of the North Atlantic, with continuous land (really, of course, pack ice) connecting Northern Europe to Greenland and to North America. The problem is that the maps were drawn when more was known about America, and hence the mapmakers may have added additional information to them. MAP 6 (*right*), drawn by Icelander Jón Gudmonson in 1640, shows *America pars* (part of America) on a landmass labeled *Terra florida*. MAP 5 (*left*), a 1670 copy of a map drawn in 1590 (not 1570 as on the cartouche), was originally drawn by Sigurdur Stefánsson, another Icelander, and shows *Helleland,* said to be Eiriksson's first landfall (probably Baffin Island) and *Markland* (Labrador), as well as the *Promontorium Winlandiæ,* Vinland, which looks strikingly like Newfoundland's Northern Peninsula.

MAP 7 (*right*).
This is the famous Vinland Map, which the balance of academic opinion now considers a fake. The island to the left is Vinland, which if it were genuine would be the first representation—1440—of any part of America on a map. If it is a fake, it is a remarkably clever deception. Its authenticity has been debated since it was revealed to the world by Yale University in 1965.

Corte-Real (see page 12), is claimed by some Portuguese historians as the real discoverer of America. He is said to have reached Newfoundland in 1472, with Scolvus as his pilot.

These accounts were not necessarily hoaxes, but flights of fancy in an age when it was often genuinely difficult to tell where you were when at sea, especially longitudinally. And they hail from a time when historical accuracy and scientific method were largely undeveloped.

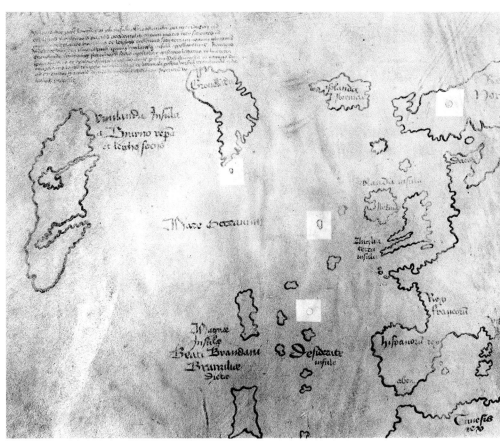

A New World Found

No book on North American exploration would seem complete without mention of the pioneering Christopher Columbus, yet he never actually reached the mainland of North America, just offshore islands and South America.

By Columbus's time, many educated Europeans were quite aware that the Earth was round; much earlier works of Ptolemy and others also confirmed this. And if the world was round, surely it must be possible to sail in either direction. In 1475 Columbus was corresponding with a Florentine physician named Paolo dal Pozzo Toscanelli who had developed a theory that there must be a short route to the East west across the Atlantic.

While living in the Madeira Islands around 1480, Columbus would have heard tales of lands to the west. There were stories of apparently Oriental-looking persons both dead and alive who had from time to time washed up on the Atlantic shores of Europe—presumably native people from the east coast of North America who had come to grief while on coastal sorties. Driftwood also washed up on European shores. Marco Polo's account of his considerable and famous travels to China included an East Asian coastline that was about 30° farther to the east that it really was.

Putting together all the information he could find, Columbus decided that not only could he reach the Indies by sailing west rather than east, but that the distance would be such that it would take him less than twenty-eight days. Famously unable to interest the Portuguese king in his ideas, Columbus moved to Spain in 1485, where it still took him another seven years to pique the interest of King Ferdinand and Queen Isabella enough that they agreed to back his venture.

Following his notion of the supposed distance, the supplies he took with him were designed to last not much more than twenty-eight days. Nevertheless, it must have taken a great deal of nerve to sail out away from the sight of land into a completely unknown ocean, without benefit of the relatively short hops between land taken by the Norse farther north five centuries before.

Columbus considered that the distance to the Indies by a westward route would be about the same as it actually is from Spain to the Bahamas. Thus when he made his landfall at the island he called San Salvador—Holy Savior (either Watling [Guanahani] Island or, according to some historians, Samana Cay nearby)—it was clear to him where he was. His calculations had proven correct, he thought. That he had in fact landed in a "new world," a hitherto unsuspected continent, was never really acknowledged by Columbus to his dying day, although after his third voyage, to South America in 1498, he did write of being in an "other world."

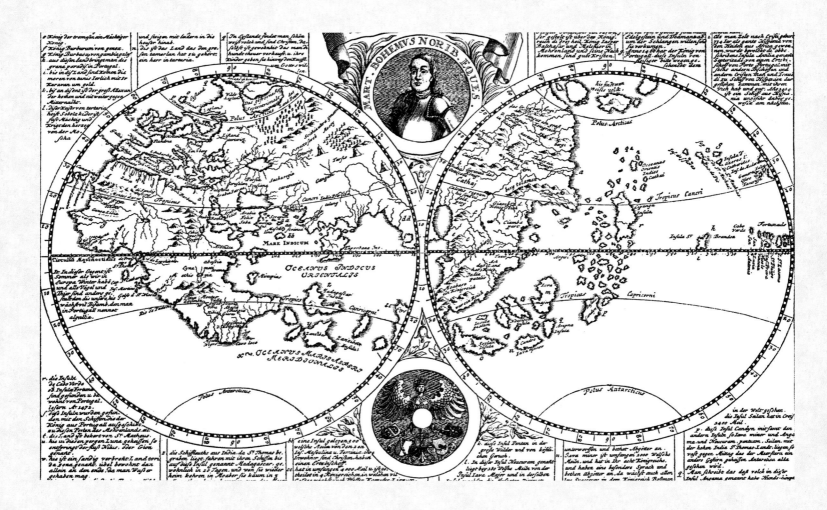

Columbus's three little ships, the *Niña, Pinta,* and *Santa María,* had left the harbor of San Sebastián, on the island of Gomera, the westernmost of the Canary Islands and the farthest outpost of Spain, on 6 September 1492 and arrived at a landfall in the Bahamas on 12 October after a thirty-four-day voyage.

One of the first acts of our exploring pioneer Columbus was one that would be followed by many from various European countries in the years to come: he claimed his discovery for his king and queen, utterly disregarding the fact that he could see that the land was occupied, in this case by what he called "naked people" whom he surely expected would be vassals of the Great Khan. It was considered that a Christian state had preemptive rights over any non-Christian one in any case. Europeans thereafter claimed territory for their sovereigns and imposed their religious beliefs on vast regions of the new continent. In accordance with his belief that he had reached the Indies, he referred to the inhabitants as "Indians," a name for the aboriginal people of North America that stuck.

Columbus may not have actually reached the North American mainland, but he was the first in a centuries-long process of European exploration and then colonization and settlement that ultimately would transform the continent.

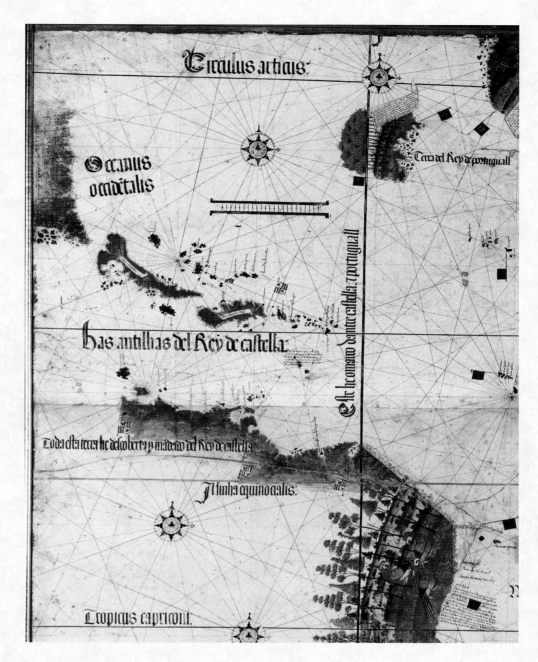

MAP 8 (*left*).
A map of the world as it appeared on the Martin Behaim globe in 1492, drawn before Columbus returned. This is a 1730 copy. No North American continent interrupts a voyage west to Asia. This was Columbus's conception of the world when he first sailed westwards .

MAP 9 (*right, top*).
Part of a world map drawn in 1502. The coast of South America is better defined than any North American counterpart, but the Caribbean islands of Hispaniola (now Haiti and the Dominican Republic) and Cuba are shown, together with what must be Florida, although this is a considerable mystery, as no known expedition to Florida had taken place at this time. It could possibly be a misplaced Yucatan Peninsula.

At *top left* is an image of Columbus from a 1594 map by Theodor De Bry.

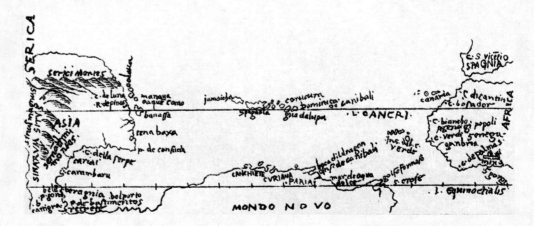

MAP 10.
This map, drawn by Columbus's brother Bartolommeo about 1503, shows the relationship of Europe to North America, marked *Asia*. Somehow *spagnola* (Hispaniola) and other Caribbean islands are shown in mid-Atlantic.

To the Shores of Cathay

The English king Henry VII had in 1488 turned down a proposal to sponsor Christopher Columbus's voyage to the west only to see him find what promised to be a land of immense wealth on behalf of the Spanish king. So when another Italian navigator, Giovanni Caboto, came knocking in 1496 with a proposal to sail a course farther to the north than Columbus, it was accepted rather readily.

In fact Caboto, who soon anglicized his name to John Cabot, was sponsored primarily by the merchants of Bristol, a west-coast English city then a major trade center. The merchants were keen to find an alternate source for the dried cod that made a major con-

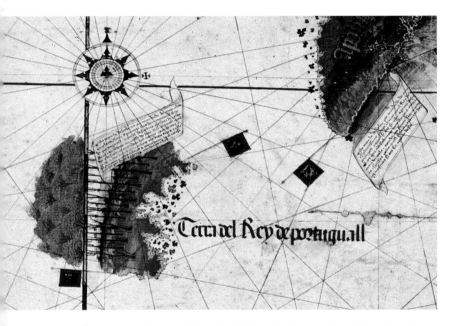

tribution to their coffers, for their existing trade with Iceland was threatened by a trade war with their rivals in the Hanseatic League, a cartel of Baltic-port merchants. Cod at this time was a very significant commodity since the Church mandated that one-third of the days in a year had to be meatless.

It is now thought that Cabot first sailed west in 1496; there is a reference to a first voyage that year in a likely authentic letter found in a Spanish archive in 1955. But the voyage for which Cabot is famous took place the following year. Cabot set sail from Bristol in his ship the *Matthew* in May 1497 and made a North American landfall on 24 June. Where he made that landfall is still a matter of some speculation. The most accepted place is Cape Bonavista in Newfoundland (which was the site of an anniversary reenactment in 1997), but it could equally well have been Nova Scotia. Landing only briefly, Cabot did not encounter native people, but he did see signs of habitation.

The land was not promising, but the waters were. Cabot found them teeming with so many fish that they could be caught with but a weighted basket. It was great news for his financial backers, and within a few years an entirely new fishing industry arose based on Newfoundland's Grand Banks. King Henry was so pleased

that he awarded Cabot £10 from his privy purse "to hym that found the new isle."

Cabot thought he had reached an easternmost part of Asia, the "land of the Great Khan," as he put it. And so the following year he sailed again, this time with five ships and priests, a significant addition in that they could perform acts of possession for the English. Running into a fierce storm in mid-Atlantic, one ship returned to England, while the other four continued. And that was the last that was heard of John Cabot.

There is some evidence that Cabot may have reached Newfoundland once more, and yet further evidence that he may have sailed south along the east coast of North America. In 1500, when Gaspar Corte-Real found Newfoundland for the Portuguese, he kidnapped some native people and took them back to Portugal. Two of the natives had in their possession a broken sword hilt and two silver earrings apparently made in Venice. Since Cabot made no contact with natives on his 1497 voyage, this may show he reached there in 1498.

Juan de la Cosa, creator of MAP 13 (*right, bottom*), was a pilot with the Spanish explorer of the Caribbean, Alonso de Hojeda, in 1499. On his map, drawn in 1500, La Cosa showed the discoveries of Cabot merging with those of the Spanish explorers. It seems that the only way La Cosa could have obtained this information at that date is if he acquired it from Cabot. We also know that Hojeda, who was known for his brutality, was awarded a gift of land by his king in 1501 for his "stopping of the English." Since there was no other known English expedition in the region this early, it seems quite probable that the English who were "stopped" were those of Cabot's expedition. And if not Cabot, who? It is all very intriguing, and conclusive evidence one way or the other will likely never be found.

In 1499 the Portuguese began to sail to the west. In that year João Fernandes found Greenland, naming it Tiera de Lavrador because he was a *lavrador*, the Portuguese name for a small landowner. This name eventually migrated across Davis Strait to become Labrador.

In 1500 another Portuguese explorer, Gaspar Corte-Real, sailed west to a probable landfall in Newfoundland, and many maps of the early sixteenth century show Newfoundland as Terra de Corte-Real. In 1501 another expedition by Corte-Real was lost as it sailed southwards along the North American coast. A rescue voyage by his brother Miguel set out in 1502, but also never returned. Exploration of an unknown shore in small ships was clearly a hazardous occupation.

Map 11 (*left*).
This 1502 map shows an explored west coast of Newfoundland as the *Terra del Rey de portuguall,* the "Land of the King of Portugal," following claims by Gaspar Corte-Real.

Map 13 (*below*).
Spanish pilot Juan de la Cosa's map on an ox-hide drawn about 1500. The line of flags marks the discoveries of John Cabot. At the western end of the Caribbean (off the part of the map shown here), an image of Saint Christopher obscured the map, hedging La Cosa's bets about a passage to the Pacific.

Map 12 (*above*).
The early explorers, like Columbus, thought that they had reached an eastern part of Asia. This map, printed by Johann Ruysch in Rome in 1507 or 1508, illustrates the conception well. Europe is at far right, and the northernmost peninsula to Europe is Greenland, south of which is Newfoundland and perhaps also Nova Scotia, all at the eastern end of an arm of Asia, to the left and top. The Caribbean is open at its western end, thus allowing a passage to Cathay, the passage Cabot was likely aiming for on his last voyage, when the North American continent—and perhaps also the Spanish—so inconveniently got in his way.

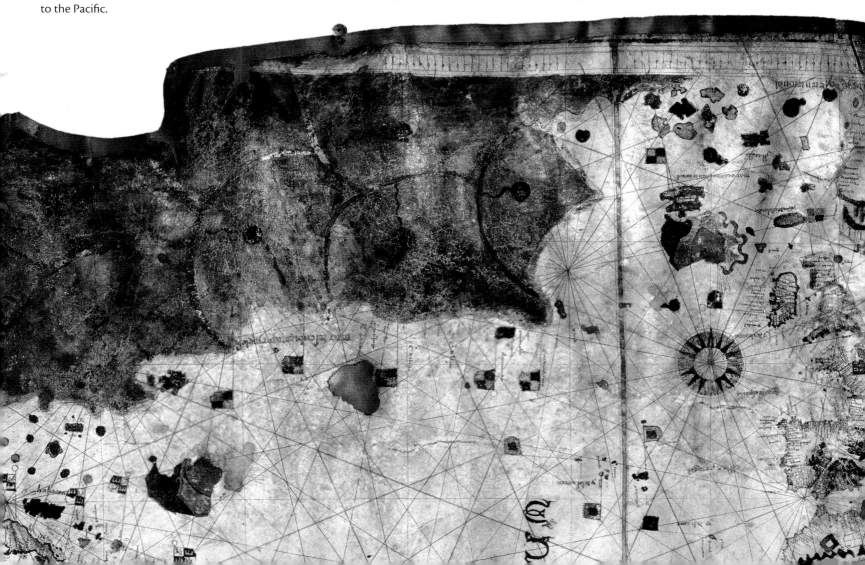

A Mainland Discovered

The Spanish explored and exploited their new-found islands in the Caribbean for two decades after Columbus found them, focusing otherwise on South America, the shape of which appeared on maps long before that of North America. Not until 1513 were the first attempts made to visit the North American mainland.

In March 1513 the governor of Puerto Rico, Ponce de León, who had once sailed with Columbus, obtained a royal license from his king to discover and occupy land he might find to the north. He was partly motivated by reports of an island called Bimini, which was reputed to contain the veritable fountain of youth. But the island he found was not a fountain of youth—though it would one day become a retirement center—but Florida. De León sighted an unknown coast on 2 April, during the Spanish festival of Pasqua

Florida, and named the island he thought he had discovered after it. The name was applied to the entire southeast for two centuries.

De León had found the east coast of Florida, and when he tried to sail south once more he discovered something else that he had not bargained for: a strong current flowing north. It was the Gulf Stream, and Spanish galleons would henceforth use it to carry the riches of the New World back to the Old. Turning north to explore the west coast of the Florida peninsula he was attacked twice by fleets of warlike natives in canoes, and landings were attempted only at great risk. De León sailed back to Puerto Rico after realizing that he would need many more resources if he wanted to colonize the place. It was not until 1521 that de León made it back, this time with two hundred and fifty men. He tried to set up a settlement in

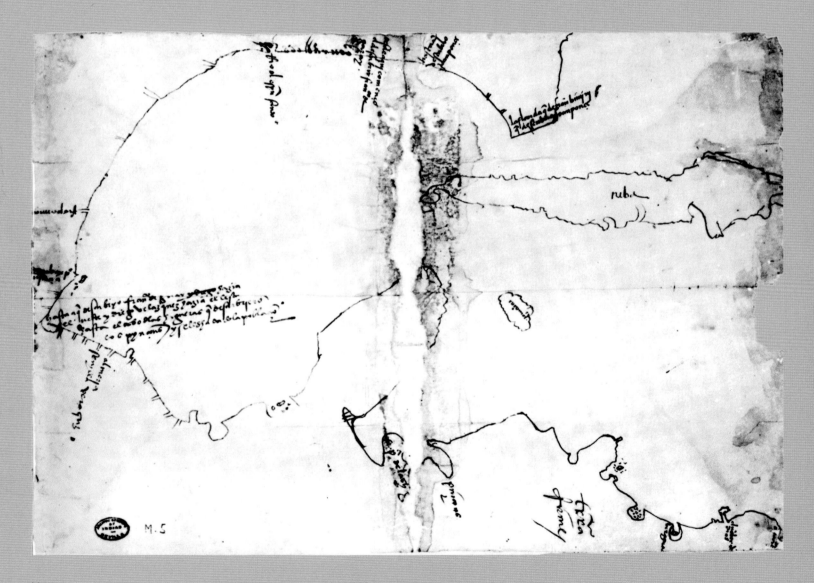

MAP 14.
Alonzo Alvarez de Pineda's map of 1519. This was the first map to more or less correctly show the outline of the Gulf of Mexico, the northern shores of which were mapped personally by him. The map was attached to the royal grant of land to Francisco de Garay in 1521. Pineda was the first to determine that Florida was a peninsula joined by land west to Mexico, rather than an island as had originally been assumed. This for the first time conclusively showed that there was no passage to the Pacific from the Gulf.

Map 15 (*left*).
Ponce de León and a map showing a native attack on the west coast of Florida, either at Charlotte Harbor or Tampa Bay. The illustration is from a Spanish history published in 1728.

Tampa Bay, only to be driven out by ferocious native attacks, one of which killed de León himself.

In 1519 Alonzo Alvarez de Pineda was sent to explore the Florida coastline by the governor of Jamaica, Francisco de Garay. Pineda followed the coast from Florida westwards, thus showing that it was not an island but part of the North American mainland. Pineda's chart (Map 14, *left*) was the first to show the entire outline of the Gulf of Mexico. Pineda's voyage also showed that the Gulf of Mexico was not open at its western end; there would be no strait to Cathay here. This map was attached to a royal grant of land given to Garay in 1521. When Garay attempted to claim his prize he was thwarted by the arch-conquistador Hernan Cortes, who did not want rivals

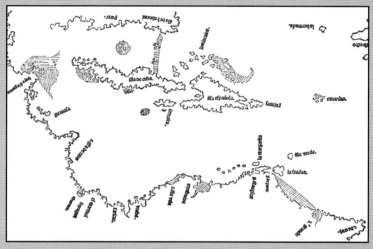

Map 16 (*above*).
Prior to Pineda's voyage in 1519, some maps of the Gulf of Mexico showed a possible opening at the western end, such as in this map by historian Peter Martyr, drawn in 1511.

in what he saw as his zone of influence. But for some time Spanish maps showed Garay's grant (see, for example, Map 20, *overleaf*).

The Spanish king was very liberal at this time with licenses to explore, wanting more territory to fall into the hands of a growing Spanish empire. In 1520 a license was granted to Lucas Vásquez de Ayllón, a Hispaniola judge, to search for new lands to the north. He dispatched Francisco Gordillo, who, the following year, enlisted the help of Pedro de Quexos, captain of a slave ship, who was no doubt interested because he might find new sources of slaves.

They found the mouth of a large river that they called the Rio de San Juan Bautista, which may have been Winyah Bay at the

Map 17.
Showing the same geography as the 1502 map on page 11 (Map 9), this example shows a detailed labeling of places along what appears to be the west coast of Florida yet, as with Map 9, is dated prior to any known expeditions to the North American mainland.

Map 18.
Part of a world map by Juan Vespucci, nephew of Amerigo, drawn in 1526. Coasts are not shown where Vespucci felt there was not enough information. On the American coast is *trá nueva de ayllón* (new land of Ayllón) marked with a Spanish flag. This map was the first to include information from Ayllón's explorations.

mouth of the Pee Dee River north of today's Charleston, South Carolina. After some exploration a hundred and fifty natives were taken on board Quexos's ship as slaves, contrary to Ayllón's orders; he later arranged for them to be returned.

Ayllón went to Spain to obtain permission to settle the new land they had found and in 1525 sent Quexos north once more to further explore the coast. He may have reached as far north as Chesapeake Bay on this voyage. Ayllón himself sailed north in June 1526 intending to found a colony. He took with him six hundred men, some women, and some African slaves, the first time such slaves had been transported to mainland America; it would not be the last.

After a false start somewhere on the South Carolina coast he ended up back at Winyah Bay, where a settlement named San Miguel de Gualdape was begun. But it was not a success. Ayllón

became ill and died, and the colonists gave up and sailed back to Hispaniola in the winter of 1527. Three-quarters of them had died on the inhospitable coast. Map 20 (*right*) shows the *Tiera de Ayllón* in the approximate position of South Carolina.

Independent of all this searching for places to establish colonies and exploit the land was a voyage commissioned by Charles V of Spain directly to find a way through it. Although Ferdinand Magellan had found for Spain the strait that bears his name at the extreme southerly tip of South America in 1520, it was widely thought that there might be another such strait farther north, which would hence provide a much easier route to the East. The French thought so too and in 1524 dispatched Giovanni Verrazano to find it first (see page 18). Pineda's recent voyage had squelched any notions that the western end of the Gulf of Mexico might reveal such a strait. In Spain, one Estévan Gomez, a Portuguese pilot in the service of Spain who had been with Magellan (though he deserted once he had reached the Pacific), argued for the existence of such a strait, and in September 1524, on the very heels of Verrazano, Gomez sailed to investigate. Right away Gomez found the most promising possible strait—the Gulf of St. Lawrence, which he penetrated as far as Prince

Edward Island, which he named St. John. (The island remained the French Île St-Jean until after taken over by the British in 1763.) But it was now February 1525 and Gomez decided not to risk the ice.

Looking all the time for the elusive break in the coastline that might prove to be a passage to the Indies, Gomez sailed southwards, particularly probing Penobscot Bay, Maine, a large bay full of islands that he thought promising. We do not know how far south he explored, but finding no passage, Gomez returned to Spain in August. The features Gomez drew on his maps showed up on maps for the rest of the century, especially his striking representation of Penobscot Bay (MAP 19).

MAP 19 (*above*).
Part of a map drawn in 1534 or 1535 showing the coast of Maine and Nova Scotia explored by Estévan Gomez in 1525, with Penobscot Bay and its many islands as a major feature, looking much like a possible strait to Cathay.

MAP 20 (*below*).
America as a Spanish province. This summary map made by Diogo Ribiero in 1529 shows as number of *tieras* (lands). On this portion, the southernmost is the *Tiera de Garay*, the royal grant to Francisco de Garay, the governor of Jamaica awarded it in 1521 but who never lived to see it. He was captured by his rival Cortes in 1523 as he attempted to occupy his lands. With typical Spanish overstatement they had been described in his royal grant as abounding in gold and with eighty towns on the banks of a mighty river. It was Garay who had sent out Pineda in 1519 to explore the Gulf Coast. Farther north is the *Tiera de Ayllon,* the land that Ayllon was to colonize from his base at Winyah Bay, South Carolina. The *Tiera de Estevā Gomez* is the region explored by Gomez, from the Gulf of St. Lawrence to an undetermined point farther down the coast. Penobscot Bay is the major coastal feature. *Tiera Nova de Cortereal,* the only Portuguese claim shown on the map, is Newfoundland.

Foundations of a French Empire

The French had been excluded from the Pope's 1494 division of the New World into Portuguese and Spanish domains at Tordesillas, and had been kept busy in Europe fighting wars at the beginning of the sixteenth century. With the reign of François I, which began in 1515, France became more interested in seaborne trade. The seafaring province of Brittany was added to the realm of the French crown through his marriage, and French eyes were cast at the apparent blank on the map between the English discoveries of Newfoundland and the Spanish of Florida. If a passage to Cathay could be found here, the freight on silk would be much lowered. But who to send to explore?

The Spanish had found Columbus, the English Cabot, both from Italy, and so French merchants, allied to Florentine bankers, turned to another Italian navigator, the Florentine Giovanni Verrazano. In 1523 Verrazano received a commission from the king to search westwards for a strait to Cathay.

Verrazano sailed from the Portuguese Madeira Islands in January 1524 in his ship *La Dauphine.* Approaching the American coast he barely survived a massive storm. A few days later "there appeared to us," he wrote, "a new land never before seen by anyone, ancient or modern." It was the coast near Cape Fear, at about 34° N. From here he sailed southwards, looking for a harbor in which to rest. Not finding one, and not wishing to encroach on what he considered Spanish territory, he turned north. He saw that there were inhabitants on the shore and had several friendly encounters. The new land had indeed been seen before.

North of Cape Fear there is a string of narrow offshore islands created from sandbanks. North and south of Cape Hatteras these islands are far from land, and it was here, likely just south of the cape, that Verrazano made the mistake that made him famous. Looking over the narrow islands to Pamlico Sound beyond, and not being able to see the low-lying mainland coast twenty miles distant, he decided that he had found the "oriental sea," the one, he wrote later, "without doubt which goes about the extremity of India, China, and Cathay." This great gulf is shown on his brother Girolamo's map (MAP 22, *right*), the surviving map of the expedition. Since these words were written on his return, and since he perhaps did not want to disappoint his financial backers, who after all had sent him to look for a strait, it is possible that Verrazano decided to make this "mistake," so as not to have failed in his mission. No one really knows if Verrazano really thought he had found the eastern sea. At any rate, no usable entrance to Pamlico Sound was found and he continued to sail northwards.

Opposite Albemarle Sound at about Kitty Hawk (site of the Wright brothers' first flight nearly four hundred years later), Verrazano, delighting in its sublime beauty, named the place Arcadia, after the philosopher Virgil's ideal landscape. Unlike most of Verrazano's names, this one survived, but not in that place. It was gradually moved northwards by mapmakers and became Acadia, the French name for what is now Nova Scotia.

Considering that he was supposed to be looking for a strait, it is perhaps surprising that Verrazano missed the entrance to Chesapeake Bay, an eleven-mile-wide opening. But such were the vagaries of weather and visibility that he did. Verrazano eventually found his harbor farther north still, at New York, where he anchored on 17 April. To this day the entrance to New York Harbor is the Verrazano Narrows. It was, he wrote, "a very agreeable situation located within two small prominent hills, in the midst of which flowed to the sea a very great river"—the Hudson River.

Now sailing eastwards, following the trend of the coastline, Verrazano came upon an island off the tip of Long Island, the shape of which reminded him of Rhodes. He named it Luisa after the French king's mother, but later, in 1637, the name *Rhode* was attributed to an island in nearby Narragansett Bay by the founder of an English colony there, Roger Williams. Thus did Verrazano inadvertently name one of the states, Rhode Island.

La Dauphine was anchored for fifteen days in Newport Harbor, during which time the crew explored inland as far as Pawtucket. Avoiding many shoals, Verrazano rounded Cape Cod and sailed northwards, along the Maine and Nova Scotia coasts as far as Cape Breton, which is shown on his map. At this point, running low on provisions, Verrazano sailed back to France, arriving in Dieppe on 8 July. It had

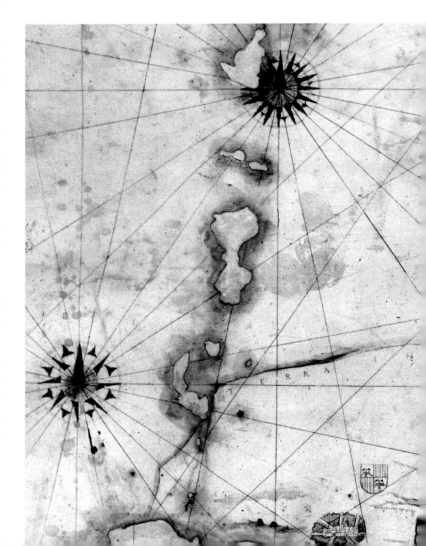

been a relatively quick reconnaissance, but it laid the foundation for a French empire in America. Verrazano, however, did not live much longer. Four years later, on another exploration, this time in the Caribbean, he was attacked and killed by cannibals.

MAP 21 (*right*).
Verrazano's famous "oriental sea" showed up on some maps in various forms during the sixteenth century. This beautifully bizarre example was drawn by Michael Lok, a promoter of a Northwest Passage, in 1582, following the voyages of Martin Frobisher, which he financed and which ruined him. The *Mare de Verrazano 1524* is well shown. This map also notes the presence of Sir Francis Drake on the west coast of America (see page 38) with the words *Anglorum* [English] *1580* [actually 1579].

MAP 22 (*below*).
Girolamo Verrazano's map of his brother Giovanni's 1524 explorations along the east coast of North America, drawn in 1529. The "Sea of Verrazano" arcs away from a small gap in the North Carolina coast. The entire region to the north is *Nova Gallia*—New Gaul, New France. This was the first French claim to America, later to be restricted to what is now eastern Canada before spreading south down the Mississippi in the wake of La Salle (see page 75). The two coastal indentations to the northwest are Cabot Strait and the Strait of Belle Isle, defining the south and north of Newfoundland, here *Terra Nova*. Two small parallel lines between the middle black flag and the westernmost one likely mark the position of New York Harbour—Verrazano Narrows, and east of that the island *Luisa* is shown enclosed in a little triangle below the middle flag. This is the island that reminded Verrazano of Rhodes and which eventually gave its name to Rhode Island. Farther to the east a sandbank is marked at the coastline's change of direction, which is presumably Cape Cod. The ship at bottom right is thought to be Verrazano's *La Dauphine*.

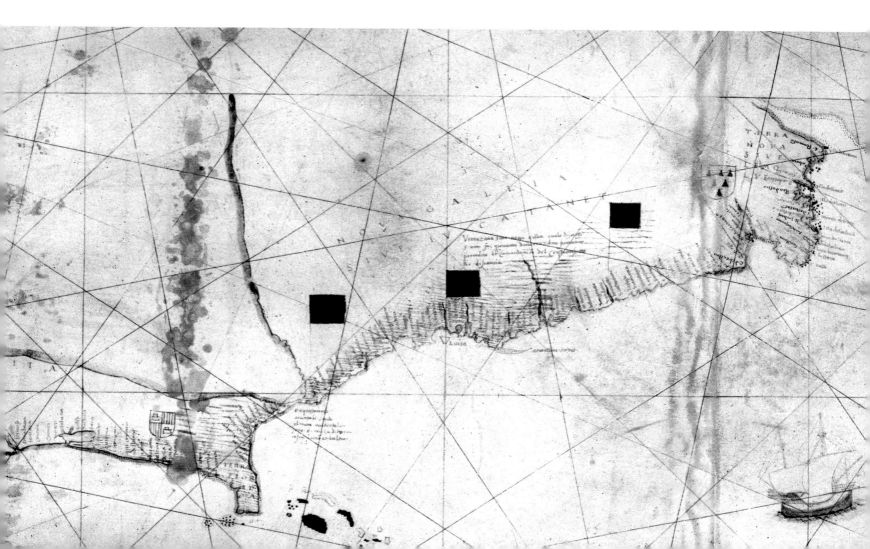

Wanderings in the Wilderness

In April 1536 a small group of Spanish slave hunters in Sinaloa, then the most northerly part of Spanish influence in New Spain (Mexico), came upon a sight they could hardly believe. Three naked Spaniards and a Moroccan stumbled out of the desert accompanied by a horde of Indians, who were escorting them believing them to be gods. And what a story they had to tell. They had crossed the continent from Florida, the last survivors of a major Spanish expedition eight years before.

The conquest of Mexico—now New Spain—by Hernan Cortés in 1519 had encouraged other Spanish adventurers to seek their fortunes elsewhere, south, in Peru, and north, in the new land called Florida, which at the time encompassed, in a very undefined way, all of what is now northern Mexico and the southern United States.

On one such expedition, Pánfilo de Narváez, who had managed to get himself named governor of this huge territory, brought an army of four hundred conquistadors to Tampa Bay, on the west coast of the Florida peninsula, in April 1528. Accompanying the expedition as an agent of the king and Narváez's second-in-command was Alvar Núñez Cabeza de Vaca. Almost immediately they had the notion that the gold they sought was to the north, and so off they went. Because Narváez thought he was still quite close to the western end of the Gulf of Mexico, he dismissed his ships. It was a fatal mistake.

Soon they ran into Indians who were fierce and aggressive, and their numbers dwindled. By the time they had reached the Apalachicola River (in the Florida panhandle just west of today's Tallahassee) the expedition was in dreadful shape and fearing for their lives. Somehow the 242 of them still alive cobbled together five boats and, thinking Mexico was not far off, coasted westwards along the Gulf shore. A promontory was rounded that proved to be the mouth of a very large river, for the current swept them away from

the coast. But it did have one benefit; they were able to obtain fresh water from the sea. It was, of course, the mouth of the Mississippi.

After a storm, the five boats were shipwrecked. Cabeza de Vaca found himself on Galveston Island. Eighty men had survived at this point, and the Indians were friendly though impoverished and were not able to give much help. Soon many more were dead.

In the six years between 1528 and 1534 Cabeza de Vaca and four others lived as slaves of several Indian tribes that lived in the region between today's Houston and Austin, Texas. At times Cabeza de Vaca ventured farther afield, reporting seeing the buffalo; some accounts state that he got as far as Oklahoma.

The tribes used to meet once a year during the one season when there was enough for everyone to eat. This was when the opuntia (prickly pear cactus) was ripe. At one such gathering Cabeza de Vaca and three others, including the Moroccan, Estéban, met up after being separated in slavery for many years, and they made plans to escape. In fall 1534 they fled, going first southwards along the Gulf Coast in hopes of making for Santisteban del Puerto (now Tampico), a Spanish settlement that had been established in 1523 on the Rio Pánuco north of Veracruz. It is a measure of their hopeless sense of where they were that they turned up the valley of the Colorado River of Texas away from the coast, on a trek that was to add thousands of miles to their journey. The purpose, wrote Cabeza de Vaca, was to avoid the cruel tribes of the coast and travel towards the sunset, surely the direction of the South Sea where they would find their salvation.

By the fall of 1535 they were well up the Rio Grande, where they turned southwest towards the Gulf of California. Fortunately

for them, the tribes of the interior were a great deal more friendly than those of the coast, often treating them as though they were gods miraculously appeared to heal or otherwise provide. Estéban's blackness also helped in this regard; none like him had ever been seen before. The Indians provided for Cabeza de Vaca and the other three, sometimes showering them with gifts and often accompanying the group as throngs of hangers-on cum worshippers. Thus it was in April 1536 when they chanced upon the Spanish slave hunters, who at least knew more or less where they were.

By July Cabeza de Vaca was in Mexico City, telling his incredible story to a new viceroy, Antonio de Medoza. Some of the gifts Cabeza de Vaca brought back with him included stones thought to be emeralds, corals and turquoises, enough to convince the viceroy that a new Peru had been found to the north. The stones came, according to Cabeza de Vaca's information, from high mountains to the north, where there were cities with large houses.

But here was a basic problem in communication. The groups of mud huts that the natives told Cabeza de Vaca about were cities of

MAP 23.
This map of the southern part of North America is almost contemporary with Núñez Cabeza de Vaca. It was drawn in 1544. There is a wealth of names along the coast but almost nothing shown inland. The newly discovered Sea of Cortes—the Gulf of California—is for some unknown reason shown like the Red Sea often was on maps of this time—colored red. The Baja California peninsula had been first mapped only nine years before (MAP 27, page 24).

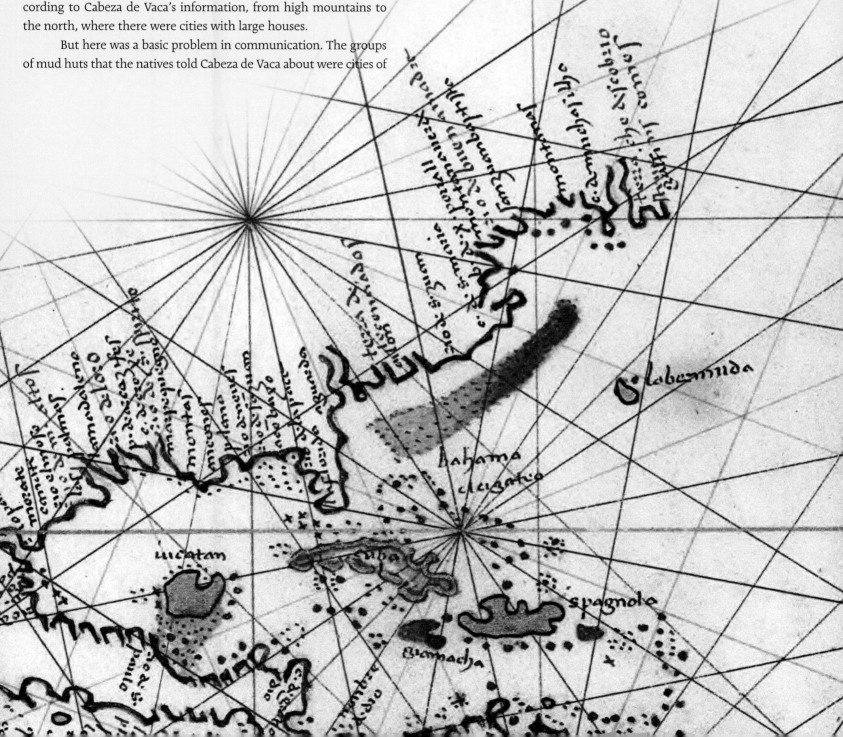

gold in the viceroy's mind, for, as a Spaniard unable to comprehend native cultures he interpreted the words as he would in Spain—large cities with an appropriately rich social infrastructure to match—and many rich people meant much plunder. After a reconnaissance by Estéban, this information, based on the Zuñi pueblos, emerged as a story of seven rich cities of gold—the Seven Cities of Cibola.

You would have thought that at least Cabeza de Vaca himself would know better, but he went back to Spain in 1537 to try a obtain a royal license to conquer his northern lands. He did not get it; instead he began a new series of adventures, this time in South America. The king had other plans. He commissioned Hernando de Soto to explore—and plunder—the new Florida.

Hernando de Soto, who is remembered as much for his brutality as for his explorations, was sent to Florida with an army in 1539. He had previously been in Peru and no doubt expected to find rich ancient civilizations as he had there. De Soto ordered natives to find gold, and when they could not, cut off their hands and feet as a punishment. And any Indians who posed a threat were massacred wholesale. It was a very sorry episode in European-native relations.

De Soto took an army of 720 men and 237 horses to Cuba in 1538, and then to Tampa Bay in May 1539. He was intending to find the Seven Cities, although he did not quite know where. He was better organized than Narváez had been, but ultimately it made little difference; finding the nonexistent has always been somewhat difficult.

De Soto did cover a lot of ground. By May 1540 he was in North Carolina and by the end of that month was making the first European crossing of the Appalachians, over the Blue Ridge Mountains to the Tennessee River valley. Then he marched south again and in October, near today's Montgomery, Alabama, attacked the Choctaw Indians, killing 2,500 of them. Here he heard that his ships were waiting at a prearranged rendezvous on the coast at Pensacola Bay, but he had not yet found the gold he was determined to have and hid the news from his men, choosing instead to continue his murderous wanderings to the west.

In June 1541 De Soto became the first European to cross the Mississippi, the Spanish Rio del Spirito Santo, near Memphis. Following a twisted route probably motivated by rumors of gold, the army marched up the Arkansas River. Still no gold could be found, and they returned to the Mississippi. By now the Indians had killed many of De Soto's men and even his equipment was wearing out. The failure of the expedition was suddenly becoming evident. In 1542 De Soto died of a fever. Luís de Moscoso took over command and, remembering Cabeza de Vaca's experiences, tried to lead his men overland back to New Spain. He got only as far as mid-Texas before turning back, unable to find food. In July 1543 they built boats on the Mississippi and coasted down the river and along the coast, reaching the Spanish settlement on the Rio Pánuco in September. Three hundred and eleven men survived the ordeal.

Meanwhile, in 1540 Antonio de Mendoza, the viceroy of New Spain, had finally put together an expedition of his own to capitalize on Cabeza de Vaca's reports of glistening cities of gold to the north. When he heard of the De Soto expedition this spurred him on, for these were expeditions financed by investors and he wanted to secure a return on his money before De Soto could claim the prize.

Another Spanish army was assembled, this time led by the governor of the province of New Galicia in northern New Spain, Francisco Vásquez de Coronado. The army comprised about 330 men with 220 horses, plus another thousand native allies and servants. In February 1543 they marched north.

Following a trail of gold that was but a receding rumor, Coronado did find the Seven Cities of Cibola, but they proved a disappointment—they were villages of mud and thatch.

To cover as much ground as possible, Coronado sent out smaller exploring parties. One of these, led by López de Cárdenas, searched for a river route to the Pacific and found the Grand Canyon. They were the first Europeans to see it. Another party, under Hernando de Alvarado, went

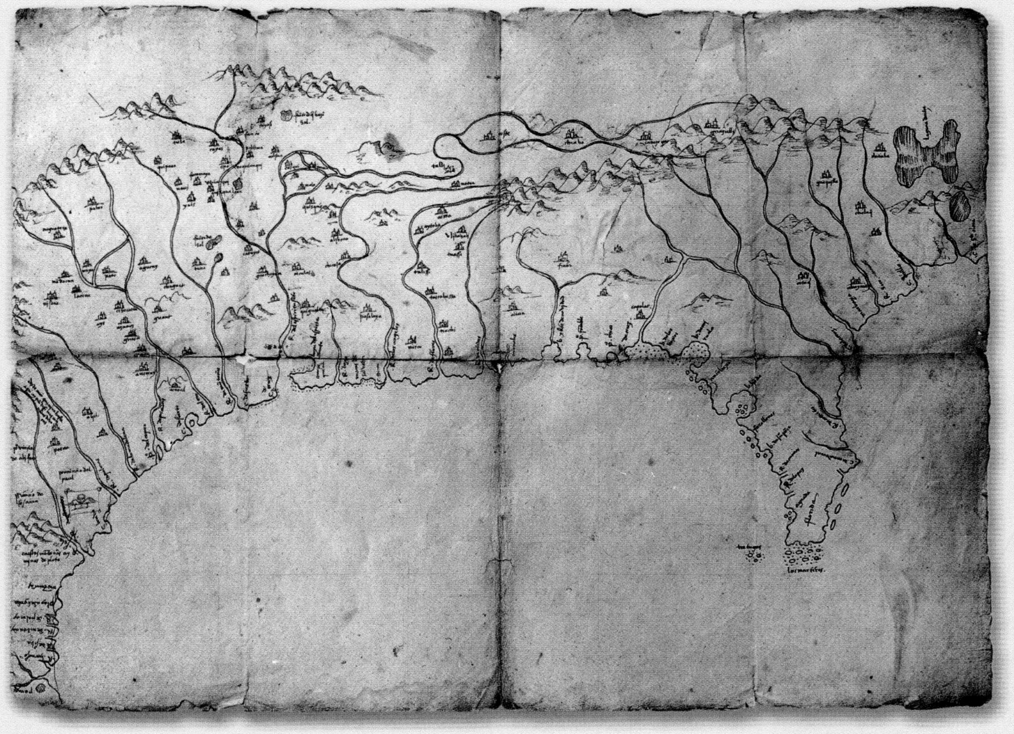

MAP 24.
The only contemporary map to show the country explored by Hernando de Soto is this one by the Spanish royal cartographer Alonzo de Santa Cruz, who compiled it about 1544 from reports by the survivors of the expedition.

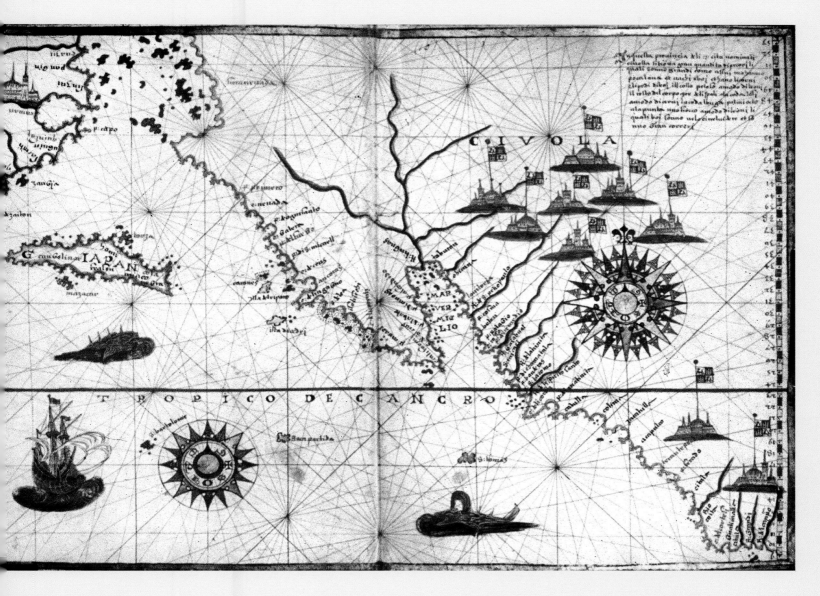

Map 25 (*above*).
The Seven Cities of Cibola, shown as they were imagined rather than as they were, on a map by Joan Martines drawn in 1578.

Map 26 (*right*).
Famous mapmaker Abraham Ortelius included this map of *La Florida*, the country explored by De Soto, in the 1584 edition of his atlas, *Theatrum Orbis Terrarum*.

north and east to the edge of the Great Plains and brought back an Indian who described a city of gold called Quivira. Excited by this news Coronado, who was then at the pueblos of the upper Rio Grande, marched northeast and found Quivira, near today's Kansas City. He reported "land as level as the sea" and enormous buffalo herds, but found no gold. Although he did not know it, while at Quivira, Coronado was only about three hundred miles from De Soto's expedition. But, like De Soto, he had come for gold and found none, and so, from Coronado's point of view, his expedition was also a failure.

The Shores of the South Sea

As early as 1513 the Spanish had seen the sea to the west, the sea to which they were all trying so hard to find a connecting strait. In that year Vasco Núñez de Balboa crossed the Isthmus of Panama and saw the Pacific Ocean—the Mar del Sur, or South Sea. Balboa waded into the ocean and in one of the most preposterous ceremonies of this kind, laid claim to the entire ocean and any shores it might wash. For centuries after, the Spanish regarded the Pacific Ocean as a Spanish lake.

In 1528 the conqueror of Mexico, Hernan Cortés, was granted a royal license to explore and subjugate the Pacific coast to the northwest. The second expedition sent north, in 1533, found what they thought was an island. It was the tip of Baja California. In 1535 Cortés himself led a third expedition, which established the settlement of Santa Cruz (today La Paz), on the east coast of the peninsula. This was to serve as a base for a search for pearls. The settlement did not last and was abandoned two years later.

In 1539 Cortés sent Francisco de Ulloa north. He sailed into the Gulf of California (at the time called the Sea of Cortés) and up to the head of the gulf, then back around Cabo St. Lucas and up the Pacific coast at least as far as Islas de Cedros, about halfway up the

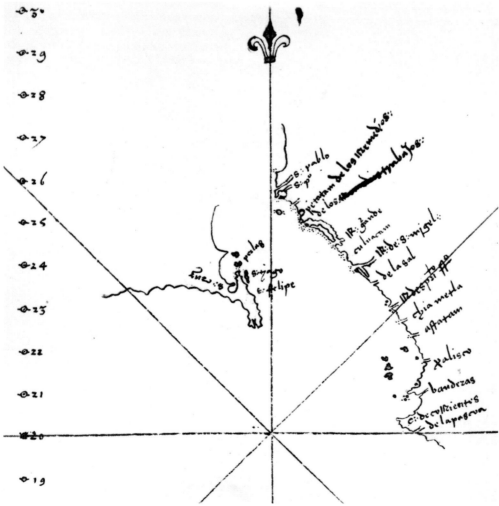

Map 27 (*left*).
Hernan Cortés's map of Baja California, 1535, the first map of that peninsula. Cortés thought it an island, yet showed the shores widening as if to join with the rest of the continent.

Map 28 (*above*).
The Baja region from Abraham Ortelius's 1570 atlas. Six of the Seven Cities of Cibola are shown, and the map incorporates Cortés's map of the tip of the peninsula. A river that could be a misplaced Colorado flows correctly into the head of the Gulf of California, but the rest of the map is largely imaginary.

Map 29 (*right*).
Part of a world map published in 1562 by Italian mapmaker Paolo Forlani. Baja is correctly shown as a peninsula but the principal feature is an enormous river that flows virtually from Alaska to empty into the Gulf of California. On this map Alaska is also the location of *Quivera*, which rapidly became a mythical land of riches that migrated all over the map. Note the *Mar del Sur*, the South Sea. *La Florida* has interestingly been placed back on the Florida peninsula.

peninsula. This voyage established that Baja was a peninsula rather than an island, although judging from the number of later maps that show California as an island, you would never know it.

Hernando de Alarcón was the next sent north. His mission was specific: he was to find and resupply the Coronado expedition. Reaching the head of the gulf, Alarcón entered the Colorado River with two small boats, which his men dragged upriver for ninety miles to the confluence of the Gila River, looking for Coronado. He did not find him and wisely decided that it was not feasible to continue the search.

About 1541, rumors were circulating that the Portuguese had found a northern strait between the Atlantic and the Pacific. Another conquistador, Juan Rodríguez Cabrillo, was ordered to sail much farther north to investigate this possibility. And, of course, he was to search for gold at the same time. Cabrillo sailed from La Navidad on the Mexican Pacific coast in June 1542. As later navigators were to

find, it was difficult to sail north in sight of the coast, due to winds and currents, and it took Cabrillo until the end of September to find a harbor he called San Miguel. It was San Diego, and he was the first European to visit the coast of what is today the state of California.

Continuing north, Cabrillo sailed offshore and thus did not see the harbors of Monterey or San Francisco. He reached just north of the latter before being driven back by storms. He retreated to one of the Channel Islands off Los Angeles, but Cabrillo died there while overwintering.

The expedition was taken over by Cabrillo's chief pilot, Bartolomé Ferrelo, who once again sailed north to try to carry out the orders to search for a strait. Ferrelo is thought to have reached the latitude of Cape Blanco (just north of today's California-Oregon boundary) in late February 1543 before deciding that no strait was to be found and returning to Mexico.

No Passage but an Empire

The Treaty of Tordesillas, signed in 1494 at the behest of the Pope, had divided the world into two spheres of influence. Those lands east of a north-south line at about 48° W were supposed to belong to Portugal, while those to the west were allocated to Spain. No one really knew where the line was, because no one could measure longitude. Nevertheless, from this Portugal derived her claims to both Brazil—which was partly east of the line—and to Newfoundland—which was not. Thus the first French exploratory foray by Giovanni Verrazano (see page 18) was essentially a surreptitious affair, with the explorer keeping to the north, out of the region where he might expect to find Spaniards.

But in 1533 the situation changed. François I persuaded the Pope that Tordesillas should only apply to lands discovered up to that time, and thus France became free to search out new lands for itself. France could resume the search for a passage through North America and perhaps find gold as well; Verrazano had reported—completely without basis—that gold was to be found in the northern regions.

It did not take long to find the right man for the job. He was Jacques Cartier, a master mariner from Saint-Malo on the Brittany coast. He had been presented to the king in 1532 as a suitable captain for such a job, and now that a voyage was planned he was the obvious choice. Cartier received a commission from the king to find a passage to Cathay and to find precious metals. But the merchants of Saint-Malo were not cooperative. Fearing a shortage of manpower for their fishing boats they tried to prevent their men from signing on with Cartier. Despite this, Cartier gathered a crew and sailed from Saint-Malo on 20 April 1534.

Cartier had been ordered to head for the Strait of Belle Isle between Newfoundland and Labrador, which was known to the French at this time through reports from fishing boats, which had been frequenting this area since the turn of the century. After making a landfall at Cape Bonavista, Cartier headed north and soon found the Strait of Belle Isle.

Cruising along the coast of Labrador he gave it the famous moniker "the land God gave to Cain," on account of its barren appearance. Then he followed the west coast of Newfoundland south, finding the Îles de la Madeleine (Magdalen Islands) in the middle of the Gulf of St. Lawrence. Here he correctly deduced from the tides that there was another entrance to the gulf not far away. This was Cabot Strait. Continuing south he came to Prince Edward Island and sailed west along its shores, then north up the coast of New Brunswick until he came to what looked like a strait trending west. Turning west, he sailed until he could no more. This was the Baie des Chaleurs—the Bay of Warmth—so named by Cartier for its inviting temperatures. At another, smaller bay just to the north of its entrance, Gaspé Bay, Cartier anchored to perform the requisite ceremony of possession for the French king. Here he met about two

hundred Laurentian Iroquois. With their chief, Donnacona, they were on their annual fishing trip from their base at Stadacona, the site of the city of Québec. Cartier took on board—whether willingly or otherwise is not known—the chief's two sons, whom he took back to France and used as pathfinders the following year.

Continuing north, Cartier sailed to Anticosti Island, somehow missing the southern channel of the St. Lawrence, which he thought was another bay. On the north side of the island westward progress—in what is today called Détroit (Strait) de Jacques-Cartier—became difficult because of the current flowing out of the river, and on 2 August he decided to return to France and return next season. Passing once more through the Strait of Belle Isle, Cartier was back in Saint-Malo on 5 September. Map 30 shows the results of Cartier's first voyage. He had found and mapped a large gulf with a promising possible strait leading west.

King François thought it likely that the passage to Cathay that he sought was the very channel in which Cartier had turned back, and so the Saint-Malo mariner quickly received another commission to continue his explorations the following year. On 19 May 1535 Cartier again sailed from Saint-Malo, this time with three ships and

Illa de fonde londe quhar men goeth a fishing

Illa daffa

Map 30 (*above*).
The only surviving map to show Jacques Cartier's first voyage is this superb map drawn by Jean Rotz, ironically for the English king. South is at the top. Newfoundland, shown as an archipelago, is to the left, while the Gulf of St. Lawrence is outlined, with Anticosti Island shown attached to the mainland beside the only open passage west, the St. Lawrence River. This map shows the first depiction on any European document of a wigwam or tepee.

Map 31 (*below*).
A rather stylized map of Hochelaga drawn by Venetian mapmaker Giacomo Gastaldi in 1556. It is the first map of any North American settlement.

over a hundred men under his command. The crossing took much longer than the one the previous year—seven weeks, and although he headed directly for Détroit de Jacques-Cartier, it was later in the year when he reached it than when he had turned back the year before. But this time this did not concern him, for he had determined to stay all winter if he did not reach southern climes through this passage to Cathay. It did not take long for Cartier to recognize that he was in a very large river rather than a sea passage. Donnacona's sons guided him to their winter village, Stadacona—in a land they seemed to call *kanata,* and which Cartier interpreted as *Canada*—but would not take him any farther upstream, to where other tribes lived.

But Cartier did not give up this easily. With his smallest ship towing longboats he sailed to Lac Saint-Pierre and then continued in just the longboats. He arrived at a large fortified Iroquois

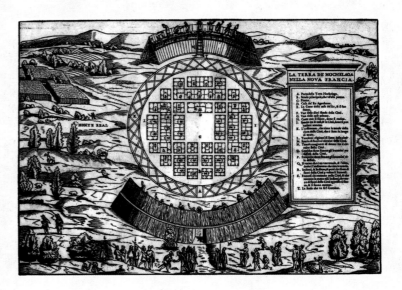

MAP 32.

This work of art is a map showing Roberval's colonists at France-Roy, a settlement briefly established by the French at Québec. South is at the top, as is common with maps drawn at this time. Known as the Vallard map, it was drawn in 1547 by an unknown mapmaker from Dieppe, France, home of a group of mapmakers who created maps for their wealthy shipowner clients. Here Newfoundland is shown more correctly almost as a single large island. *Rio do canada* (River of Canada) is named; the name *St. Lawrence* was first used by Cartier on his second voyage for a small harbor on the north side of the gulf (*La baye sainct Lawrens*) and came to be applied to both the river and the gulf. Thus did Cartier unwittingly leave his stamp on the land.

encampment called Hochelaga, on the site of modern Montréal. On 3 October, deliberately dressing in all his finery with the hope to impress, Cartier took twenty volunteers and marched towards the settlement, which was under a hill he named Mont Réal. He was well received, with the natives seemingly thinking he was a god of some sort. Cartier had trumpets blown to further the effect.

Cartier could explore no farther: the Lachine Rapids on the St. Lawrence blocked his way. For centuries men would go no farther except by canoe. But Cartier's interest was piqued, for the natives led him to believe (or he interpreted their signs to mean) that beyond the rapids lay another river—the Ottawa—which was the source of gold.

Cartier and his men spent a miserable winter at Stadacona, averting death from scurvy by using the native remedy, the bark of the arborvitae tree. And Donnacona conjured up more tales of gold and precious stones in a kingdom called Saguenay. This was surely worth investigating, Cartier no doubt thought, but it would have to await another expedition. He set sail for France on 6 May 1536 and was back in Saint-Malo on 16 July. This time he had Donnacona himself with him.

Donnacona proved to be somewhat of a celebrity in France, regaling the French court with tales of gold and emeralds, then spices and pomegranates, all of which could be found, he said, in his kingdom of Saguenay. It was soon resolved to send out yet another expedition to locate all these riches, but a two-year European war between France and Spain delayed it, and the expedition did not depart until 1541.

This time Cartier was not nominally the leader, for the plan was to establish a colony as well as explore for gold. The leader was Jean-François de la Roque, Sieur de Roberval, but Cartier went ahead with five ships and several hundred colonists, out of contact with Roberval. The plans went awry, and after several abortive attempts at exploration, they overwintered, losing thirty-five men to scurvy and attacks by the increasingly unfriendly natives. Cartier had

had enough. Roberval had not appeared, and he was now undermanned. He sailed back to France, meeting Roberval briefly in the harbor at St. John's, Newfoundland, but ignoring his orders to follow him back to Canada.

Roberval did briefly establish a French colony at Stadacona—he called it France-Roy—but like Cartier's, it was not a success and did not endure. But it did create the foundation of a French claim to the new northern land called Canada.

One of Roberval's pilots, Jean Alfonce, explored up the Saguenay River, which flows into the St. Lawrence below Québec. He interpreted this wide fiord to be an arm of the sea, a passage to "la mer du Cattay." If he had gone far enough upstream, Alfonce would have come to the Chicoutimi Rapids and been disavowed of his illusion.

MAP 33.
A map by Roberval's pilot, Jean Alfonce, drawn about 1544. It shows the Gulf of St. Lawrence. The island is Anticosti, and the river flowing into the gulf from the west (at left) is the St. Lawrence River. On the north shore is the Saguenay, shown as a strait leading to another sea. In fact the Saguenay River flows from a lake, Lac Saint-Jean, and this was Alfonce's Mer du Saguenay. He had drawn his map from native reports and, of course, interpreted them through his own expectations.

The French in Florida

If gold could not be found directly, the next best thing might be to take it from the Spanish, who had found it in Mexico and Peru. And so the next attempts to establish a French colony in North America were to the south, in today's Georgia. The idea was to build a hidden fort behind the offshore islands and from there prey on Spanish treasure fleets passing by on the Gulf Stream. Like many later colonies, refuge would also be provided for a persecuted religious community, in this case the Huguenots, a Protestant group. Like any venture of this kind, it required investors, but it seemed like a good bet, and even Catherine de Medici, the mother of the French queen, thought it worthwhile to risk her money.

Perhaps the most experienced mariner in France at the time was Jean Ribaut, and he was appointed to head the expedition. He

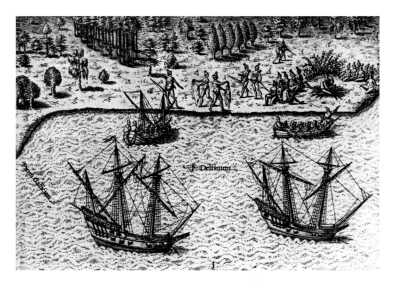

sailed with 150 colonists from Le Havre in February 1562 and made a landfall on the Florida coast near Saint Augustine, at a point he named Cap François. Then he turned north, searching the labyrinth of river mouths and islands for a suitable spot for his colony. On 1 May he entered the St. Johns River, which flows to the sea at Jacksonville, naming it the River of May. The river was explored a

short distance, and the requisite ceremony of possession was carried out, with a stone marker erected. Farther up the coast Ribaut found what he was looking for: a hidden and defensible site for his base. It was a harbor he named Port Royal, which he thought "one of the greatest and fayrest havens in the world." On Parris Island,

The French exploration and colonization attempts in the Southeast are well illustrated in a multivolume German history, *America*, by Theodor De Bry, published in 1591. The pictomaps on this page are from his book.

MAP 34 (*left, top*) shows the French ships setting off to explore one of the many rivers.

MAP 35 (*left, bottom*) is the French arrival at Port Royal Sound, South Carolina, where they would build Charlesfort.

MAP 36 (*above*) shows the French in longboats entering the River of May, the St. Johns River at Jacksonville, Florida.

MAP 37.
This De Bry pictomap shows the French sailing north towards Charlesfort and discovering six other rivers. The Florida, Georgia, and South Carolina coasts in this region are full of rivers and offshore islands, making it an ideal place to hide a fort or settlement.

Beaufort, South Carolina, about thirty miles north of Savannah, Georgia, Ribaut built Charlesfort.

Ribaut himself returned to France for supplies for his colony, but when he arrived he found a war raging between the Huguenots and the Catholics. After fighting for some time, Ribaut fled to England, where he was imprisoned as a spy. Ribaut's colonists soon ran out of food and decided to sail back to France themselves. Desperately hungry, they resorted to cannibalism to survive. They were saved only because an English ship happened to see them.

A peace in 1563 allowed a new colonization attempt, and in 1564 René de Laudonnière, who had been with Ribaut two years before, was chosen as its leader. He sailed back to Florida and built Fort Caroline on the St. Johns River, his River of May. From this base a number of short explorations were made into the interior of Florida and Georgia, searching for the precious metals thought to be found there. But the colony, like the first, did not prosper; the Indians were at war with each other and hardships created mutinies within the French colonies.

The colony was considerably buoyed by the arrival of the English buccaneer John Hawkins, whose fleet was on the way back to England after a slave-trading voyage. He provided the French with food and noted in his journal a strange habit of the Indians, who put a dried herb in a cup, lit it, and "doe sucke thorow [a] cane the smoke thereof." The herb, of course, was tobacco.

On the very day in August 1565 that the colonists had decided to abandon their colony, Jean Ribaut arrived with seven ships and hundreds of new colonists. He had escaped from his prison back to France and had been sent once again to take command of the French efforts at colonization.

Ribaut was a much better leader than Laudonnière, but it was to make little difference, because the Spanish had learned of the French incursions into what they considered their territory and sent a new and ruthless governor of Florida, Pedro Menéndez de Avilés, to rid themselves of the French. Ribaut and his men were no match for Menéndez's large fleet and army, and Ribaut was shipwrecked during a hurricane, putting him at a further disadvantage. Menéndez killed

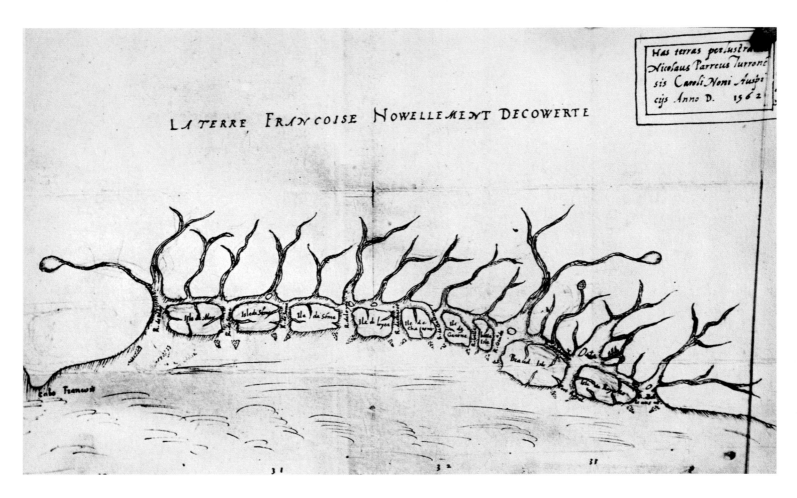

LA TERRE FRANCOISE NOWELLEMENT DECOWERTE

Has terras per.iustr...
Nicolaus Parreus Turron...
sis Caroli Noni Auspi...
cijs Anno D. 1562

Map 38 (*above*).
"The newly discovered French lands" are shown on this map, a contemporary Spanish spy's copy of a map, now lost, by Nicolas Barré, who was Jean Ribaut's pilot on his expedition of 1562. It may well have been that as a result of seeing this map, the king of Spain decided to dispatch Menéndez to wipe out the French colonies in what he viewed as his domain.

Map 39 (*below*).
French Florida *de la Main de Marc Lescarbot*, published in 1609. Lescarbot was with Samuel de Champlain in Acadia until 1606, and when he returned to France he wrote a history of French exploration and colonization attempts. The result was his *Histoire de la Nouvelle France*, in which this map appeared. Cap François is shown at the bottom, and Charlesfort at the top. The inland sea at top left was derived from native reports but was fictitious.

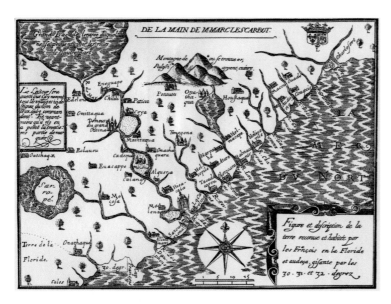

most of them, ending French thoughts about colonies to the south. Ribaut himself was killed but Laudonnière escaped to France, as did a painter with the colonists, Jacques Le Moyne de Morgues, who drew the splendid summary map of Florida opposite (Map 40).

Menéndez built a fort at Port Royal that he called Fort Felipe, and Port Royal became the Spanish Santa Elena. Excavations on Parris Island have several times mistaken later Spanish forts for Ribaut's original French one, the location of which is still not certain. Menéndez also built a fort at San Mateo, on the site of the French Fort Caroline, and established San Agustin. As Saint Augustine, it became the oldest continously occupied European city in North America.

Menéndez sent exploration parties to the upper St. Johns River in search of a reported passage across the peninsula, but it was another Spaniard, Juan Pardo, who did the most exploring. He arrived in 1566 and Menéndez ordered him to explore the interior to find a route to Mexico and, of course, to search for gold and silver. Pardo undertook two expeditions far to the west. He went up the Savannah River valley and across the Appalachians into the valley of the Tennessee, where he turned south, reaching central Alabama before returning. His expedition produced reports of a mountain of diamonds—Los Diamantes—which Pardo was unable to find. The reports were likely of quartz or mica crystals found by the natives.

The Spanish outposts, like the French, did not flourish, and in 1586 Saint Augustine was attacked and destroyed by an English fleet under Francis Drake. After that the Spanish presence was restricted to the Florida peninsula.

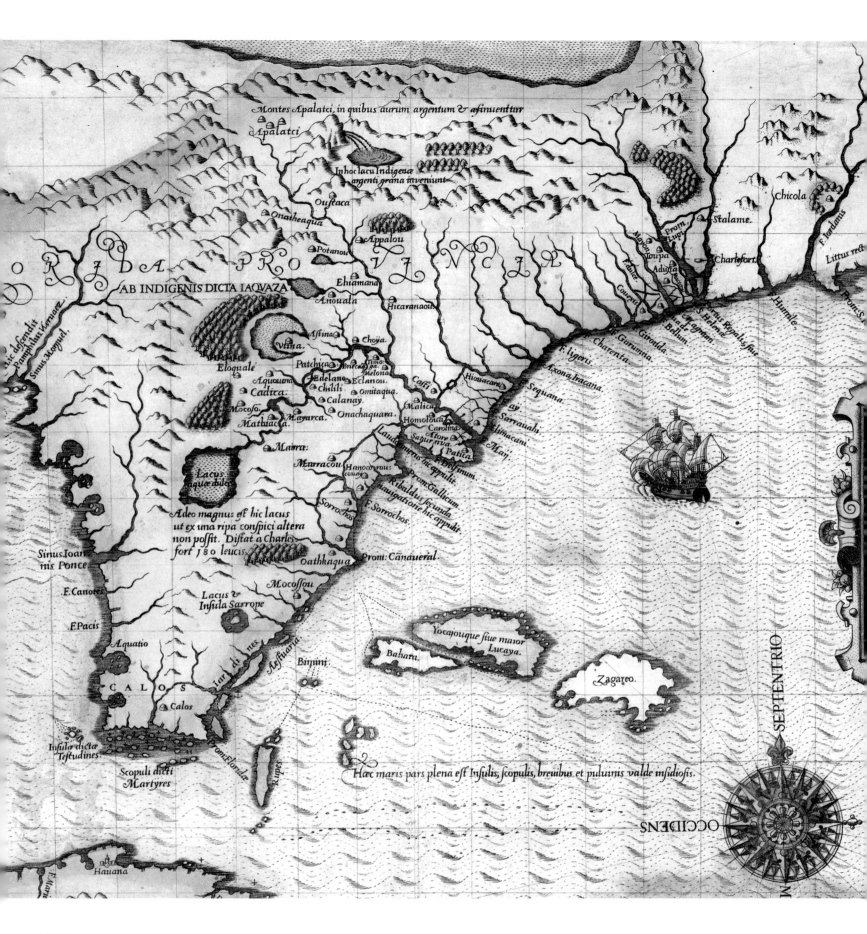

MAP 40.

Another De Bry engraving, this is the map of Florida originally drawn by Jacques Le Moyne de Morgues, an artist who was with Laudonnière in 1564–65. *Prom. Gallicum*, De Bry's Latin name, is Ribaut's Cap François, at the same latitude as the ship. Just to the north is the *Maii*, the River of May, St. Johns River, which is correctly shown flowing from the south to its mouth at present-day Jacksonville, Florida. At the north end of the coast is *Charlefort*, Ribaut's fort on Port Royal Sound. Le Moyne died in 1588, and De Bry published the map in his book *America* in 1591.

Fact and Fantasy

By 1570, when Dutch mapmaker Abraham Ortelius published his atlas *Theatrum Orbis Terrarum*—"Theater of the World"—the exploration of North America had come a long way in eighty-two years. From being a literal blank on the map it was now a full and recognizable continent. Nevertheless, there were still huge areas unexplored and huge geographical misconceptions to be corrected. Much of the West on Ortelius's map was in fact conjectural; he just happened to draw a shape that bears some resemblance to the real thing.

In the northeast, Cartier's St. Lawrence penetrates to the center of the continent, with another river, which could be a nascent Colorado, flowing from the other side of the mountains to the Gulf of California. Some maps of this period show the St. Lawrence the way Cartier wanted it, as a strait cutting right through the continent. The southern part of the continent is well defined coastally, but with little more than the legends of the interior. The Mississippi is not yet in evidence, but the Florida peninsula is somewhat correctly shown, as is Baja California, mapped by Cortés in 1535. California was destined to spend another century defined as an island, contrary to all the exploratory evidence thus far. Coronado's Seven Cities of Cibola grace the Southwest, but Quivira, which he also investigated on the Great Plains, has somehow been transposed to the Northwest. To the north again is Anian, another mythical land on the shores of a passage between the continents of North America and Asia that would one day be known as Bering Strait. Yet in 1570 there was no exploration that we know of that could have defined such a strait. Even more mysterious is a great bay on the north shore of North America that looks remarkably like Hudson Bay. Yet again there is no evidence of it being found before 1610, though some have argued ardently for a Portuguese voyage to the region, perhaps by Sebastian Cabot, John Cabot's son. Once again, however, this is mere conjecture. And then there is the startling clear passage across

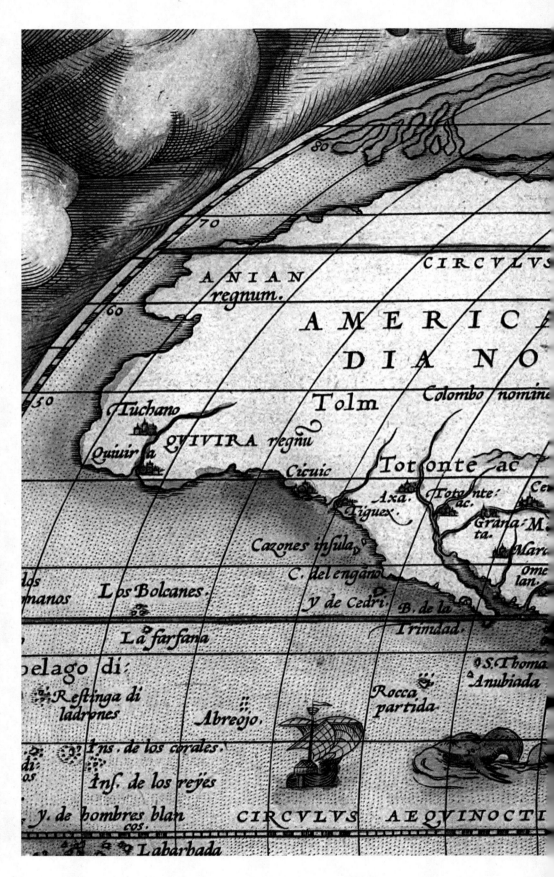

the top of the continent—the fabled Northwest Passage. This easy passage from Europe to the East was fixed in the European mind for centuries and drove men to sail against immeasurable odds to brave the icy wastes of the Arctic seas, many never to return.

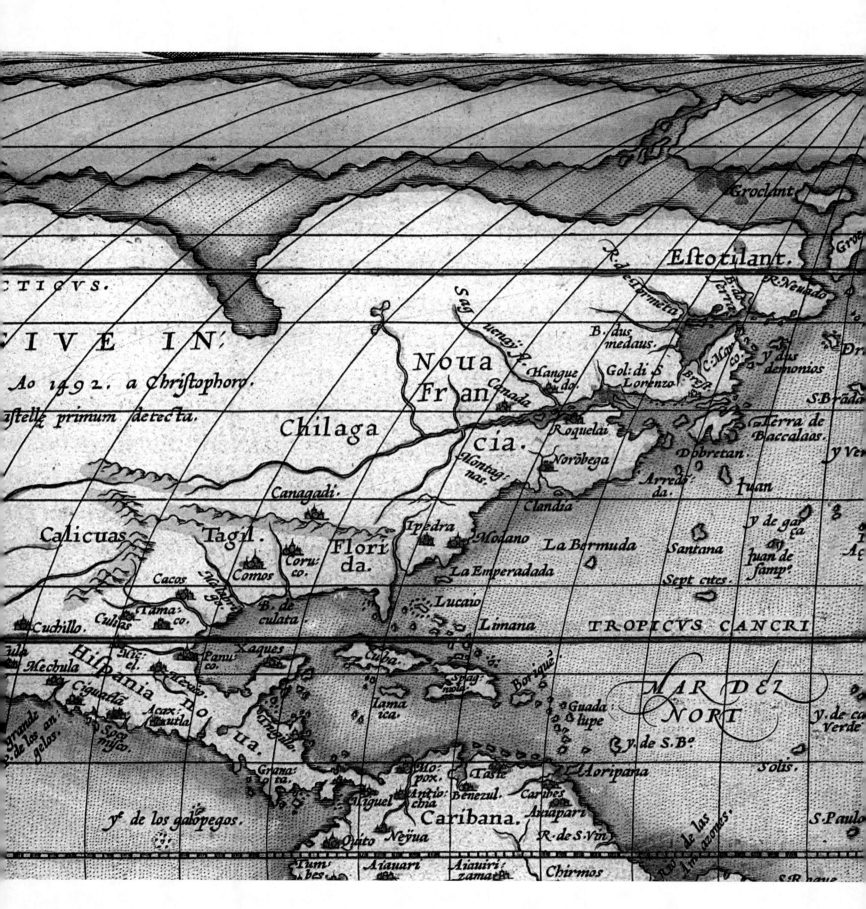

Map 41.

The North American part of Abraham Ortelius's map of the world, published in 1570.

A Northern Passage

For years the merchants of England dreamed of finding an easy passage to Cathay and the Spice Islands that avoided the trade routes of the Portuguese and the Spanish, who between them seemed to have preempted the best seaways. In 1553, on the recommendation of Sebastian Cabot, then Pilot Major of England, several voyages to try to find a Northeast Passage were undertaken. When these failed, attention turned to the possibility of a Northwest Passage across the top of North America. Maps such as that of Abraham Ortelius (Map 41, *previous page*) showed such a clear and unequivocal passage that no one could doubt that it existed. Indeed, of course, it does exist, but choked by ice impassable in a sailing ship.

Thus when an opportunist obsessed by fame and fortune named Martin Frobisher proposed a voyage to find the Northwest Passage in 1575, the merchants of London were easily persuaded. Choreographed by passage promoter Michael Lok, the financing was put together, and Frobisher sailed in June 1576 with three ships. One was lost and the other turned back when ice was encountered, leaving Frobisher alone in his ship *Gabriel* to continue.

Frobisher sailed into Davis Strait and found the bay now named after him on the southeast tip of Baffin Island. He was convinced it was the strait he had been looking for. And so "Frobisher's Streytes" it became. He lost five men to the Inuit when he landed on a small island, named Hall's Island after his sailing master, Christopher Hall. A few stones were picked up either as a ceremony of possession or simply as souvenirs, and then he sailed back to England.

Those few stones turned out to hold major significance for Frobisher. Through some underhand promotion—someone wanted to make a killing on stock, no doubt—the stones were pronounced gold ore. Here at once was England's Peru. Now England could rival Spain in wealth. New financial backing flowed in,

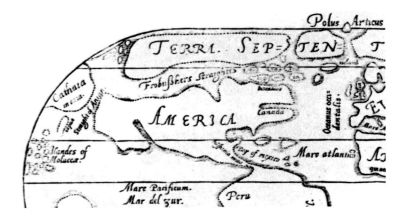

MAP 43.
This map by one of Martin Frobisher's officers, George Best, shows clearly what Frobisher *thought* he had discovered—a clear and wide strait to the East across the top of the continent—here *Frobusshers Straights*.

and even Queen Elizabeth herself made an investment. Suddenly the venture had become much more than merely an exploration to find a passage to Cathay. Why go all the way to Cathay if riches were so much nearer?

In 1577, and again in 1578, Frobisher led voyages to mine the supposed gold ore from the barren shores of his bay. Three ships in 1577 brought back 200 tons of the rock. This was somehow again pronounced to be gold ore by assayers who likely knew better, leading to a veritable armada of fifteen ships that sailed for Baffin Island in 1578, with three hundred miners and another hundred who were to found a colony for England. This third and final Frobisher voyage brought back an astonishing 1,350 tons of the imagined ore. A ship carrying house timbers was lost, leading to the abandonment of the colony idea, and the "ore" ended up being used to build walls and pave roads—surely some of the most expensive construction materials ever.

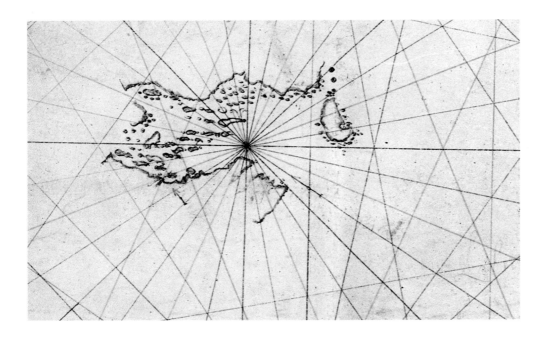

MAP 42 (*left*).
Frobisher took with him on his first voyage a base map, a "carte of navigation . . . ruled playne," drawn by William Borough, commander of the Muscovy Company of England, and who had himself sailed to try to find a Northeast Passage. On this base Frobisher drew in what he had found. Here was the eastern end of his "strait," in fact Frobisher Bay shown open at its western end. This is the earliest example of a map of any part of the North American continent drawn in the field by an explorer.

But Frobisher had showed the way. Perhaps there was still a strait to Cathay somewhere in the region. In 1584 merchants in London and in Exeter revived the idea. The English were concerned that some other nation might discover a passage before them, preempting yet another route to riches. One of the wealthiest merchants, William Sanderson, led a group that financed John Davis on three separate voyages, in 1585, 1586, and 1587, in which Davis reached successively higher latitudes in his strait—Davis Strait, which separates Baffin Island from Greenland. And even when Davis returned from his third voyage he still tried for a fourth. "I have bene in 73 degrees, finding the sea all open, and forty leagues between land and land," he wrote, "the passage is most probable, the execution easie." But after three voyages with no financial return, he could find no more backers.

During Frobisher's last voyage, some of his ships had sailed in error into Hudson Strait, and John Davis had noted "whirling and overfalling" at the entrance to the strait, caused by a meeting of tides. This would later also have to be investigated as a possible route to the East, leading to the 1610 voyage of Henry Hudson (see page 54).

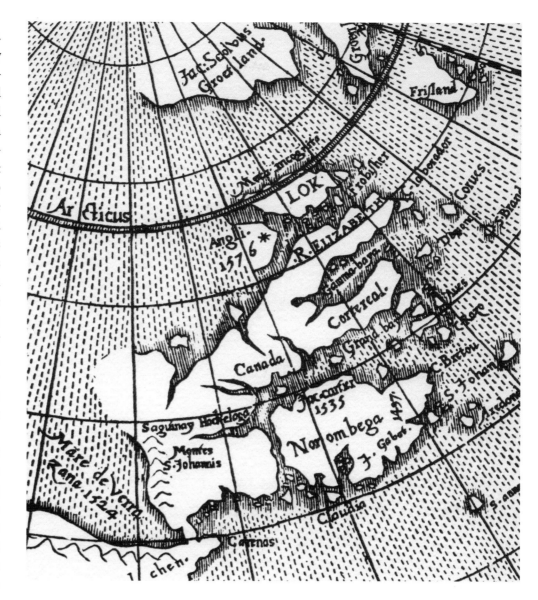

MAP 44 (right, top).
Northwest Passage promoter Michael Lok's map of North America, published in 1582. *Frobisher* marks the strait, within which is *Angli 1576** (English 1576). The northern shore is *Lok*. Note also *Cortereal* (Newfoundland), *Canada* (Cartier's discoveries), and *Mare de Verrazana 1524*, Verrazano's sea.

MAP 45 (right).
Mathematician Edward Wright constructed a map of the world in 1599, notable because he was one of the first to use Mercator's new projection. He included on the map the latest information from John Davis, and it shows *Fretum Davis*—Davis Strait. Frobisher Strait is now shown incorrectly, displaced east to the tip of Greenland, the result of Frobisher's inability to tell how far west he was. The measurement of longitude was an ongoing problem for maritime explorers until towards the end of the eighteenth century.

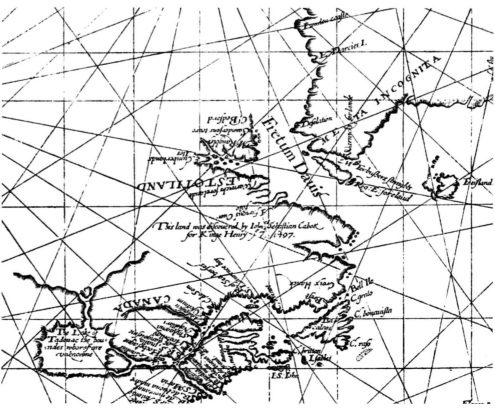

New Albion

New Albion, the Latin form of New England, was the name applied by Sir Francis Drake when he claimed the west coast of America for his queen, Elizabeth I, in 1579. The moniker persisted for centuries after and was one of the bases of English claims to the Northwest.

During the period 1577 to 1580 Drake circumnavigated the world on what is known as his "famous voyage." This was the first circumnavigation in which the captain also completed the voyage; on the first, Ferdinand Magellan's in 1519–22, Magellan was killed by natives in the Moluccas. His ship circumnavigated, but he did not.

It was during Drake's circumnavigation that he visited the west coast of America, landing to career and repair his ship the *Golden Hinde* at a harbor shown on maps as Portus Novus Albion.

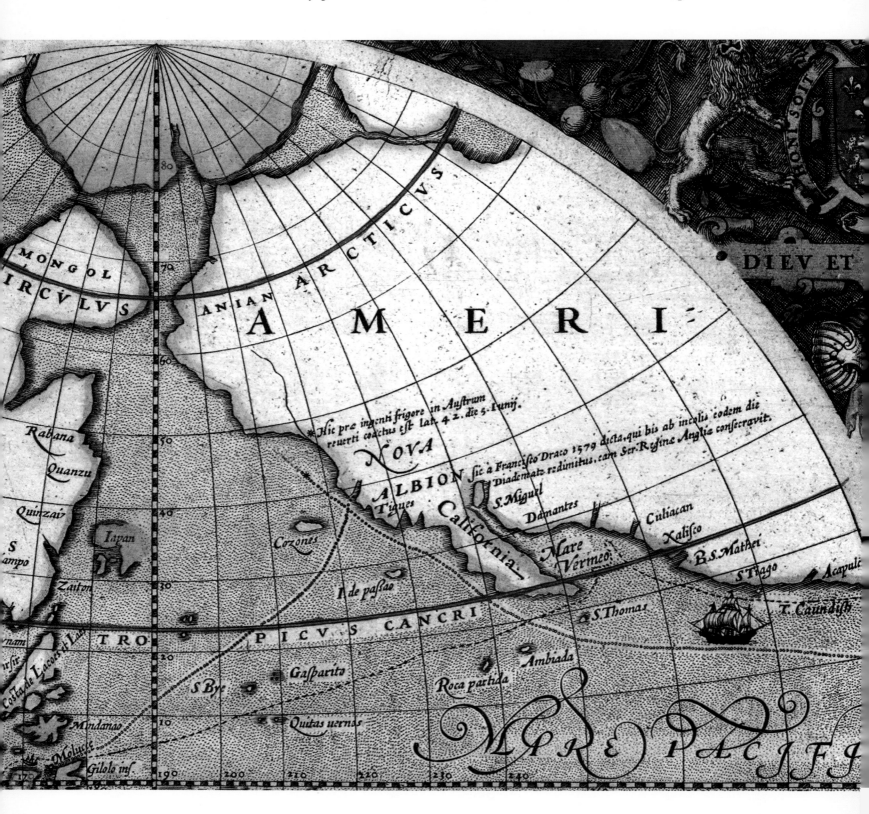

The exact location of this cove has been disputed for years, but the most likely candidate is Drake's Harbor, on the south side of Point Reyes, California. After the ship was repaired Drake explored inland some undefined distance in the company of Indians—likely Miwoks—whom he had befriended at the coast. They visited several native villages and hunted. With this thirty-six-day visit to California, England claimed the entire region.

Before arriving at Drake's Harbor, Drake had sailed northwards, perhaps with the intention of searching for the western entrance to the Northwest Passage as an easy escape from the Spanish, whom he presumed might be pursuing him since he was laden with gold looted from a Spanish galleon earlier in his voyage. Although the evidence is that he only reached about 48° N, there are endless theories (but that is all they are) that he reached much farther north, perhaps even to Alaska. The theories maintain that the evidence was suppressed in order to conceal from the Spanish where Drake had been. The Spanish spy network in England was well developed at this time, however, and it seems unlikely that any shenanigans could have been kept from them for long.

There is indirect cartographic evidence of some knowledge of the northwest American coast contained in a map published in 1647 by Robert Dudley, a son of the Earl of Leicester, who was one of Drake's financial backers and therefore presumably privy to inside information. The cape at the northern point of the map (MAP 48, *right*) does bear a resemblance to Cape Flattery, at the northwestern corner of the Olympic Peninsula, in Washington State. Then the two indentations on the coastline south of the cape could be Grays Harbor and the Columbia estuary, respectively.

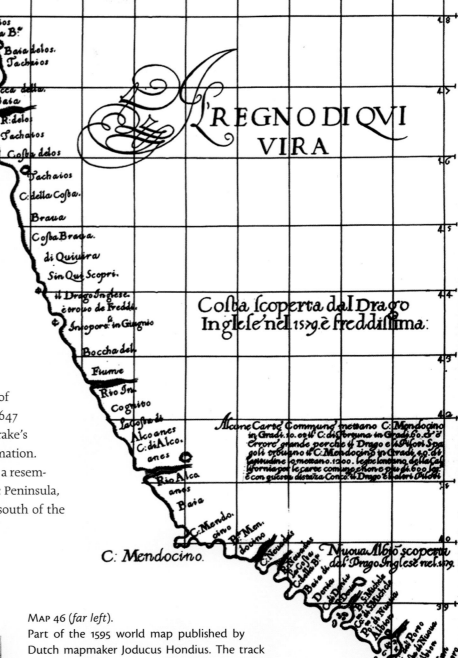

MAP 46 (*far left*).
Part of the 1595 world map published by Dutch mapmaker Joducus Hondius. The track of Drake's ship is shown. An indentation on the coast at 38° N is *Portus Nova Albionis*, which is shown in detail in an inset on the same map (MAP 47, *left*). The track of Drake's ship peters out just below 50° N, likely because, in fog, Drake did not know exactly how far north he was, yet it is fodder for those who contend that he sailed much farther north but that somehow the evidence was altered or suppressed.

MAP 48 (*above*).
Robert Dudley's map of the west coast of North America. If the northernmost cape is in fact Cape Flattery, it is in approximately the correct latitude. The map was published in 1647 in an atlas of copper-engraved maps, *Dell' Arcano del Mare* ("Concerning the secrets of the sea"). It was the first English sea atlas, intended to be carried aboard ships for navigation, and used Mercator's new projection, which was ideal for navigation because lines of constant bearing (rhumb lines) are straight lines.

A Plantation at Roanoke Island

By 1565, both Spain and France had colonies in the New World. In 1563 Sir Thomas Stukeley, an English buccaneer in the tradition of Drake and Frobisher (though perhaps even worse), had intended to set up a colony in Florida, or rather, take over the French one. He was no doubt attracted by the thought of having a hidden base from which to raid the rich Spanish galleons passing so close by. Stukeley had actually set sail with the fugitive Jean Ribaut (founder of Charlesfort) as his forced pilot. When Ribaut escaped overboard while the ships were off Gravesend, he had been arrested as a spy to keep him from informing the French (see page 31). But Stukeley was really much more concerned with easy prey, and the pickings turned out to be too good close to home to warrant a foray to far-off Florida.

John Hawkins brought back a favorable report on the French colony to England when he returned in 1565. In 1566 Sir Humfrey Gilbert wrote a treatise (though it was not published until 1576) promoting the goals of finding a Northwest Passage and establishing English colonies, increasing royal power and promoting trade. It has been called the first important document of the Elizabethan age on exploration and voyaging. Delayed by wars in Ireland, Gilbert intended to set up a colony in Norumbega (New England) in 1583 but his five ships got only as far as St. John's, Newfoundland. Sailing south, ships were wrecked in a storm, and Gilbert was returning to England to try again the following year when his ship foundered and he was drowned.

But the idea of "planting" a colony did not die. Colonies could be sources of wealth just as passages could make trade easier. In March 1584, Gilbert's half-brother, Walter Ralegh (often spelled "Raleigh," despite the fact that he never spelled it that way and there are about forty other ways it was spelled), obtained a patent from Queen Elizabeth to possess all newly discovered territories. At the same time Adrian Gilbert, Humfrey's younger brother, obtained a patent for discovering the Northwest Passage, and it was under this authority that the voyages of John Davis (see page 37) were undertaken. Ralegh quickly put together an expedition. Two ships were dispatched, under captains Philip Amadas and Arthur Barlowe, together with a Portuguese pilot, Simão Fernandez, who had served with Gilbert and had an abiding hatred of the Spanish. This was a reconnaissance voyage to determine where a colony might be placed. The idea, as with the French, was to create a hidden base from which Spanish shipping could be attacked. Fernandez's copy of a Spanish chart, in turn copied by the English polymath John Dee (MAP 49, *below*), shows why the coast of what is now North Carolina had been selected as a possible site for a colony. The only bay with any islands (to hide behind) is *B*[ahia] *de S*[anta] *Maria,* which just happens to be at the latitude of the North Carolina banks. And so this is where they headed for, by the circuitous route the English had to follow to pick up favorable winds, first to the West Indies and then north.

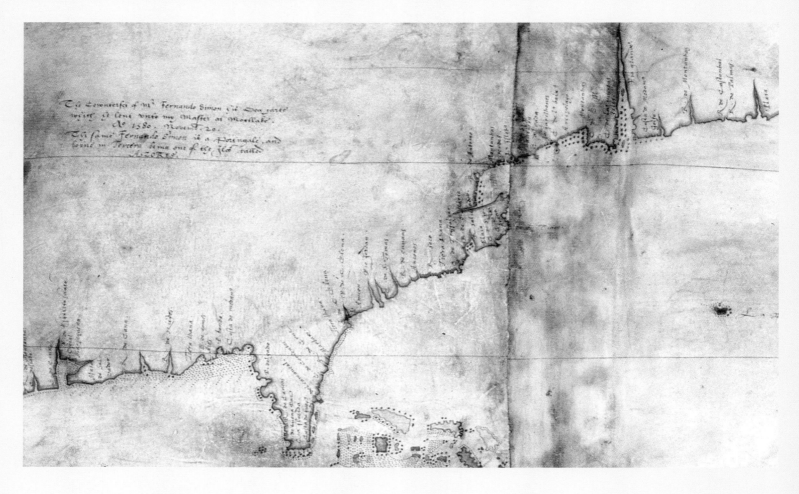

On 13 July they arrived at the outer coast, and Fernandez found a gap between the sandbanks at Hatarask, into which they took their boats. Three days later they made contact with the Indians, led by a chief named Wingina, who were friendly. The next six weeks were spent exploring the immediate area, and then the ships sailed for England, bringing word of the suitability of the region for settlement and taking back two of the natives, Manteo and Wanchese. The lack of a good harbor, essential on this hurricane-prone coast, seems to have been overlooked, as were the shallow entrances through the outer sandbanks.

Colonization fever ran high in England on their return. Richard Hakluyt wrote a *Discourse on Western Planting* at Ralegh's request while Amadas and Barlowe were still away, colonial propaganda to interest investors. In January 1585 Ralegh was knighted, and Queen Elizabeth permitted him to name his new colony-to-be Virginia in her honor.

Seven ships under Sir Richard Grenville left England in April 1585, bound for Virginia. With the fleet was John White, an artist who later produced superb paintings of native life and two maps (MAP 53, *overleaf*), and Thomas Hariot, a mathematician who was to record data on the climate, the flora and fauna, and the geology—preferably rocks containing gold.

They arrived on the coast by July, after the voyage via the West Indies and several groundings on the sandbars of the banks, which damaged some of the stores. Grenville immediately set about trying to find a harbor suitable for the larger ships. With a pinnace (a small ship) and three boats Grenville took sixty men to comb Pamlico Sound, the water behind the banks, and they visited several native villages, including the main village of Secoton.

MAP 50 (*above*).
Part of a pictomap engraved by Theodor De Bry and published in 1591, showing the arrival of the English at Roanoke Island in 1584. Note the sunken ships on offshore sandbanks.

MAP 51 (*below*).
The first map of Virginia, a sketch likely drawn by John White or Thomas Hariot in 1585. The entrance through the banks is that of Wococon, the first entrance found (approaching from the south). It is identified as *the port of saynt maris wher we arivid first*, for this is where they expected to find the *Bahia de Santa Maria* marked on the Dee map.

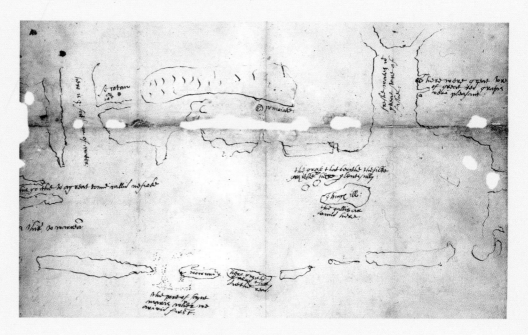

MAP 49 (*left*).
The reason why the North Carolina banks were selected as a location for a colony. John Dee's copy of Simão Fernandez's map of the East Coast, itself a copy of a Spanish map, shows at that latitude B[ahia] de S[anta] Maria, with its islands the English wanted to hide behind.

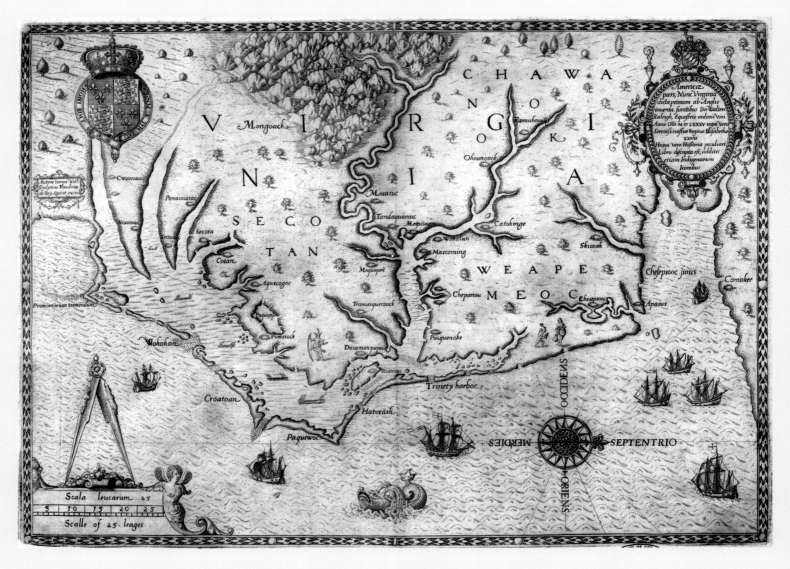

Although the Indians had remained friendly, the loss of a silver cup presumed to have been stolen led to the only kind of response English commanders of Grenville's age knew of: he burned the village and its fields. Grenville had been involved recently in bloody fighting in Ireland so this sort of thing came naturally to him. But it was a mistake; from that point relations with the natives only went downhill.

A site for a fort was agreed upon at the northern end of Roanoke Island, although, without a harbor, it could only be temporary. In August, Amadas took a party into Albemarle Sound to explore. Later that month Grenville departed for England, leaving Ralph Lane in command of the colony. Taking "a great amass of good things" with him to convince Ralegh and other investors of the fecundity of the new land, Grenville soon found another source of wealth: a Spanish ship that he attacked, seizing a great store of sugar, ginger, ivory, hides, and cochineal. With this he was assured of a tremendous reception from the investors in England, for, after all, the intent of the colony had been to use it as a base to raid Spanish ships.

In the fall, Lane sent an exploring party north to Chesapeake Bay to find somewhere that might be more suitable for a settlement. Here they camped in the vicinity of today's Norfolk, Virginia, among the "Chesepians" over the winter. It seems that Lane intended to move the colony north to a new site once a relief ship arrived from England. In March and April 1586 he himself led an expedition west to the head of Albemarle Sound and up the Roanoke River, looking for "a good mine, or a passage to Southsea," and up the Chowan River (which flows from the north into the western end of Albemarle Sound) looking for a good overland route to Chesapeake Bay. The natives of the region had now turned unfriendly, having heard of the depravations on the local tribes during the winter. But Lane was a soldier, a veteran of the Irish wars, and he simply overpowered the Indians by force of arms.

No relief ship arrived. But in June a fleet under Sir Francis Drake unexpectedly arrived, on his way back to England after fighting with the Spanish in the Caribbean (and fresh from the sacking of Saint Augustine on the coast of Florida). Drake supplied the colonists with everything from food and ammunition to a new pinnace for exploration, but then a storm struck, sinking the new ship and scattering the supplies. Lane accepted Drake's offer of a passage back to England. Just after they had all left, the relief ship arrived, but, finding no one, turned and headed home. Grenville also arrived a little later. Determined to hold the colony, he landed fifteen men as a token force, and then sailed for England. But the men left behind did not survive in a now hostile land.

In January of the following year, 1587, Ralegh tried again, sending John White with three ships and 150 men, women, and children, including White's own newly married daughter, Elenore Dare. After picking up Grenville's men, they were to establish a new settlement on Chesapeake Bay—"the citie of Ralegh in Virginia," which had a coat of arms though no existence in reality.

Largely due to the apparent incompetence of the pilot Fernandez, who wanted to attack Spanish shipping at every opportunity, they ended up back at Roanoke in July and went no farther. Now White was to pay the price of Lane's aggression the year before. The Roanoke Indians immediately began a war of attrition against the colonists.

White was selected to return to England with the ships to press their case for more support. Elenore Dare had just given birth to a daughter, named Virginia, of course, and the colonists reasoned that White would not abandon his relatives.

They had reckoned without Queen Elizabeth. The growing threat of a Spanish attack on England led her to forbid the removal of any ships needed for the defence of the realm. White did slip away on a pirate ship, but it was attacked by a larger ship and forced to return to England. The Spanish Armada was defeated in the summer of 1588, but still no relief was authorized until 1590. When White finally arrived back at Roanoke Island in August 1590 his colony had disappeared. No one really knows what happened to the "lost colony," but it seems inevitable that it was overwhelmed by the superior numbers of natives. England's colonial aspirations would have to await the new century. Nevertheless, the possibilities of the New World had been revealed, not least by the publication in 1588 of Thomas Hariot's *Briefe and true report of Virginia.*

MAP 52 (*above, left*).
The map of Virginia published in Thomas Hariot's *Briefe and true report of Virginia* in 1588.

MAP 53 (*right*).
John White's classic finished map of the region of the first English settlement in North Carolina, including all the information gained from exploration parties. The first copies of White's maps and drawings were lost when a storm hit the boats loading Drake's ships in June 1586. The map shows that a remarkable amount of exploration had been done in the short time available. It was likely drawn in England in late 1586 or in 1587.

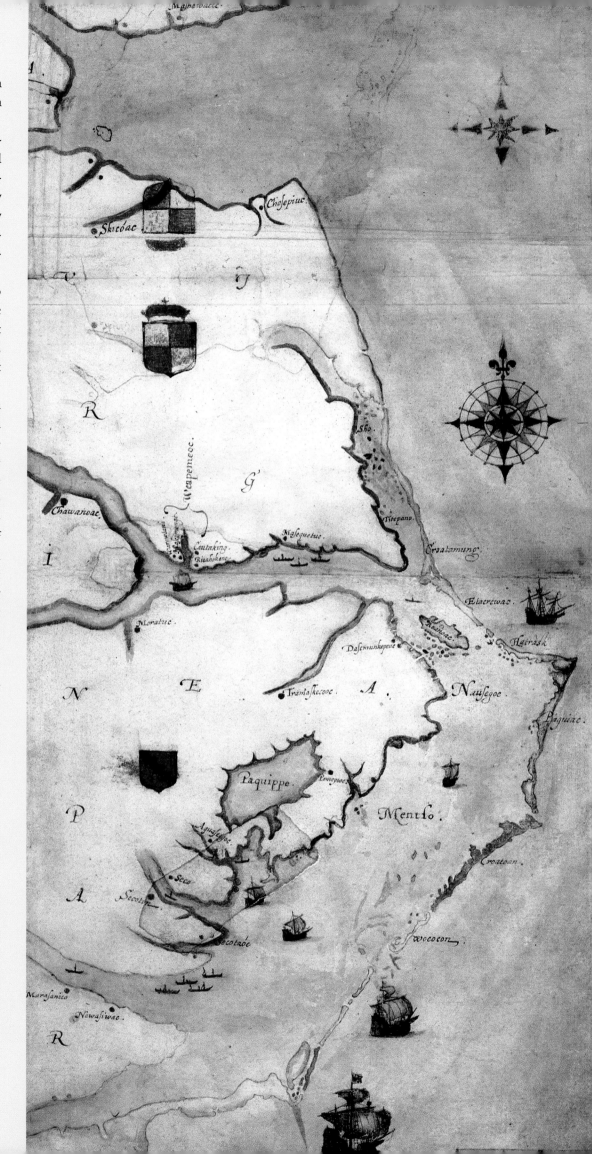

After the disastrous end to the French colonizing efforts in Georgia and South Carolina, French efforts were directed farther north, out of the way of Spanish claims. Like those of the English, these ventures were directed by groups of investors in companies chartered usually as a monopoly by the crown, rather than by any direct royal or state involvement. But it was clear from the continued flow of fish and, increasingly, furs, that there was money to be made even in the north.

The first French colonization attempt was on Sable Island, off the coast of Nova Scotia, in 1598, when two shiploads of convicts were landed. For obvious reasons, settlement on this barren, windswept isle was not a success. The monopoly passed to Pierre Chauvin, who established a fur-trading post at Tadoussac, on the north shore of the St. Lawrence, in 1600. When he died in 1603 the royal favor was granted to a new company led by the governor of Dieppe, Aymar de Chaste. He sent out an expedition in 1603 led by François Pont-Gravé, who found Samuel de Champlain, already a competent navigator, to accompany him.

That year Champlain sailed to Tadoussac. During the summer he explored as far as Montréal in a pinnace that had been carried disassembled in the larger ship's hold. He also went about fifty miles up the Saguenay, which Jean Alfonce had argued was the way to the Pacific (see page 29). It was not, but Champlain did hear from the Indians about a great saltwater bay to the north—Hudson Bay.

On his return to France in September, he found that De Chaste had died, and the monopoly passed on once again, this time to Pierre du Gua, Sieur de Monts, who rehired Champlain. The following year three ships were sent out, but two were to make for Nova Scotia—Acadie—where, De Monts had been persuaded, the climate was more favorable for colonization.

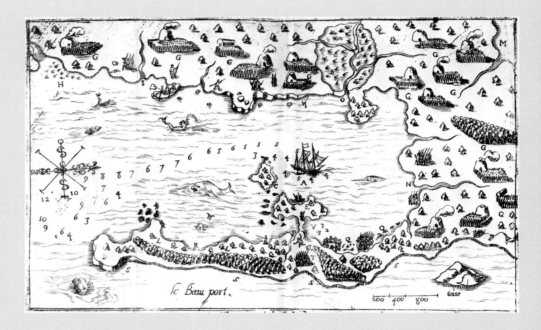

MAP 54 (*right*).
One of the best local maps made by Champlain was this one drawn during his third southward foray to New England. It shows his *Le Beau Port*, today Gloucester Harbor, originally drawn in September 1606. The pinnace is shown anchored at *A*, behind Ten Pound Island just to its left on this representation, today still a favorite anchoring place for pleasure boats.

MAP 55 (*left*).
This pictomap from Champlain's 1613 book shows the attack on the French by the Nauset Indians at Stage Harbor, Chatham, Massachusetts (at the southeast corner of Cape Cod), in October 1606. With some artistic license, probably by the engraver, a sequence of events is depicted. At *A* and *B* natives are shown attacking a tent where some of the Frenchmen were baking bread; at *L* and *M* natives are attacking the shallop (in fact the French were in the boat rather than natives, as shown). The pinnace is at *N*.

Champlain arrived in Nova Scotia in early May 1604 and was immediately put to the task of locating a suitable spot for a colony. Champlain explored the entire shore of the Bay of Fundy in this quest, mapping a number of possible harbors. He did this again in September, reaching south to the large island-filled Penobscot Bay, explored by Estévan Gomez in 1525 as a possible passage to Cathay (see page 17).

But the best site was not chosen, probably because defense was considered the overriding factor. Because of this, an island was chosen in the St. Croix River, which is today the international boundary between Canada and the United States. Here the would-be colonists spent a miserable winter. Thirty-five out of seventy-five men perished. The winter seems to have been particularly long and harsh that year. "Il y a six mois d'uyer en ce pays," wrote Champlain. "There are six months of winter in this country."

In June and July the following year, Champlain was again sent to explore the coast for possible new settlement sites, and this time he ranged farther south, sailing in the pinnace as far as Cape Cod, mapping all the harbors he could find. Despite the discovery of a number of possibilities, De Monts decided to move the colony just across the Bay of Fundy to the Annapolis Basin, where he established Port Royal. Although still not ideal—twelve more died that winter—it was better than St. Croix.

In 1606 a further exploration of the coast to the south was made, and in 1607, in a shallop with nine men, Champlain explored and mapped the coast of Nova Scotia as far north as Canso.

Champlain's explorations produced the first reasonably accurate detailed maps of the coast from Canso to Cape Cod and the first maps of many of the harbors along this coast; many were incorporated into his maps of New France (such as that of 1632, MAP 73, page 59). Champlain went back to France in September 1607, never to return to Acadia. Instead, the following year he established a permanent French presence on the St. Lawrence at Québec (see page 58).

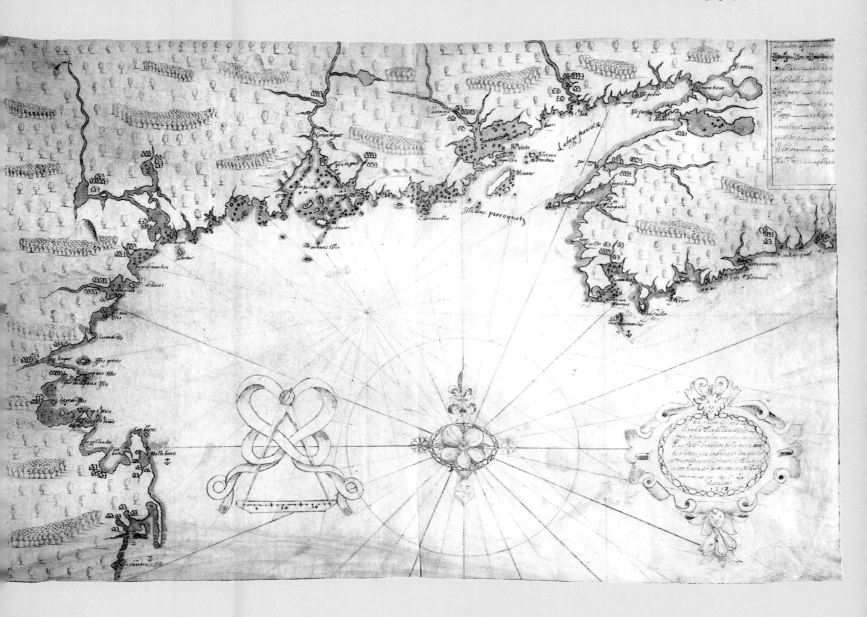

MAP 56.
Champlain's quite accurate summary map of his exploration of the outer New England, New Brunswick, and Nova Scotia coasts, from Cape Cod (*Cap blanc*) to Liverpool, Nova Scotia (*P. au Rossignol*). The long promontory at the southern end of the map is the island of Monomoy, at the elbow of Cape Cod; *S. Loiiis* is Plymouth; *Pentagoet* marks Penobscot Bay; and *La baye francaise* is the Bay of Fundy. The map was drawn in 1607.

Harbors for Ships and Men

The Philippines had been taken over by the Spanish in 1565 by an army under Miguel López de Legazpi. His pilot, Andrés de Urdaneta, figured out how to get back to New Spain by sailing first northwards to utilize the westerly winds at about 43° N, and his theory had been proven by Alonso de Arellano, one of Legazpi's captains, the same year. For the next 250 years, the Manila galleon, as it was called, annually hauled the treasures of the Philippines back to New Spain.

The required route took the galleons down the coast of California, and it was not long before the Spanish realized that it would be useful to know the location of harbors where the galleons could take refuge. Some galleons had made landings on the coast, but these ships were so large and laden that it was not practical for them to do any coastal exploration. In 1587 one galleon, under Pedro de Unamuno, landed at Morro Bay, near San Luis Obispo, and there was some limited exploration of the country around, but the main event was a ceremony of possession for the Spanish king. In 1595, another galleon, under Sebastian Cermeño, landed at Drake's Bay on Point Reyes, the very same bay likely used by Sir Francis Drake to career his ship sixteen years before, but Cermeño came to grief; his ship grounded and he and his crew only escaped by cruising down the coast in a longboat.

In 1602, Sebastian Vizcaíno, a merchant involved with the Philippines trade, was authorized to sail north from Acapulco to find harbors. With three ships, he rediscovered San Diego, first found by Juan Cabrillo in 1542 (see page 25); the Spanish, overdoing their secrecy, were not in the habit of giving an explorer the most up-to-date maps, and this led to much rediscovery—and a confusion of names—over the three hundred years of Spanish exploration of the West Coast.

Vizcaíno mapped the coast in some detail and discovered Monterey Bay. One of the ships, commanded by ensign Martín de Aguilar, was separated from the others in a storm and forced northwards beyond Cape Blanco, where a large river was discovered, which they named the Rio Santa Iñez.

This "entrance of Martin Aguilar" showed up on maps for centuries afterwards as either the western entrance to the Strait of Anian—leading to the Atlantic—or the mouth of the River of the West, long thought hopefully to flow to the Pacific from deep within the continent. Some thought it the Strait of Juan de Fuca, which

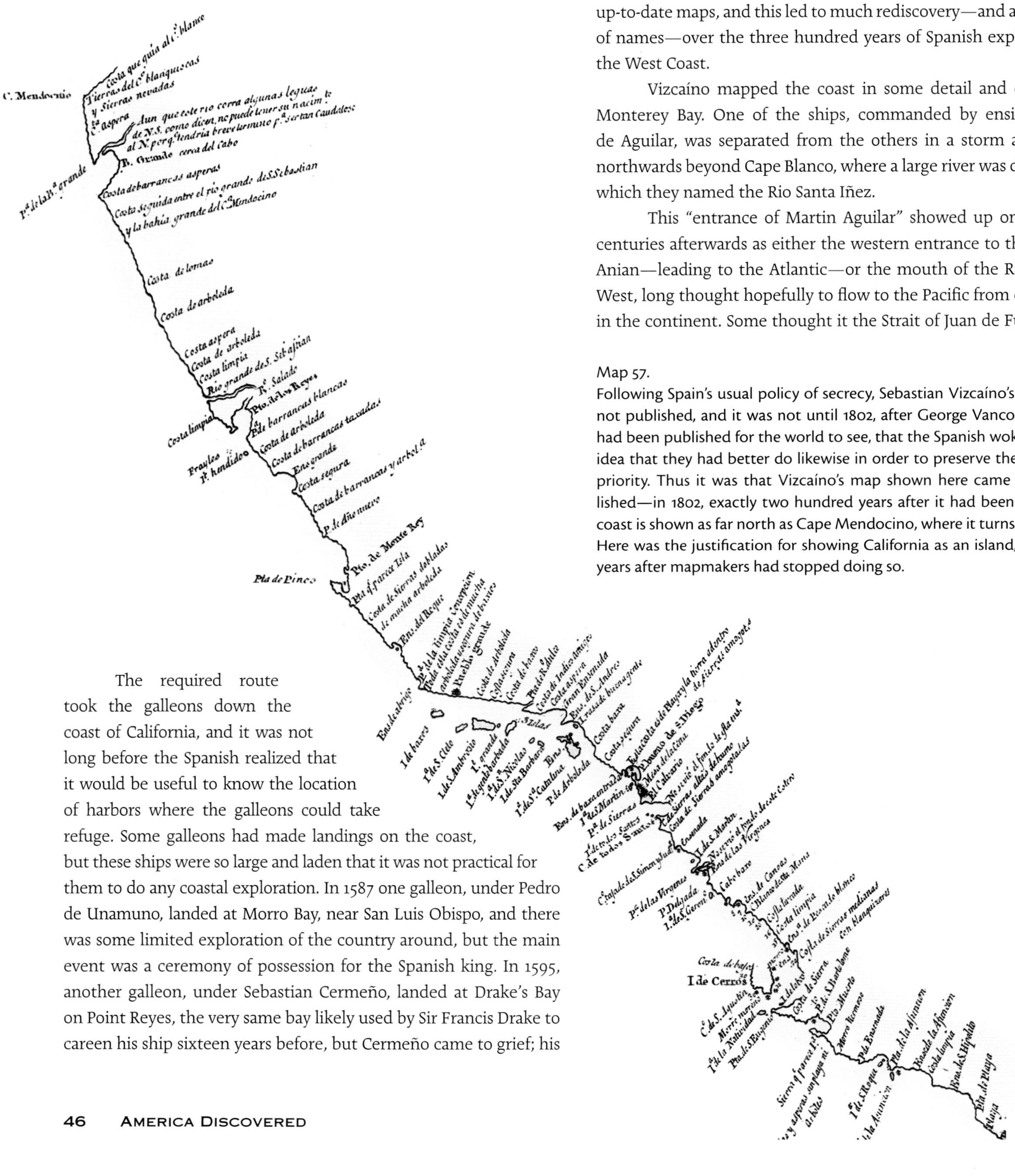

Map 57.
Following Spain's usual policy of secrecy, Sebastian Vizcaíno's maps were not published, and it was not until 1802, after George Vancouver's work had been published for the world to see, that the Spanish woke up to the idea that they had better do likewise in order to preserve their claims of priority. Thus it was that Vizcaíno's map shown here came to be published—in 1802, exactly two hundred years after it had been made! The coast is shown as far north as Cape Mendocino, where it turns to the east. Here was the justification for showing California as an island, a hundred years after mapmakers had stopped doing so.

was reputed to have been found in 1592 by a pilot of the same name, but records of such a voyage have never been found.

Vizcaíno had been instructed to follow a westward-trending coast towards Asia, but found instead that the coast north of Cape Mendocino turned eastwards, and so he did not follow it. This eastward bend in the coast was used as justification by some cartographers for showing California as an island; here, clearly, was the northern tip.

Vizcaíno's expedition lasted only one year, but that of another, contemporaneous Spanish expedition lasted for no less than seven. This was the inland foray of Juan de Oñate, the governor of New Mexico, to Spain's frontier lands to the north of its Mexican domains. Not only was Oñate's expedition long, it was also large: 400 men, 130 families, 83 carts, and 7,000 cattle. Was this an exploration? New ground was discovered and mapped, yet the principal purpose was one of colonization.

Most of the time a new Spanish policy of better treatment of Indians was followed; friars accompanying the expedition set up missions in the pueblo country. In 1601 Oñate led a party northeast in search of the elusive Quivira, coming into contact with Apache and seeing the vast buffalo herds of the plains. In 1604–05 he led another expedition down the Colorado River to the Gulf of California. Oñate was recalled in 1608, but the Spanish friars went on to establish a mission at Santa Fe in 1610—the original settlement seems to have been in 1607 or 1608—and it became the capital of their northern region and the Holy Grail of western explorers wanting to establish trade routes for two centuries thereafter.

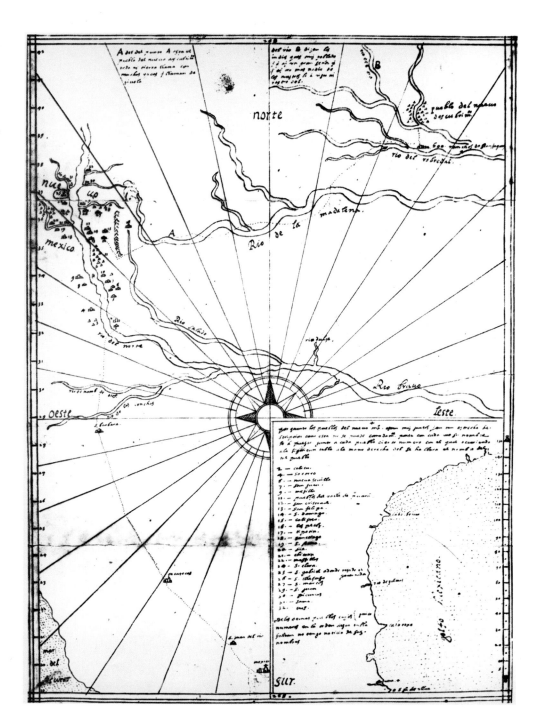

MAP 58 (*above*).
Map by Juan de Oñate of his expedition in 1601 to search for Quivira, the fabled city of legend. This is shown as *Pueblo del nuevo describimento* at top right, at a location about twenty-five miles northwest of modern Wichita, Kansas. The *rio del robrodal* is today's Arkansas River. The more populated region at top left is the valley of the Rio Grande, shown as the *rio del norte*, where the Spanish would establish Santa Fe about 1607. The *Rio salada* is the Pecos River, and the *Rio de la madalena* is the Canadian River. This map is probably the earliest surviving map of any part of western North America made by an explorer in the field.

Excursions from the Chesapeake

Although the English intended to move to the shore of Chesapeake Bay in 1587, they never made it. Not until April 1607 was a new effort made to settle, on the James River. A Spanish Jesuit mission had been established somewhere on the lower James in 1570, but it had lasted only a year before being wiped out. Some of Ralph Lane's men had spent a winter on the lower James in 1585–86. And in 1588, a Spanish expedition under Vincente González (who had transported the Jesuits in 1570) searched Chesapeake Bay for any signs of intruding Englishmen.

The new Virginia Company organized the 1607 attempt to found a permanent colony at Jamestown, a site on the north side of the James River, sixty miles upstream from Chesapeake Bay. Captain John Smith, though not the original leader of the expedition, soon emerged as such, and it was he who did most of the initial exploration of the region.

Just a month after arriving in Virginia, Smith accompanied Christopher Newport up the James River to the falls (at Richmond).

Expectations were, as usual, unrealistic. Newport had instructions "not to returne without a lumpe of gold, a certainty of the south-sea or one of the lost colony of Sir Walter Rawley." They returned without these but not empty-handed, for they had persuaded a native to draw them a map, which showed not a South Sea but mountains to the west.

In December 1607 and January 1608 Smith led a small party up the Chickahominy River (which flows into the James) and overland to the Rappahannock. During this expedition he was captured by the chief Powhatan and saved—if we are to believe Smith's account—by the intervention of the chief's daughter, Pocahontas.

Between January and July 1608 Smith explored the intricate shore of Chesapeake Bay in a small boat. He ventured as far north as today's Baltimore and he found the "Patowomek" (Potomac) River, which he ascended to just past the site of today's Washington, D.C., in search of a "big sea water" the Indians had told him of, in fact perhaps one of the Great Lakes.

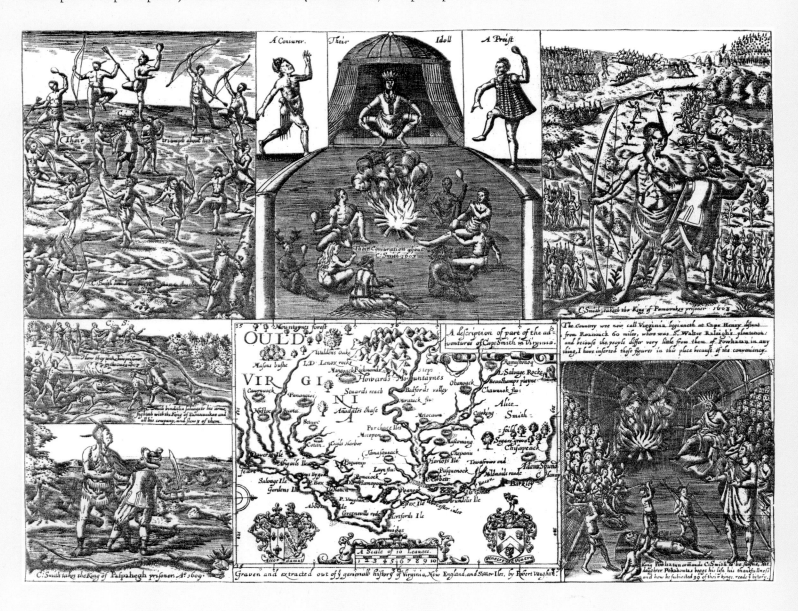

Map 59 (*left*).

This extensively illustrated map appeared in John Smith's *Generall History of Virginia, the Somer Iles* [Bermuda], *and New England*, published in 1624. It was compiled and drawn by Robert Vaughan to illustrate the adventures of Smith. Most of the scenes are taken from engravings made by Theodor De Bry, as is the map of "ould Virginia," referring to Walter Ralegh's patent, the region in which the English tried to settle in the 1580s, which De Bry in turn copied from John White (**Map 53**, page 43). Vaughan drew Smith into the scenes wherever he could.

Map 60 (*above*).

John Smith's map of Virginia, drawn in 1611 and first published the following year in the explanatory booklet *A Map of Virginia, With a Description of the Country*; this copy is from his 1624 *Generall History of Virginia*. The engraver, William Hole, was supplied with a basic sketch map by Smith augmented with other sketched details from his explorations upriver, to which were added some verbal descriptions from native sources. Hole integrated these to produce this detailed first map of Virginia. There are, if you look carefully, small crosses on many of the rivers. These mark the limits of Smith's own explorations; everything above them was drawn from native information. The combination on a map of an explorer's own work with native information beyond firsthand exploration was common until the middle of the nineteenth century.

In July 1608 Smith began another expedition, which took him to the very head of Chesapeake Bay, to the Susquehanna River. On entering the "river of Tockwogh, the Salvages all armed, in a fleete of boats, after their barbarous manner, round invironed us." Nevertheless, one spoke the language of Powhatan, and a "friendly parley was arranged." Smith's account of his explorations of Chesapeake Bay and the rivers draining into it make it abundantly clear that he was in a region quite heavily populated with native people. He sometimes had to resort to unusual means to prevent his boat from being attacked. At one point in 1608, with more than half his dozen men ill, he displayed their hats on sticks in his boat to make the natives think there were more of them.

Smith's main hope still was to find a route to the Pacific. Even half a century later this was still thought to be just a few miles from the other side of the mountains. Perceptions of distance were a little off. Smith himself soon decided, more correctly, that the sea he kept hearing about was to the north rather than to the west, and was likely a reference to either the Great Lakes or the great bay to the north reported by Henry Hudson's men.

Hudson Finds His River

By 1600 the English were becoming interested in a region they had previously ignored, the region between New Jersey and Maine that they called North Virginia. In the space of a few years, most of it would be transformed into the second primary English settlement in America, New England.

The voyage of Bartholomew Gosnold was the first attempt to establish a colony in the region. Privately financed by the Earl of Southampton, Gosnold sailed for New England in 1602 with twenty would-be colonists aboard. A colony was established on Cuttyhunk Island, a very small island south of modern New Bedford, Massachusetts. A good defensive site, the island was hopelessly inadequate for a colony, which quickly failed, largely because of Indian hostility. Nevertheless, the English continued to be interested in this apparently fertile land. Gosnold named both Cape Cod and Martha's Vineyard, the latter after his mother, a name originally applied to a nearby island, and the former because "here we found excellent Cod." Gosnold was later one of the organizers of the Virginia Company and captain of *Godspeed,* one of the three ships that took settlers to Jamestown (see page 48).

Three years after Gosnold, another English navigator, George Waymouth, sailed up the St. George River, in Maine, on a voyage intended to find the Northwest Passage. He did not find it in the Maine countryside, but he was impressed by the fertility of the land, and thus in 1607 the new Virginia Company established a little colony led by George Popham around Fort St. George at the mouth of the Kennebec River. This lasted only one year and was abandoned after an exceptionally hard winter, similar to that the French had found so difficult on this coast at much the same time just slightly farther to the north (see page 45). The site of Fort St. George was located as recently as 1997.

The principal explorer of the region in the years before the establishment of permanent colonies was also an Englishman, although he was working at the time for the Dutch. This was Henry Hudson, one of the most persistent at trying to find a route to Cathay and also one of the most experienced navigators of his age.

In 1607, at the instigation of the English Muscovy Company, he had attempted to sail over the supposedly ice-free North Pole to the East. The next year he tried to find a Northeast Passage; he got as far as Novaya Zemlya, north of Russia, but, once again, found no usable route. In 1609 he was invited to try once again towards the northeast by the Dutch East India Company, but this time his crew mutinied (he had language problems; his crew was Dutch) and instead, on his own initiative, Hudson decided to sail west and look for a Northwest Passage. He had reckoned without his mutinous crew,

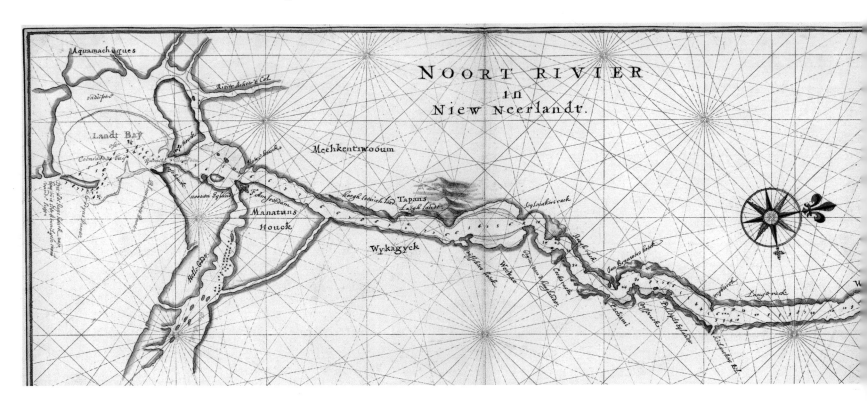

MAP 61.
The Hudson River, called the Noort Rivier by the Dutch, from New York Harbor (at left) to Albany. This is a later Dutch map, drawn in 1639 by Joan Vingtboons, and shows F[ort] *Amsterdam* on the site of Manhattan and F[ort] *Orange* at Albany. The wide part of the river is marked *Tapans,* today still the Tappan Zee. North is to the right. The map of the river is drawn in two sections, but is shown here connected together.

who insisted he try farther south than he had intended. Thus it was that in the summer of 1609 Henry Hudson in his ship *Half Moon* was probing the inlets of the east coast of North America for passages to Cathay.

Hudson sailed as far south as North Carolina before turning north. He did not enter Chesapeake Bay to visit John Smith, probably because he was in the employ of a foreign power, but he did note Delaware Bay. To the Dutch this became the South River.

On 10 September Hudson thought he might have finally found what he was looking for. Entering the narrows found by Giovanni Verrazano eighty-five years before, he found a spacious harbor. This was New York Harbor. He then entered a large channel, which turned north. It was the river that would later be known as the Hudson River. The Dutch called it the Noort Rivier, the North River.

On 12 September Hudson entered his river, trading "Oysters and Beanes" from the natives. Two days later he reached "a Strieght between tow points" where the river is a mile wide. This was the Tappan Zee, a considerable widening of the river that must have encouraged Hudson to think he was on the right path to the South Sea. Hudson sailed 150 miles up the river, as far as today's Albany, and sent boats out another 25 miles. But it was only a river; the boats "found it to be at an end for shipping to goe in." There were mere seven-foot depths, and so Hudson, no doubt reluctantly, turned back.

When Hudson returned to Europe later in 1609 he stopped first at the mouth of the Thames in England. Here he was arrested by an annoyed government for "voyaging to the detriment of his country."

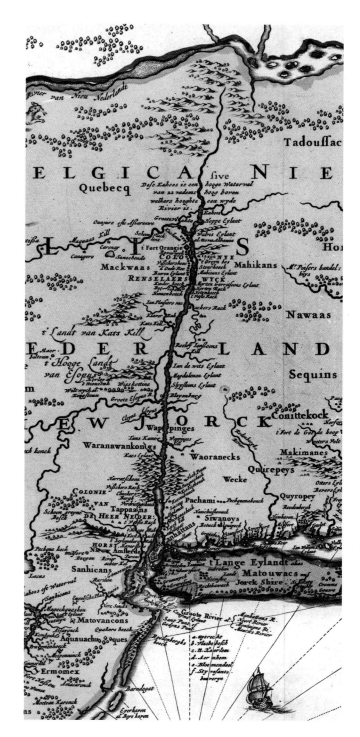

Map 62 (*right*).
The course of the Hudson River through the New Netherlands is shown in this map drawn by Dutch mapmaker Nicolas Visscher probably about 1651. This edition was not published until 1685, by which time the Dutch had been ousted from their American domain for twenty years.

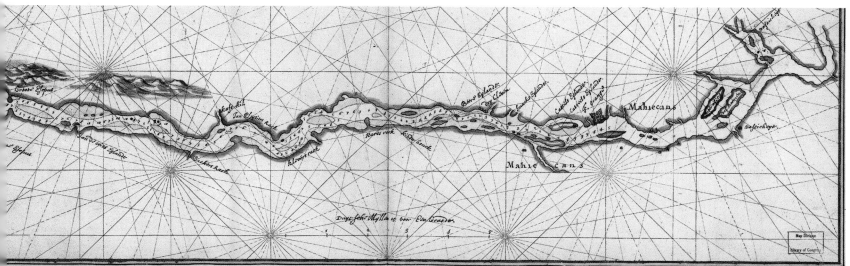

Indeed it was to England's detriment; soon after the Dutch New Netherlands Company capitalized on Hudson's findings, claiming the whole region for Holland, and Dutch fur traders were soon making the voyage west. One such trader was Adriaen Block, who in 1614 found Manhattan's East River. He had lost his ship to fire and built a new one from the trees of Manhattan Island, and the new ship was blown one day into the river. Calling it Hellegat—"Hell's Gate"—because of the tide rips, he sailed through it and found Long Island Sound beyond. Sailing around the eastern tip of Long Island he was the first to realize that it was an island, and, of course, he claimed it all for his country. He also found an island off the tip of Long Island he called after himself, Adriaen Block's eylandt, today just Block Island.

New Netherlands was the province of the Dutch, under first the New Netherlands Company and then the Dutch East India Company, until 1664, when control was wrested from them by the English.

At the same time that Block was sailing around Long Island, Captain John Smith of Virginia fame (see page 48) made an exploratory voyage to the region. It was, in fact, Smith who seems to have coined the name *New England* to replace Norumbega, the name by which the region was previously generally known, a name Smith no

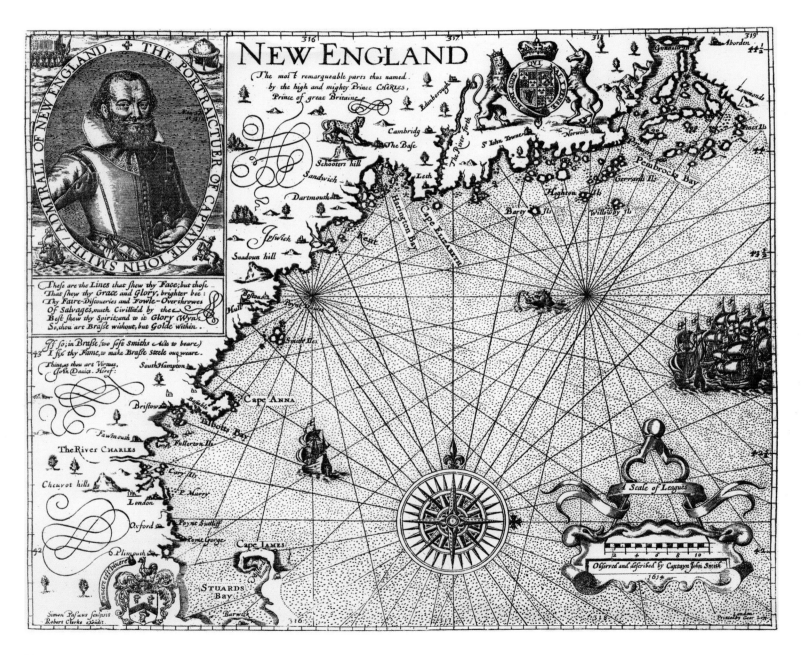

MAP 63.

The map of New England from Cape Cod to the Penobscot River that appeared in John Smith's *Generall History of Virginia* in 1624. The original grant of Virginia by James I in 1606 defined it as extending from 34° to 44° N, which included most of New England. The map was drawn by Simon van der Passe from John Smith's 1614 explorations and went through many editions; this is an early one. Little detail is shown beyond the coastline; *Cape James* (at bottom) is easily recognizable as Cape Cod. The latter was first named by Bartholomew Gosnold in 1602 on account of all the fish he found there, and it was renamed Cape James by Prince Charles (later Charles I of England) at Smith's request. The original name was the one that prevailed. One of Smith's names did endure, however—New England.

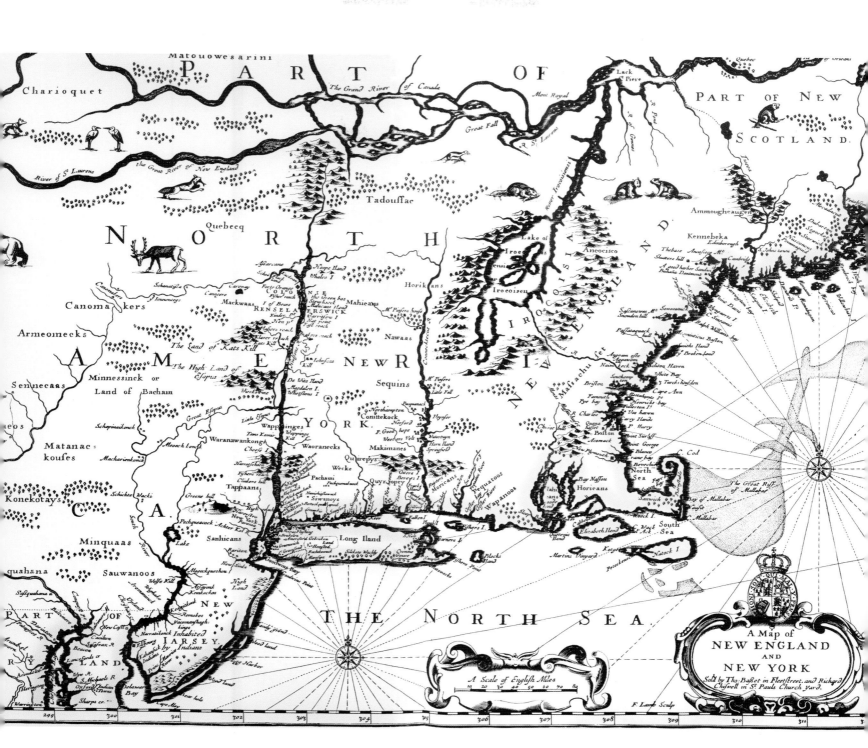

MAP 64.
New England and New York, 1627, by English mapmaker John Speed, published in his *Prospect of the Most Famous Parts of the World*, the first general atlas produced in England. New York at this time referred to the country between the Connecticut and Hudson Rivers; the Dutch were still ensconced in New Amsterdam and claimed much of the lands here apparently attributed to England. You would hardly know from this map that the Dutch had any presence in the region at all. The large lake in New England is Lake Champlain, drastically misplaced towards the east. Noted by Samuel de Champlain in 1609, it had been incorrectly located on his 1613 published map and simply copied, mistakes and all, by Speed. The interior of New England was relatively unknown in 1627, but was about to be explored by colonists wishing to expand their horizons (see page 62).

doubt thought sounded too Spanish. Other names were deliberately anglicized; the English king, Charles I, confirmed the name New England, and "did change the barbarous names . . . for such English, that posterity may say, King Charles was their godfather." It was an attempt at civilization by nomenclature; with familiar-sounding names, colonists might more easily be induced to settle.

Smith explored the coast as far north as the Penobscot River, with his eye on the resources that might be of use to settlers. He wrote that the coast of Massachusetts had in some places "Quaries of stones" that were "so strangely divided with tinctured veines of divers colours: as Freestone for building, Slate for tyling, smooth stone to make Furnasses and Forges for Glasse and Iron, and Iron Ore sufficient conveniently to melt in them." And soon the settlers would come, in 1620 creating the first permanent English colony in Smith's "New England."

Searches to the North

Henry Hudson was too valuable a navigator to stay imprisoned for long. Despite his detention for aiding a foreign power, Holland, in 1609 (see page 51), the following year he was released and sent on what was to prove his final voyage. It seems likely that his principal sponsor, Sir Thomas Smythe, who was governor of both the Virginia Company and the English East India Company at the time, bailed him out because he wanted him to lead an expedition to find a Northwest Passage. This, he thought, would recoup losses he had recently incurred when a fleet sailing to Virginia was scattered in a storm and lost.

The lure of the Northwest Passage was so strong, and the passage considered so real—but just not yet found—that wealthy men would risk their fortunes on such a venture. But men have always been attracted to the promise of easy money.

If anyone could find a passage, it was Henry Hudson, the foremost Arctic explorer of his time, with several northern voyages already to his name. Hudson was to investigate some of the "passages which [John] Davis saw" on his voyage of 1587 (see page 37).

Of particular interest was the place where Davis had encountered a "whirling and overfalling" as he sailed south from Frobisher Bay. This was the strait that Hudson took and that would come to bear his name. The disturbed seas, in fact a meeting of tides, were presumed to indicate a passage to another ocean.

Hudson sailed in April 1610 in his ship *Discovery*, the very same ship as that used by George Waymouth in 1605 (see page 50). By August he had located Davis's whirling strait and passed through it, entering Hudson Bay. So vast was the bay that Hudson was convinced he had passed through the Northwest Passage and into the South Sea.

But it was awfully chilly for a South Sea. In accordance with his expectations Hudson sailed south, and one can sympathize with his likely reaction when he reached the "bottom of the bay"—James Bay—and found he could go no farther. Worse, the winter had started to close in, and ice prevented him from returning north. And so he was forced to spend a miserable winter—for which he was totally unprepared—trapped in the ice.

Yet worse was to come. In an attempt to be fair to all, Hudson ordered that no food was to be hoarded. To enforce this, he ordered that all the men's trunks be broken open and food found there redistributed. It was too much for some of the men. A mutiny followed in which Hudson, his son, the sick, and those who had supported him were put into an open shallop and set adrift. Hudson was never seen again; his gravestone is his eponymous bay.

By June the ice had cleared sufficiently to allow an attempt to return north. Command was assumed by Robert Bylot, one of the few who, from the available evidence, does not appear to have been directly involved in the mutiny. Certainly one can imagine that many kept their mouths shut when Hudson was being set adrift for fear of being cast in with him.

The mutineers did manage to get back to England, where they were arrested, but lack of evidence allowed them to go free. There have been recent claims that Hudson was not ordered to find a Northwest Passage at all but to search for—what else—gold mines on the barren shores of northern Canada. This is a possibility, but no direct evidence for this has yet been found. Hudson put his bay clearly on the

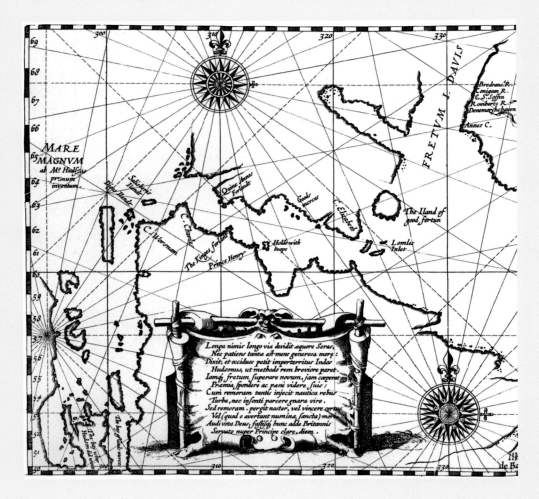

MAP 65.
Dutch mapmaker Hessel Gerritsz's *Tabula Nautica*, the first map to show Henry Hudson's discovery, Hudson Bay. It is not known why the bottom of the bay was shown with a fictional peninsula, but this feature continued to show up on maps for some time, as mapmakers copied each other.

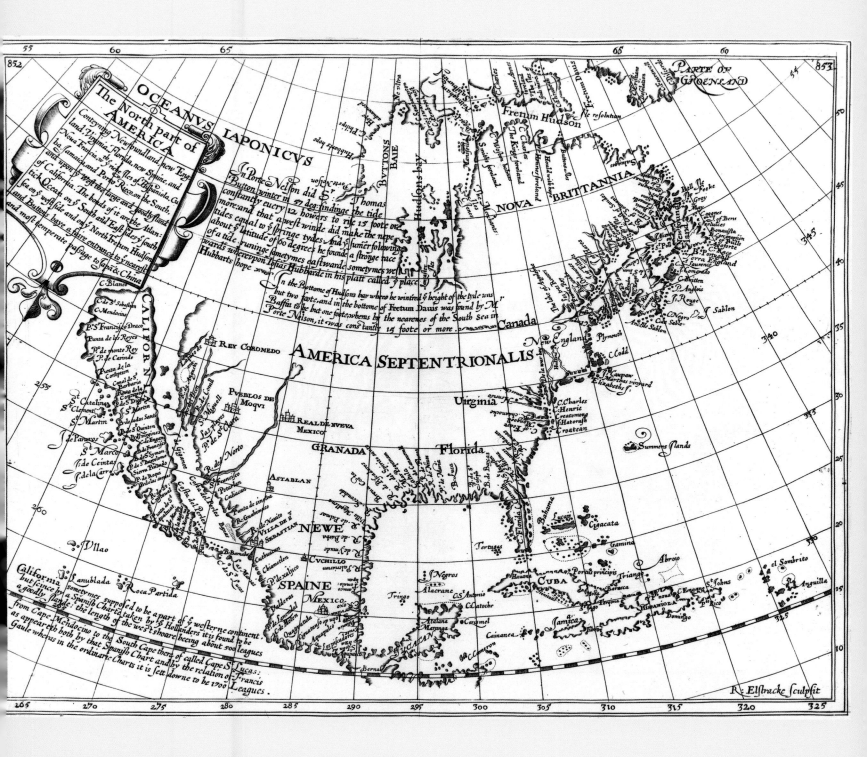

The map bears numerous inscriptions and place names, including "OCEANVS IAPONICVS", "The North part of AMERICA", "CALIFORNIA", "AMERICA SEPTENTRIONALIS", "NOVA BRITTANNIA", "PARTE OF GROENLAND", "Canada", "New England", "Virginia", "Florida", "GRANADA", "NEWE SPAINE", "MEXICO", "CUBA", "Jamica", "HISPANIOLA", "BUTTONS BAIE", "Hudsons bay", "Fretum Hudson", and "R. Elstracke sculpsit".

map, or at least its eastern half, and in so doing firmly established later English claims to the region, claims that would be parlayed into the entire drainage basin of the bay, which would become the Rupert's Land of the Hudson's Bay Company sixty years later.

In England there arose a popular rumor that Hudson had found a Northwest Passage before the mutiny. Another group of investors formed a new company with the presupposing name of the Company of the Merchants Discoverers of the Northwest Passage, or the Northwest Company, and hired a Welshman, Thomas Button, to determine what had happened to Hudson and to complete "ye full and perfect discovery of the North-west Passage."

With two ships, *Resolution* and *Discovery* (the latter being Hudson's ship), and taking Robert Bylot with him, Button sailed into Hudson Bay in 1612 and immediately headed westwards, in which

MAP 66.

This map by Henry Briggs, published in 1625, was the first to show the results of Button's explorations. The western half of Hudson Bay is *Buttons Baie*. *Ne ultra* is Roe's Welcome Sound, in fact not a bay, though it leads only to Foxe Basin to the north and was choked with ice when Button was there. Briggs's map, *The North Part of America*, is famous not so much for its depiction of Button's voyage as for being one of the earliest to show California as an island, a myth that lasted until 1702 (see page 84).

direction he expected to find the passage, making a landfall on the west side of the bay at a place he named, for obvious reasons, Hopes Checkt. No effort at all was made to find Hudson. Button overwintered at the mouth of the Nelson River (which he named after Robert Nelson, the master of the *Resolution*) on the western shore, the first to do so, then headed north looking for passages west. He was stopped at a place he named *Ne ultra* ("Go no farther"), and, having determined that there were no passages leading out of the bay, at least in the right direction, he sailed back to England.

The next year the Northwest Company, still convinced of their purpose, sent Button's cousin William Gibbons, who had been with Button the year before, to continue the search. Gibbons did much less than Button, reaching only the Labrador coast, where he spent ten weeks at a place his crew christened Gibbons, His Hole.

Two years later, in 1615, the Northwest Company investors tried yet again. This time they sent Robert Bylot, from Hudson's crew, together with William Baffin, an experienced Arctic navigator, as his pilot. They sailed into Hudson Strait and at its western end made many measurements of tides, which, it was thought, would indicate whether or not the strait led to another sea (Map 67). Baffin correctly concluded that the strait would not lead them anywhere.

You would think that the poor investors would have given up by now, but the following year, Bylot and Baffin were sent to try yet once more, but this time farther to the north. They sailed through John Davis's strait, continued north up the west coast of Greenland, and reached 77° N, a "farthest north" that would not be bettered until 1852, by Edward Inglefield. They then sailed south along the east coast of Ellesmere Island, probing for openings to the west.

Baffin mapped three openings that he thought were bays; in fact all were passages, and one, which Baffin named Sir James Lancaster's Sound (after one of the investors), is in fact the true eastern entrance to the Northwest Passage. But because it was ice-filled, Baffin did not recognize it as such. It would be just over two centuries before someone (W. Edward Parry in 1819) sailed west through Lancaster Sound. The other openings, also named after investors, were Sir Thomas Smith's Sound (Smith Sound), which leads only poleward, and Alderman Jones Sound (Jones Sound), which leads northwest. Baffin's work for some reason baffled the principal chronicler of such voyages, Samuel Purchas. His map and journal, wrote Purchas, "were somewhat

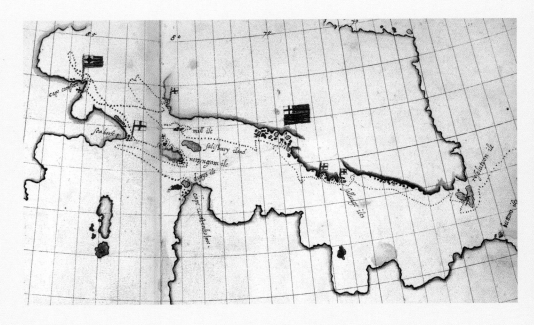

MAP 67 (*above*).
William Baffin's own map of his explorations with Robert Bylot in 1615 in Hudson Strait. The track of his ship is shown by a "red prickle line" and the flags are at locations where Baffin landed to make "tryall of the tyde," that is, to measure the tides to try to determine if they were being generated from another sea to the west.

MAP 68 (*below*).
Baffin Bay, drawn in 1628 by Hessel Gerritsz and showing the three openings mapped by Baffin.

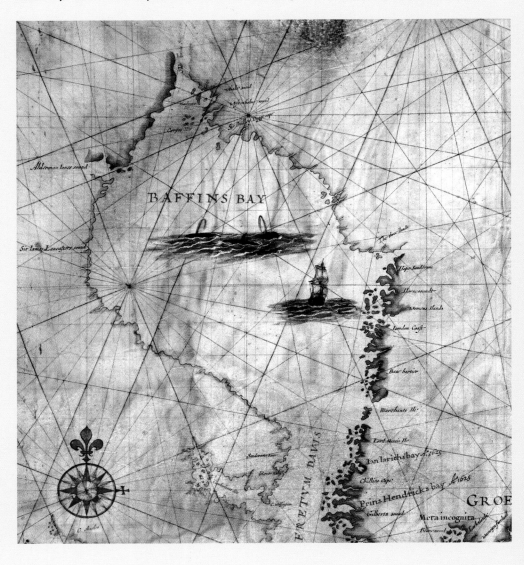

too troublesome and too costly to insert." And thus Baffin's mapping of his entire bay languished, and by the 1800s, when serious consideration was once again being given to possible openings westward, Baffin Bay was not even considered certain to exist at all.

Up to now, all this searching had been the purview of the English, but in 1624 the Danes got into the act. Their king did not want the English discovering a passage in the North, where the Danish were active in whaling. And so in 1624, Jens Ericksen Munk, the most experienced naval officer in the Danish navy, was sent to find a passage for Denmark. He ended up on the west side of Hudson Bay at the mouth of the Churchill River, where, over the winter of 1624–25, so many of his crew of sixty-four died of cold and scurvy that it was a minor miracle that he was able to get back to Denmark at all. As it was, the ship arrived back in Denmark manned by a weakened Munk and just two others.

Only thirteen years passed after Baffin before English investors were ready to risk their money once more. A new group of investors in London, which included Henry Briggs (maker of MAP 66), formed the Company of Adventurers and obtained permission from the king, Charles I, to try again. The king even lent the group a ship, named after him the *Charles,* and a captain, Luke Foxe, was hired. But then another group of merchants in Bristol, fearing that the London investors would find a passage and exclude them from trading through it, also obtained permission from the king for a venture. The Bristol group secured a ship, which they named *Henrietta Maria,* after the queen, and hired Thomas James to lead the expedition. Both ships left England within days of each other, both carrying letters from the king to the emperor of Japan.

James crossed Hudson Bay and then cruised to the south, naming Cape Henrietta Maria after his queen and his ship. With the winter closing in he sailed to the bottom of the bay, with the more reasonable intention of finding not a passage to the South Sea but one to the St. Lawrence. He found neither and ended up, like Hudson before him, trapped for the winter. He spent it on Charlton Island and temporarily sank his ship to protect it from a pounding surf. It must have been an unnerving experience for all. The large bay at the southern end of Hudson Bay became *James his baye* on his map, and James Bay it has been since.

Luke Foxe took a different tack. He first sailed northwards, for he thought that if a passage existed it would have to be in the northwest part of Hudson Bay. Foxe found a passage, choked with ice, but he could make no headway through it. This was Foxe Channel, and it led to what is today Foxe Basin. Unlike James, Foxe decided not to overwinter and arrived back in England on 31 October. Neither James nor Foxe had found a Northwest Passage but, like others before them, they had added to the knowledge of the North.

MAP 69 (*above*).
A pictomap showing Jens Munk's expedition overwintering at the mouth of the Churchill River on the west side of Hudson Bay. One of the men is already being buried.

MAP 70 (*below*).
Map of Luke Foxe's voyage, showing Foxe Channel (not named) at the northwestern end of Hudson Strait. The name *New Yorkshire* has been used for the land southwest of Hudson Bay; Foxe came from Yorkshire in England. On *T. Roes Welcome* (upside down) where Briggs had written *Ne Ultra* ("Go no farther") Foxe had written *Ut ultra* ("Go farther"). After his voyage Foxe was sure that if a Northwest Passage existed, it would have to be here.

A Short Route to China by Way of the River

Samuel de Champlain has been dubbed "the Father of New France" for establishing the first French colony in North America that lasted. But he was also an explorer, covering many thousands of miles, many of these in a quest for a western sea he felt sure was not far away, and more to reconnoiter the country for furs and other resources to supply his infant colony.

It was the early summer of 1608 when Champlain arrived once more in North America, stopping at Tadoussac as he had before to assemble a knocked-down pinnace transported in the hold of his ship. With the pinnace he sailed up the St. Lawrence to look for a suitable site for a fur-trading post. He found what he was looking for at Québec and on 3 July 1608 landed his men to begin building a fort.

The first winter at Québec was terrible; out of the twenty-four men left there, only eight survived. It took, it seems, a great deal of tenaciousness to establish a viable colony in those days.

The first order of business was to secure the colony. In order to obtain the allegiance of the nearby Huron, Algonkin and Montagnais Champlain agreed to assist them in their ongoing war against the Iroquois. Unfortunately this would incur the wrath of the Iroquois and mean that they would harass the French for almost another hundred years. (A peace was finally arranged in 1701.)

Reinforcements arrived from France in the spring, and in June, with a large native army, ascended the Richelieu River to a large lake, which Champlain later named after himself. It was exploration by force indeed. The Iroquois were defeated at Ticonderoga in a battle in which Champlain and his men used their arquebuses to devastating effect, firing four balls at once.

It was at this time that Champlain realized that the light birchbark native canoe was far superior for getting around in this country, and from this time on, that is what was used not only by Champlain but by all who came after him.

Champlain was to learn a great deal from the natives, not least of all the geography of the lands to the west. In 1610 he sent Étienne Brûlé to live among the Indians, learn their languages, scout for furs, and locate a route to the western ocean; he did all but the last. Brûlé is credited as the first European over the Toronto carrying-place north of Lake Ontario—and site of the modern city—to Lake Huron beyond. Indeed, Brûlé may well have been the first to reach as far west as Lake Superior.

Champlain was in Paris in 1612 attending to the publication of a book about his travels (*Les Voyages du Sieur de Champlain,* 1613) when he heard of Henry Hudson's discovery of Hudson Bay. He then hastily prepared a map that extended his own to incorporate this new information (Map 71, *left*). Back in Canada in 1613, Champlain journeyed up the Ottawa River in an Indian canoe as far as Allumette Island (near Pembroke, Ontario). On native advice a shortcut was taken to avoid rapids on the Ottawa, but Champlain lost his precious astrolabe (used to take sightings of the sun and determine latitude). In 1867 an astrolabe was found on this route; it was

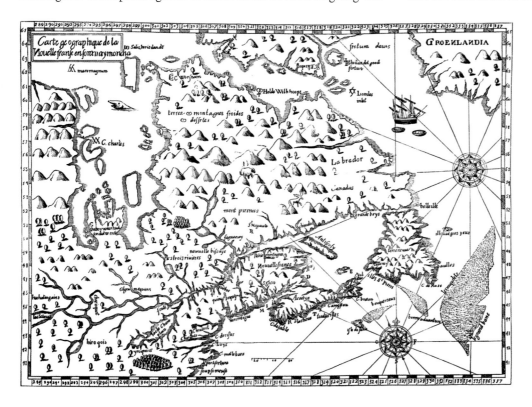

MAP 71 (*above*).
A map of New France drawn by Champlain in 1612 and published in his book in 1613 to incorporate the latest information about Hudson Bay that he learned of while in Europe that year. This was the first map to show a significant part of the North American continent, including Hudson Bay. *Lac de Champlain* is marked, but none of the Great Lakes.

MAP 72 (*left*).
Part of a revision of the same map published later in 1613 (in later editions of Champlain's book) to include information from his expedition up the Ottawa as far as Allumette Island in May and June 1613. The cross indicates the farthest point he reached.

of the right age and type and seems almost certainly to have been Champlain's. A revised version of his map (Map 71, *left, bottom*) added the details of this journey. During this trip he learned of Lake Huron (*Mer douce* on Map 73, *above*), and in 1615 he embarked on a second expedition during which he reached the lake, which he had hoped was a westward-leading strait or sea. In 1616 he drew a map with the geography of Map 73 showing Lake Huron connected to another lake to the west (Lake Superior), which to the end of his days he thought a probable passage to the South Sea.

In Paris again in 1618 to drum up investor support for the French-Canadian enterprise, he was specific. "One may hope to find a short route to China by way of the River St. Lawrence; . . . and it is certain that we shall succeed in finding it without much difficulty; and the voyage could be made in six months," he said to the chamber of commerce. He got the backing he sought.

Champlain himself made no further major explorations, but from his base at Québec he administered his colony and accumulated information from his own men and from native sources, building an increasingly accurate view of the geography to the west.

Map 73.

This was the final map Champlain produced, published in 1632, but shows everything he knew only up until about 1620. *Grand lac* is Lake Superior, for which his information came from Étienne Brûlé. It is still conveniently open on the western side, reflecting the possibility, or perhaps the desire, that it was a way to China. *Lac St. Louis* is Lake Ontario, and *Mer douce* is Lake Huron. Lakes Erie and Michigan are not shown, except possibly as a suggestion. The west side of Hudson Bay is but a peninsula, again the result of wishful thinking. A later version of this map published by French geographer Pierre Du Val goes so far as to show this complete coast with a ship's track marked "route to Cathay." *Nouvelle France* now covers the entire northern part of the continent. Despite the fantasies, the map is a remarkably accurate document for its time.

Towards the Pole Articke

Newfoundland may have been the first land found by the Northern European powers, and it was considerably closer to that continent than the lands farther south, but it was not the first to be explored away from the coasts. The rocky, windswept country held little attraction for those in search of fertile lands and had no promise of gold. The exploration of Newfoundland began only once the English had established foothold colonies on the shoreline, themselves set up to exploit the rich inshore fishery, which required a place to lay out the fish to dry. Augustine Fitzhugh's superb map shown here (MAP 75, *right*) was drawn in 1693 and still emphasizes fishing, making as much of the Grand Banks as of the land.

The Newfoundland Company was founded in 1610 and sent John Guy as its governor to set up a colony at Cupid's Cove (now Cupids), on the western shore of Conception Bay. Exploration was difficult along the coast because of the presence of pirates who attacked the fishing fleets in the summer, but late in 1612, Guy led an expedition to find out more about the land on which they had settled. He sailed, he wrote, "towards the pole Articke," actually into Trinity Bay, which is the next major bay northwest of Conception Bay. He wanted to know if the Avalon Peninsula was an island, which it very nearly is. He no doubt had seen the many maps of the time that showed Newfoundland as an archipelago. Guy found his way barred by the narrow isthmus that connects the peninsula to the rest of Newfoundland. He was probably at the northern end of Bull Arm, from where it is only five miles overland to Placentia Bay.

Guy left Newfoundland in 1613 and was replaced by John Mason, an experienced sea captain thought better able to deal with the pirates than Guy. Mason spent the summers of 1616 and 1617 exploring and mapping the southern coastline of Newfoundland all the way to St. George's Bay, at the southwestern tip of the island. The result was the first map of the whole island to be drawn from actual exploration (MAP 74, *below*).

English colonization of Newfoundland persisted, but was very marginal. One of the more famous failures is the colony of George Calvert, Lord Baltimore, established at Ferryland in 1621. It was moved in 1632 to Maryland, where the city of Baltimore commemorates his name.

MAP 74 (*below*).
John Mason's map of Newfoundland, the first to be drawn from exploration. Although drawn in 1616–17, it was not published until 1625, as part of a book designed to encourage colonization.

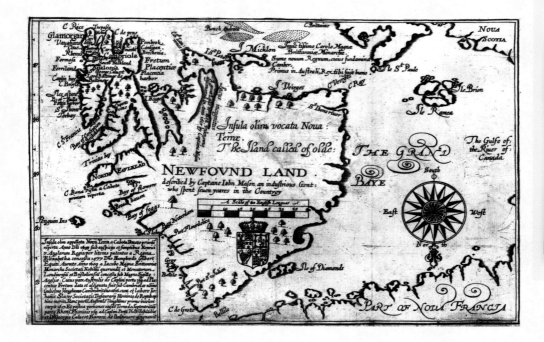

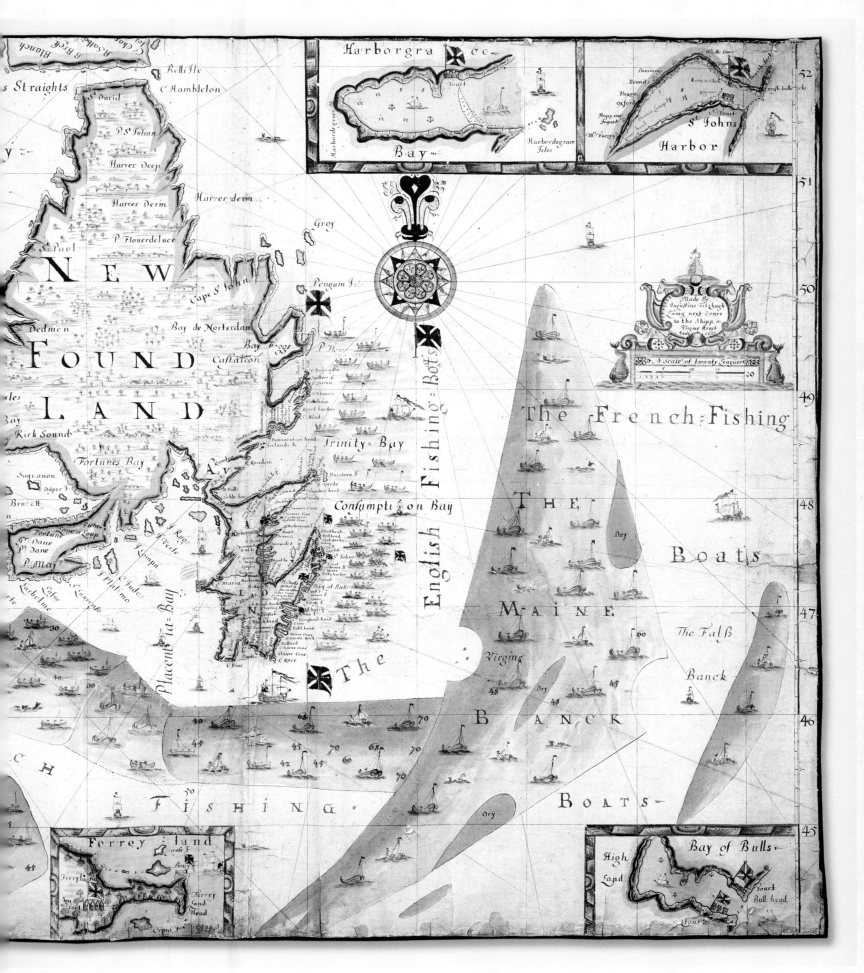

Map 75.

English Newfoundland, 1693, by Augustine Fitzhugh, with inset maps of settlements. Nothing is known of Fitzhugh, who may have been a London merchant in the fish trade, other than that he was "living next doare to the Shipp in Virgine street."

First Steps Inland

Once permanent settlements had been established on the New England seaboard from 1620 on, there was some limited exploration of the interior, or routes from one part of the coast to another, by colonists looking for new fields of endeavor. This was usually as a result of simply wanting more fertile lands or as a result of a search for freedom from religious persecution, the reason most colonists had come to America in the first place. For example, in 1636 Roger Williams and his followers were expelled from the Massachusetts Bay Colony and trekked overland to the Narragansett region, which would later become a separate colony, Rhode Island.

Beyond the coastal region, however, it was the search for other sources of wealth, especially furs, that drove exploration. In 1633, after invitation by the Indians, who saw value in the fur trade,

Edward Winslow explored up the Connecticut River and established a trading post at what is now Hartford. A year later John Oldham opened up a trail from Boston to Hartford. This was used by William Pynchon to access the river, which he explored farther north in his quest to find more furs, establishing Springfield in 1636. In much the same way Simon Willard had led a group northwards along the Merrimac River to found Concord in 1635, and in the following years he explored farther upstream, always trying to broaden his sources for furs. Many of the fur traders did not document their journeys, however, because they did not want settlers following in their wake; settlement and the fur trade were always at odds with each other.

As early as 1629 an attempt had been made to explore up the Piscataqua River farther north (from what is now Portsmouth, New

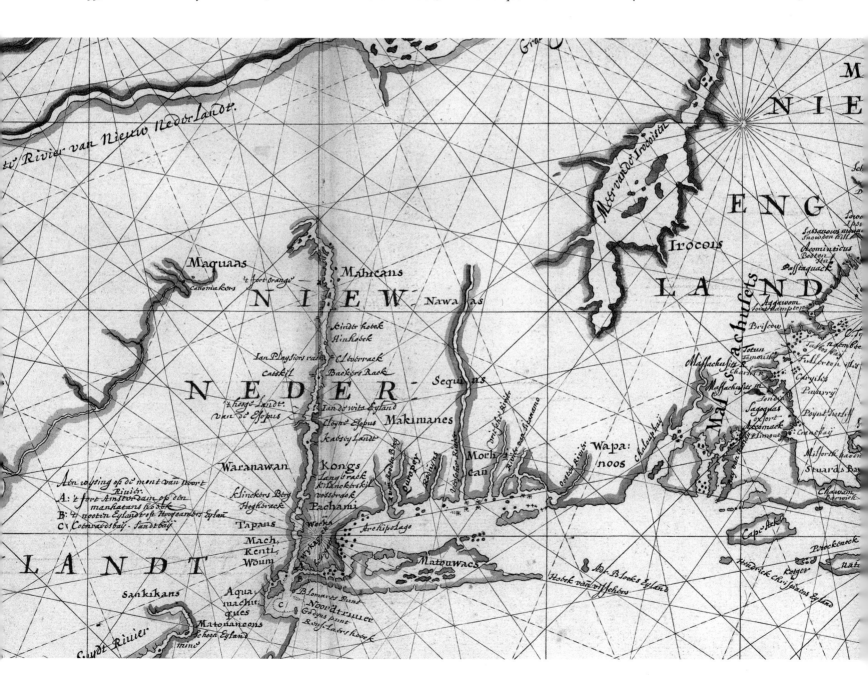

Hampshire) by Waltar Neale, governor of the Laconia Company, which had been established to find a route to Lake Champlain for an anticipated lucrative fur trade. But the lake was not so far east as thought and certainly was not accessible by such a route.

In 1642, Darby Field explored the White Mountains in the same area and thought that he could see the St. Lawrence from the summit.

Another motivation for exploration was the disputes between colonies as to their boundaries, often ill-defined in charters drawn up in England. It was the result of an exploration by John Sherman and Jonathan Ince in 1652 that made Massachusetts interpret its charter in a way that allowed it to annex Maine.

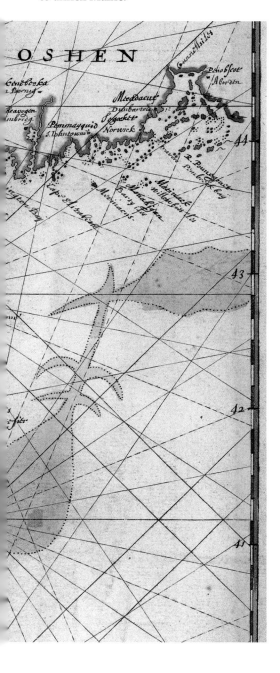

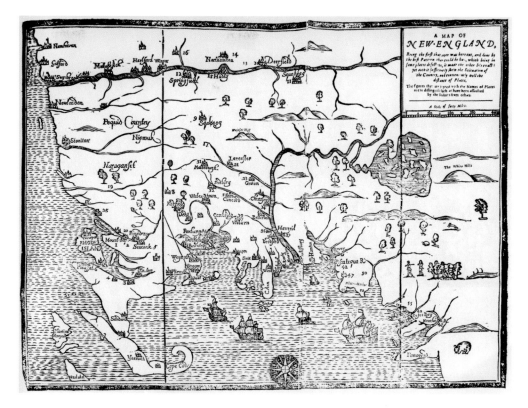

Map 76 (*left*).
This map of New England and the New Netherlands was drawn by Dutch mapmaker Joan Vingtboons in 1639. The rivers are shown as far as they were known at that date. Most prominent is the Hudson, with the Dutch stronghold of Fort Orange (Albany) at its northern end. Just to its west are the headwaters of the Susquehanna. Between the New Netherlands and New England is the Connecticut River. Looming large in New England is the *Mere van der Irocoisin*, Lake Champlain, vastly oversized and considerably misplaced to the east. The conception explains why men ascended rivers from the New England coast looking for this lake.

Map 77 (*above*).
New England in 1677. Many of the interior rivers are now known and many have settlements on them. This edition of this map shows the White Hills, the White Mountains explored by Darby Field in 1642. The prominent river is the Merrimack, flowing from an oversized Lake Winnipesaukee. This map was the first map to be drawn, engraved, and printed in America, to illustrate a book on Indian uprisings called *Narrative of the troubles with the Indians in New England*, by William Hubbard. It was published by John Foster.

Other explorers and fur traders trekked much farther west in the latter half of the seventeenth century, but failed to leave any record of their journeys. The Dutch explored westwards from Fort Orange (Albany) as early as 1616. Some discontented settlers went west in 1642 to found another settlement at Schenectady. After 1664, when the English ousted the Dutch, efforts were made to attract native fur traders to Albany at the expense of the French. In 1685 James Rosebloom, guided by deserters from the French, traveled all the way to Michilimackinac (where Lakes Michigan and Huron meet) to trade furs with the Ottawa Indians. He presumably must have roamed through northern New York, southern Ontario, and into Michigan, but his route is uncertain, for he left no record. Similarly, from 1692 to 1694 Arnout Viele, an interpreter, went west to the Susquehanna and then down the Ohio to the vicinity of today's Cincinnati to establish a trade with the Shawnee. Again, his exact route is not known.

Farther south, in the English colony of Virginia, one of the early motivations for exploration was the search for a passage to the South Sea. As late as the 1650s maps still showed the Pacific Ocean on the other side of the Appalachians, and expeditions were still going forth

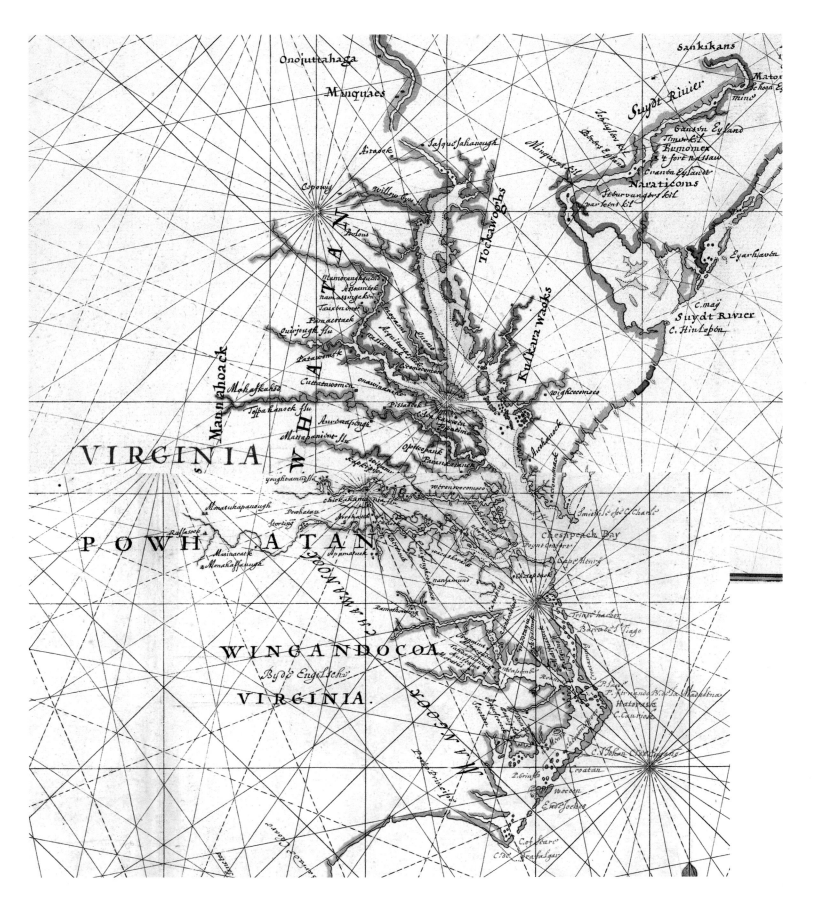

Onojuttahaga

Minquaes

Sankikans

Suydt Riuier

VIRGINIA

Mangahoack

WHATAN

Tockawoghs

Kuskarawaoks

Naraticons

Suydt Rivier
C. Hinlopen

POWHATAN

WINGANDOCOA
By de Engelsche
VIRGINIA.

Chesapeack Bay

MAP 78.
This composite of two maps by Dutch mapmaker Joan Vingtboons shows the extent of European knowledge of the East Coast in 1639. The coast itself is quite well defined and some of the major rivers are known, but beyond that the land is a blank. The Carolina coast is defined as a result of the initial English attempts at colonization in the 1580s, and knowledge of Chesapeake Bay and its tributary rivers is largely the work of John Smith and others in the Virginia Company, starting in 1607. Farther north, the Delaware River and Bay (here *Suydt Rivier,* South River) had been mapped by the Dutch. A year before this map was drawn a Swedish colony had been established on the site of today's Wilmington.

in the 1670s to find it. It would take a number of these expeditions before the reality would be accepted and the notion put to rest.

Abraham Wood was the commander of Fort Henry at the falls of the Appomattox River. He had built the fort in 1646 at the request of the Virginia General Assembly to counter Indian raids. Wood, a longtime believer in the proximity of the Pacific, first wanted to increase Indian trade at his fort, and so in 1650, with Edward Bland, he went on an expedition south to the Roanoke River (approximately where Roanoke Rapids, just inside the North Carolina boundary, sits today). Bland published a book about their journey the following year, called *The Discoverie of New Britaine,* and it was enthusiastic about the fertile soil, which Bland thought could be used in the future for growing tobacco. In the meantime, Wood seems to have increased the native fur trade at his fort as a result of his explorations.

For Bland's book, John Farrer, an English merchant so keen on Virginia that he named his daughter after the colony, drew a map that illustrated the conception of the geography of Virginia, and which showed the Pacific Ocean just over the mountains. Farrer's first effort was the rough sketch shown below (MAP 79). This was then refined, and the result was the engraved map overleaf (MAP 80).

As the notation on the map makes clear, the Pacific was expected but ten days' march from the headwaters of the James River. This notion of a Western Sea "just over the next hill" would drive explorers westwards for another century and a half, with the sea always receding before them (see page 90).

The governor of Virginia, William Berkeley, was a another believer in the proximity of the Pacific. In 1670 he commissioned John Lederer to explore to the west. Lederer undertook three expeditions in 1669 and 1670 to the Blue Ridge Mountains and the Piedmont of North Carolina. His three "marches," as he called them,

MAP 79.
John Farrer's first map of Virginia, incorporating the explorations of Edward Bland and Abraham Wood in 1650. The *West Sea where Sr Francis Drake was 1597 [sic, 1579]* is shown at top (west). The large river is *Hudsons River* and connects with the *Head River Canada* (the St. Lawrence) and the *West Sea.* This map is inserted into Farrer's own copy of a promotional book on Virginia by Edward Williams (now in the New York Public Library), the title of which leaves little doubt about its contents: *Virgo Triumphans: or, Virginia richly and truly valued; more especially the south part therof; viz the fertile Carolana, and no less excellent isle of Roanoak.*

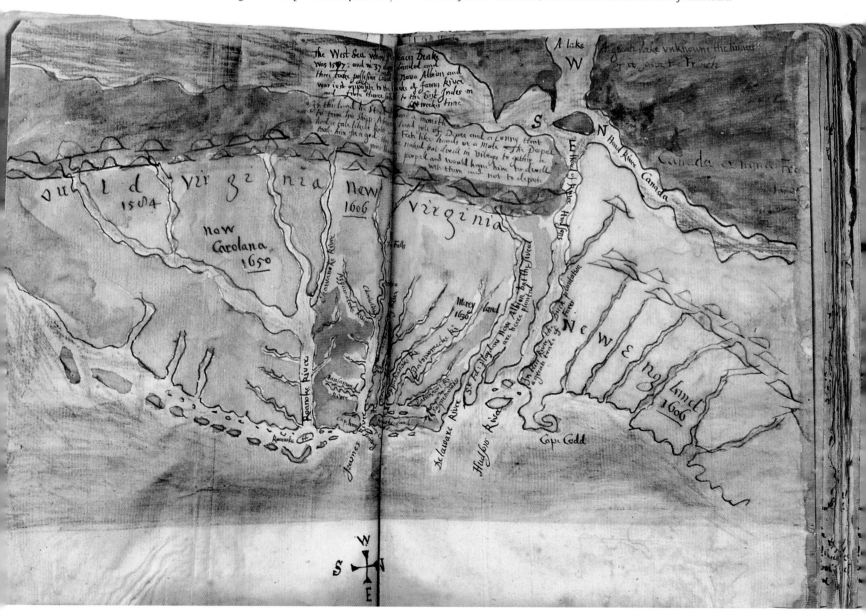

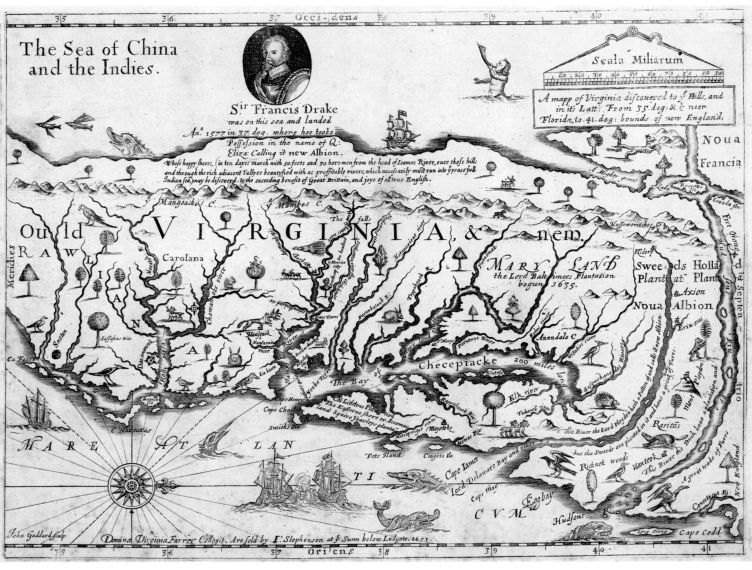

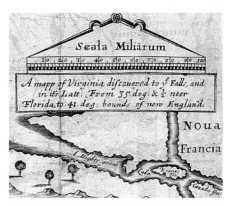

MAP 80 (*above*).
An engraved version of John Farrer's map, published in 1651 in Edward Bland's book *The Discoverie of New Britaine.* Now the West Sea has become the less ambiguous—but still egregiously misplaced—*Sea of China and the Indies.* The sea is now separated from the river systems by a small isthmus (top right); in the first edition of this map earlier in 1651 (see **MAP 81**, *right*) this was only a little peninsula, still allowing connection of rivers and sea. A little hedging was clearly going on! The notation under Drake's picture reads: *Sir Francis Drake was on this sea and landed Ano 1577 in 37 deg. where he tooke Possession in the name of Q: Eliza calling it new Albion. Whole happy shores, (in 10 dayes march with 50 foote and 30 horsemen from the head of James River, over those hills and through the rich adjacent Vallyes beautyfied with as proffitable rivers, which necessarily must run into ye peacefull Indian Sea,) may be discovered to the exceeding benefit of Great Brittain, and joye of all true English.*

are shown on **MAP 82** (*right*). His first expedition (the middle dashed line, marked 1 on the map) took him to the Blue Ridge near Swift Run Gap, northwest of Charlottesville, Virginia, where he was discouraged to see more mountains beyond, and so he returned. His second "march," between May and July 1670, was initially with men from Fort Henry, who later abandoned the determined Lederer, who pushed on with only the company of one Susquehanna Indian. He traveled southeast to the Catawba River near today's Rock Hill, South Carolina, where he met the Esaw of Ushery Indians. Here Lederer thought he saw the glint of water in the distance and at-

tributed it to a large but fictitious lake that mapmakers had been placing in the region for fifty years or more (see, for example, **MAP 39**, page 32). The lake is thus shown on Lederer's map (at top left on the map). Lederer understood from the Indians that only two and a half days' journey to the southwest "a powerful Nation of Bearded men were seated," which, he wrote, "I suppose to be the Spaniards, because the Indians never have any [beards]." He did not continue because he was afraid the Spanish would arrest him as a spy. Although he had not found an ocean, this expedition did find a route that would soon be used to open a fur trade with the Cherokee.

Lederer must have been a man of some energy, for almost immediately he left on another expedition (the right-hand dashed line on the map) that reached the summit of the Blue Ridge, but here once more he could see endless mountain ranges receding into the distance where he had once been certain of a South Sea. "They are certainly in a great errour," he wrote, "who imagine that the Continent of North-America is but eight or ten days over from the Atlantick to the Indian Ocean, which all reasonable men must acknowledge."

But men, otherwise reasonable, did not yet acknowledge reality. In the foreword to Lederer's book, published in 1672, William Talbot wrote: "From this discourse it is clear that the long looked-for discovery of the Indian Sea does nearly approach." In 1671 Abraham Wood dispatched his relative Thomas Wood (who died on the journey) west with Thomas Batts and Robert Fallam. They reached approximately the present boundary between Virginia and Kentucky. Here they found the New River, which they were convinced ebbed

and flowed, which they attributed to its being tidal. Clearly the Western Sea could not be far away. Batts later determined that the river in fact flowed into the Ohio, and this would lead to English claims to the entire Ohio Valley.

Wood sent out another expedition in 1673, this time with the intention of finding new sources of furs. James Needham, a trader, and Gabriel Arthur, an illiterate assistant, reached the headwaters of the Tennessee, but Needham was murdered by an Indian guide. Arthur was captured by Tomahitan Indians and spent a year accompanying them on their raids on other tribes. He gained considerable knowledge of the Southeast, but was unable to record his experiences. He escaped and managed to return to Fort Henry in June 1674.

Once the English in Virginia heard of the discovery of the Mississippi by the French (see page 72), they realized that land rather than sea must lie over the mountains. But not until the next century would they begin to explore it.

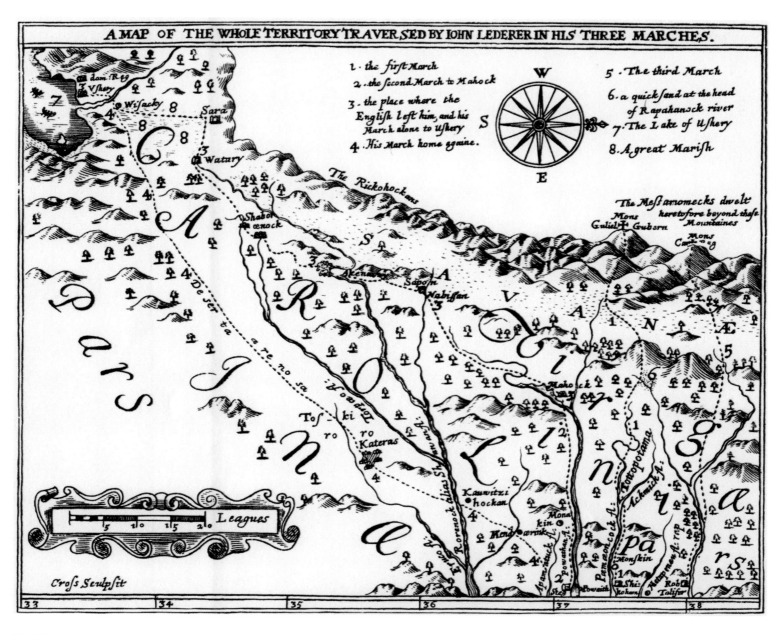

MAP 82.
John Lederer's map of his three expeditions, published in his book in 1672. Note that west is at the top of the map.

Seeking Furs and Lost Souls

In New France, Samuel de Champlain realized that ultimately he would not stand against a concerted native effort to oust him; his colonists were simply vastly outnumbered. The solution, he thought, was to convert the natives to the Catholic faith, and to this end he introduced Récollet friars to Canada. The Récollets were not energetic proselytizers, probably because they valued their own lives. In 1625 Champlain invited Jesuits to replace them, for the Jesuits believed that martyrdom was the way to heaven, and thus were much less fearful in the face of danger. And danger there was; many of them achieved horrible martyrdoms at the hands of the Iroquois, traditional foe of the Huron. But the Jesuits actively went in search of souls to convert, and in so doing they explored a considerable part of the continent centered around the Great Lakes.

By 1634 Jesuits had moved to live among the Huron in today's western Ontario, bordering Lake Huron. From this base individual Jesuits traveled west. They were not always the first. In that year trader Jean Nicollet de Belleborne went as far as eastern Lake Superior and established a trade with the Winnebago of that region. He was so certain he would reach China that he took with him a damask Chinese-style robe. The Winnebagos must have been impressed.

The Jesuits had chosen first to convert the Huron, but in the decade of the 1630s they were decimated by smallpox, some of which may have been introduced by the missionaries themselves, and the Iroquois, seeing the weakened state of their foe, attacked and annihilated the Huron during the following decade. This, however, was considered just part of God's design to the Jesuits, for now they had to move farther to the west.

Also exploring westward were the *coureurs du bois*, unlicensed independent fur traders looking for new sources of furs. They made contact with natives in order to trade with them. Two such traders were Pierre Esprit Radisson and Médard Chouart des Groseilliers. In 1656 Radisson had reached Lake Michigan and in 1659 with Des Groseilliers traveled along the south shore of Lake Superior before going inland in the region of what is now Wisconsin.

From 1665 on, a new French intendant at Québec, Jean Talon, began to send out exploration parties to search for minerals. His aim was to make the colony more independent as well as claim more territory for France. In 1668 a merchant, Jean Peré, was sent to find copper, and Adrien Jolliet joined him the following year. Peré was as much interested in furs as copper, but it mattered not what the motivation was, exploration was still required. Peré and Jolliet explored the region north of Lake Superior but, unusually, it was their return journey that was of greater significance, for instead of taking the route along the Ottawa and Mattawa Rivers that all had used up to that time, they went farther south and opened up an alternative route using Lakes Erie and Ontario.

It was at this time that Radisson and Des Groseilliers defected to the English. They journeyed to London in 1665 to offer their services to the English king, but could not have arrived at a worse time, for the

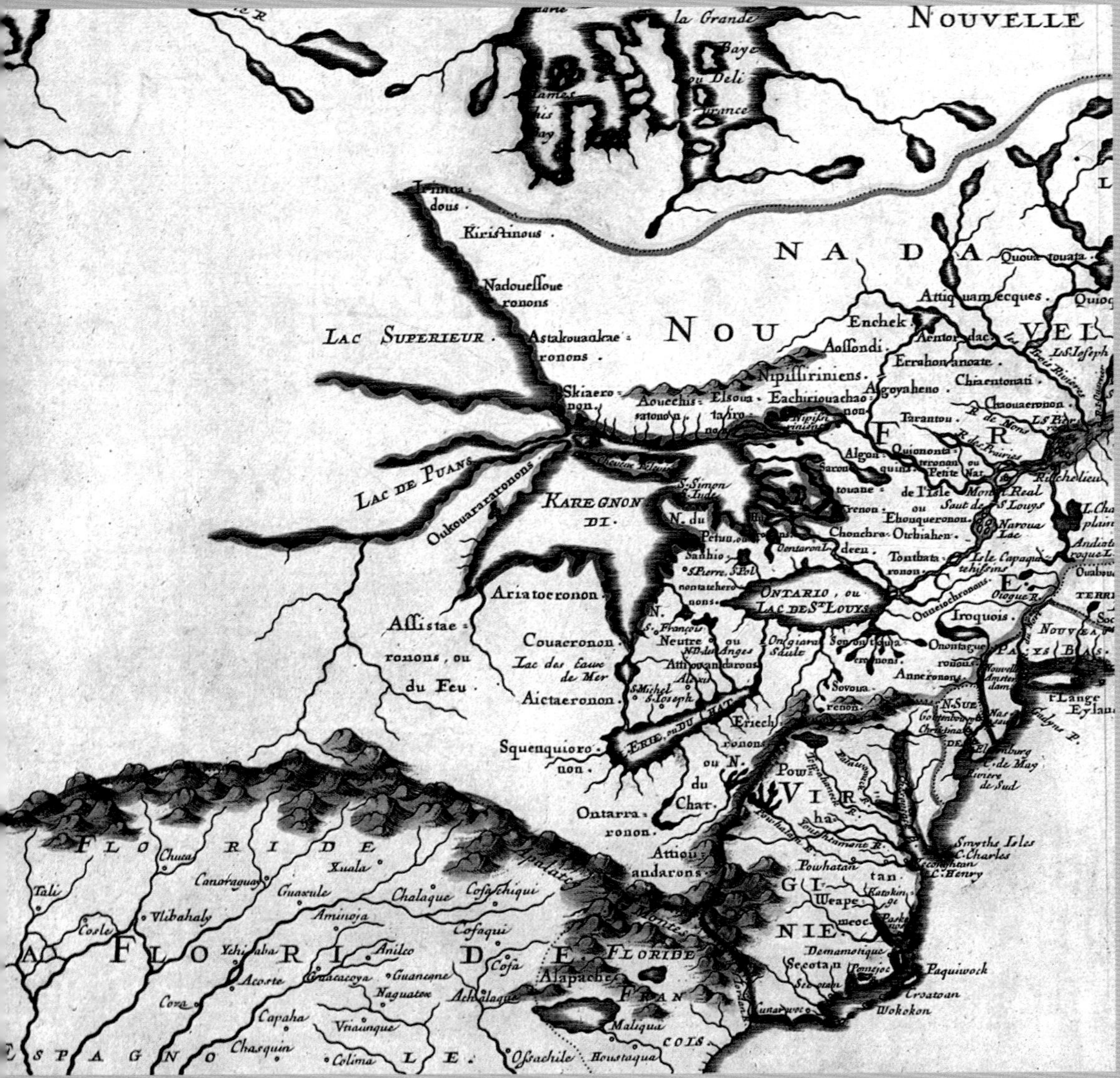

Map 83.
Part of a map by Nicolas Sanson d'Abbeville, geographer to the French king, published in 1656, incorporating information from Jesuit missionary-explorers. This was the first map to show at least some of all five of the Great Lakes. The western and southern extents of Lakes Superior and Michigan have not yet been defined.

MAP 84.
Map of the Huron country drawn by a Jesuit priest, perhaps Jean de Brébeuf, one of the first missionaries to reach the region. The map was drawn sometime between 1639 and 1648. The presence of the mission of Ste. Marie-among-the-Hurons shows that the date cannot be 1651, as indicated, because the mission was destroyed in 1649. The date may refer to slight later changes. Lake Huron is to the left and top, the latter part being Georgian Bay. *Lac Oventaren* is Lake Simcoe, and Lake Ontario is at bottom right.

Great Plague of London was followed in short order by the Great Fire of London, and it took them until 1668 to interest enough English investors to finance a voyage to Hudson Bay. For this was their revolutionary idea. Why travel all the way to Montréal to ship furs back to Europe when Hudson Bay was so much closer? The French, fearing a bypassing of their colony on the St. Lawrence, naturally were not so keen on this rerouting of trade. Hence the pair had gone to the English.

After the 1668 voyage, which was a test of the idea, the Hudson's Bay Company was incorporated by royal charter of the English king in 1670. From now on the French would have rivals in the fur trade. As it happened, the English were largely content to let natives come to them, and so they stayed on the shores of the bay. The one major exception was the exploration of Henry Kelsey, who in 1690 was sent west to drum up business. Unfortunately his journal was lost, and so we do not know for sure how far west he got, but it seems likely that he reached Cedar Lake, just west of Lake Winnipeg, and he may have been the first European to see the Canadian Prairies.

In 1669, the Jesuit Claude Allouez followed the route of Jean Nicollet to Green Bay, on the western side of Lake Michigan, and continued south to found a mission

among the Fox Indians of Wisconsin. Here he learned that he was only six days away from a large river flowing south—the Mississippi. He was joined the following year by another Jesuit, Claude Dablon, and together they explored Lake Superior (MAP 85).

At Sault Ste. Marie on 4 June 1671, French government spokesperson Simon-François Daumont de Saint-Lusson, surrounded by representatives of fourteen Indian tribes and backed up by Jesuit missionaries, held a ceremony claiming all the territory to the west, south, and north for France, which to the French, at any rate, gave legitimacy to their explorations. And the stage was set for future conflicts.

In was not long after this that Louis Jolliet and Jesuit Jacques Marquette found the way to the Mississippi. Their explorations, and those of René Robert Cavelier, Sieur de La Salle, in 1682, led ultimately to the incorporation of the new province of Louisiana into the French realm (see page 72).

By 1680 there were perhaps a thousand French *coureurs du bois* in the West. Each was pursuing his own goal, universally that of acquiring more furs and hence more wealth, but with such coverage (for each tried to find territory untapped by the others), a great deal of the middle part of the continent was revealed. And French mapmakers in the employ of the government used the cumulative snippets of information to compile composite maps of the new "French" territories. Sometimes, of course, the information was not

MAP 85.
A map of Lake Superior and part of the other Great Lakes attributed to Jesuits Claude Allouez and Claude Dablon and published in the *Relation* for 1671. The *Relation* was a journal of events in the lands the Jesuits were working, intended to aid in fund-raising; it was published until 1672. Father Allouez was the most far-ranging of the Jesuit explorers, second only to Jacques Marquette, explorer of the Mississippi.

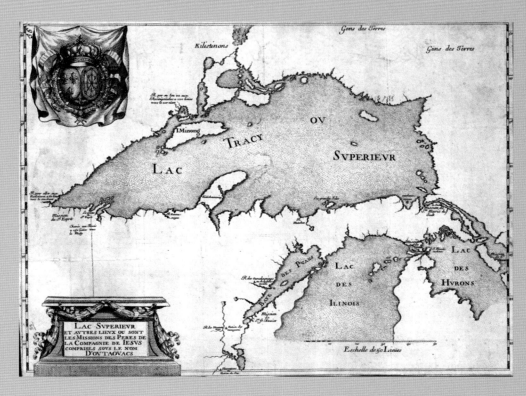

reliable, and this led to errors on the map that might be corrected later, and might not. One such master mapmaker was Jean-Baptiste-Louis Franquelin, the king's hydrographer of New France between 1687 and 1697. His maps were superb works of art that were much copied by other mapmakers back in Europe. MAP 93 on page 75 is an example of Franquelin's work.

During the period 1678 to 1687 Daniel Greysolon, Sieur Du Lhut (sometimes spelled Dulhut or Du Luth), a French military officer, traveled twice to the western end of Lake Superior, to where

the city named after him now stands, Duluth. He then continued into Minnesota and found the headwaters of the Mississippi. He had been sent to try to negotiate a peace between warring tribes, for natives at war were not paying much attention to the fur trade. He managed to broker a peace treaty in 1679. Du Lhut sent some of his men yet farther westwards to find the western ocean that must be very close by now. His men returned the following summer with evidence of an ocean—or so they thought. It was salt, given to them by natives. But where did it come from? Perhaps it was from the Great Salt Lake of Utah? We know that some commodities traveled very long distances being passed through Indian trade networks, so this is a possibility. It certainly got Du Lhut excited.

A discovery of major significance was made in 1688. On a journey from Fort Nipigon, which had been built by Du Lhut in 1684, young *coureur* Jacques de Noyon found the Kaministiquia River and a portage past its Kakabeka Falls (near Thunder Bay) to Rainy Lake and Lake of the Woods. This was a major new route that would allow the opening of the West by canoe. The English after 1763 used a slightly different route up the Pigeon River from Grand Portage, but when this was cut off by the new United States boundary, enforced in 1794, the Kaministiquia was again found and was the route to and from the entire West until at least 1821.

Particularly after the French heard of the English incursion into Hudson Bay in 1670, there was renewed interest in finding routes to the north. As early as 1647 the Jesuit Jean de Quen had ascended the Saguenay River as far as Lac Saint-Jean, a lake that from native information Jean Alfonce had thought a sea in 1542. In 1671, intendant Jean Talon asked Jesuit Charles Albanel, who had been with Quen and also with Radisson and Des Groseilliers, to penetrate yet farther north by this route and check on the English presence in Hudson Bay. Talon also was interested in the possibility of establishing a food storage depot to assist ships going through the Northwest Passage, still thought, despite the fact that many had tried and failed to find it, to exist somewhere on the west shore of Hudson Bay.

Albanel made it to the shores of the bay, thus demonstrating the practicality of the Saguenay route, but found only

MAP 86 (*above*).
The route from the St. Lawrence at Taddoussac (at bottom right) to Hudson Bay (at top left) is shown on this map by king's hydrographer Jean-Baptiste-Louis Franquelin, drawn in 1681.

MAP 87.
Published in 1685, this map by Alexis Hubert Jaillot shows the French approaches to Hudson Bay. Charles Albanel's route from Tadoussac to James Bay is shown. *Lac Timagaming* is Lac Mistassini and *Anglois* is Charles Fort. Also shown is the route up the Ottawa (*Riviere des Outaouacs*) to Lake Abitibi (*Lac des Tabitibis*) and the Abitibi River (*R. des Tabitibis*). The English forts, marked *Anglois*, on the west side of James Bay are Moose Fort (southernmost) and Fort Albany.

an abandoned English fort at Charles Fort (*Ruperts River* on MAP 88, *below*). Albanel's route to the bay is shown on MAP 86 (*left*). Another exploration to Hudson Bay was carried out in 1679 by the now renowned explorer Louis Jolliet, back from his explorations of the Mississippi. He traveled over much the same route as Albanel and returned after meeting with Hudson's Bay Company governor Charles Bayly, who offered him considerable sums if he would defect to the English. Jolliet refused, but he was convinced of the richness of Hudson Bay for the fur trade.

After 1682, rivalry between the French and English became more pronounced. In that year the Compagnie du Nord was formed to directly challenge the Hudson's Bay Company, and in 1689 war was officially declared between England and France. Explorations became more like armed interventions. Already in 1686 a French force of ninety men under Pierre de Troyes had ascended the Ottawa River, portaged to Lake Abitibi, and then descended the James

River to James Bay, where they had surprised and taken over the English Hudson's Bay Company forts at the bottom of the bay. Struggle for control of the bay continued until the Treaty of Utrecht in 1713. By that time the southern part of the bay was well known to both sides.

MAP 88.
Hudson Bay in 1709, drawn by London mapmaker Samuel Thornton. The map was commissioned by the Hudson's Bay Company either for the captains of supply ships or for reference in London. Company forts at the bottom of the bay are shown, as is York Fort at the mouth of the Nelson River. One of the islands in James Bay is Charlton Island, where Thomas James spent the winter of 1631–32 (see page 57). Thornton has drawn a demarcation line separating French and English territories, but it was purely his own invention.

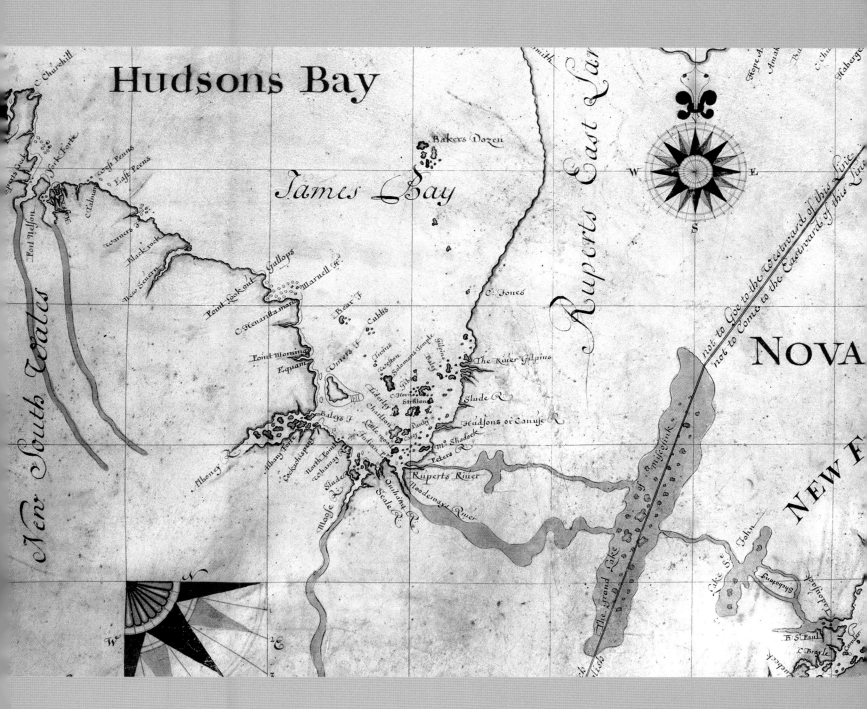

Finding the Mississippi

Persistent Indian reports of a great river to the south of the Great Lakes prodded the French into commissioning an official exploration to investigate. This river, they hoped, would flow into the Pacific and finally prove to be the passage to China that had been sought for years. New France intendant Jean Talon thought that even if the way to China was not found, new sources of furs and minerals might be; new Indian tribes would be brought under the influence of the French, and new territory added to the French empire in North America.

After the French ceremonially claimed all the lands about to be discovered—the proclamation by Simon-François Daumont de Saint-Lusson at Sault Ste. Marie in 1671 (see page 69)—Louis Jolliet was chosen to find the new southern river. But the French government's desire to see the river found did not run to actually financing the expedition. For that Jolliet had to resort to the usual method: finding investors who thought they could get a return on their money.

Taking Jesuit Jacques Marquette to convert any heathen they might find along the way, and five voyageurs, Jolliet left Fort Michilimackinac at the strait between Lakes Huron and Michigan in May 1673 and headed first into Lake Michigan, then into Green Bay, and

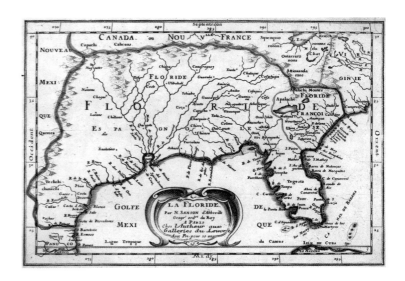

MAP 89 (*above*).
There was no Mississippi on this 1657 map of Florida (which covers all of what is now the southern United States), but the mouth had been noted by Alvar Núñez Cabeza de Vaca in 1529 and the river crossed by Hernando de Soto in 1541 (see pages 20 and 22).

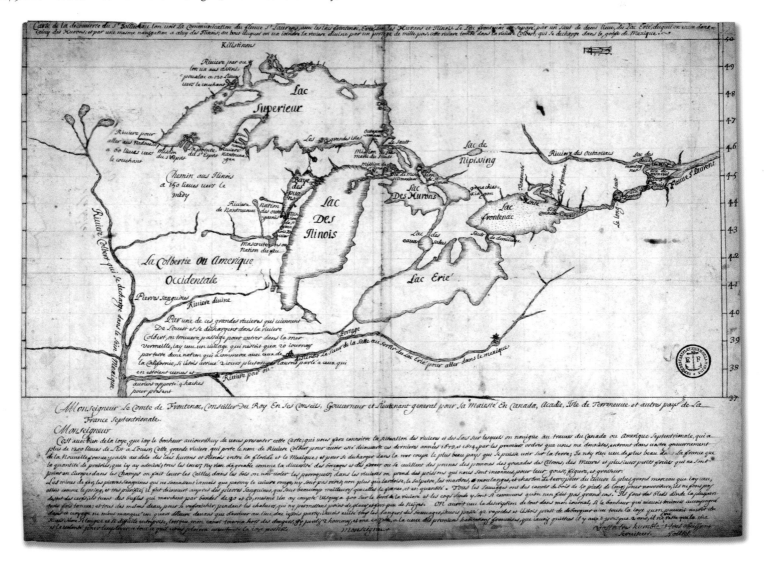

then up the Fox River, which drains into that bay. Jolliet thought he knew the route because he had spent the winter collecting native information and making a map (which has, like all of Jolliet's writings about this expedition, been lost). He did. Disregarding Indian tales of monsters and demons, they crossed a short portage to the Wisconsin River—which drains into the Mississippi.

Here they encountered fertile lands, a virtual paradise, but surprisingly no native people, a vacuum temporarily created by Indian wars. Indeed, two hundred miles went by before any were seen; luckily they were friendly Illinois. A little farther south the tranquil Mississippi was disturbed by another mighty river flowing in from the west. This was the Pekitanoui, the Muddy River—the Missouri. This river, they were told, really did lead to a western ocean. Jolliet reported that he had been to a village only five days' journey away from a tribe "which trade with the natives of California."

After another one hundred and thirty miles another great river flowed in, this time from the east. This was the Ouabougkigou, or Ohio.

Map 90 (left).

Jolliet's original map has been lost, but this map appears to be one of a small number of copies of it. Drawn about 1675, it clearly shows the connections of the Mississippi with the routes down the Wisconsin River and the Illinois River, but what is controversial is the course of the Ohio River, attributed on the map to the discoveries of René Robert Cavalier, Sieur de La Salle. He reported that he had reached the Ohio in 1669, but it now seems that this was a fabrication. Nevertheless, the Ohio is shown more or less in its correct position, and a possible route to it via the Maumee River and a portage to the Wabash is also indicated, although not very correctly. Perhaps La Salle, or the Sulphican missionaries who were with him (François Dollier de Casson and René de Bréhant de Galinée) received reports of the Ohio from natives. Yet the region is not shown at all on a map of the eastern Great Lakes drawn in 1670 by Bréhant de Galinée. The mapping of the Ohio on this map remains one of those exploration mysteries caused by lack of documentation. Jolliet interpolated the course of the river from the La Salle report south of Lake Erie to the confluence with the Mississippi.

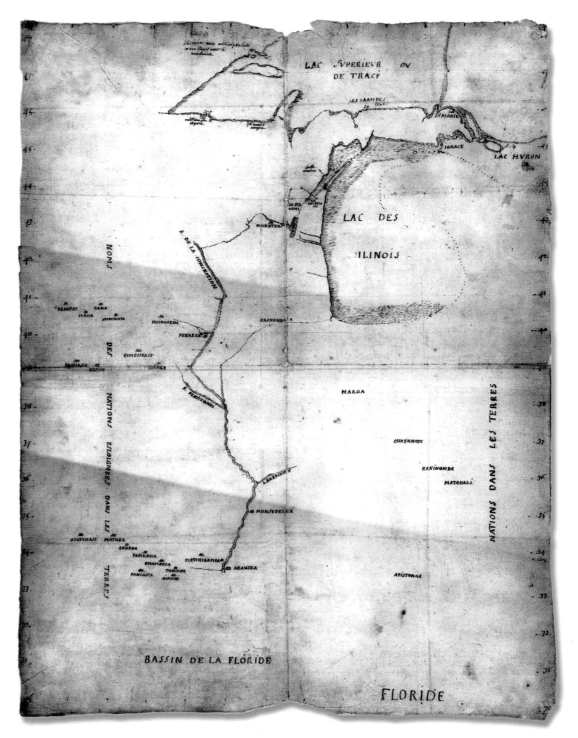

Map 91.

Father Jacques Marquette's map showing the route he and Jolliet took in 1673 from Lake Michigan (*Lac des Ilinois*) to the Arkansas River. An undefined *Bassin de la Floride* is at the south. *Pekittan8i* is the Missouri and *8ab8skig8* is the Ohio. The return route using the Illinois River to the southern end of Lake Michigan is also shown.

On they went, for another 450 miles, but then they thought they were entering Spanish territory and so, still 400 miles from the Gulf, at the approximate location of the Arkansas River, they decided to turn back. On their return they ascended the Illinois River, which joins the Mississippi just north of the Missouri, and then the Des Plaines River, finding the important portage to the Chicago River and Lake Michigan. Here was a route that would provide a real and viable link to the Mississippi River system from the Great Lakes.

Not until 1678, however, were further efforts made to explore the Mississippi; as always, funding had to be raised privately and was forthcoming only with the promise of a return.

René Robert Cavelier, Sieur de La Salle, who had arrived in New France in

MAP 92.

A map drawn in 1681 that shows clearly the results of Jolliet and Marquette's exploration of the Mississippi in 1673, but refuses to speculate on where the mighty river leads, even though by now it seems fairly obvious. This refusal to speculate means that the map also shows quite well the extent of French geographical knowledge elsewhere at this time. To the south the Ohio is known, but to the north Lake Winnipeg has not yet been reached. Everything to the west of the Mississippi is *Terres Inconnues*—unknown lands.

Map 93.

Jean-Baptiste-Louis Franquelin's wonderfully anachronistic general map of North America, drawn in 1678, incorporating Jolliet and Marquette's journey down the Mississippi in 1673—and the extrapolation of the river to the Gulf. Despite its errors it was a reasonable synthesis of geographical knowedge at the time. The Mississippi was assumed to rise somewhere on what are now the Canadian Prairies, much too far north, near a presumed Arctic coast and a presumed Pacific coast. It was an error only corrected towards the end of the eighteenth century.

1667 to take up a grant of land, soon saw more profit to be made in the fur trade and in finding a way to China. In 1670 he built Fort Conti on the site that would later be Fort Niagara. On Lake Erie he built the *Griffin,* the first sailing ship on the western Great Lakes.

Aided by his lieutenants Henri de Tonti and Louis Hennepin, La Salle established Fort St. Joseph in 1679, on the river of the same name at the southern end of Lake Michigan, and found here another portage, this one to the Kankakee River, a tributary of the Illinois. Farther down the river, on the Illinois near Peoria, Fort Crèvacoeur was built in 1680. Hennepin, meanwhile, journeyed to the northwest, getting himself captured by the Sioux in the process; he was only saved by the intervention of Du Lhut, who happened to be in the area at this time (see page 70).

La Salle was finally ready for the attempt on the Mississippi in 1681. He left Montréal in August and reached the river in February 1682. With Tonti he reached the "farthest south" of Jolliet and Marquette by mid-March and, traveling fast downstream, arrived at the

mouth of the Mississippi on 6 April. The delta region was explored, and of course a ceremony was held to claim the land for France, naming it Louisiane after King Louis XIV. Then he returned northwards, reaching Fort Michilimackinac by September. Relatively speedy travel was possible on the new river because, unlike most of the rivers on which the French had traveled up to this point, the Mississippi had no rapids. La Salle's was the first exploration of a vast new country that France would soon officially add to its North American empire.

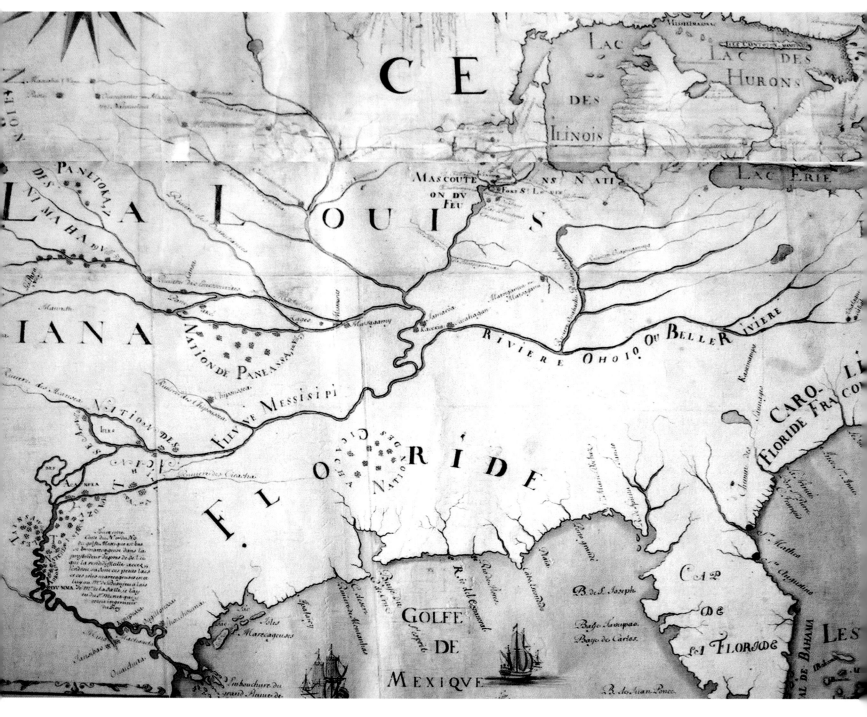

Map 94.

This 1699 map, with the course of the Mississippi copied from a 1688 map by Franquelin, shows La Salle's Mississippi flowing to the Gulf where he placed it, too far west. Following his own maps, La Salle returned to the Gulf Coast by sea in 1685 looking far to the west for the river he had descended.

La Salle, it seems, was not a very good navigator. Following a river to the sea was one thing, but showing its course on a map was quite another. He is also known to have broken his compass during the outward journey. At any rate, his maps showed an inexplicable jog in the river—if six hundred miles can be called a jog—to the west beginning just below the Ohio, pretty much from where Jolliet's maps ended. La Salle's maps have disappeared, but there were copies made by Jean-Baptiste-Louis Franquelin, incorporated in a more general map of North America (Map 94, *above*), and then, of course, copied by numerous other mapmakers who had no way to know anything different.

La Salle went back to France in 1683 to present plans for the establishment of a colony at the mouth of the Mississippi. They were approved and he arrived on the Gulf Coast in January 1685 with four ships and over three hundred men. But, following his own map, he went too far west and ended up at Matagorda Bay, in Texas. Here he built Fort Saint-Louis. La Salle knew he was not where he wanted to be, but still seemed unsure of his location, for he intiated a series of searches for the Mississippi first by going west, where he found not the Mississippi but the Rio Grande, which he ascended for more than three hundred miles. He also tried to find the river overland to the northeast, finding only the Trinity River in eastern Texas. Another expedition in the same direction in 1687 led to his murder by some of his men, likely upset at his failures. Almost all of his colonists were massacred by Indians. France's first attempt to populate their newly found lands ended in dismal failure.

The Spanish government, having heard of La Salle's venture, determined to find the colony and destroy it. To them, it was intruding into their territory. Numerous expeditions, by both land and sea, were sent out. Alonso de León led five overland expeditions north from New Spain, one each year between 1686 and 1690. In 1689 he located the remains of Fort Saint-Louis and burnt it to the ground. He found only a few French children, the only survivors of the colony. The Spanish seemed obsessed with the apparent threat of the French colony, for they also sent out five naval expeditions to find it. Searching the coast quite carefully, the Spanish reexplored a number of bays previously known to them but forgotten; the policy of Spanish secrecy worked to their own disadvantage. One expedition, that of Andrés de Pez and López de Gamarra, rediscovered Pensacola Bay, where, in 1698, a Spanish fort would be built.

MAP 95 (*above*).
Louis Hennepin published this map of the Mississippi in 1697. The river has a more correct north-south orientation but its course is still too far west.

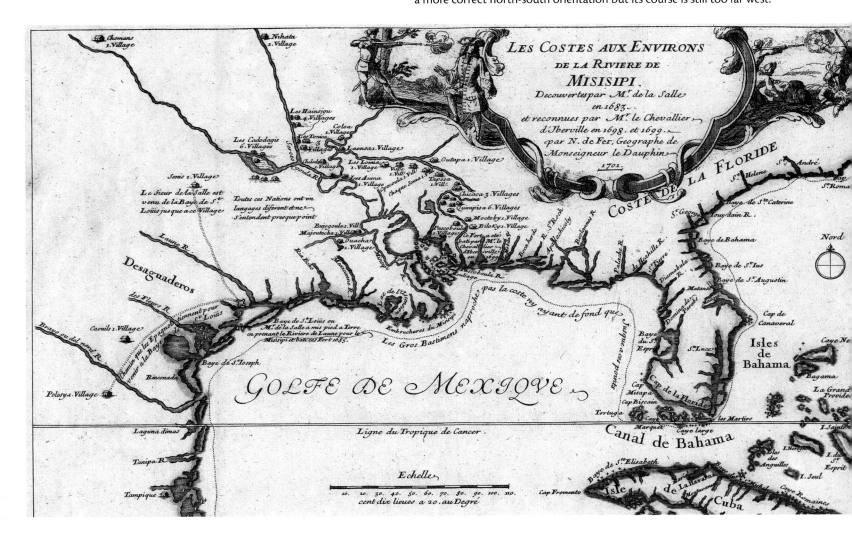

MAP 96.
Nicolas de Fer drew this map of the Gulf Coast in 1701. It shows the discoveries of La Salle together with those of D'Iberville and Bienville in 1698 and 1699. There is some detail in the delta region showing Indian villages. In the west, the *Chemin que les Espanols* (route of the Spanish) is the approximate route of the Alonzo de León expedition of 1689 that found La Salle's Fort Saint-Louis.

The French were slow to consider establishing another colony in La Salle's Louisiana, the latter's failure giving pause for thought, and it was not until rumors of an English claim to the region arrived in Paris that a decision was made to try again. Pierre le Moyne d'Iberville, a hero of the recent war, was chosen to lead the expedition. With him in October 1698 went his brother, Jean-Baptiste le Moyne de Bienville, four ships, and about four hundred men.

First the Mississippi had to be found. After being repulsed by the Spanish at Pensacola and searching Mobile Bay, his boats located the North Pass entrance to the great river on 2 March 1699. They were the first Europeans to enter the Mississippi from the sea. The delta area was explored, then a base established at Biloxi Bay, called Fort Maurepas. D'Iberville went back to France for reinforcements, returning in January 1700. This time a search was made for an easier exit from the river to the sea, for the river here juts out fifty miles to sea beyond the rest of its delta. Bienville, with trader Louis Juchereau de Saint-Denis, and following Indian advice, found a short portage from the river to Lake Pontchartrain, at the location where Bienville would

build New Orleans in 1718. Bienville got a shock one day during his explorations of the delta. He found himself suddenly face-to-face with an armed English ship, under Captain William Bond, who had been sent out by Daniel Coxe to claim his grant of "Carolana" (see page 80). Bienville managed to convince Bond that the region was already claimed and in the possession of France.

Bienville and Saint-Denis explored deep inland in 1700. Bienville reached as far as Oklahoma, while Saint-Denis explored the Red River and then, the following year, the region between the Red and Ouachita Rivers, and the results were compiled by Guillaume De L'Isle later that year from information brought to France by D'Iberville (MAP 97).

Another explorer who was with D'Iberville, on his second arrival at the Mississippi, was Pierre-Charles Le Sueur. In 1700 he ascended the river with twenty-five men as far as the Falls of St. Anthony—site of today's Minneapolis—where he turned southwest up the Minnesota River and finally the Blue Earth River. Here he found what he had been looking for: what he thought was copper ore. He wintered in a

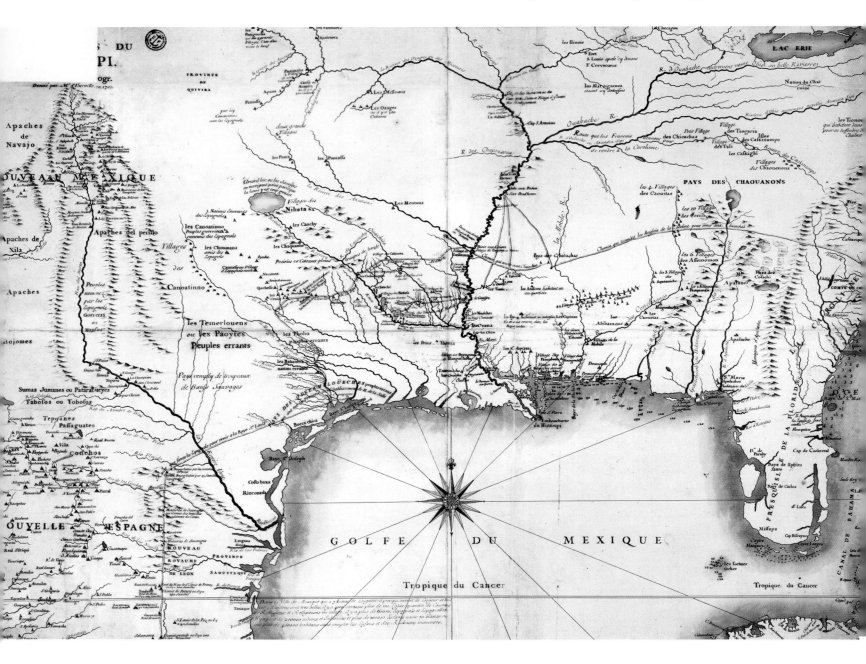

fort he built there. The rock was not copper ore at all, but Le Sueur's explorations of the upper Mississippi improved French knowledge of that region. MAP 98 (*right*) shows the area of Le Sueur's explorations.

Le Sueur and D'Iberville never returned to Louisiana after 1710, but Bienville stayed on, founding New Orleans in 1718. Saint-Denis became the foremost explorer of Texas. In 1714, because of his experience, the governor of Louisiana, Antoine de La Mothe Cadillac (earlier the founder of Detroit), commissioned him to find a trade route to New Spain. Saint-Denis left Mobile in September 1713, ascended the Red River, and established a post at Natchitoches. From there he set out overland to the southwest, crossing all of what is now Texas and arriving at the Spanish frontier settlement of San Juan Bautista, on the Rio Grande near Eagle Pass, Texas. But the Spanish were not interested in trade with the French; Saint-Denis was arrested and only freed after being taken to Mexico City. Saint-Denis's route is shown on Guillaume De L'Isle's seminal map of 1718 (MAP 107, page 86). Saint-Denis was freed because he agreed to act as a guide for a Spanish expedition intended to settle East Texas. This expedition, led by Domingo Ramón in 1716, took a more northerly route, also shown on MAP 107, because the Spanish wanted to establish missions along the way.

The Spanish had decided that expansion was the best way to prevent continued encroachment by the French (a fact that was demonstrated to them by maps drawn by Saint-Denis when in Mexico City). In 1709 an expedition under Pedro de Aguirre had escorted missionaries Antonio de Olivares and Isidro de Espinosa to meet the Tejas Indians; Aguirre was instructed to determine how far the French had penetrated. They reached the Colorado River of Texas before turning back. This route would become known as the Camino Real.

In 1718 Martín de Alarcón followed this route to found the mission settlement of San Antonio. The French began to seize missions in East Texas in 1719, and that year Marqués de San Miguel de Aguayo was sent to retrieve them. Guided by Espinosa, he spent several years crisscrossing East Texas, establishing a greater Spanish presence there. But the French presence in nearby—and ill-defined—Louisiana was to continue until 1762.

MAP 97 (*left*).
This superb map was drawn in 1701 by French geographer *suprême* Guillaume De L'Isle. It incorporates the discoveries of D'Iberville, Bienville, and Saint-Denis in 1699–1701. The "road taken by the English" (*Chemin que tiennént les Anglois*) from Carolina to the Mississippi is also shown. *Ouabache R.* is the Ohio, *La Riviere des Ozagesou ou des Missouris* is the Missouri, *La Riviere des Akansa* is the Arkansas River, and *Riviere Rouge* is the Red. On the coast, *Bilocchy* is Biloxi, with its fort.

MAP 98 (*right*).
Another map by Guillaume De L'Isle, this is a five-sheet composite of the entire course of the Mississippi River as known to the French by 1701. *Portage des égarez* is the portage from the Mississippi to Lake Pontchartrain found by Bienville and Saint-Denis in 1700, the site of New Orleans. In the north, the region of Pierre-Charles Le Sueur's explorations is marked. *R. St. Pierre* is the Minnesota River; *le Fort Vert* and *mine de Terre Verte* are Le Sueur's fort and mine. *Saut de St. Antoine* is the Falls of St. Anthony.

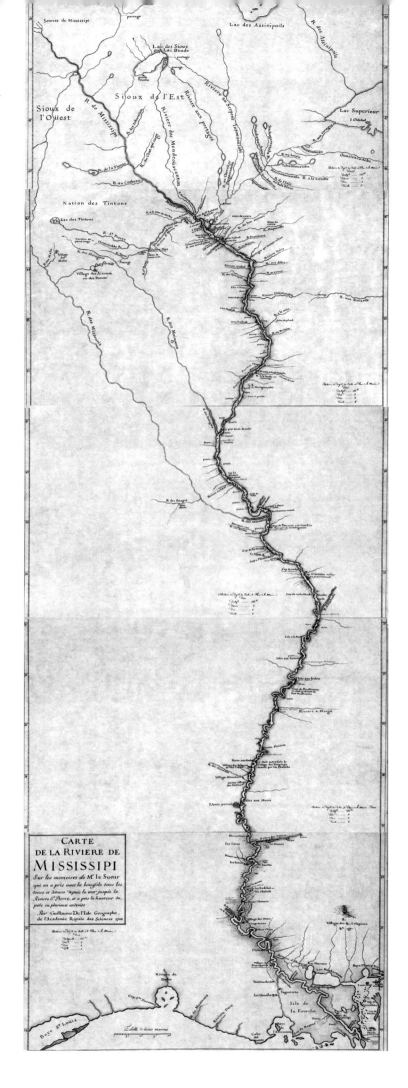

West from Carolina

The English ship encountered by Bienville on the Lower Mississippi in 1700 was sent by Daniel Coxe from England via Charlestown (Charleston), South Carolina, to investigate the country to which he had purchased an original 1629 land grant from the English crown (the *Carolana* grant); this grant had been superseded by another grant, of *Carolina,* to eight "lords proprietors" in 1663. Nonetheless, Coxe intended to test his rights.

Although this particular show of English might came to nothing, there were English claims to the entire territory west to the Mississippi based on the 1663 grant, which, in common with other East Coast grants, extended west well beyond any geographical knowledge at the time.

From the 1670s on, various explorations had been made from Carolina to trade with Indians or search for minerals. Few are recorded. Henry Woodward made a series of trips from Charlestown: north to the Santee River to trade with the Catawba in 1670, west to the Savannah River and the Westo Indians in 1674, and west to the Creek country in 1685. Then the native trail skirting the southern end of the Appalachians was found by traders from Charlestown and opened up the route to the Mississippi Valley. It is shown on Map 100 (*right*) and also on the French map on page 78 (MAP 97). Thomas Welch followed this trail to the Mississippi in 1698, and he even built a trading post on the river close to its confluence with the Tennessee.

The following year Jean Couture, a French trader reputedly with a knowledge of many Indian languages, who had deserted, followed the same trail and reached the mouth of the Arkansas—where he had been in charge of a French post in the 1680s.

The English traders tended to be successful because they usually offered better and cheaper goods than the Spanish or French. The English also developed a trade in Indian slaves, which they sent to the plantations of the West Indies.

In 1708 Thomas Nairne trekked across the Southeast and traded with the Talapoosie Indians north of the Spanish fort at Pensacola before continuing to the lower Mississippi, well within territory he knew was claimed by the French. Nairne, who produced the map shown here (MAP 100), was killed in 1715 by Indians in northern Florida. Nairne had been to southern Florida in 1702 (while on a slave-hunting expedition) and had acquired the idea that the southern

MAP 99 (*above*).
Carolina on the map attached to the land grant to the eight lords proprietors in 1663, attributed to the philosopher John Locke. Carolina stretches right across the continent. Maps such as this gave English traders apparent legitimacy to trade to the Mississippi from the East Coast.

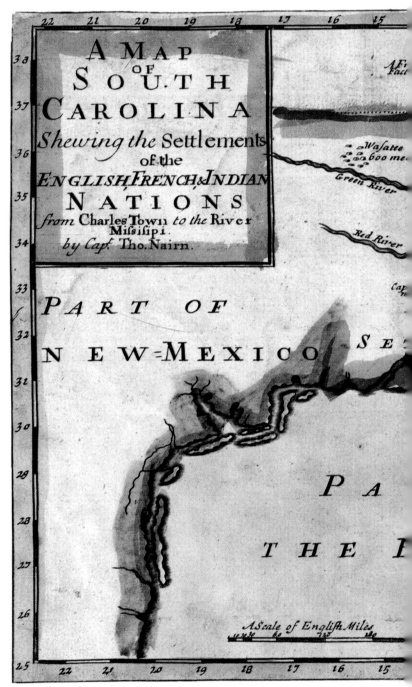

Florida peninsula was an archipelago, as shown on his map. His expedition was the first recorded into the Everglades.

In 1713 Pryce Hughes, a Welshman with a vision of a Welsh colony at Port Royal, arrived in Charlestown, but he soon planned instead to establish his colony on the Mississippi. He never did, but his perambulations around the Southeast alarmed the French, for he planned to cut the link between the French settlements in Louisiana and those in Canada. The land, he thought, was worth a fight if need be. "I've been a considerable way to the Westwd. upon the branches of the Mesisipi," he wrote in 1713, and was impressed with the country; there are "many fine navigable rivers, pleasant savannahs, plenty

MAP 100.
This beautiful map was produced by Thomas Nairne in 1711. It was an inset on a larger map of Carolina by Edward Crisp. The Indian trails across the Southeast are shown. The *Cussate alias Hockelegie River* is the Tennessee. The map also shows Nairne's idea of Florida as an archipelago, derived from his visit to the Everglades in 1702.

of coal, lead, iron, lime and freestone wth several salt springs . . . and as fine timber as the largest I ever saw in England."

But the English did not have to fight the French; they had to fight the Indians, some of whom were becoming increasingly upset at the European intrusion onto their lands. Nairne suffered at their hands as did Thomas Lawson, a trader from Charlestown killed as he explored northwards towards Virginia in 1711.

One of the most important maps to be made in colonial America was a summary drawn about 1716 by John Barnwell, also of Charlestown. "Tuscarora Jack," as he was known, researched all the routes, trails, and tracks forged by most of the explorers to the west at this time, mapped all the Indian trails, included some information from his own explorations, and added details of the coastal colony of Carolina. The result was what has been called a "mother map," one used by later mapmakers to construct their own maps. Barnwell's map, shown here (MAP 102), was used by Henry Popple for his monumental multisheet *Map of the English Empire in America,* published in 1733, and by John Mitchell for his seminal *Map of the British and French Dominions in North America,* originally published in 1755 but issued in several later editions with the same basic information. The 1775 edition of this map was used to define the boundaries of the new United States of America for the Treaty of Paris in 1783.

MAP 102 (*right*).
John Barnwell's "mother map" of 1716, showing all the routes and trails from Charlestown known at the time. One of the most significant maps of colonial America, this map was widely copied by mapmakers, many of whom became better known than Barnwell himself.

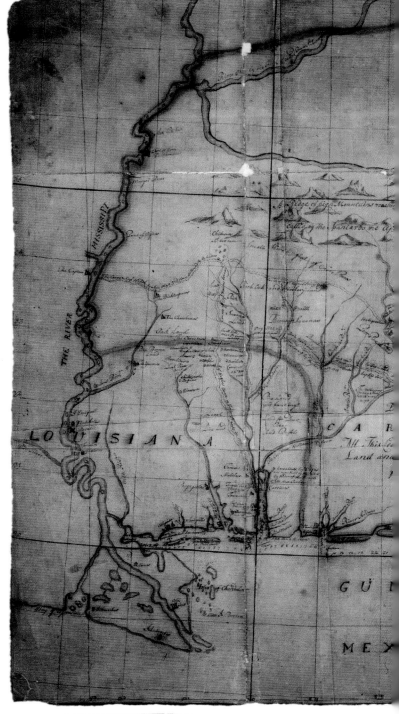

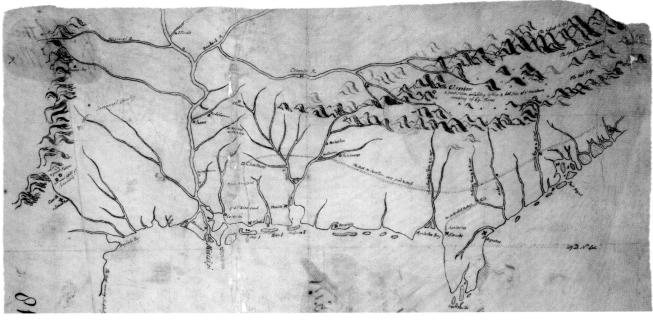

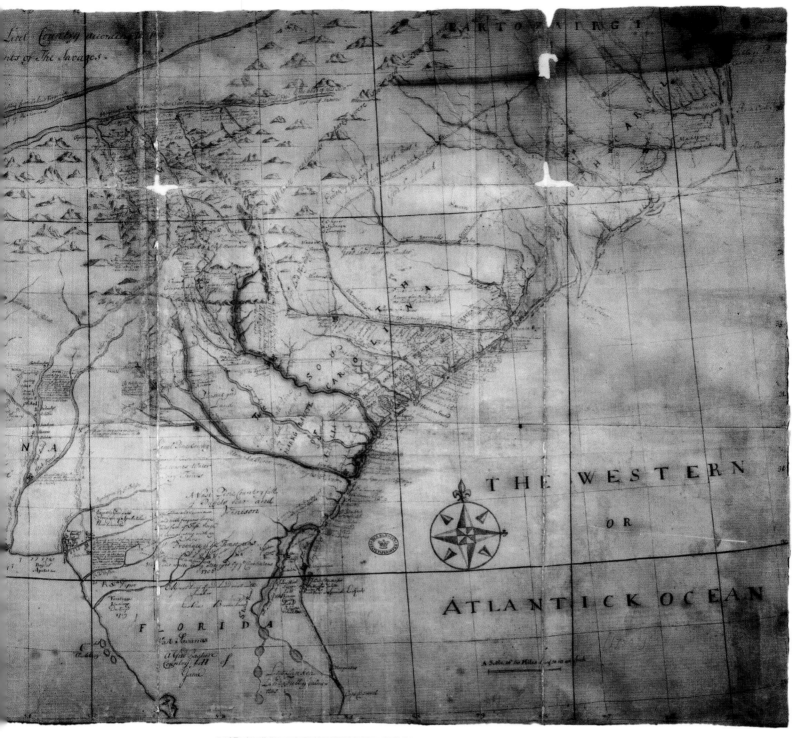

MAP 101 (left).
Pryce Hughes's map of the Southeast, drawn in 1713, which was copied by Alexander Spotswood in 1720.

MAP 103 (right).
Part of a map of North America published by English mapmaker Herman Moll in 1720. This map, like Barnwell's, shows many details of routes and trails, and also includes details of Thomas Nairne's episode in the Everglades of Florida in 1702.

An Island No More

Beyond the initial forays of the Spanish into the frontiers of New Spain, which had demonstrated that gold and other easy treasures were not easily found in this region, the principal Spanish explorations were carried out by missionaries anxious to found missions and convert the Indians. There was also an occasional burst of exploration activity when Spain felt threatened by encroaching French traders.

One of the most far-ranging missionaries was Father Eusebio Kino. In 1687 he built a mission of Nuestra Señora de los Dolores in northern New Spain, at a location close to the present United States–Mexico boundary south of Tucson, Arizona. From here he made over forty expeditions to the north and west. By 1691 he was in Arizona, and he founded the mission of San Xavier del Bac near Tucson in 1699.

From native reports Kino had decided that the land to the west, California and Baja California, was part of the mainland, not, as was normally shown on maps of this period, an island (MAP 106, *right, bottom,* and see also MAP 66, page 55). Although earlier Spanish explorations had demonstrated that Baja was not an island, the information had somehow become lost to Spain and the world. By 1700 Kino had reached the confluence of the Gila and Colorado Rivers and realized that he was north of the Gulf of California. Further explorations in 1701 and 1702 down the Gila and Colorado Rivers to the head of the Gulf led him to conclude that Baja was a peninsula, for here he could see the continuance of land to the northwest of the Gulf. He incorporated a map in his report (MAP 104, *below*) that showed the region closer to reality than it had been depicted before. It was the first map of Arizona based on actual exploration.

MAP 104 (*left*).
An English edition of Eusebio Kino's map showing the connection by land across the head of the Gulf of California (here the *Sea of California*), and the Colorado and Gila Rivers.

MAP 105 (*above*).
Francisco Alvarez Barriero's map of the frontier regions of New Spain, from Texas to California, drawn in 1729. The long river cutting the map more or less in two is the *Rio del Norte*, the Rio Grande. Barriero's depiction of the West is incorrect. The river entering the sea at 34° N is presumably the Colorado, but the Gulf of California (which actually terminates at 32° N) continues northwards beyond this point

MAP 106 (*right*).
California as an island is typically shown on this 1685 English map by Philip Lea.

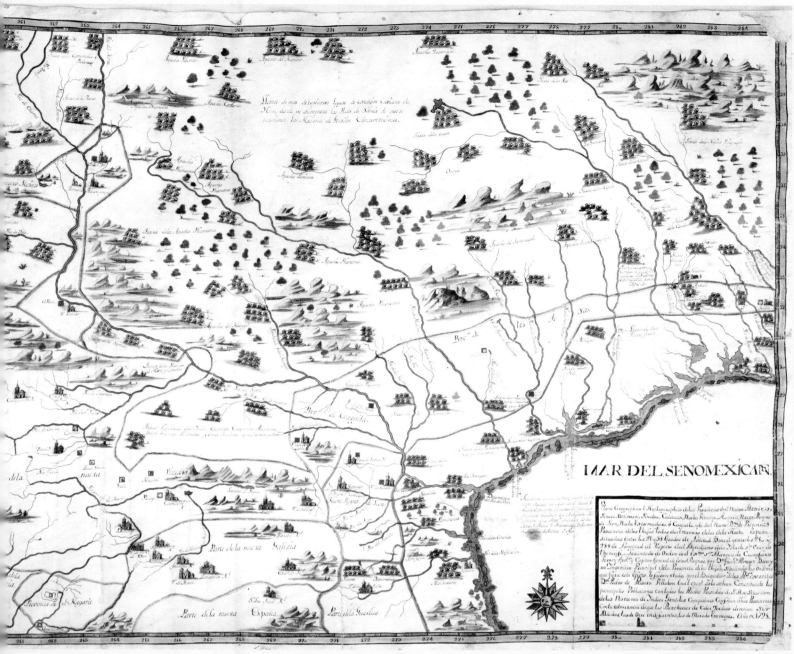

Although many cartographers accepted Kino's conclusion that California was not an island, since he had not journeyed to the Pacific himself, there was still an element of doubt. It took another missionary, Father Fernando Consag, to prove the matter once and for all. In 1746 he sailed right around the Gulf, and as a result the king of Spain issued a decree proclaiming that California was not an island.

Despite the sparseness of Spanish settlement in the frontier regions, Spain by 1724 thought that the cost of their administration was too high and dispatched an expedition under Pedro de Riviera y Villalón to survey them and recommend economies. With the expedition was a military engineer, Francisco Alvarez Barriero, who had been with Martín de Alarcón in 1718 (see page 79). All the presidios and missions in northern New Spain were visited on a four-year and seven-thousand-mile journey that crisscrossed the area now occupied by Texas, New Mexico, Arizona, and California. Barriero's map (MAP 105) was a uniquely comprehensive view of the region in the first half of the eighteenth century.

Ascending the Missouri

The Missouri River, which would prove to be the major highway west, was explored at least as far as the Platte River in 1714 by a French explorer who has certainly not received his fair share of recognition: Étienne de Véniard, Sieur de Bourgmont.

One of the main concerns the French had at this time was encroachment upon their territory by the Spanish; no one knew where the boundaries of each other's territories were anyhow.

Bourgmont (whose name has sometimes been spelled Bourgmond) had been commandant of Fort Detroit during the absence of Antoine Laumet de Lamothe Cadillac, the virtual owner of the fort. In 1712 he had, it seems, deserted, and spent five or six years living among the Missouri Indians, taking an Indian wife. He thus gained an intimate knowledge of the Lower Missouri, and it was during this time that he ascended the river to the Platte, and perhaps beyond, noting as he went the information required for a map (MAP 108).

In 1719, Claude Charles du Tisné, one of the officers of the Sieur de Bienville, governor of Louisiana (and founder of New Orleans), was sent to attempt to make peace with Indians in the Lower Missouri to clear the way for French expansion of trade, but was stopped by Pawnee (called Panis by the French) beyond the head of the Osage River at about the location of Chelsea, Oklahoma.

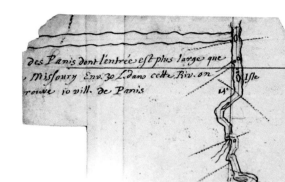

MAP 107 (*below*).

This detailed and famous map of Louisiana by French geographer Guillaume De L'Isle was published in 1718. *Natchitoches* is shown on the Red River (*Riviere Rouge*). The next northernmost major west bank tributary of the Mississippi is the Arkansas and the next *le Missouri R*, into which flows the *Grande Riviere des Cansez*, the Kansas River. The villages of the *Panis* (Pawnee) and *Padoucas* (Comanche) are also depicted. Earlier explorers' routes, such as that of La Salle, are also shown. This map included information from Louis Juchereau de Saint-Denis, including his 1714 (marked 1713) and 1716 tracks (see page 78), and from François Le Maire, a missionary at Mobile.

Map 108 (*below, center*).
Bourgmont kept a journal of his ascent of the Missouri in 1714 entitled *Routte qu'il faut tenir pour monter la rivière Missoury* ("The route to be taken to ascend the River Missouri"). This passed into the hands of Guillaume De L'Isle, who used it to construct this map of the Missouri about 1716. It is the first reasonably accurate map of the Missouri drawn from exploration. The Mississippi is at lower right, the Platte at top left.

Map 109 (*right*).
A plan of Fort D'Orleans, built on the banks of the Missouri by Bourgmont in the winter of 1723–24. It is not known how much of this was actually built and how much only proposed. Certainly it is an apparently large and elaborate structure. It could even have been an exaggerated fantasy designed to impress colonial officials.

Some of the letters and numerals from the key: *A* the commandant's house; *B* officers' quarters; *C* chapel; *D* blacksmith's house; *E* forge; *F* chaplain's house; *G* storekeeper's house; *H* store; *I* guardhouse; *K* drummer's house; *L* laundry; *O* barracks; *Q* powder magazine; *R* embrasures for cannon; *1* Bourgmont's house; *2* poultry house; *3* oven; *4* ice house; *5* big garden; *6* yard; *7* little garden; *8* store; *9* field of tobacco; *10* kitchen garden; *18* parade ground; *19* pond; *20* island; *21* prairie; *22* big hills two leagues from the fort; *23* road from the river to the fort; *24* 15-foot embankment.

The fort was not a success and was abandoned in 1728. The site has never been found, probably because the shifting river erased all the evidence.

Much the same thing seems to have happened to Jean-Baptiste Bénard, Sieur de La Harpe. He was also sent to Pawnee country by Bienville for the same reason, but by a different route. In 1718–19 he ascended the Red River from Natchitoches, the post established in 1714 by Louis de Saint-Denis (see page 79) and where La Harpe built a fort, then took off across country to reach the Arkansas River. He ranged a short distance east and west along the Arkansas but did not get any farther. La Harpe was proficient enough to make detailed notes in his journal and draw maps, but none of these have survived. A larger area map made using his notes is extant, however (Map 110, *right*). La Harpe was content to establish a trading post on the Red River, near present-day Texarkana, on the Texas-Arkansas state line.

When Bourgmont later returned to France he was honored and reenlisted for another expedition, to the Padouca (Comanche) territory up the Kansas River and beyond, where he was to form alliances with this tribe as a bulwark against Spanish intrusions. News had by now reached Paris of a Spanish force of a hundred soldiers headed by Pedro de Villasur that had been sent north from Santa Fe to counter the *French* intrusion into their territory. (Both the French and the Spanish thought that the Missouri and Santa Fe were closer than they really are.) In addition, excitement—and speculation—had recently been at fever pitch over the Compagnie des Indes, created in 1719 with a trade monopoly over all French New World trade, including that of Louisiana. This had been sensationalized in the press with stories of gold, easy trade routes to Mexico, and the like.

In this environment Bourgmont was appointed "Commandant of the Missouri River," ordered to facilitate a peace between the Indians, especially the Padouca, and promised ennoblement if he succeeded. After making peace with the Indians, he was also to establish trade with the Spanish in Santa Fe—the Missouri being thought of as the route to that city. It was an essentially impossible task; the last thing the Spanish wanted to do was establish a trade with the French.

After a fearsome voyage and near death from malaria, Bourgmont reached the vicinity of New Orleans just in time for the hurricane of the century, which struck the region 9–11 September 1722. A further delay ensued, heightened by bureaucratic bungling by local officials and the opposition of Bienville, who wanted to organize his own expeditions, and only in February 1723 did the expedition finally set out.

During the winter of 1723–24 Bourgmont established Fort D'Orleans on the Lower Missouri near present-day Miami, Missouri. The fort was named after the Duc D'Orleans, at the time the French regent to the underage Louis XV. From this base, between September and November 1724 Bourgmont, often accompanied by hundreds of Kansa Indians, ranged westwards, going first up the Kansas River and then towards the Arkansas River. Bourgmont established contact and made an alliance with Indians thought to be the Padouca, although it is possible they were Apache east of their normal hunting range. At any rate, the alliance proved to be unsustainable in the too-far-flung French territory. In 1728 even Fort D'Orleans was abandoned. Nevertheless, much geographical knowledge of this previously unknown region was gained. And Bourgmont got what he wanted: when he returned to France he was made an *écuyer*, a squire.

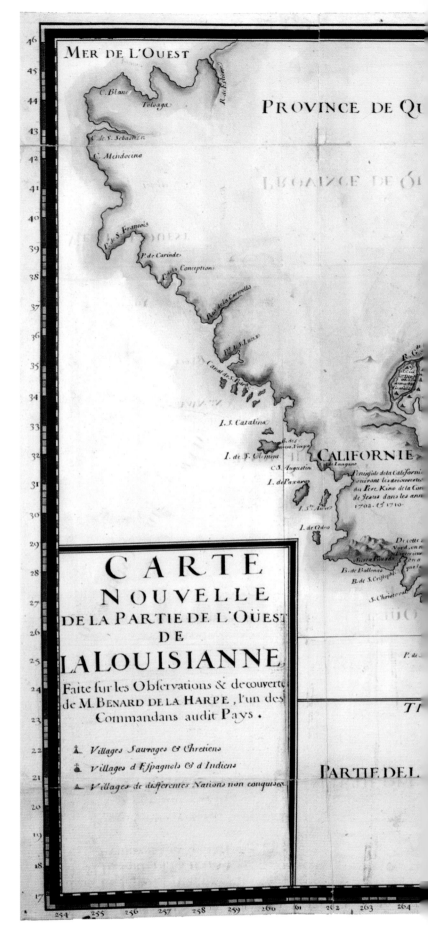

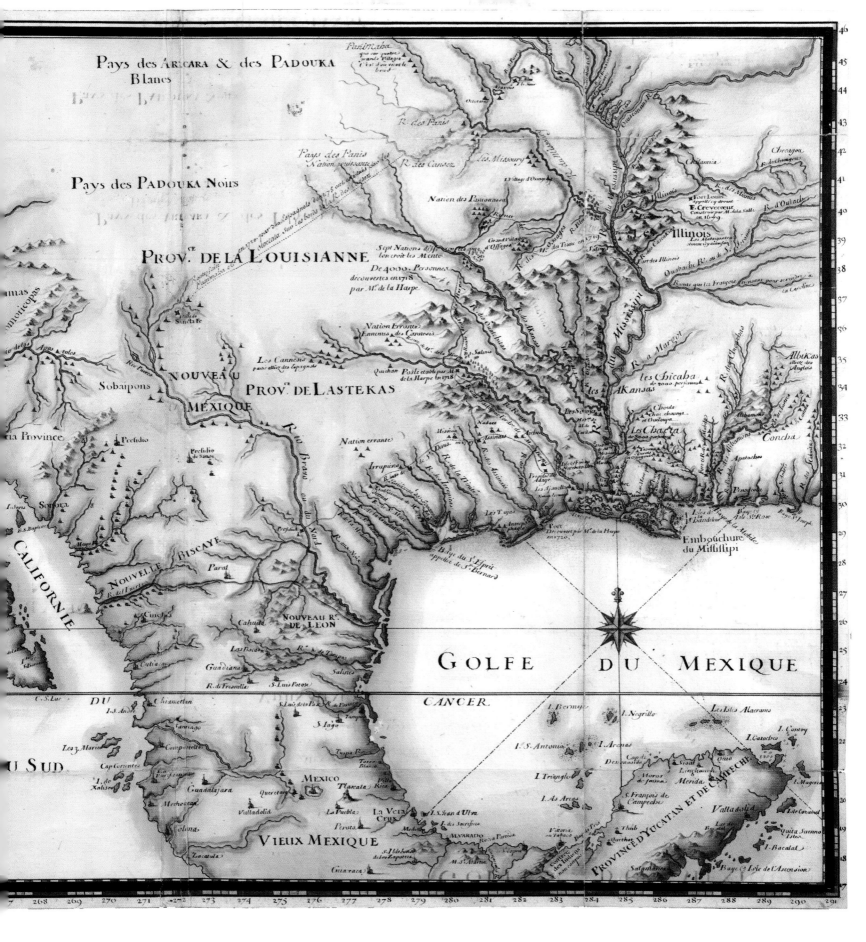

MAP 110.

This stunning map, drawn in 1723–25, is found in Bénard de La Harpe's journal, now in the Library of Congress. It was drawn by Jean de Beaurain to illustrate the journal, which was dedicated to the French king and presumably intended for presentation to him. Although the map covers a much larger area than that known to La Harpe, his travels up the Red River and overland to the Arkansas River are shown by a red line, leading to land *découvertes* [discovered] *en 1718* [sic, 1719] *par Mr. de la Harpe*. Also shown is the route of Pedro de Villasur's *300 Espanols* (300 Spaniards) in 1720, soldiers searching for Bourgmont, the French intruder into the Spanish sphere. A blank *Province de Quivire* covers much of the West Coast.

Explorers' Myths — The Sea of the West

Until the end of the seventeenth century the Pacific Ocean was thought to lie just over the Virginian mountains. With the French discovery of the Mississippi and the explorations of the Virginians beyond the mountains, most realized that the sea was not that close. Where was the sea? Until the third voyage of Captain James Cook in 1778–79, no one really knew how wide the North American continent was. Measuring longitude was a difficult and laborious process using techniques learned by only a few. Explorers were often told of seas to the west, even salt ones. These were undoubtedly tales of large lakes that did indeed appear to be seas to people who had never seen the boundless ocean. And so mapmakers made the sea come to the explorers. Maps such as those on these pages

MAP 111.
Published about 1780, this map of North America exhibits the concept of a Sea of the West—*Mer de l'Ouest*—extending far inland, in this case about as far as Nebraska, a sea of water replacing a sea of grass. The sea is open to the Pacific at a cutoff Californian coast, labeled New Albion. Equally well-defined is a Northwest Passage leading from the Western Sea north to the northwest corner of Hudson Bay, where explorations by the British in the 1740s (see page 100) had demonstrated that no such passage existed. The geography of the Northwest is bizarrely wrong yet is placed in a North American continent otherwise quite recognizable. Note that Alaska is shown as an island, which it was thought to be by some at this time, and the Mississippi takes the pronounced westward jog to the Gulf of Mexico that was known to be incorrect from about 1700 on.

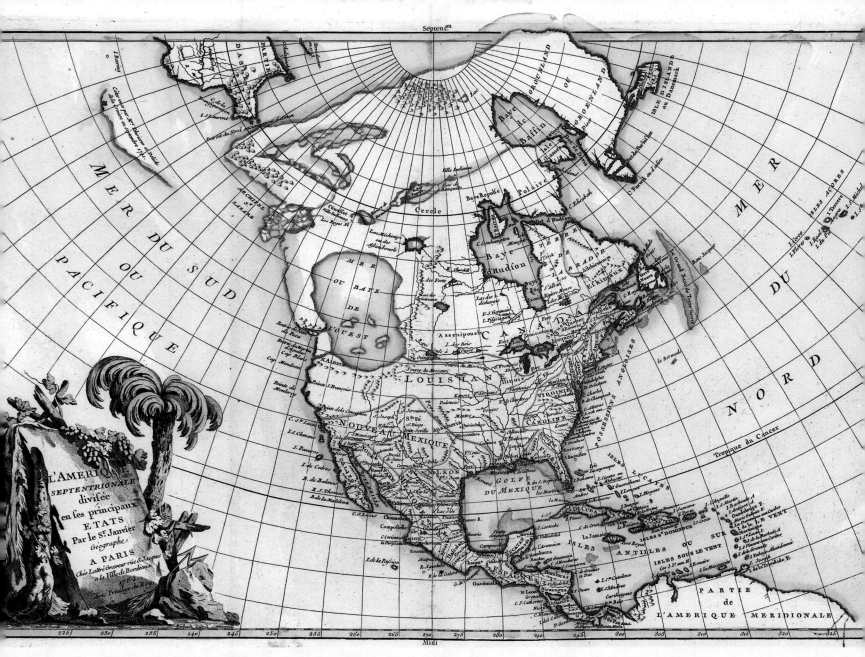

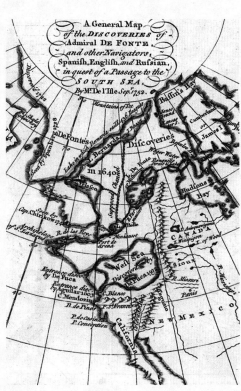

Map 112 (*above*).
This artistically superb and geographically absurd map was published by French mapmaker Jean Janvier in 1762. Here the *Mer ou Baye de L'Ouest* has two entrances, a northern one through the Strait of Juan de Fuca and another farther south through the *Entrée de Martin d' Aguilar*, the opening reported by one of Sebastian Vizcaíno's captains in 1602 (see page 46). The geography of the Northwest on these maps reflects the supposed voyage of a Spanish admiral named Bartolomew De Fonte in 1640 to Baffin Bay and Hudson Bay from the west.

Map 113 (*right*).
A map by Joseph-Nicolas De L'Isle, drawn in 1752, showing the geography of the De Fonte voyage and a *West Sea discover'd by De Fuca 1592*, which like the others has nonexistent islands in an imaginary sea.

demonstrate the mythical Sea of the West as it appeared on maps of the eighteenth century, a huge embayment of the Pacific often entered through the Strait of Juan de Fuca, supposedly discovered in 1592 by the Greek pilot of a Spanish ship, but for which no record has ever been found. It was a convenient opening for a sea that, explorers reported, had been said to exist over the next mountain in numerous locations in the West.

It was not until Cook defined the trend and the position of the west coast in 1778 (see page 126) and Alexander Mackenzie reached the waters of the Pacific in 1793 (see page 135) that mapmakers as well as explorers came to the conclusion that a Western Sea so near and so convenient was but a myth.

Explorers' Myths — The River of the West

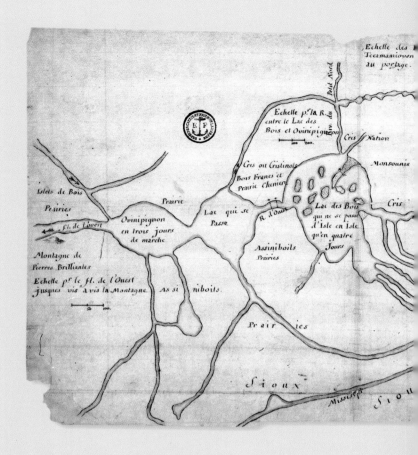

Equally as powerful as the concept of a Sea of the West was that of an easy way to get there: a long and straight river flowing from the center of the continent to the western ocean, the River of the West. This concept, of course, had a little more reality to it, in that there was a long river flowing to the west, the Columbia. And myths with an element of reality are usually more tenacious in that they are harder to disprove.

The first apparent documentation of the River of the West was the account of Louis Armand de Lom d'Arce, Baron de Lahontan (or La Hontan). His book, *Nouveaux Voyages dans l'Amérique Septentrionale*, published in 1703, was an account of an expedition he said he had made down a mysterious, westward-flowing river that was a tributary of the Upper Mississippi. Quite how it could be westward-flowing is not clear. This he called the Long River. Lahontan did leave from Fort Michilimackinac in September 1688 but his wanderings for the next eight months or so are not known. It was during this period that he claimed to have found the Long River. It seems clear now that Lahontan's work was a mixture of fact, fiction, misinterpretation of native reports, exaggeration, and just plain lies, but nevertheless, no one knew this at the time, and his book was enormously influential, as books of fiction parading as fact often are. His book went through a number of editions, though the content did not change, and the most popular was that of 1735. The idea that there was another great river west of the Missouri did not seem unreasonable, and the Long River began to show up on maps as fact.

Another book that was completely fictitious contributed to the illusion. This was the *Histoire de la Louisiane* of Le Page du Pratz, published in 1758 although pirated before then, in 1753. Du Pratz had lived in Louisiana for sixteen years and thought he would have a little fun with history. He invented a character named Moncacht-Apé, one of whose improbable adventures took him down a large and long river called the Beautiful River to the Pacific. Again, at the time no one could tell fact from fiction, and the book reinforced the idea that such a river existed flowing to the west.

MAP 114 (*below*).
Baron Lahontan's influential map of the "Long River" he claimed to have discovered in 1688–89, published in his book in 1703. To the east of the Mississippi the geography is reasonably accurate. Perhaps Lahontan heard Indian reports of a west bank tributary of the Mississippi, even a misplaced Missouri (though that river is shown at the bottom of the map), together with reports of a westward-flowing river (such as the Snake or Columbia) on the other side of mountains not realized to be a high barrier. But Lahontan claimed to have journeyed down this river.

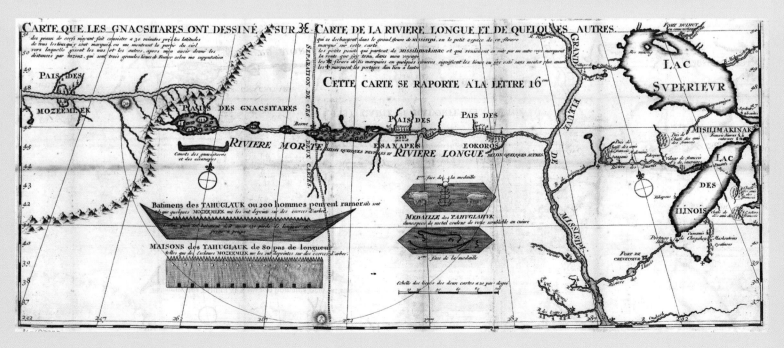

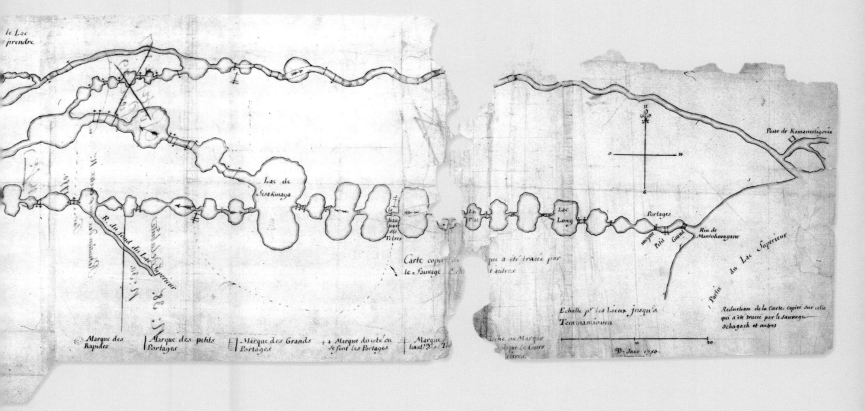

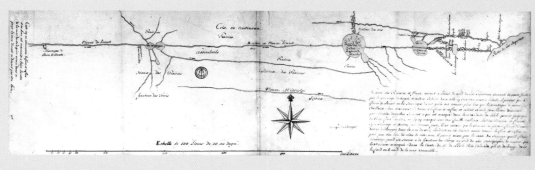

Map 115 (*above*) and Map 116 (*right, middle*). French copies of a map drawn by Auchagah, a Cree, for the explorer Pierre La Vérendrye in 1727 (see page 96). The original was drawn on bark with charcoal. Map 115 is a depiction of the river and lake system from Lake Superior (at right) to Lake Winnipeg and beyond, drawn as a sort of route map in a straight line, with the scale getting smaller to the west. At the western side of Map 115 is *fl*[euve] *de L'ouest,* the River of the West, now apparently westward flowing. Map 116 shows a French redrawn map more to scale with an extension of the river westwards to integrate European beliefs with what they thought Auchagah was showing them. Now a clear *Fleuve de l'ouest* runs straight to a note on the western edge about tides in that location—the sea. *Lac de bois* on both maps is Lake of the Woods, and the lake *Ouinipignon* or *Ouinipigon* is Lake Winnipeg.

Map 117 (*right*).

Part of a map of North America published by the British mapmaker William Faden in 1785. It shows a very long *River of the West* flowing northwest from the middle of North America to Juan de Fuca's strait. Faden had hedged his bets as to its mouth, showing the river also flowing to Nootka Sound, found by James Cook in 1778; this information was published in 1784. Along the course of the River of the West is the notation *Ascended by Moncachtapé.* Le Page du Pratz's fictional character was being used to give authority to a nonexistent river.

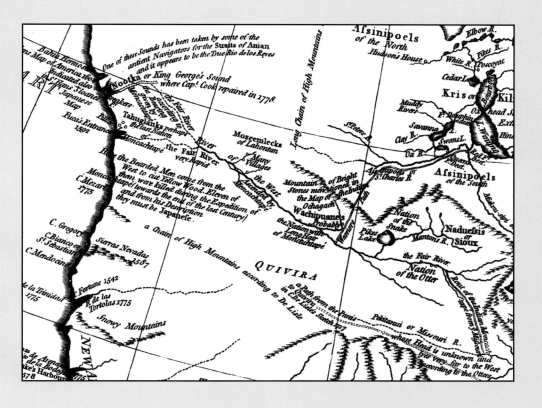

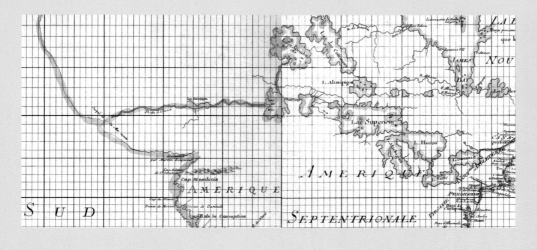

The next episode in the River of the West story was also influential because of a book. In 1766 Jonathan Carver was sent to explore "uncharted western territories" by Robert Rogers, an army captain who was very keen on finding a Northwest Passage by land or by sea. Carver traveled only as far west as the Minnesota River, a tributary of the Upper Mississippi, but he wrote a book, *Travels Through the Interior Parts of North-America in the Years 1766, 1767, and 1768*, which was a major best-seller, going through thirty editions in several languages. The book contained two maps. One, of the western Great Lakes and Upper Mississippi drainage basin, showed at its western end a little lake with a river leading west (MAP 119), with the notation *Heads of Origan*. The other, a general map of North America, showed this river labeled first *Mantons R.*, and then *River of the West*. It flowed to the Pacific through a channel *Discovered by Aguilar*, and was connected to the strait *Discovered by Juan de Fuca*. Here, then, was an incipient Oregon River, the Columbia. But, of course, Carver depicted the river flowing from the longitude of Lake Winnipeg, halfway across the continent. It sprang from the region in which rivers flowing to the Gulf of Mexico, the Atlantic, and Hudson Bay also arose.

Geographical experts by the end of the eighteenth century agreed that there must be an interior "height of land" somewhere in the west, a common source from which the major rivers of the continent fanned out to flow to each of its shores. The discovery in 1792 of the Columbia as a river by Robert Gray in his ship *Columbia Rediviva*—from whence the river derived its name—merely lent credence to this idea; here was where the westward-flowing River of the West entered the Pacific. Thus the idea was that the Columbia, the Mississippi, the St. Lawrence, and the Nelson Rivers flowed from a central point, with headwaters within thirty miles of each other.

The transcontinental journey of Meriwether Lewis and William Clark from

MAP 118 (*above, left*).
A map showing the River of the West published by Isaac Brouckner in 1749. The river flows out of *Lac de Bois* (Lake of the Woods) to the Pacific.

MAP 119 (*above, right*).
The western edge of Jonathan Carver's map of the Great Lakes and Upper Mississippi showed an unnamed little lake and a river flowing off the map with the notation *Heads of Origan*. Carver's use of an original Indian word is considered to be the origin of the name *Oregon*, in this case applied to the Oregon River, the Columbia. Carver's superior officer Robert Rogers first used the name *Ouragan* or *Ourigan* in his proposal for an expedition in 1765.

1804 to 1806 (see page 138), finally put an end to the common height of land concept, but did find rivers flowing to the Pacific from the Rocky Mountains, that immense barrier to travel that few had conceived of until near the end of the eighteenth century. Here was not a River of the West, but the Columbia.

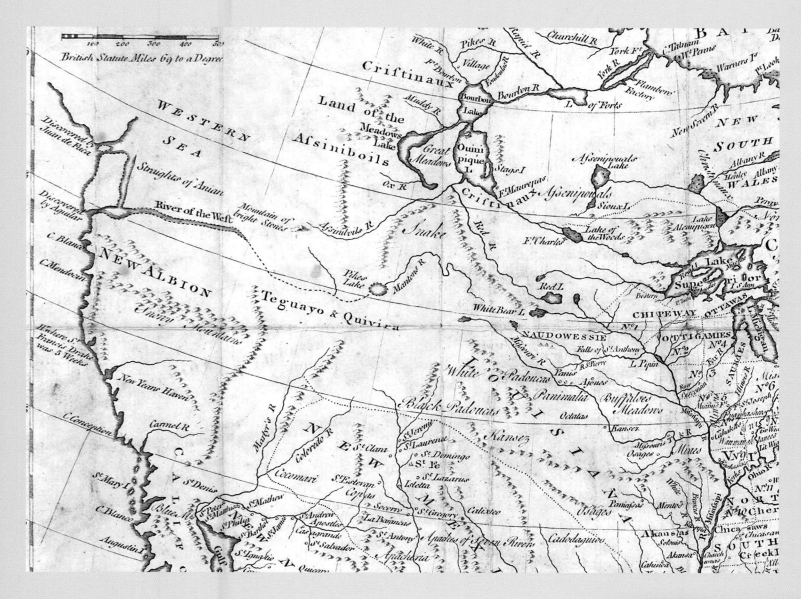

MAP 120 (*left*).
The River of the West shown on a map of North America published by British mapmaker Robert Sayer in 1750. The river flows from *Winipigue Lake* (Lake Winnipeg), which is also depicted connected to Red Lake, shown on **MAP 119**, and enters the Pacific at Martin Aguilar's entrance (see page 46).

MAP 121 (*above*).
The map of North America in Jonathan Carver's 1778 book. The River of the West is tentatively connected to *Mantons R*, actually the Upper Missouri but not shown as such. The mouth of the river is through the two entrances of De Fuca and Aguilar, as for a Sea of the West on **MAP 112**, page 91.

MAP 122 (*right*).
French geographer Jacques-Nicolas Bellin published this map in 1743 incorporating a Lahontan-Auchagah-style depiction of a River of the West flowing almost—but not quite—to the Pacific.

Searching for an Illusion

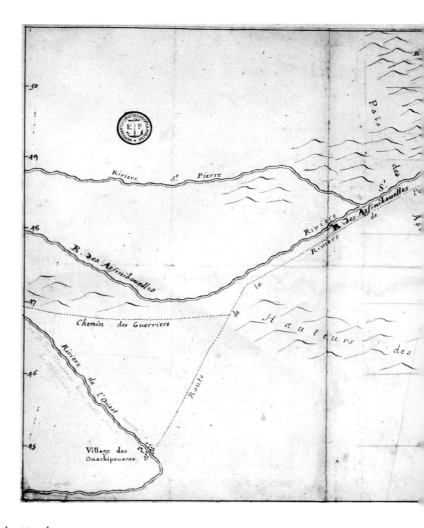

One explorer who tracked westward expecting to find a Sea of the West with a River of the West leading to it was the French explorer Pierre Gaultier de Varennes et de La Vérendrye, with his sons and nephew. It was for him that the Cree Auchagah drew the map illustrated on pages 92–93 (MAP 115).

The French need to push westwards had been exacerbated by the 1713 Treaty of Utrecht, which closed Hudson Bay to them. A plan was evolved to establish forts, called *postes du nord,* in strategic positions to intercept natives taking their furs to the British forts on the bay. Yet by 1728 there were still only three French forts in the Northwest, all around Lake Superior: Kaministiquia, Nipigon, and Michipicoten. That year La Vérendrye was appointed commandant of these forts and instructed to further expand the French fur trade network. In 1731 he received a three-year monopoly on the fur trade, which was supposed to finance his operations and, specifically, allow him to find the rumored River and Sea of the West for France. As usual, the French government wanted to expand and wanted to claim territory before others could, but did not want to pay for it. As a result, although La Vérendrye did his best, he did not do nearly as much as he could have because he was always having to establish posts to bring in the furs to continue. And he also had to concern himself with getting his monopoly renewed every few years. Nevertheless, La Vérendrye succeeded in increasing European knowledge of a vast region of the Northwest.

In 1686 Jacques de Noyon had found the important route up the Kaministiquia River and reached Lake of the Woods (see page 70). It was this route that La Vérendrye took in 1731. His nephew, Christophe Dufrost de La Jemerais, established Fort St. Pierre on Rainy Lake that year, and the next year Fort St. Charles was built on Lake of the Woods. By 1734 they had found Lake Winnipeg, building Fort Maurepas on the lower Red River. Lake Winnipeg was likely the Sea of the West the natives had told them about.

But where was the River of the West? The best bet seemed to be the Assiniboine River, which flows into the Red River at today's Winnipeg, Manitoba. La Vérendrye was hampered by the need to finance himself, and it would take him some years to investigate this river. In 1736 his nephew La Jemerais died of disease, and the same year his oldest son was killed along with a Jesuit, Father Jean-Pierre Alneau, and nineteen others by a Dakota war party at Lake of the Woods, at a place now named Massacre Island. La Vérendrye had traded in not only furs to finance his explorations but also Dakota slaves.

By 1737 he was in trouble for not exploring fast enough, despite opening up the entire country west to Lake Winnipeg for the French. He was able to show the governor of New France, the Marquis de Beauharnois, maps such as the one by La Jemerais (MAP 123), which in their western extremities contained information only from Indian report. In this case reports of the Missouri River had been interpreted to mean it was the River of the West, which was as reasonable an interpretation as any. La Vérendrye promised to speed up his explorations and in 1738 built Fort La Reine on the Assiniboine near today's Portage la Prairie, south of Lake Manitoba. Thinking that the river he sought might be to the south, he set off to the southwest in 1738, likely reaching the Mandan villages on the Upper Missouri. Yet he referred in his journal to a river that ran to the *west,* which could hardly have been the Missouri.

After a period of building more forts and yet again having to justify his actions to the government in Québec, he dispatched his two sons, Louis-Joseph and François (known as the

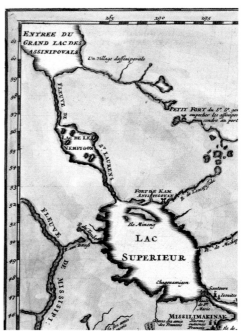

MAP 124.
The route from Lake Superior to Lake Winnipeg as it was perceived in 1719 by French mapmaker Henri Chatelain. *Entree du Grand Lac des Assinipovals* is Lake Winnipeg; *Lac de le Nempigon* is Lake of the Woods; *Petit Fort* is Fort Nipigon; and *Fort de Kamanistigoyan* is Fort Kaministiquia.

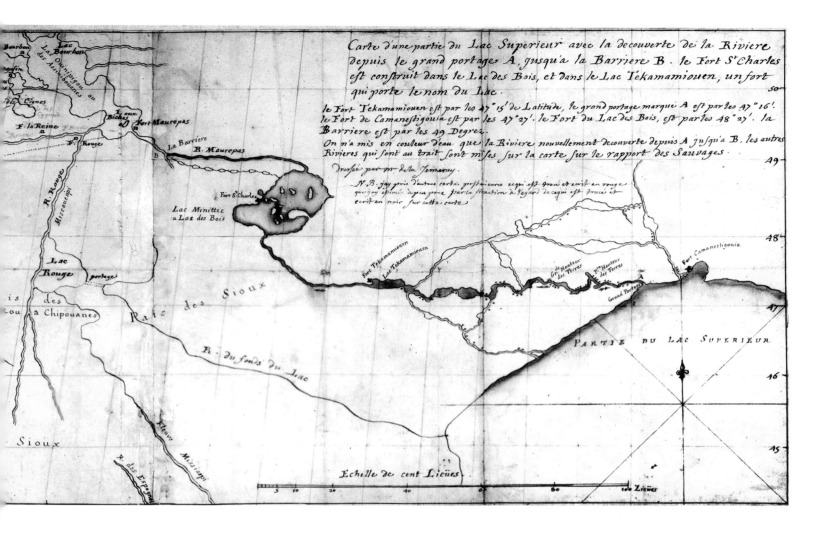

MAP 123 (*above*).
Christophe Dufrost de La Jemerais's map of the West, 1733. Lake Superior is at right. *Fort St. Charles* is shown on *Lac Minittie ou Lac des Bois* (Lake of the Woods); *Lac Ouinipigou ou des Assinibouenes* is Lake Winnipeg; *F. Rouge* is Fort Rouge at today's Winnipeg; *Riviere St. Charles*, also marked *R. des Assinibouelles* in red, is the Asssiniboine River; the *Village des Ouachipouanes* are the Mandan villages on the Missouri; and the *Riviere de l'ouest* is the Missouri. The notations in red were added in 1742.

Chevalier), to search for the River of the West and the elusive Western Sea. With two others, they set off to the southwest from Fort La Reine in April 1742 and did not return until the following year. Unfortunately there is no clear record of where they went. They did report coming within sight of a range of mountains, and these were likely the Big Horn Mountains, an outlying range of the Rockies in northern Wyoming, but they could also have been the Black Hills of western South Dakota, nearly a hundred miles farther east. What seems certain is that they reached the vicinity of Pierre, South Dakota, for in 1913 a lead plate claiming possession of the land for Louis XV was found, and it appears to be genuine.

The French government was furious that the Vérendryes had not discovered at least a River of the West. It seemed they could do nothing right. La Vérendrye senior lost his position as commandant of the *postes du nord* that he had founded, but not before establishing his final one, Fort Paskoya, on the Saskatchewan River near Cedar Lake, the site of modern The Pas, Manitoba. In 1746 La Vérendrye was reappointed, a tacit recognition that the job he had done was not so bad. But he died in 1749.

It was an impossible task: find a nonexistent river and sea. But the penny-pinching French government got a great deal of new geographical insight for its Scrooge-like behavior. If it had not been so tight-fisted there seems little doubt the Vérendryes would have reached at least the Rocky Mountains. As it was, another fifty years would pass before a Briton rather than a Frenchman reached the Western Sea—Alexander Mackenzie in 1793 (see page 135). By that time all the North American governments had changed.

As the explorations of the Vérendryes were winding down, other French explorers were ascending the Missouri searching for another illusion: that of a Santa Fe as an El Dorado. French traders had long been interested in finding a route to Santa Fe for trade, thinking it contained silver such as the Spanish had found farther to the south. It did not, but this did not lessen the desire to pursue the mirage. Even the route was wrong; the Missouri, thought to lead to Santa Fe, did not.

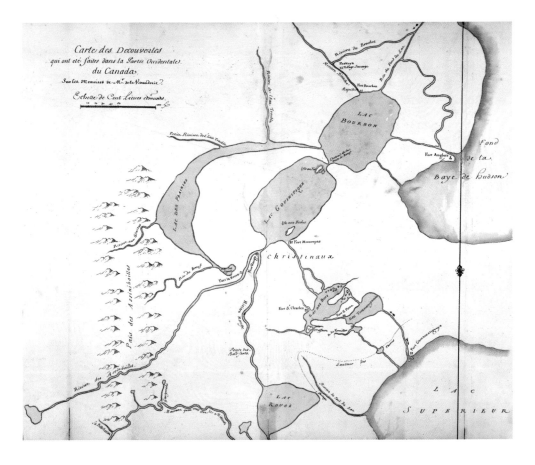

In May 1739 the Mallet brothers, Pierre and Paul, reached a point on the Missouri, today at the northeastern tip of Nebraska, where they were advised by Pawnee to cut back to the southwest, overland. Braving lands thought to be inhabited by hostile Indians, they reached Santa Fe in July, where they were welcomed, despite it being illegal for Spaniards to trade with the French. The Mallets had lost their trade goods crossing the Salinas River anyhow.

The brothers found their way back to New Orleans the following year by way of the Pecos, Canadian, and Arkansas Rivers, and the French realized that these rivers would provide a much more usable route to Santa Fe. The Santa Fe Trail, which would become one of the major routes west, had been found. The search for an illusion had produced a practical result.

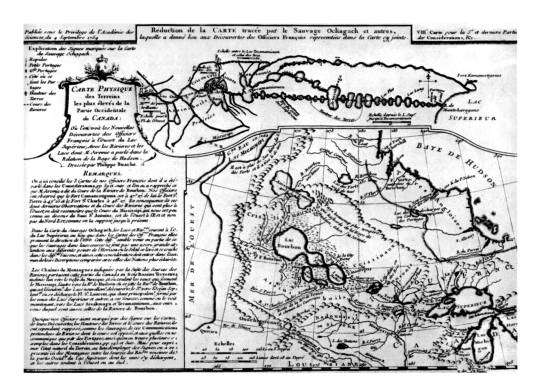

MAP 125 (*left*).
A map of the discoveries of La Vérendrye and the network of forts he set up, drawn by Jacques-Nicolas Bellin in 1752, a copy of an anonymous map drawn about 1740. James Bay, the southern extension of Hudson Bay, is at top right, and Lake Superior at bottom right. From it rivers flow to or from Lake Winnipeg (*Lac Gouinipique*) via Rainy Lake (*Lac Tecamanigouin*) and Lake of the Woods (*Lac des Bois*). *Lac Bourbon* is the northern part of Lake Winnipeg, while the curving arc of *Lac des Prairies* is a combination of Lake Manitoba, Lake Winnipegosis, and probably Cedar Lake as well. *Lac Rouge* is Red Lake, Minnesota. The map has been drawn with north at the top, but the distances, especially from James Bay to the western lakes, are very compressed. All the forts established by La Vérendrye are shown, from Fort St. Pierre (*Ft S. Piere*) on Rainy Lake and *Fort St. Charles* on Lake of the Woods west to *Fort Bourbon*, where the Saskatchewan River is shown entering the northern part of Lake Winnipeg, *Lac Bourbon* (it actually enters Cedar Lake), *Fort Paskoya* (Poskoya, at The Pas), and *Fort la Reine* (at Portage la Prairie). *Fort Maurepas* is shown at its second location, where the Winnipeg River enters Lake Winnipeg, and also shown is *Fort Rouge*, at the junction of the Red and Assiniboine Rivers, where Winnipeg now stands. Fort Kaministiquia (*Fort Gainanesfigouya*) is shown on the Lake Superior shore. This route to the west would be rediscovered by the North West Company after the Grand Portage route immediately south of it was denied to the company after the American Revolution. Fort Kaministiquia would become Fort William, and is now part of Thunder Bay, Ontario. The map shows the beginnings of the European understanding of the geography of the Northwest.

MAP 126 (*left, bottom*).
A map published by French mapmaker Philippe Buache in 1754 showing the geography to the west of Lake Superior as he (mis)understood it, together with a representation of Auchagah's map (see MAP 115, pages 92–93).

MAP 127.

This map shows a river that could either be a representation of the Assiniboine or the Saskatchewan (since it leaves Lake Winnipeg on its western side), which flows to or from a sea—*Mer Inconnuë* ("Unknown sea"). It does this via a lake (*Lac de la hauteur,* "Lake of the heights") astride a mountain range—the Rockies? This was the map sent to governor Beauharnois in 1737 to support further renewal of La Vérendrye's fur trade monopoly, and since this was dependent on exploration, a map showing a clear River of the West all the way to the sea was an obvious incentive. Unfortunately for the Vérendryes, the river they had heard of from Indian report—which probably was the Saskatchewan—did not defy physics and flow up mountain ranges; their political masters were bound to be disappointed. The map is oriented approximately with the top left corner to the north. On the top edge is Hudson Bay, on the top right edge Lake Superior, at the bottom right edge is perhaps intended to be the Gulf of California—it may have been derived from the Great Salt Lake of Utah. *Lac 8inipigon* is Lake Winnipeg, and *Lac Rouge* is Red Lake, Minnesota.

Even more long-lived, and even more tenacious than the myths of the Sea of the West and the River of the West was the myth of a navigable Northwest Passage. Despite earlier failures to find the route, the myth had not died but merely been put on hold as "not found."

The Hudson's Bay Company up to 1713 had been too busy worrying about their trade in the face of French aggression to concern themselves with trying to find a passage. In 1719 a new bayside governor, James Knight, persuaded that sources of copper and gold were near at hand, sailed with two ships north along the west coast of the bay. He was never heard from again; the ships were wrecked on Marble Island, just south of Chesterfield Inlet, and he and all his men perished. The company was not keen to try again.

All further attempts to find a Northwest Pasage in the eighteenth century were largely due to the drive and enthusiasm—and unflagging optimism—of one man, Arthur Dobbs. He was a wealthy Ulster landowner who was convinced of the commercial and imperial advantages that would accrue to Britain if the passage was found. He managed to convince Sir Charles Wager, First Lord of the Admiralty, to speak to King George II about it. The king thought it such a "trifle" that he approved a naval expedition.

Christopher Middleton, an experienced Bay Company captain, was recruited to lead the attempt. Two ships were outfitted: *Furnace* and *Discovery,* the latter under William Moor, another company captain. The ships sailed in June 1741, reaching the west side of Hudson Bay too late in the season to continue. They overwintered at the mouth of the Churchill, and after a difficult winter, sailed north on 1 July 1742. Middleton discovered a considerable inlet, which was explored in boats, though not to its end. He named it, after the first lord, Wager's River (now Wager Bay). Continuing north he passed a cape that had land trending to the west. Middleton wrote that it gave him "great Joy and hopes of it's being the extream Part of America, on which Account I named it C. Hope." But hope was not enough; it was in fact a large bay, which he named Repulse Bay.

MAP 128.
Wager Bay has become *Wager Strait* in this map by John Wigate, Middleton's clerk on the *Furnace.* It was published in 1746. Frozen Strait, to the east of *Repulse Bay,* is now not shown. *Wager Strait,* on the other hand, is drawn to suggest a westward opening.

Returning south Middleton found Rankin Inlet, but not Chesterfield Inlet. He also investigated the tides in Roes Welcome Sound, which Dobbs had been convinced came from a nearby Northwest Passage; Middleton determined, correctly, that they came from Frozen Strait, which leads only north to Foxe Basin.

Middleton returned to Britain to an outraged Dobbs, who, convinced he could not have been wrong, insisted Middleton had falsified his log and maps. The government had no stomach for another attempt, but instead offered a reward of £10,000 for discovery

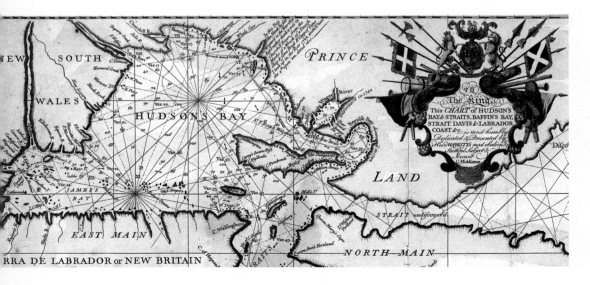

MAP 129 (*left*).
Christopher Middleton's map of his exploration of the northwest part of Hudson Bay, published in 1743. North is to the right. The track of Middleton's ships is shown up the west side of Hudson Bay and into *Repulse Bay,* which he had hoped would be the entrance to the Northwest Passage. *C. Dobbs* is at the entrance to *Wager River* (Wager Inlet). *The Frozen Strait* leads from Repulse Bay to the east rather than to the west. It was the source of tides in *Sr T. Roe's Welcome* (Roes Welcome Sound), thought by Arthur Dobbs to indicate the presence of a passage west.

of a Northwest Passage. This allowed Dobbs to interest enough private investors to finance another voyage.

This time William Moor was joined by Francis Smith and the pair sailed on a voyage in 1746 similar to that of Middleton's, in 1747 finding Chesterfield Inlet and investigating Wager Bay to its western end. Henry Ellis, Dobbs's agent on the voyage, wrote that they "had the Mortification to see clearly that our hitherto imagined Strait ended in two small unnavigable rivers."

Dobbs was furious once more. Clutching at straits like straws, he now claimed that Chesterfield Inlet was the true Northwest Passage, for it had not been examined to its western end. But he could not convince any more investors, and Dobbs instead turned his considerable energies to attacking the Hudson's Bay Company. There would be no more talk of Northwest Passages until the following century.

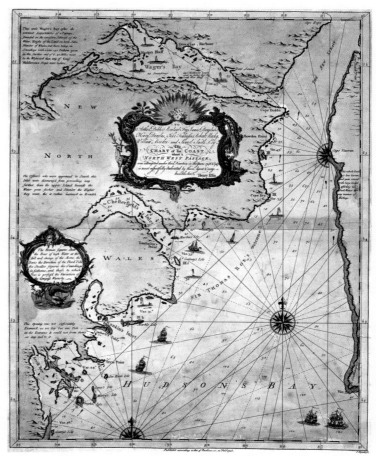

Map 132 (*above*).
A 1748 map by Henry Ellis, Arthur Dobbs's agent on the voyage of William Moor and Francis Smith in 1746–47. The notation at the western end of *Wager's Bay* reads in part: *thus ends Wager's Bay after the warmest expectations of a Passage.*

Map 133 (*below*).
A book published in 1768 by Alexander Cluny reported on his supposed journey north on the west side of Hudson Bay in 1744 and across a peninsula bearing a superficial resemblance to the real Melville Peninsula in this region, but it is likely the report, and the map, was but a hoax.

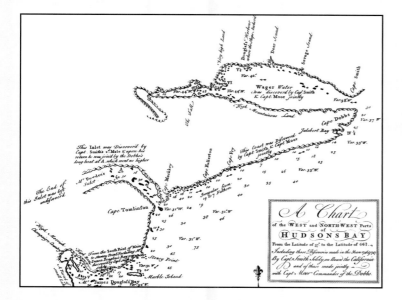

Map 130 (*above*).
Map illustrating the voyage of William Moor and Francis Smith in 1746–47. *Mr Bowden's Inlet* is Chesterfield Inlet. Note *The End of this Inlet was left undiscovered,* allowing Dobbs a further straw.

Map 131 (*below*).
Indian reports of an inlet on the east side of Hudson Bay prompted the Hudson's Bay Company to send William Coats to investigate in 1749. He found it to be only the location of a large lake. This 1744 map, as seems usual for this period, showed every possible inlet as a new sea or strait, in this case taking up most of the peninsula of Labrador.

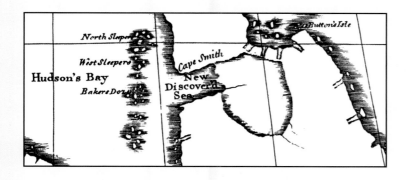

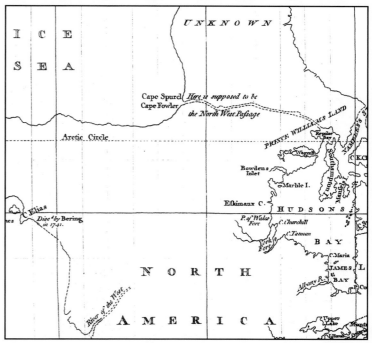

The Russian Discovery of America

North America was discovered by Europeans not only from the east but also from the west. Danish captain Vitus Bering together with Russian Aleksei Chirikov both found the west coast of what is now Alaska in 1741, and claimed it for Russia.

Europeans had been aware for some time of a probable continent to the east of the eastern shore of Asia. Maerten Vries was sent from the Dutch East Indies in 1643 to search for reputed islands of silver and gold. He found Japan and the Kuril Islands north of it, marking the northernmost one Compagnies Land, after his Dutch East India Company. At this time North America was thought to stretch right across the Pacific and so, within a year, Compagnies Land became Americae Pars—"part of America"—on some maps.

Almost a hundred years later the Russian emperor Peter the Great dispatched a Danish captain employed in his navy, Vitus

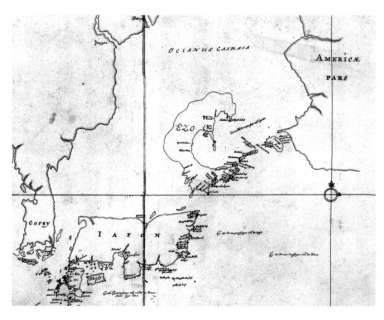

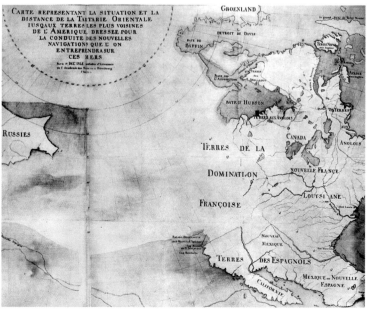

Bering, to determine just where America was in relation to his own domains and, in particular, to determine if it was joined to Asia. The Russians had forgotten that a fur trader named Semen Dezhnev had sailed right around the eastern extremity of Asia in 1648, thus proving that Asia and America were not joined. Bering sailed northeast from the Kamchatka Peninsula in 1728 to the strait that now bears his name; but he did not see the coast of Alaska and so could not say for sure where America was. The first sighting of America was four years later, by Mikhail Gvozdev, who saw a coast east of the Diomede Islands in Bering Strait. He could not land because of contrary winds but was told of the "Big Land" by natives.

On his return from his less than completely satisfactory voyage of 1728, Bering proposed a new effort to locate and map America as part of a larger scientific expedition to Eastern Siberia called the Second Kamchatka Expedition. (The first was his 1728 voyage.) This was a massive effort with many men involved and included voyages to Japan. Transportation in Russia was so bad that to get all the supplies to Kamchatka took many years, and it was not until the spring of 1741 that two ships, *Sviatoi Petr* and *Sviatoi Pavel* (*St. Peter* and *St. Paul*), commanded by Bering and Aleksei Chirikov, sailed east to find America. The map they had with them is shown here (MAP 135); their job was to fill in the blanks!

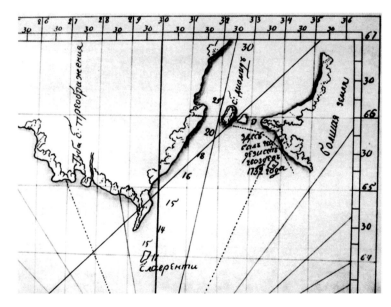

MAP 134 (*left, top*).
The discovery of *Americæ Pars*—"part of America"—by Maerten Vries in 1643, shown on a map drawn the following year. It was not America but Ostrov Urup, one of the Kiril Islands chain. But America was known to be somewhere in that direction, and might even stretch across the Pacific.

MAP 135 (*left, bottom*).
This map illustrates all that was known about the northwestern part of America and the North Pacific in 1730. It was drawn by Joseph-Nicolas de L'Isle to guide Vitus Bering on his voyage of discovery to America.

Map 136 (*left, center*).
Part of a map of Mikhail Gvozdev's discovery of the North American continent in 1732. The map was drawn in 1734. It shows Bering Strait and the Diomedes Islands, with Cape Prince of Wales, the westernmost part of the North American mainland, to the right.

Map 137 (*right*).
This was the latest information in 1724 when Peter the Great asked Bering to investigate the location of America. It is part of a map published by Johann Baptist Homann in 1723. *Incognita* is, perhaps, America, and comes from an earlier map drawn by Ivan Lvov in 1710.

Map 138 (*below, top*).
Map of the voyage of Vitus Bering to America in 1741–42, drawn by his surviving lieutenant Sven Waxell in late 1742 or in 1743. Kayak Iskand, Bering's landfall, is shown at top right.

Map 139 (*below, bottom*).
Map of the voyage of Aleksei Chirikov in 1741, drawn by Ivan Elagin, Chirikov's pilot, in 1742. His landfall in Alaska is shown at top right—twice. This is because he plotted his position using dead reckoning from a known point (Kamchatka), and there were differences in the errors outbound and inbound. Bering's track is also shown on this map, with the landfall farther north than Chirikov's.

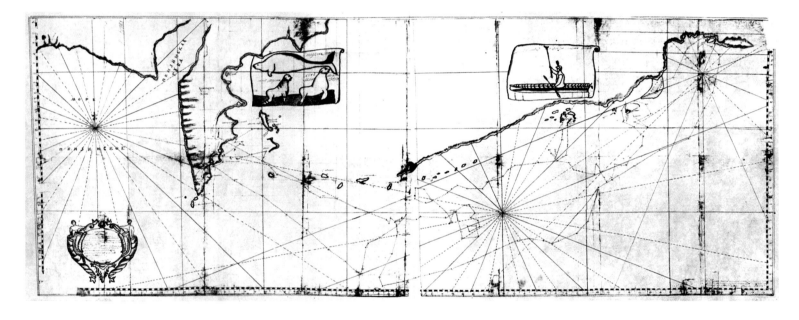

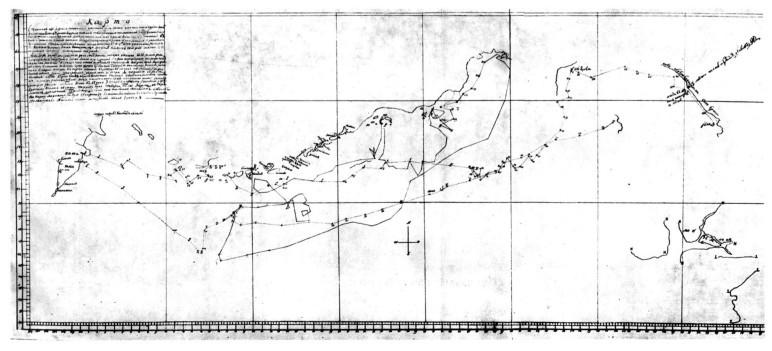

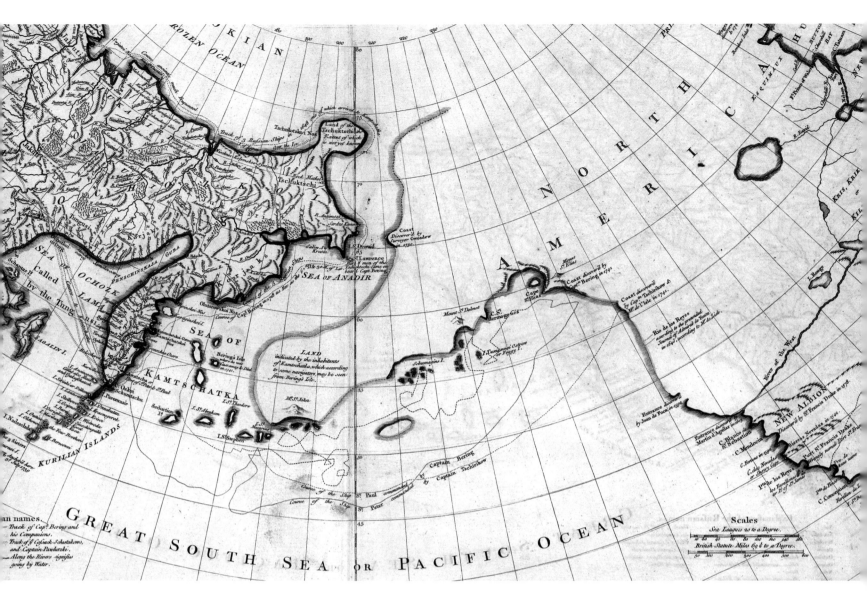

Map 140 (above).

German scientist Gerhard Müller, who had been a member of the Second Kamchatka Expedition, drew this map in 1754 based on his interpretation of information from Bering's and Chirikov's voyages. Müller was confused by the Aleutian Islands chain, and the result was a mainland peninsula of America jutting hundreds of miles into the North Pacific. This geography was copied by many mapmakers for several decades. The map is a 1768 copy by British mapmaker Thomas Jefferys.

Map 141 (below).

Potap Zaikov's map of the Aleutian Islands, drawn in 1779. It was the first map of the whole chain.

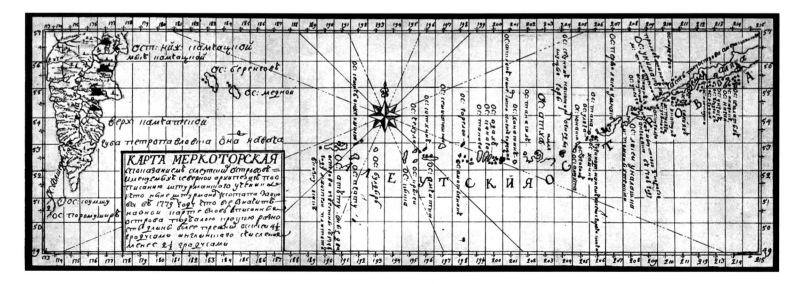

This map caused a lot of problems, for it showed lands sup-posed seen by Jean de Gama (south of Kamchatka on MAP 135) on an earlier, probably apocryphal, voyage. Bering and Chirikov spent so much time looking for Gama Land that they became separated, and each proceeded towards America on his own.

Chirikov reached his landfall on 15 July 1741, a few days before Bering, at Baker Island, on the west coast of Prince of Wales Island at 55° 20´ N. He then coasted north looking for an anchorage, find-ing none. Off Baranof Island Chirikov sent off a boat to locate an anchorage, but it disappeared. After a week, he sent another to find it; this boat was never seen again either. Finally, concluding his men must have been attacked by natives—this was the land of the fierce Tlingit—and having no more boats, Chirikov sailed back along the Aleutian chain to Kamchatka. At Adak, the largest of the Andreanov group, natives approached and were given gifts, but again Chirikov did not land due to his lack of boats.

But at least he made it back to Kamchatka; Bering did not. He had made a landfall a few days after Chirikov's farther south, at Kayak Island, within sight of Mount St. Elias, the name Bering gave only the island, not the mountain. Bering spent but ten hours at Kayak Island, during which time his scientist, the renowned Georg Steller, scurried about doing research that should have taken weeks.

On his way back to Kamchatka Bering was wrecked on what is now Bering Island, quite close to the Kamchatka shore. They were forced to overwinter on the island, and many died, including Bering himself. A new ship was constructed from the timbers of the first and Bering's first officer, Sven Waxell, sailed it back to Petropavlovsk, Kamchatka, where they arrived on 5 September 1742.

Other Russian explorers followed in Bering and Chirikov's tracks, slowly revealing the true shape of Alaska, which was for some time thought to be a peninsula (MAP 140, *left*)—a deception due to the chainlike pattern of the Aleutians—and then only a series of islands (as in MAP 142).

Before 1750 the westernmost Aleutians, Attu, Agattu, and the Semichi group, all part of the Near Islands, were discovered by M. Nevotchikov, and St. Matthew Island was found by S. Novikov and Ivan Bakhov. Other Aleutians were discovered and by 1761 G. Pushkarev found the Alaskan mainland, though he thought it just another island. Kodiak Island was reached by Stepan Glotov in 1763. These were private fur-hunting expeditions and produced few maps, but in 1762 Catherine II came to power in Russia, and she was interested in ex-ploration and expansion of her empire. And so in 1764 she sent out one of the survivors of the Bering expedition, Ivan Synd. He found many islands, as might be expected, and plotted them on a map, not altogether accurately, it would seem (MAP 142); as a result Alaska was shown as an island on maps for a while.

Another official expedition was sent out in 1768. Petr Krenitsyn and Mikhail Levashev were sent to find out if any other powers (especially Spain) were encroaching on what the Russians were increasingly coming to think of as their domains. Between 1768 and 1769 Kren-itsyn and Levashev explored and mapped part of the Aleutians and the western end of the Alaska Peninsula, but it was left to another fur hunter, Potap Zaikov, to produce the first map of the entire Aleutian chain (MAP 141, *left*). In 1786–87 Gavriil Pribilof found the small and isolated, but later economically valuable, Pribilof Islands.

By the end of the century, Russian influence had extended over much of coastal Alaska, and in 1799 the Russian-American Company was established to monopolize and co-ordinate fur hunting and trading in the now Russian Northwest.

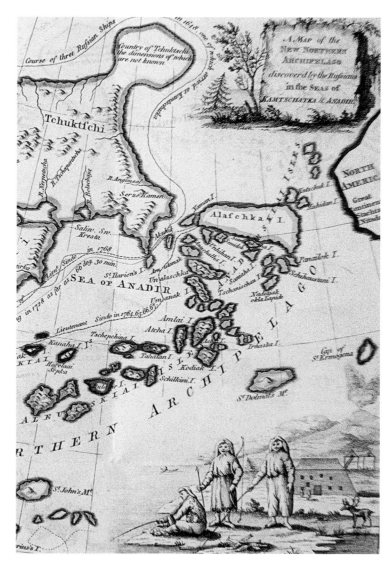

MAP 142 (*above*).
A map published by Jacob von Stählin in a book in 1774, based on his interpretation of informa-tion from the voyage of Ivan Synd. The map is famous for confusing Captain James Cook, who had it with him on his third voyage in 1778 (see page 126).

MAP 143 (*below*).
Part of a map of the Russian Empire published in 1776. The Aleutians nearest to Siberia are shown at the extreme northeastern corner of the map.

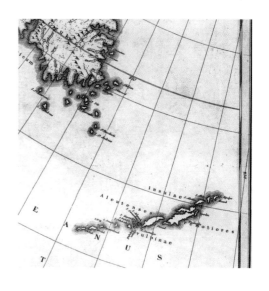

Crossing the Mountains

The first forays of the East Coast colonists across the mountain ranges that lay behind them were to search out the Western Sea that they felt sure was an easy march away. Once they realized that land, not water lay on the other side of the mountains, the more intrepid among them set out to find what bounty the land might hold. The easier way west was around the mountain ranges rather than over them, and traders from Charlestown, South Carolina, first took advantage of this. But there were passes through the mountains if one could find them.

Virginian Cadwaller Jones wrote *An Essay: Louissiania and Virginia Improved* and sent it to the governor, Frances Nicolson, in 1699. It advocated a rapid expansion of English trade and settlement for English benefit and French containment.

A new lieutenant governor, Alexander Spotswood, likely read Jones's writing. He was an active promoter of westward expansion and in 1716 led what appears to have been a largely ceremonial exploration, if there is such a thing. He led sixty or so colonial gentlemen dubbed Knights of the Golden Horseshoe, together with their retinues, through Swift Run Gap across the Blue Ridge Mountains to the Shenandoah Valley. To this day the road leading to Swift Run is the Spotswood Trail. A map copied by Spotswood, that of Pryce Hughes depicting the lands towards the Mississippi, is shown as Map 101, page 82.

It was in the Ohio Valley that the British and the French would clash in competition for Indian trade and, later, land. The French had generally used the Lake Michigan portages to the Mississippi until Indian unrest in the early part of the eighteenth century caused them to divert their traffic to the Ohio route. In 1729 the French military engineer Chaussegros de Léry surveyed the Ohio

and Allegheny Rivers, and in 1749 Céleron de Bienville took two hundred soldiers down the Ohio, nailing up lead plates to claim ownership as he went. Yet the British, who were finding their way over the mountains in increasing numbers, also claimed the region by dint of a cession from the Iroquois in 1744.

From 1744 to 1748 Britain and France were at war, and French merchants received fewer trade goods from Europe. The British trader George Croghan used this to his advantage, building trading posts in the Ohio country, but in 1752 these were attacked and destroyed by the French, who in turn built a number of forts, including Fort Duquesne (at Pittsburgh), the target of attacks by the Virginia militia under George Washington in 1754. It marked the beginning of a long war that would end with the conquest of New France in 1759 and 1760, putting an end to French influence in the region forever.

The region also became better known as a result of scientific exploration. In 1743 the naturalist John Bartram traveled to what is now upstate New York in the company of mapmaker Lewis Evans, who would incorporate information about the area into his important 1755 map (Map 147, pages 108–9)

Explorers traveling westward from Virginia also found the Ohio Valley. And one of the incentives was the land itself. It was easy for governments to give away huge tracts they had never seen, had dubious title to, and which were far removed. In 1737 the Virginia Council granted ten thousand acres to John Howard on condition that he explore west to the Mississippi. This he did in 1742. Accompanied by John Peter Salley, he set out in a boat, built on the spot, down the New and Kanawha Rivers to the Ohio, and then on to the Mississippi. Unfortunately for them, they encountered a French supply convoy. They were arrested, taken to New Orleans, and thrown in prison. Salley and some others managed to escape after two years, paddling across Lake Pontchartrain in a boat made from the hides of two bulls they killed, using the shoulder blades tied to sticks as their paddles. It took him another year to reach Virginia again. Salley's journal was used by Peter Jefferson in the making of his 1751 map (Map 150, pages 110–11).

The widest of the gaps through the Appalachian chain is the Cumberland Gap, where the boundaries of Virginia, Kentucky, and Tennessee meet. Used by the native peoples of the region for centuries, it was found by Gabriel Arthur (see page 67) and was

A view west from the summit of the Blue Ridge Mountains near Swift Run Gap, Virginia.

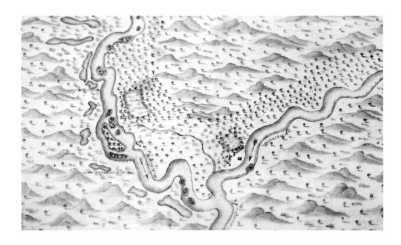

MAP 144.
This rather beautiful French map showing the confluence of the Ohio River (at right) and the Mississippi seems to have been drawn in connection with the survey of the higher parts of the Ohio Valley done by Chaussegros de Léry (père) in 1729. It was given to the French military establishment in 1752 by his son.

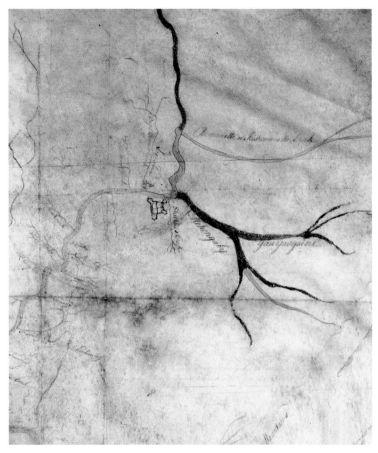

MAP 145 (*above*).
Christopher Gist's map of part of the course of the Ohio River, drawn in 1754 on an animal hide; it is difficult to see. Fort Du Quesne is shown at the forks of the Ohio. Lake Erie is off the top of the part of the map shown.

rediscovered in 1750 by Thomas Walker, who named it in honor of the Duke of Cumberland, commander of the British army. Walker was employed as the surveyor for the Loyal Land Company, which had been granted 800,000 acres of land in the valleys to the west in 1749. Walker's discovery of the Cumberland Gap as a practical route west was significant; in the period between 1775 and 1810 as many as 300,000 people passed through it on their way to settle in Kentucky.

In a similar fashion to the Loyal Land Company, the Ohio Company had been granted 200,000 acres of land along the upper Ohio, also in 1749. The company commissioned frontiersman Christopher Gist to explore and survey this land. Gist made two explorations of the Ohio country, in 1750–51 and 1751–52, finding a route across the mountains along the valley of the Potomac River. He met George Croghan and the pair negotiated with the Indians, who agreed to meet again in June 1752. At this meeting the Indians agreed to British settlement rights east of the Ohio River.

Between 1752 and 1754 Gist was employed once more by the Ohio Company, to mark the route across the mountains along the Potomac-Monongahela route he had pioneered. This he did with the help of Nemacolin, a Delaware chief. The route was later the first part of the National Road built west to Illinois in the 1840s.

Gist's report to the Ohio Company waxed eloquent about the agricultural prospects for western Pennsylvania and eastern Ohio, and recommended the confluence of the Allegheny and the Monongahela, where they come together to form the Ohio River,

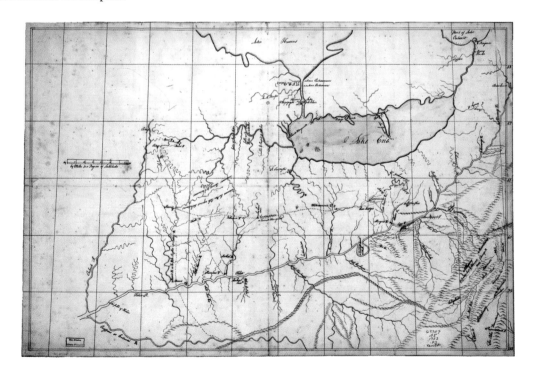

MAP 146.
A map of the Ohio drawn by a British trader in the region, John Patten, about 1752. It shows a fairly detailed knowledge of the entire watershed, some of which was no doubt based on secondhand information. Nonetheless, the map is accurate in its essentials.

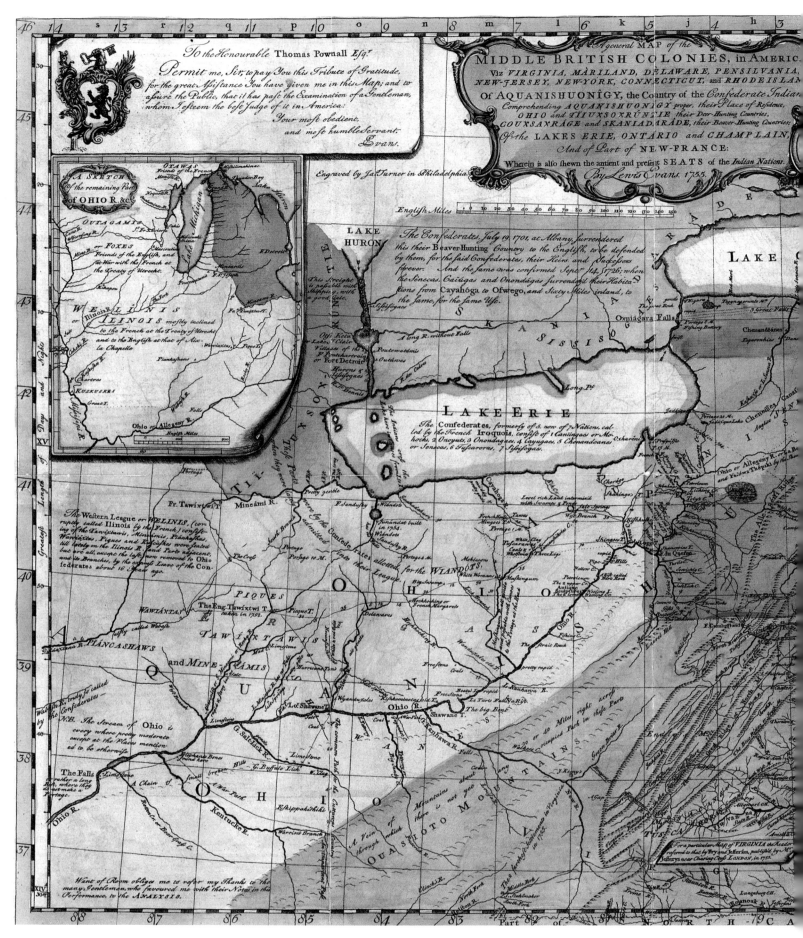

Map 147.

Lewis Evans's important *General Map of the Middle British Colonies, in America*, published in 1755. Evans was commissioned by the Pennsylvania Assembly to construct a map of the colony. It took him four years, and

he toiled often in secret to avoid his work coming to the attention of the French. In a description of the country published with the map, Evans emphasized the need for permanent settlements in the Ohio Valley border

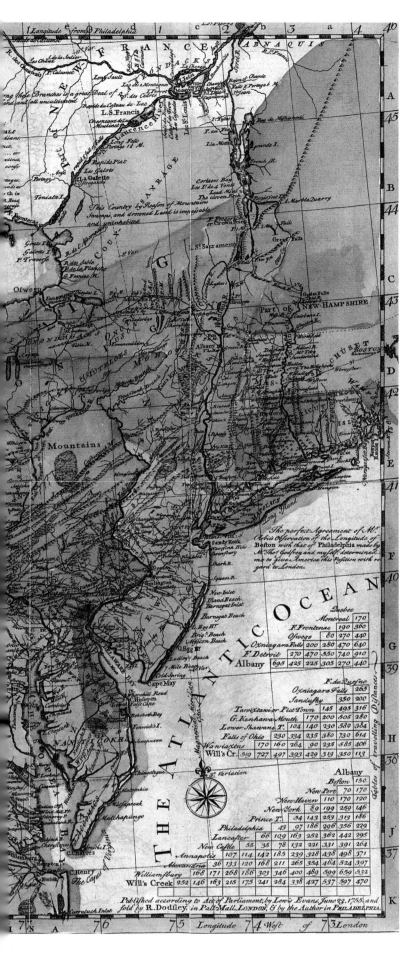

MAP 148 (*above*).
The waves of the daunting mountain ranges of the Appalachians are shown graphically in this extract from a map drawn in 1765 by British military engineers.

as a strategic location for a fort. Such a fort was under construction in 1754 when it was seized by the French; it was their Fort Duquesne until 1758, when it was retaken by the British and renamed Fort Pitt—now in Pittsburgh. Gist was enlisted by George Washington as a guide during the action against the French in 1754.

Information from Gist's perambulations was used by Joshua Fry, who with Peter Jefferson (Thomas Jefferson's father) constructed an important map of Virginia (MAP 150, *overleaf*) that would be used to guide settlers through the mountains to the Ohio Valley.

Perhaps the most famous of all the frontiersmen of this period was Daniel Boone. Between 1767 and 1775 Boone explored most of the Trans-Appalachian West, the region that is now Kentucky. He lived in western North Carolina and from his youth had developed frontier skills. In 1767 he went west across the Appalachians "in quest of the country of Kentucke," but did not reach it. In 1769, while on a hunting expedition, he reached the south fork of the Kentucky River, was captured by Shawnees, then escaped to explore down to the Ohio. On his return he was relieved of all his deerskins by Cherokee near the Cumberland Gap.

In 1773 Boone returned to Kentucky, guiding six settler families, but they were driven back by Indian attacks. The Shawnee had never ceded lands to the settlers and were becoming increasingly pressed as hunters moved into their region, wiping out their food supplies. But the human tide was not to be stopped, and in 1775 Boone and others, working for a land and colonizing organization called the Transylvania Company, blazed a trail called the Wilderness Road for two hundred miles through the Cumberland Gap to the south bank of the Kentucky River, where the settlement of Boonesborough was founded. Boone, aided by a book called *The Adventures of Daniel Boone,* published by John Filson in 1784, somehow passed into history as the romantic ideal of the American frontiersman, rugged, independent, skilled in hunting, and opener of hitherto savage lands to civilization. The truth is no doubt different, but the ideal inspired many who came after him. John Filson's *This Map of Kentucke* (MAP 149, *overleaf*) acknowledges its debt to Boone in a cartouche.

regions rather than the current trading posts. Information from his own surveys was supplemented by information from other sources, notably from George Croghan.

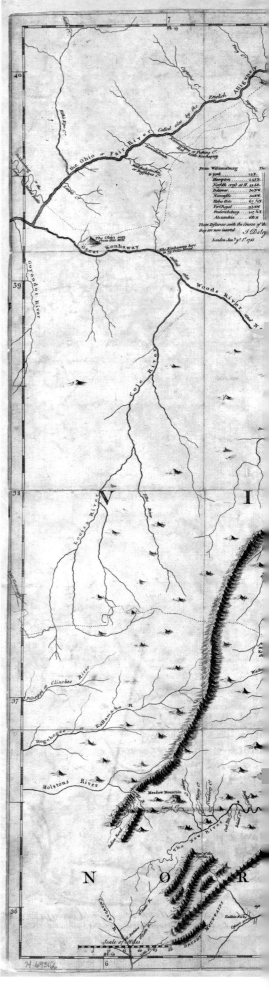

Map 149 (*above*).

John Filson's map of *Kentucke*, compiled with information from Daniel Boone and other explorers, and published in 1784. Filson's writings did much to create the image of Boone as the romantic American frontiersman.

Map 150 (*right*).

Joshua Fry and Peter Jefferson's *Map of the most Inhabited part of Virginia*, published in 1751, a collation of all the latest information from explorers and traders west of the mountains, together with information from their own surveys. Peter Jefferson was Thomas Jefferson's father. The detailed cartouche from this map is below. The map was engraved by British mapmaker Thomas Jefferys.

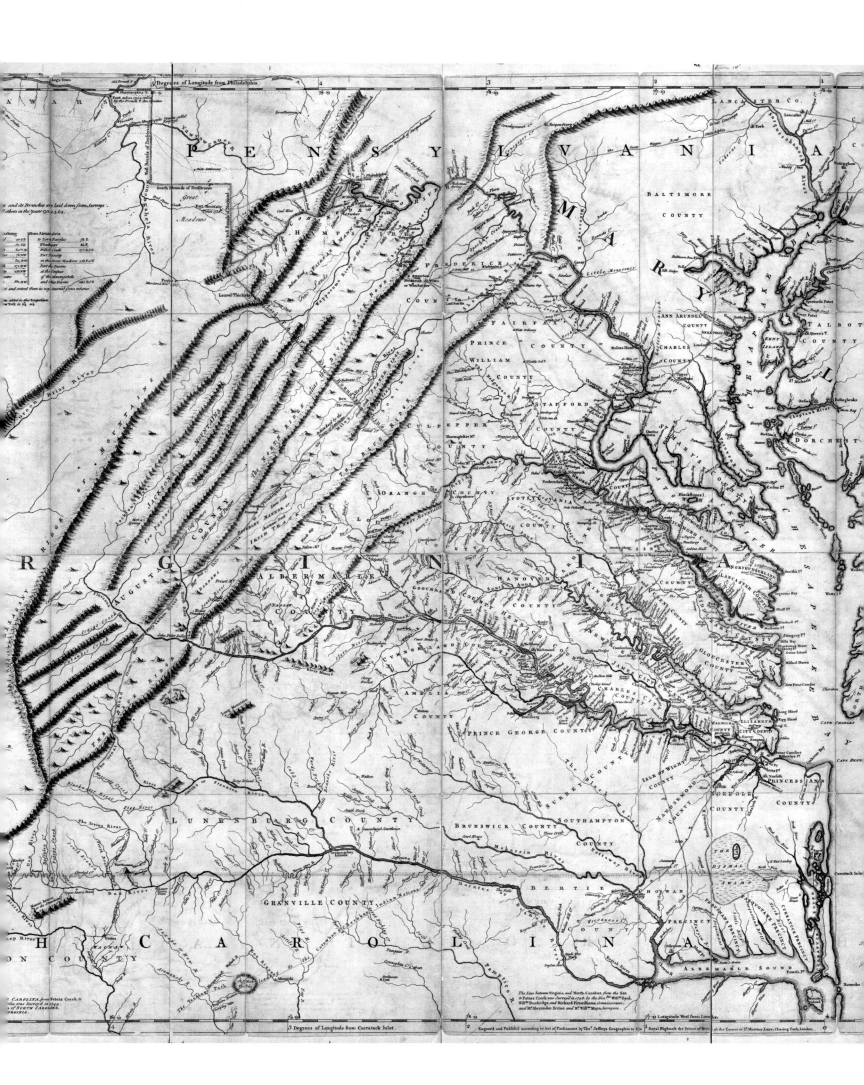

Exploring on Company Time

The North American shores of the Arctic Ocean were first reached by a European explorer, Samuel Hearne, in 1771. After a century of prodding, the Hudson's Bay Company was beginning to explore the vast lands over which it had acquired a charter.

James Isham, chief factor at York Fort, started the ball rolling. In 1754 he sent Anthony Henday on a two-year journey far to the

west. Henday may have reached within sight of the Rocky Mountains in today's Alberta, but unfortunately he left no maps and was prevaricating in his account; there are no less than four copies of his journal, but they all differ in the significant details that may have allowed a determination of his route. We do know, however, that he did not find the Northwest Passage that he was instructed to find. His main purpose commercially was to persuade any Indians he might encounter to take their furs to the Hudson Bay posts.

Fifteen years later, in 1769, Moses Norton, who was the chief factor at Prince of Wales Fort, sent Samuel Hearne into the interior, this time to search for copper—and a Northwest Passage. For years Norton had collected information from the natives about the lands to the west and north. Two Chipewyan chiefs, Matonabbee and Idotlyazee, gave him particularly juicy information in 1767, which Norton included in a map (MAP 151, *left*). Although now hard to see, this was the first look at the essential geography far to the west of Hudson Bay. In particular, it was the first map to show Great Slave Lake, the fifth-largest lake in North America, and the first to show the Mackenzie River, flowing from the western end of the lake. But what Norton was more interested in were copper mines shown at the extreme north, and it was these that Hearne was sent to find.

After two false starts in 1769 and 1770, Hearne finally began his journey in the dead of winter, December 1770, accompanied by Matonabbee and an entourage that grew to almost two hundred.

On 14 July 1771 Hearne and the natives arrived at a river he hopefully named the Coppermine, a north-flowing river that emptied into the Arctic Ocean. There Hearne found out why the Chipewyans had come in force: they planned an attack on the Inuit, against whom they harbored an undefined

MAP 151 (*left*).
Moses Norton's rendering of the information provided to him by the Chipewyan chiefs Matonabbee and Idotlyazee, drawn in 1767. For clarity the map is shown upside down from the way it was drawn, so that north is now at the top, though this varies depending on which part of the map is being looked at. The west coast of Hudson Bay and the Arctic coast on the west side of Melville Peninsula westwards is shown as a single straight coastline along the right edge of the map. The rivers flowing both to Hudson Bay and to the Arctic Ocean are shown flowing to this coast. Inland, on the left side of the map, is a triangular-shaped large lake, Great Slave Lake, out of which, at the western end, flows a large river called the *Kis-ca-Che-Wan*, a Cree name. This is today the Mackenzie River. Several bright red dots at the top of the map are indicated to be *copper mines*, those which Hearne was sent to find. In reality they were not mines but places copper had been found on the ground.

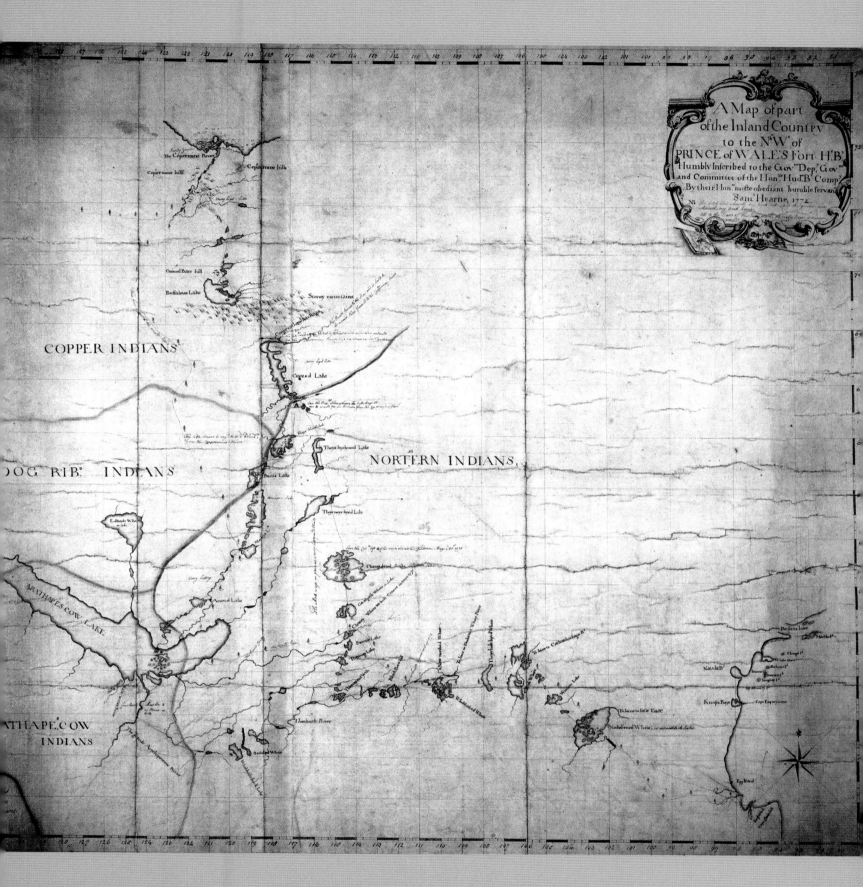

MAP 152.

Samuel Hearne's 1772 map of his expedition from Prince of Wales Fort on Hudson Bay (at bottom right) to the Coppermine River and back via Great Slave Lake, shown as *Arathapescow Lake,* at bottom left. Hearne simplified this map by including in most parts only the swath of territory over which he had actually traveled. In reality the land is covered with an undisciplined mosaic of lakes, large and small, and finding a pathway through them all would have been an impossible task. Hearne's journey was only feasible with his native guides. Note that the map shows the Mackenzie River flowing out of the western end of Great Slave Lake. This was secondhand information from the Indians.

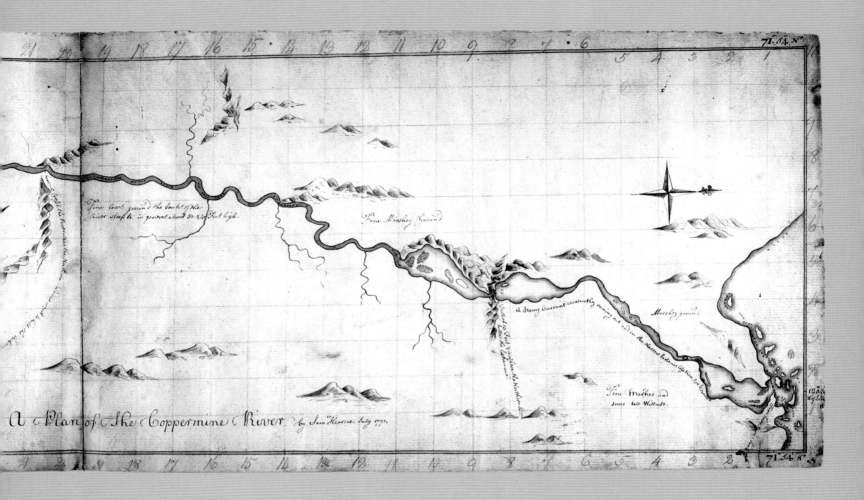

MAP 153.
Samuel Hearne's map of the mouth of the Coppermine River, where it meets the Arctic Ocean. North is to the right. Bloody Falls, the site of the Inuit massacre, is not named but has the notation *Fall of 16 Feet & is where the Northern Ind[ia]ns killd the Eskamaux*. Hearne was the first European explorer to reach the shores of the Arctic Ocean overland on the North American continent.

grudge. Hearne was powerless to prevent bloodshed. Early on 17 July, as they approached the Arctic Ocean, they came upon an Inuit encampment, which was mercilessly assaulted, and all the inhabitants massacred. Hearne was forced to watch the gruesome spectacle standing, as he put it, "neuter in the rear." He named the rapids here Bloody Falls.

Later the same day Hearne arrived at the Arctic Ocean, at a great embayment later named Coronation Gulf. Hearne found it difficult to determine that it was the sea, because the tide was out and the water was fresh on account of the river, but, he wrote, "I am certain of its being the sea, or some branch of it, by the quantity of whalebone and seal-skins which the Esquimaux had at their tents, and also by the number of seals which I saw on the ice."

It was indeed the sea, but Hearne would later have to defend himself against accusations that he had placed it at the wrong latitude. He thought he was at 71° 54′ N—this latitude is shown on his map of the Coppermine River (MAP 153, above), but he was really at 67° 49′ N, or 280 miles south of where he thought he was. Nevertheless, placed at either of these latitudes, the presence of the river here proved beyond a shadow of a doubt that there could be no Northwest Passage to the south. The myth of a passage in temperate latitudes was destroyed. However, Hearne's information was not widely known until 1795, when his book was published, posthumously. And so, predictably, the time lapse gave the proponents of such a passage a few more years of belief. Both James Cook and George Vancouver knew of Hearne's work when they came to the Northwest Coast. Cook was instructed not to begin looking for a passage until he reached 65° N for this reason.

Hearne's return took him first south to Great Slave Lake. He was the first European to see it and the first to cross it: by walking across its frozen surface at the beginning of January 1772, going from island to island and finding deer to hunt on each. He noted that the lake was "stored with great quantities of very fine fish" and abounded with beaver. Clearly this was good fur country. He also noted the aurora borealis playing across the northern winter sky.

Hearne found his way, with the continued help of his native guides, across the lake-filled Barren Lands back to Prince of Wales Fort, arriving there on 30 June, having been away for eighteen months and twenty-three days.

In an effort to increase trade, in 1772 Andrew Graham, then chief factor at York Fort, sent his second-in-command, Matthew Cocking, out to contact natives and try to persuade them to bring furs to the fort. Cocking undertook a journey westwards in June and did not return for a year. He traveled almost as far west as the current boundary between Saskatchewan and Alberta, southwest of

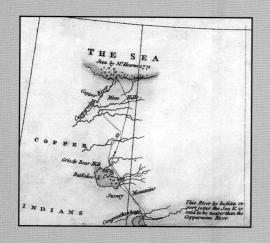

the Eagle Hills. During his time away, Cocking increasingly ran into independent fur traders who were intercepting the natives taking furs to the bay. In 1763, Britain had inherited New France with the signing of the treaty ending the French and Indian War, and quickly Scottish and English traders had moved in to take over the fur trade. Operating from Montréal, they had moved to challenge the monopoly of the Hudson's Bay Company.

Graham used information from Cocking's expedition to construct a map that showed the country as far west as the forks of the North and South Saskatchewan Rivers (MAP 155, *below*) and plot his strategy to deal with the upstart Montréal-based fur traders, later called the North West Company (see page 130). This competition would finally prod the Hudson's Bay Company to begin to explore to the limits of its Rupert's Land charter.

MAP 154 (*above*).
Hearne's discoveries on a map by London mapmaker Aaron Arrowsmith published in 1795, with revisions to 1802. The position of the Arctic coastline at the mouth of the Coppermine River has been corrected to about 68° N, close to its real position. The line of latitude shown is 70° N.

MAP 155 (*below*).
Information from Matthew Cocking's 1772–73 journey to the South Saskatchewan is shown in this map drawn by Andrew Graham in 1774. It was one of the first maps to show ethnographic divisions, here the native groups that came to Hudson Bay to trade.

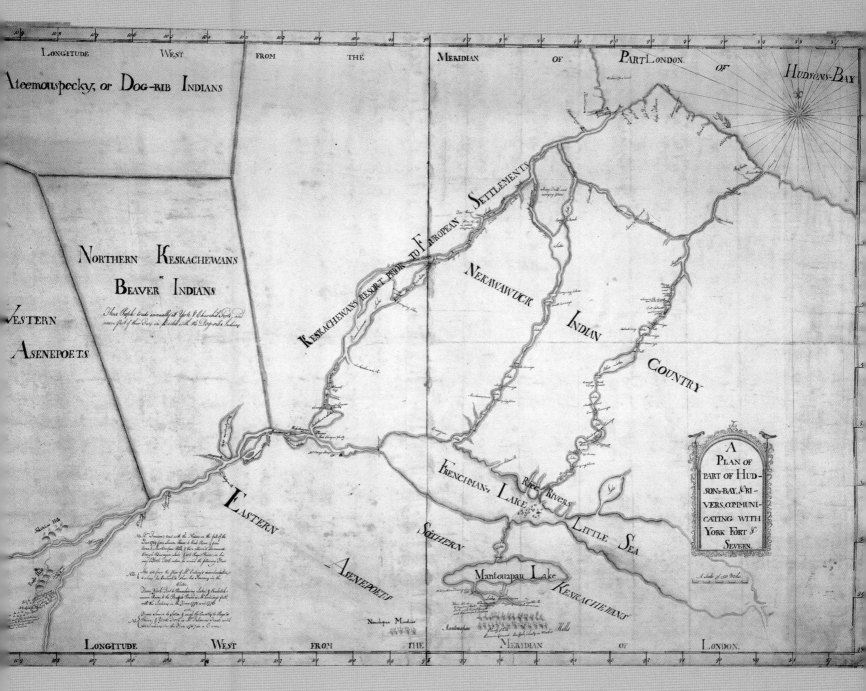

Spain Moves North

France ceded Louisiana to Spain in 1762, to prevent it falling into the hands of the British. In 1764 the British sent Commodore John Byron to search for a Northwest Passage from the west, although in fact he got nowhere near the Pacific Northwest coast. But the Spanish heard about it, as did Catherine of Russia, and exploration by both powers increased in the next few years, often as a response to the supposed encroachments of others.

The ceding of Louisiana prompted an expedition by Spain north into Texas led by the Marqués de Rubí. He was to inspect the new frontiers and to recommend places for the establishment of presidios (forts). The journey took almost two years between 1766 and 1768 and covered 7,600 miles, from Texas to Sonora and as far north as Santa Fe. With Rubí went Nicolas de Lafora, a captain in the engineers, and José de Urrútia, a cartographer. They produced several beautiful maps of the entire region, of which detail of one is shown here (Map 156, *below, left*).

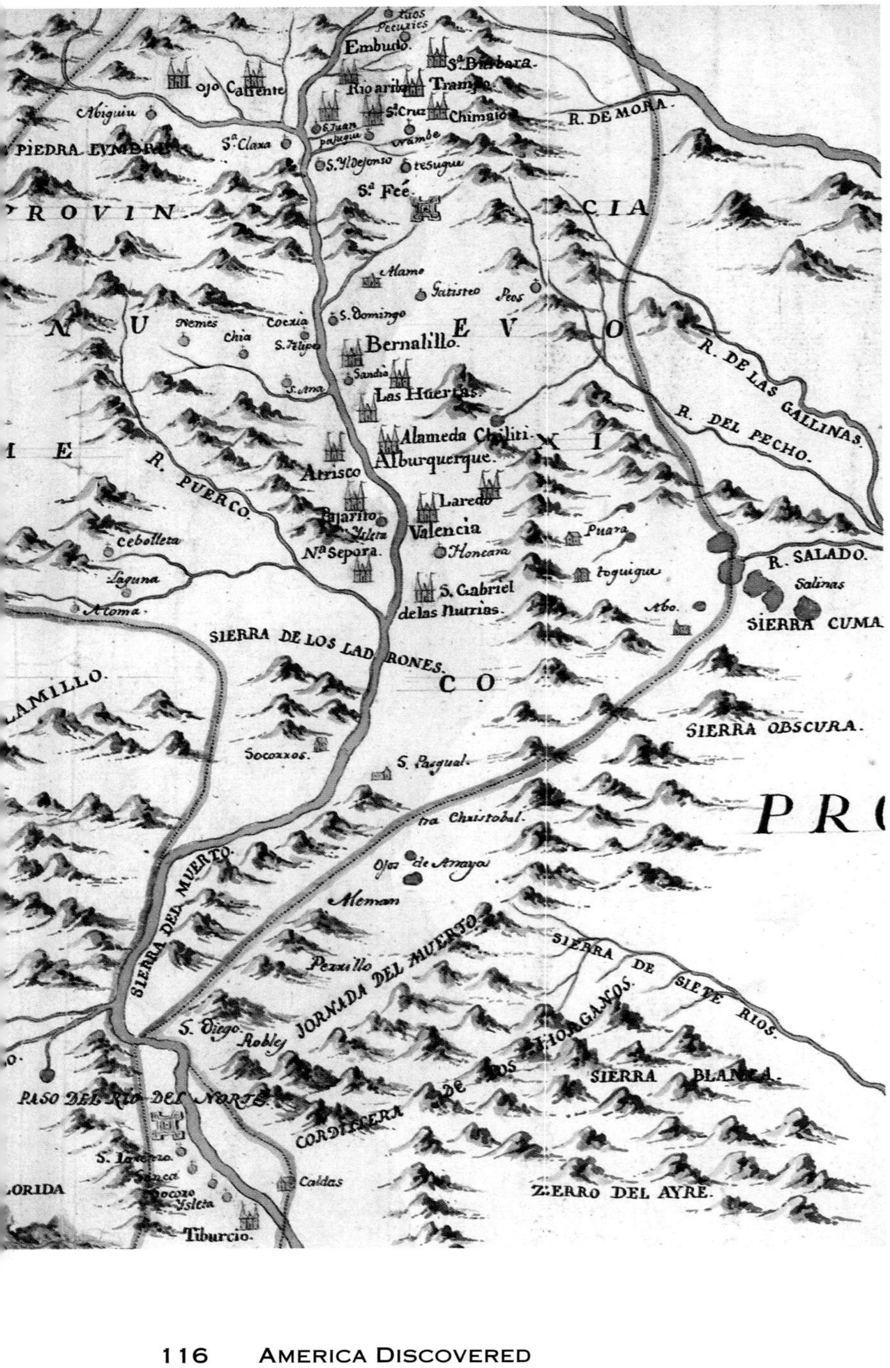

The Spanish response to the British and Russians plus a premeditated determination to extend the Spanish empire generated the next wave of interest north along the coast into Alta California. In 1769 the Spanish fleet was sent to San Diego, and an overland expedition under Gaspar de Portolá arrived shortly after. Portolá then continued northwards along the coast to Monterey, where a mission would be founded the following year. Portolá thought Monterey Bay so unlike the glowing description given it by Sebastian Vizcaíno in 1603 (see page 46) that he sent a party still farther north to search for such a bay. They found San Francisco Bay in October 1769, a magnificent bay, though not the one found by Vizcaíno. It was thought at first to be the mouth of a large river, and its true nature was not realized until 1775, when Juan de Ayala sailed through the Golden Gate, sent to prepare for the arrival of settlers trekking overland.

In 1773 Juan Bautista de Anza, sometimes called "the last conquistador" for his role in the expansion of the Spanish empire, was ordered to begin a process of settlement in Alta California that was to consolidate Spanish claims to the region. To determine that there was a land link between New Spain (other than Baja) and Alta California, in January 1774 Anza set out from the presidio of Tubac (close to the present-day Mexico-Arizona boundary at Nogales), where he was commandant, taking with him Father Francisco Tomás Garcés and thirty men. After a period when they were lost in the desert, they arrived at the mission at San Gabriel Arcángel—established in 1771 where Los Angeles now stands—on 24 March.

The following year he went north again with about three hundred soldiers and settlers. Going first to San Gabriel he then marched north to Monterey and then San Francisco, arriving on 27 March 1776, where they found "favorable conditions for establishing the presidio

Map 156 (*left*).
Part of a map drawn by Nicolas de Lafora and José de Urrútia in 1769 showing the *Rio Del Norte* (Rio Grande) and presidios, missions, and settlements. About halfway up the map is *Alburquerque* (now Albuquerque, New Mexico), founded in 1706 and named after the Duke of Alburquerque, and nearer the top is *Sa. Fée* (Santa Fe). Near the bottom edge is *Paso Del Rio Del Norte* (Pass of the River of the North), today El Paso, Texas.

Map 157 (*right*).
A summary map drawn in 1782 showing the cumulative Spanish knowledge of the Southwest as a result of the expeditions of the 1760s and 1770s. It was drawn by Manuel Agustin Mascaro. The tracks of Anza and Garcés in 1775 are shown, as is the region to the north and west of Santa Fe traversed by the Dominguez-Escalante expedition of 1776, which can be compared with Map 159, *overleaf*. The lake at the top edge of the map is the Great Salt Lake.

contemplated." Anza determined that the tip of the peninsula at today's Fort Point was the appropriate place for his presidio. Three months later, Franciscan friars from Monterey built on the peninsula a new mission, San Francisco de Asis—San Francisco.

Father Garcés had accompanied Anza on the first part of his journey north in 1776 but in February he struck out on his own to the north, in search of new spiritual fields to conquer. He went first to San Gabriel, then north to the San Joaquin Valley, then up the Colorado River, becoming the first European to see the Grand Canyon since some of the Coronado expedition in 1540. Garcés reached as far as Hopi pueblos on the Little Colorado River (near Flagstaff, Arizona) before he was forced to return by hostile Indians. It was a remarkable solo wandering. Some of his routes are shown on MAP 157 (previous page).

A similar feat, though not a solo one, was performed by the expedition from Santa Fe of Francisco Domínguez and Silvestre Vélez de Escalante, both also Franciscan friars. In 1776 they were dispatched on a probe that was intended to find a route from Santa Fe to Monterey. With them went Bernardo Miera y Pacheco, who was to provide a record of the expedition in the form of several artistic maps.

They left Santa Fe at the end of July 1776, first following the Rio Grande north and then finding a path among the headwaters of the Colorado in present-day Colorado State, where they discovered ruins of an ancient Indian settlement, a prehistoric Anasazi site. Miera was impressed with the Rocky Mountains, calling them the backbone of North America and noting that "the rivers that are born of it empty into two seas, the South Sea and the Gulf of Mexico."

Domínguez and Escalante then turned westward, finding Utah Lake and learning from the Indians of the even larger Great Salt Lake to the north. Here the expedition turned south, crossing the parched lands of southwestern Utah, part of which today is named the Escalante Desert. Here, abetted by the lack of water and running low on food, a decision was made to abandon their quest to find Monterey.

After considerable searching, they crossed the Colorado River at a place near Marble Canyon now called Crossing of the Fathers. The Little Colorado Valley then led them back to the Colorado Plateau and back to Santa Fe. It had been a vast circular tour bearing little relation—except perhaps in the wrong direction, on the way back—to a route to Monterey. Nevertheless, Domínguez and Escalante had covered country never before found by Europeans. And the maps that Miera produced revealed many details of the land, although they remained unpublished and thus not available to most of those who explored the region later.

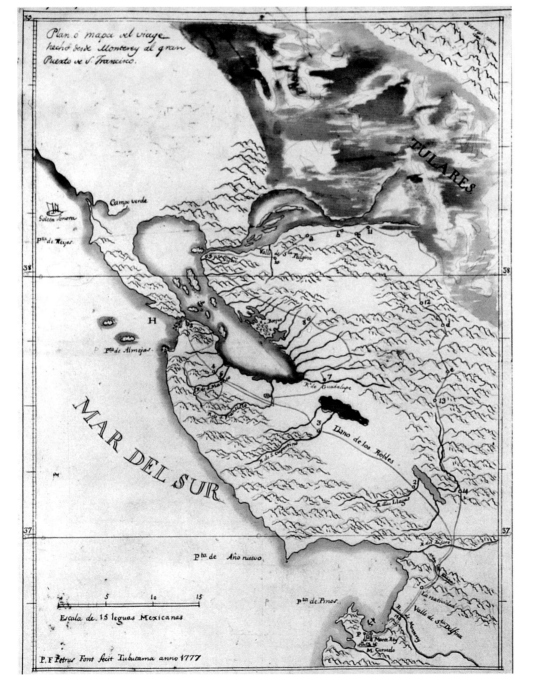

MAP 158 (left).

Map of San Francisco Bay by Pedro Font, a friar who accompanied Juan Bautista de Anza on an expedition to bring settlers to the area in 1776. The track of the expedition leads to the peninsula at the southern side of the Golden Gate, where the first mission was established. Farther up the coast is a representation of the schooner *Sonora*, a reference to Juan Francisco de Bodega y Quadra's voyage up this coast to Alaska the previous year (see page 122.)

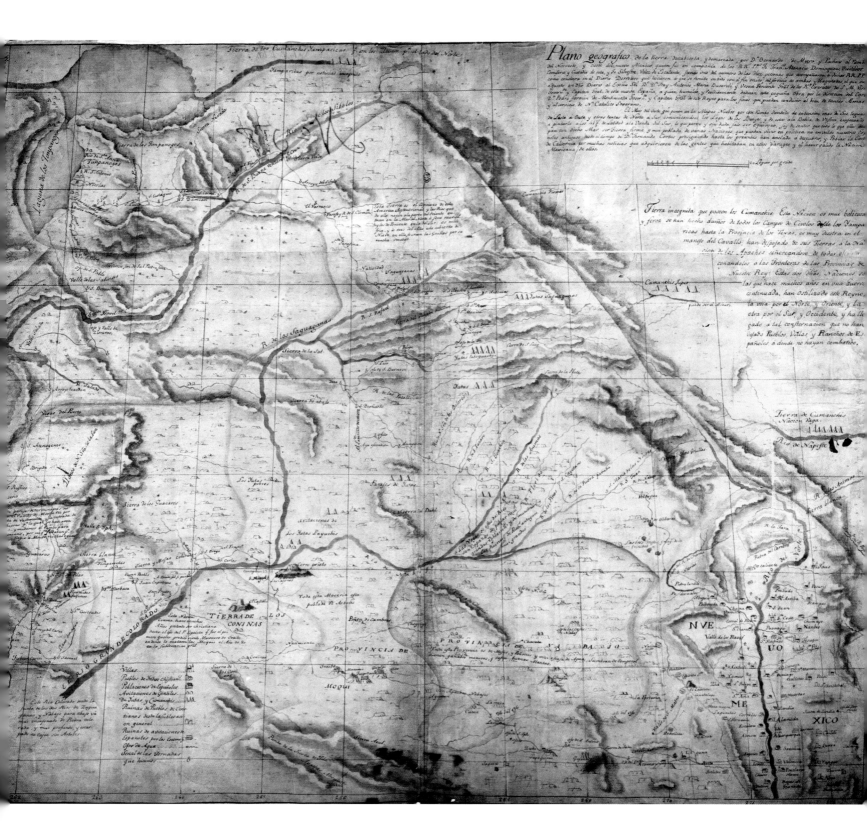

MAP 159.

One of the maps Bernardo Miera y Pacheco drew showing the country traversed by the 1776 expedition of Francisco Domínguez and Silvestre Vélez de Escalante. *Sta Fee* (Santa Fe) is in the southeast corner, among the settlements of the upper *Rio Del Norte* (Rio Grande). The Continental Divide is quite clearly shown to the north, and Miera realized that there were rivers that flowed into two oceans. In the northwest corner are Utah Lake and the Great Salt Lake, incorrectly shown as connected. South of them is *Laguna de Miera,* now the dry Sevier Lake. Miera has shown a river flowing into it called the *R. de S. Buenaventura* (San Buenaventura); it is in fact the Green River, but this river flows into the Upper Colorado, here labeled *R. de los Saguaganas,* not Sevier Lake. This Buenaventura River was to show up on maps in the future under various names as wishful thinking manifested as fact, a river flowing from the Rockies to the California coast. MAP 215 on page 160 is one example.

A supposed threat from the Russians drove another phase of Spanish northward exploration in the 1770s, that of coastal voyages to the Pacific Northwest and Alaska.

Juan José Pérez Hernández Pérez, an experienced naval captain, was ordered by the viceroy of New Spain, Antonio María de Bucareli y Ursúa, to sail north. His instructions, dated 24 December 1773, do not explicitly mention the Russians, but there is no doubt they were one of the motivations for the voyage, and he was told to look for foreign settlements. Instead the instructions take a higher tone: to make "new discoveries in unknown areas, so that their numerous Indian inhabitants . . . may receive by means of the spiritual conquest the light of the Gospel which will free them from the darkness of idolatry." As usual, he was also to keep an eye out for gold, precious stones, and spices. He was even to take tropical spices with him to show any natives he might encounter what he was looking for. Clearly the Spanish at this time had little idea of the nature of the Northwest Coast. Pérez was to sail to 60° N and return along the coast, "never losing sight of it."

Pérez sailed in January 1774 from the Mexican port of San Blas in his ship *Santiago,* with Estéban José Martínez as his senior officer. He reached Monterey on 8 May and sailed again on 6 June. Such were the conditions that he could not even get out of Monterey Bay for another eight days. Picking up favorable winds well offshore he sailed northwest, then north, until on 18 July a landfall was made at Langara Island, just off the northern tip of Graham Island, one of the Queen Charlottes. Haida immediately came to investigate, and some trading was done, but Pérez, fearing treachery from the natives in their carved canoes, did not venture ashore. Pérez found that the Haida here had some metal, in the form of half a bayonet and a piece of sword beaten into the shape of a spoon. Martínez assumed that these items had come from an attack on the landing parties

of Aleksei Chirikov thirty-three years before, and only a little farther north (see page 102), but they may also have been obtained through lost-distance native trading networks, passing from tribe to tribe.

Pérez sailed round in circles in Dixon Entrance, the channel between the Alaska Panhandle and the Queen Charlottes, never anchoring because the water was too deep. He was confused as to his latitude. He maintained that he was at 55° 24′ N when he saw a cape he named Santa Maria Magdalena, but it seems that this was Cape Muzon, at 54° 40′. The latitude is of signal importance because it is today the boundary between the United States and Canada. In 1819 the United States inherited the territorial claims of Spain under the terms of the Transcontinental Treaty of that year, and 54° 40′ was accepted as the southern limit of Russian claims based on Pérez's voyage. Then in 1846 a boundary between British territory and the United States was negotiated at 49° N, and in 1867 Russian Alaska was purchased by the United States. Thus the southern boundary of Russian claim became that of the United States. This is an excellent example of how the chance presence of an explorer could later affect the shape of nations.

Having seen no evidence of Russian settlements, Pérez decided to return south. He had a lot of problems keeping the coast in sight until he reached the west coast of Vancouver Island. He found the entrance to the spacious Nootka Sound, which would become more famous for its supposed discovery by Britain's James Cook four years later. He was unable to steer his ship into the sound because

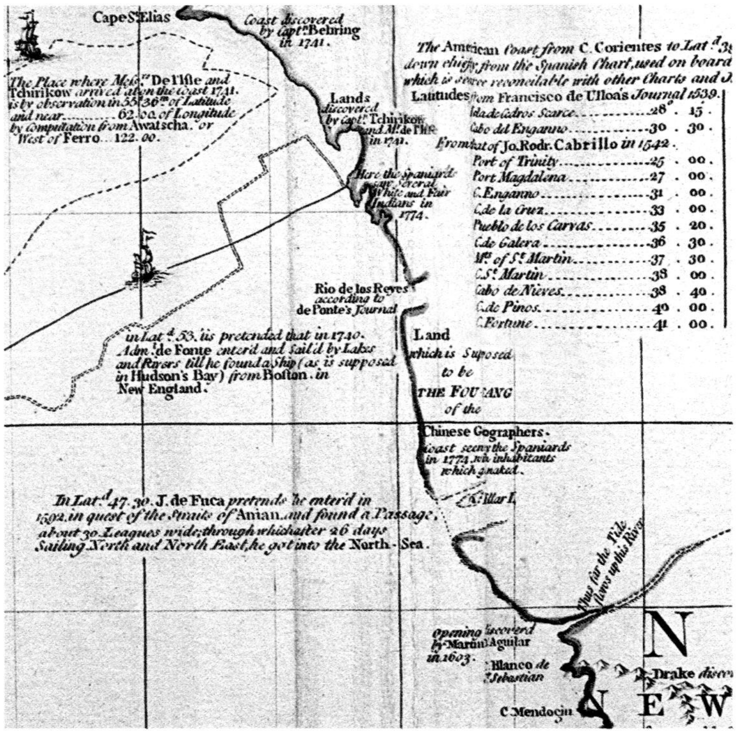

MAP 160 (*left*).
The Spanish were normally very secretive about their discoveries, and so it is a surprise to find this map that records information from the Pérez voyage, published only a year later. It comes from British mapmaker Thomas Jefferys's *American Atlas* of 1775. No geographical details are shown but there are two notations. One, at about 55° N, states: *Here the Spaniards saw several White and Fair Indians in 1774.*

MAP 161 (*right*).
The west coast of North America, from Juan Pérez's voyage in his ship the *Santiago* in 1774, drawn by his pilot, Josef de Cañizares. It is the first map of the West Coast (north of Cape Mendocino) drawn from actual exploration. The coastline shown is from Monterey, in the bottom right corner, to Dixon Entrance, today's boundary between Alaska and Canada. The large offshore islands of Vancouver Island and the Queen Charlotte Islands are merged with the mainland coast. Mountains are shown as a coastal view, as they were seen from the ship. At the north end of the map is P^{ta} *de* Sta *Maria Magdalena* (Punta de Santa Maria Magdalena), Cape Muzon, the southern tip of Dall Island, at the tip of the Alaska Panhandle; *Isla de* Sta *Christina*, Forrester Island; and P^{ta} *de* Sta *Margarita*, not a point as such but Langara Island, off the northern tip of Graham Island, the northernmost of the Queen Charlottes. Farther south, Pérez's anchorage off Nootka Sound is *Surgidero de* S^n *Lorenzo; Cerro de* Sta *Rosalia* is Mount Olympus, Washington; and P^{to} *de Monterrey* marks the entrance to Monterey Bay. This exceptionally important map was found relatively recently in the National Archives of the United States, and no one knows how it ended up in that institution. One can only guess that it had something to do with boundary negotiations, either for the forty-ninth parallel in 1846 or the 1903 Alaska boundary settlement.

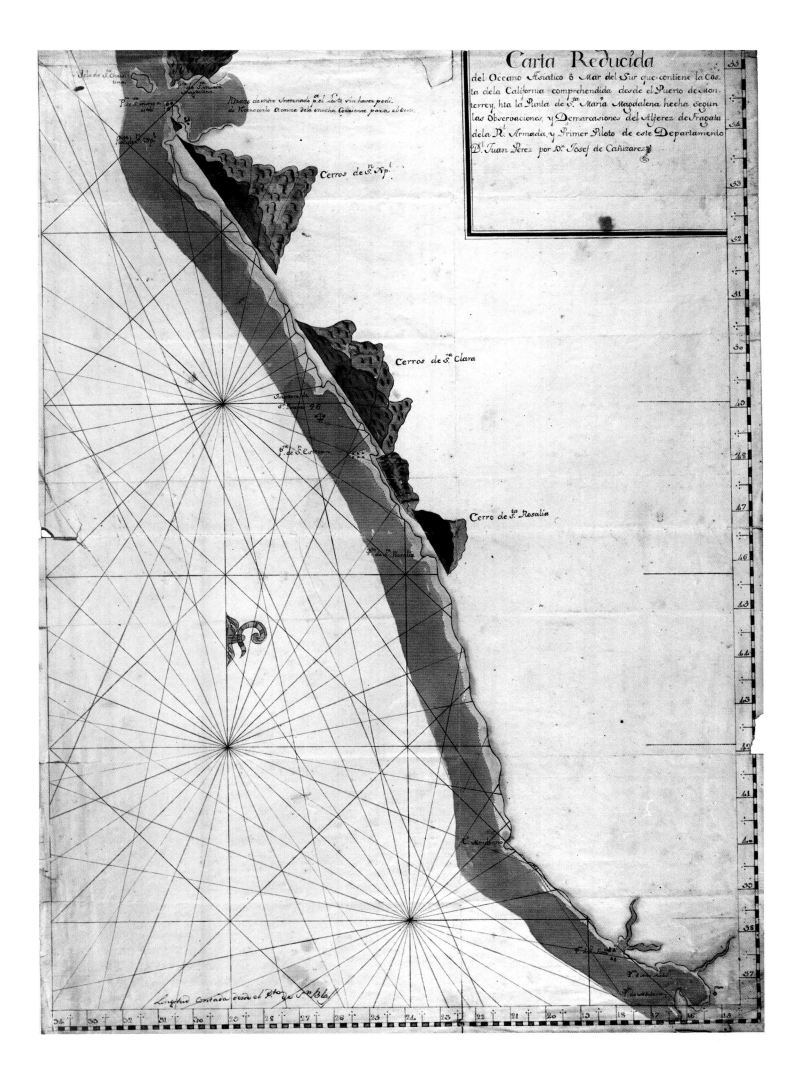

of contrary winds, but did manage to find an anchorage on 7 August just outside its entrance. Again natives came to trade. This encounter is significant in that some silver spoons belonging to Martínez were apparently pilfered. James Cook purchased the same spoons in 1778, noting in his journal that it was evidence that the Spanish had been there before him.

From Nootka Pérez sailed straight back to Monterey, where he arrived on 28 August. The map of his voyage (MAP 161, *previous page*) is the first map of the west coast of North America above Cape Mendocino drawn from exploration, and the first of anywhere in Oregon, Washington, or British Columbia.

The following year Bucareli sent Pérez north once more, but as a second officer as punishment for not following his instructions to sail to 60° N. In charge of the expedition was Bruno de Hezeta y Dudagoitia, with Pérez in the *Santiago,* and on another ship, the mere 38-feet-long *Sonora,* Juan Francisco de la Bodega y Quadra. A third ship, under Juan de Ayala, was to sail into San Francisco Bay (see page 116). Hezeta's instructions now told him to sail to 65° N.

A first landfall was made at Trinidad (just north of Eureka, in northern California). Then, after being tossed around in heavy seas off Cape Flattery, Hezeta and Bodega found themselves sailing *south* along the coast of Washington. On 13 July they anchored off Cape Elizabeth (about halfway up the coast of Washington). Here some of Hezeta's men were murdered as they went ashore to fill casks of water. Heading once more out to sea, the ships became separated.

Hezeta sailed to about 50° N in heavy seas, but had by then so many men ill that he decided to return south, following the coast. In so doing he found what appeared to be a large bay penetrating far inland. He tried to sail into it but could not due to currents of considerable force. "It may be the mouth of some great river or some passage to another sea," he wrote in his journal. He decided it was a misplaced Strait of Juan de Fuca. But it was not; it was the mouth of the Columbia, and Hezeta was the first to record sighting it, and also the first to make a map of it (MAP 163).

Bodega, meanwhile, despite sailing in a ship half the size of Hezeta's and intended only for shallow water exploring, decided to continue north. In a voyage little short of the epic he fought the

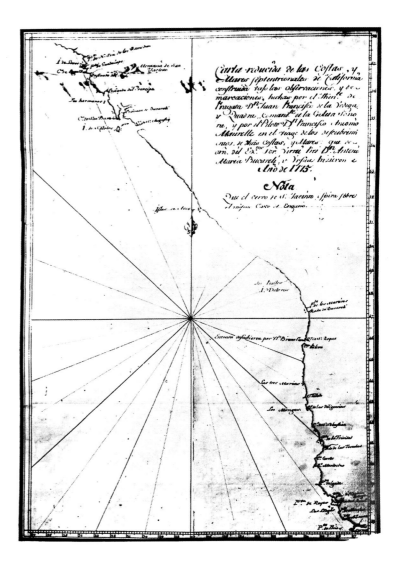

MAP 162 (*above*).
A map of the west coast of North America prepared by Juan Francisco de Bodega y Quadra in 1775 and containing information from both his voyage to Alaska and Hezeta's cruise down the coast of Oregon. There is a gap in information between the two. At top, *Montaine de San Jacinto* is Mount Edgecumbe, near Sitka. Halfway down the map is *Rada de Bucareli* (Bucareli road, or anchorage, named after the viceroy) at Cape Elizabeth, Washington. Farther south is the *Entrada* found by Hezeta, the mouth of the Columbia. *Rio de los Trinidad* is at Trinidad, near Eureka, in north California. *P^ta de Reyes* is Point Reyes, just north of San Francisco Bay, which is also shown. At the bottom of the map is Monterey Harbor.

MAP 163 (*left*).
Bruno de Hezeta's map of his *Bahia de la Asunciõn,* the mouth of the Columbia River. North is to the left.

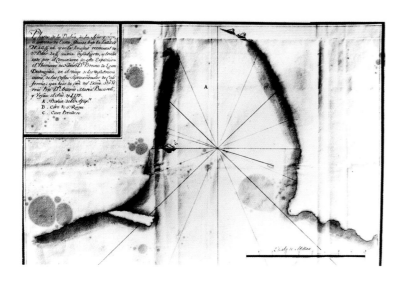

heavy seas to make a landfall on 15 August at 57° N, under the snow-capped peak of Mount Edgecumbe, just west of Sitka. He ultimately made it to 58°, just 2° short of the goal set for Pérez the year before. Here Bodega searched diligently for the strait of Bartolomew De Fonte (see MAP 112, page 91) that he expected to find in this location.

But scurvy was taking its toll on the *Sonora* as it had on the *Santiago,* and so Bodega sailed south once more to Monterey and San Blas, where he arrived on 20 November. Hezeta's voyage was long unknown to the world because of the Spanish policy of secrecy, but Bodega's became known because a copy of the journal of his first officer, Antonio Mourelle, found its way to London, where it was translated and published along with a map, an anglicized version of MAP 162.

The Spanish government's response to Hezeta's discovery of a possible Northwest Passage, the mouth of the Columbia, led to the ordering of another voyage for 1777. Diversions in Mexico causing a shortage of ships meant that the expedition did not get under way until 1779, during which period James Cook had come and gone. This was the voyage of Ignacio de Arteaga, with Bodega y Quadra. Arteaga was instructed to reach 70° N. They reached Prince William Sound and on Hinchinbrook Island, at 61° N, they performed a ceremony of possession that became the basis of Spain's claims up to that latitude. But Spain was by now increasingly unable to maintain its grip on the lands it claimed, and the Spanish were overwhelmed by a flood of British fur traders that, having discovered the sea otter, followed in the wake of Cook (see page 128).

It was not until 1788 that Spain ventured north once more. Esteban José Martínez and Gonzalo López de Haro were ordered to

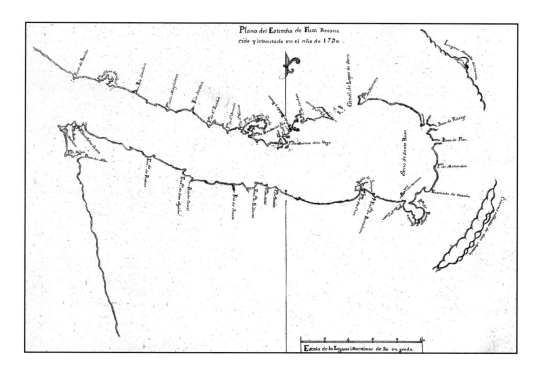

MAP 164 (*above*).
A Spanish map of their newly found and not yet fully explored Strait of Juan de Fuca at the end of 1790, attributed to pilot Gonzalo López de Haro. It reflects the explorations of Manuel Quimper that year. Just beyond the farthest point reached by Quimper, his ensign Juan de Carrasco sighted an opening he thought was a bay; it was the opening to Admiralty Inlet, which leads to Puget Sound. Here it is marked *Ensenada de Camaño*, after Jacinto Caamaño, a newly arrived naval officer at San Blas.

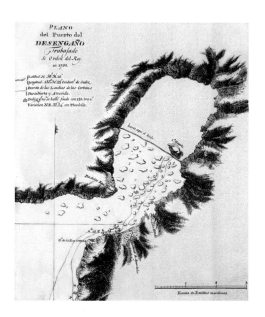

MAP 165.
Alejandro Malaspina's map of his *Puerto del Desangaño*, or Bay of Disappointment. It shows the Hubbard Glacier blocking the northeastern extension of Yakutat Bay, Alaska, blocking what he had hoped would be a Northwest Passage.

Alaska to claim possession for Spain wherever possible and make maps so that places could be found again should a decision to colonize be made later. The pair reached Prince William Sound and then continued, getting as far west as Unalaska Island in the Aleutians and actually meeting their threat—Russian traders. Potap Zaikov (see MAP 141, page 104, and page 105) got on famously with Martínez; he liked Spanish brandy as much as Martínez appreciated the Russian vodka. On his return, Martínez reported on the Russian presence and recommended that Nootka should be occupied before the Russians got there. As it happened, it was not the Russians but the British, in the form of George Vancouver, who were next to Nootka (see page 129).

Nootka was occupied by the Spanish in 1789, abandoned in October, and reoccupied in April 1790. Francisco de Eliza arrived with three ships, the other two under Salvador Fidalgo and Manuel Quimper. Fidalgo was dispatched to Alaska. He entered Prince William Sound and took possession of a bay inside, which he named Córdova, from which today's city takes its name. Fidalgo also entered Cook Inlet but, finding Russian forts there, retreated to Kodiak Island— where he found yet another Russian fort. Clearly the Russians had beaten the Spanish to Alaska.

Quimper, meanwhile, taking López de Haro as his pilot, sailed along the coast south from Nootka, ordered to search for harbors. Quimper found and surveyed a number of possible harbors along the shores of the Strait of Juan de Fuca, which itself was thought a possible entrance to a Northwest Passage. Quimper also found Haro Strait and Rosario Strait, channels that lead north into the Strait of Georgia, but did not explore them enough to realize that this was just an archipelago, today the San Juan Islands. López de Haro drew maps of the Strait of Juan de Fuca that show it as a closed-end basin (MAP 164, *above*).

The following year Eliza was instructed to examine all the remaining unknown parts of the Northwest Coast, but, finding it impossible to sail north due to the winds, he turned instead once more to the Strait of Juan de Fuca. This time probing longboats found the way through the San Juans and into the Strait of Georgia, which was named the Canal de Nuestra Señora del Rosario, a name which, in truncated form, now applies to a channel through the San Juans.

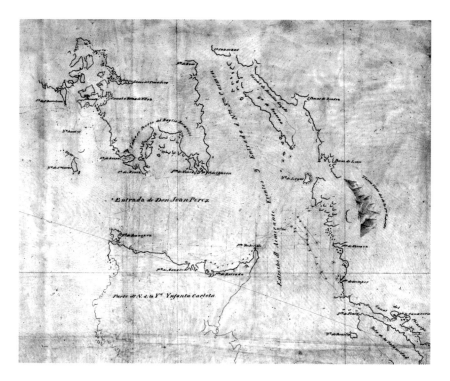

MAP 166 (above).
Jacinto Caamaño's map of the De Fonte strait he thought he had found—actually Clarence Strait, penetrating not a continent but the Alexander Archipelago of the Alaska Panhandle. Caamaño's *Estrecho dl Aimirante Fuente y Entrada d. Nstra Stra Carmen* was renamed after the Duke of Clarence by George Vancouver and his name, like many on this coast, prevailed.

Eliza then dispatched a small schooner, the *Santa Saturnina*, under José María Nárvaez, north into the Strait of Georgia. Nárvaez noted fresh water coming from a large river, the Fraser, and passed the site of today's Vancouver, British Columbia, continuing north for nearly a hundred miles. He noted in his report the presence of whales, which made him believe that this might finally be the Northwest Passage. In fact, it *is* a passage, but back to the Pacific.

The same year, the round-the-world expedition of Alejandro Malaspina reached the Northwest Coast, probing inlets in Alaska for a Northwest Passage (see MAP 165, page 123) before arriving at Nootka in August. Malaspina's voyage had been planned as a Spanish foil to that of Britain's James Cook, an attempt to recapture some world approbation for Spain. As such it was a scientific voyage, and the government approved the considerable expenditure to publish what would have been seven volumes including seventy maps with its results. But Malaspina fell afoul of political intrigue on his return to Spain and they were not published.

What proved to be the final year of Spanish explorations to the north came in 1792, with two the same year. Jacinto Caamaño was sent north to examine the last possible place where there could be a Northwest Passage, the region between the north of Vancouver Island and the Alaska Panhandle. He found, and for a while got very excited about, Clarence Sound, within the Panhandle, which is a wide strait-like body of water leading in the right direction. Thinking it was the

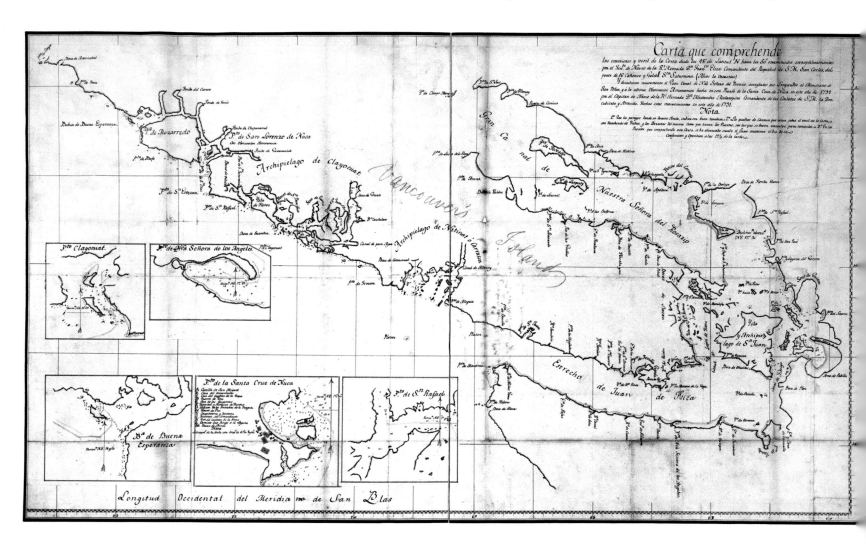

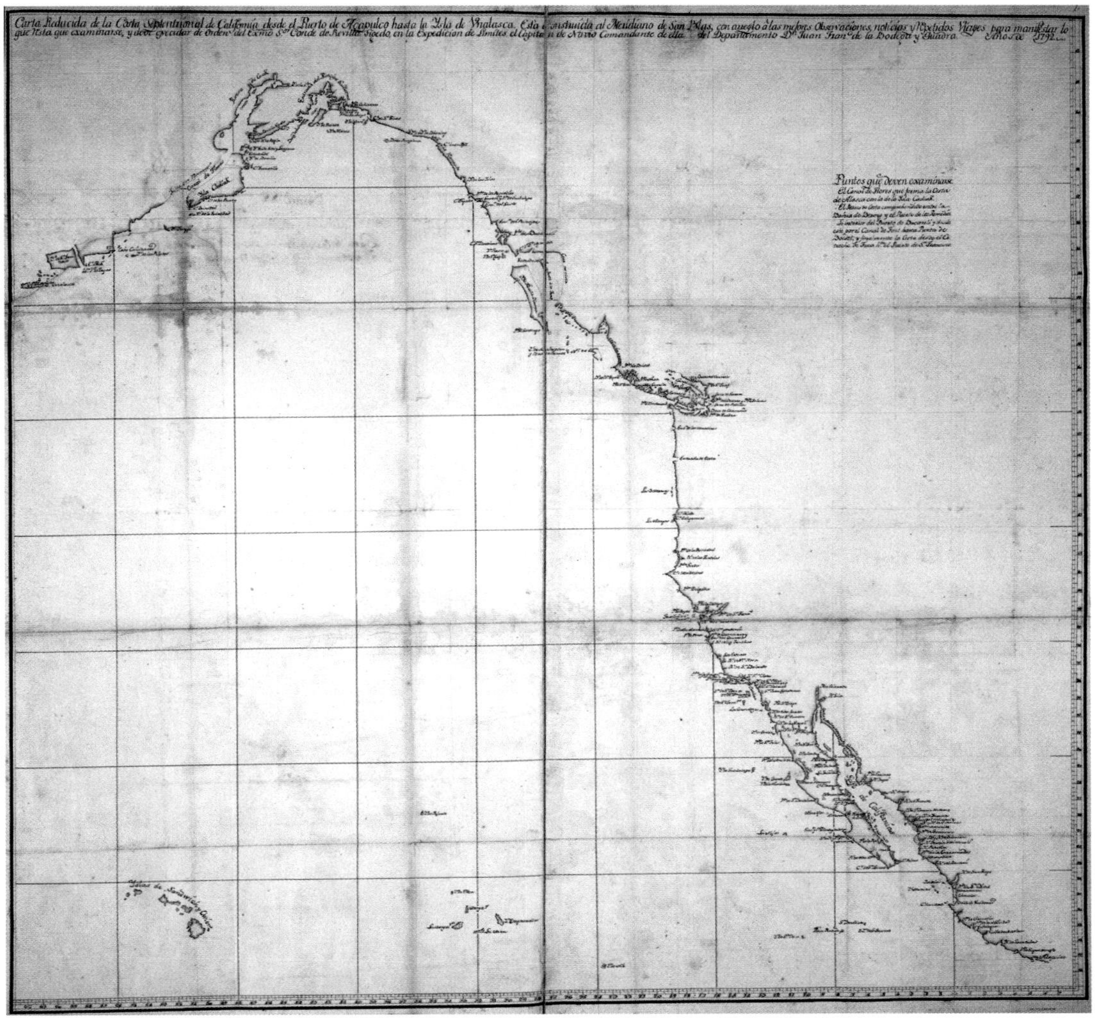

De Fonte strait, Caamaño followed it north to 55° 30´ before being forced back by bad weather. His exploration, while it had not been a success from his point of view, did establish that much of the Panhandle is an archipelago, not mainland coast, as had been presumed.

The other 1792 exploration was that of Dionisio Alcala Galiano and Cayetano Valdes, who were sent by the new Nootka commandant, Bodega y Quadra, to explore north beyond the point reached by Nárvaez the previous year. In their little schooners (*goletas*) *Sutíl* and *Mexicana,* Galiano and Valdes found the passage north of the Strait of Georgia and sailed through it back to the Pacific Ocean, becoming the first to circumnavigate Vancouver Island in the process. They produced excellent maps. They had found the Fraser River and on 14 June became the first Europeans to enter it. And near today's city of Vancouver they had met the British explorer and surveyor George Vancouver, who was also searching the mainland coast for a Northwest Passage, and they even explored together for a while.

But these last explorations determined that there were, after all, no undiscovered western entrances to the Northwest Passage, and if there was one it would have to be in Arctic latitudes. Spain's star was descending and no more would she be motivated to equip voyages to the north. These weathered shores would have to be abandoned to the Russians, the British, and, in time, the Americans. Spain would find it hard enough to hold on to New Spain, far to the south.

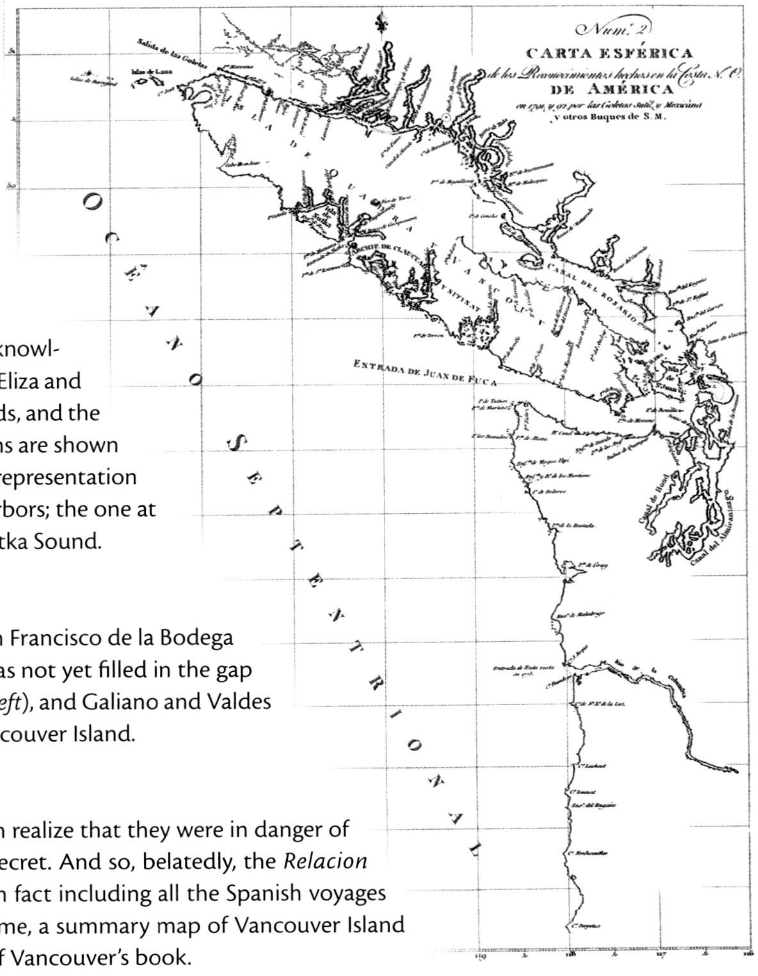

Map 167 (*left*).
This *Carta que comprehende*—"Map of all that is known"—was a summary of Spanish knowledge of southwest British Columbia and northwest Washington at the end of 1791, after Eliza and Nárvaez's explorations of the eastern end of the Strait of Juan de Fuca, the San Juan Islands, and the Strait of Georgia. Much of today's city of Vancouver is shown as water, and the San Juans are shown as a single island instead of the island group they are, but nevertheless it is a very good representation of the region in the year before George Vancouver's survey. The insets show various harbors; the one at center bottom is P[uer]*to de la Santa Cruz de Nuca,* Yuquot, or Friendly Cove, in Nootka Sound.

Map 168 (*above*).
One of the summary maps of an emerging west coast of North America drawn by Juan Francisco de la Bodega y Quadra. This one was drawn at the end of 1791 or the beginning of 1792. Caamaño has not yet filled in the gap behind the Queen Charlottes, which he would do the following year (**Map 166**, *above, left*), and Galiano and Valdes have not yet completed their circumnavigation that would prove the insularity of Vancouver Island.

Map 169 (*right*).
Only when George Vancouver's survey was published in Britain in 1798 did the Spanish realize that they were in danger of losing their claims to prior sovereignty if they continued to keep their explorations secret. And so, belatedly, the *Relacion* of 1802 was published, ostensibly about the explorations of Galiano and Valdes but in fact including all the Spanish voyages towards the Northwest since that of Vizcaíno in 1603. This is the map from that volume, a summary map of Vancouver Island and the adjacent coasts that very closely resembles one of the same area in the atlas of Vancouver's book.

A West Coast Defined

In 1776 the British government dispatched their master mariner James Cook on his third and final voyage, to the Pacific and the west coast of North America. Samuel Hearne's report of an Arctic Sea had brought forth the idea that perhaps the illusive Northwest Passage was to be found along the northern shore of the continent, and maps such as Jacob von Stählin's (MAP 142, page 105) seemed to show that the Russians had discovered a huge strait that might well be its western entrance. For this reason Cook was instructed not to begin to search for a strait until he reached 65° N.

With his two ships, *Resolution* and *Discovery,* Cook took nearly two years to get to the North Pacific, discovering Hawaii, which he called the Sandwich Islands, on 18 January 1778. He finally reached the American coast on 6 March at a place he named, with good reason, Cape Foulweather. Such was the weather and the visibility on this unmapped coast that he was forced back out to sea several times (MAP 170, *right*), missed the Strait of Juan de Fuca, and found a harbor where Juan Pérez had anchored four years before, Nootka Sound. While he was here Cook purchased some Spanish silver spoons, which seemed to him to be incontrovertible evidence that he was not the first European to arrive here (see page 122). Cook also carefully calculated his longitude, comparing the results of the land-based astronomical observation with those from the new chronometers that his expedition was carrying. His results, published in 1784 and in pirated books before that, for the first time fixed the width of the North American continent; from now on explorers heading to the Western Sea from the interior would know how far away it was. For a time, the mixture of accurate with inaccurate inland calculations made the river and lake system of the Northwest seem nearer to the ocean than it really was, encouraging Alexander Mackenzie to reach for the Pacific in 1793 (page 135).

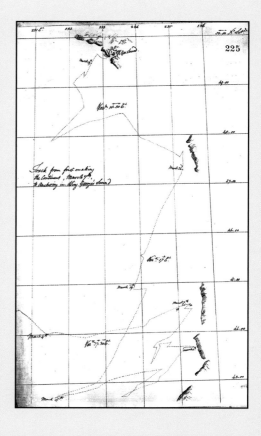

MAP 170 *(above, right).*
This page from the journal of one of Cook's officers, James Burney, shows the difficult track against the weather from the first landfall at Cape Foulweather, Oregon, to Nootka Sound (*K. Geo. Sound*).

MAP 171 *(below).*
The first map of James Cook's 1778 exploration of the Northwest Coast and Alaska. The map was sent in a letter to the Admiralty via Russian traders on Unalaska when Cook was returning south to Hawaii. It was sent on 20 October 1778 and arrived in London on 6 March 1780.

Following his instructions, Cook headed north, not actively surveying the coastline, and staying farther out to sea than he would have liked, due to the "exceeding tempestuous weather." This is why Cook's maps show only the general trend of the coast rather than any detail. Prince William Sound was explored and named, and Cook Inlet was found, though not explored to its end and named Cook's River, which in turn gave many hopes that it would connect to interior lakes. At Unalaska Cook met Russian fur traders, and maps were copied and exchanged. Searching for a way through the Aleutians, Cook had Stählin's map in hand, but he soon found it less than useful, describing it as a map "that the most illiterate of his Sea-faring men would have been ashamed to put his name to." Eventually Cook found a gap between two of the islands and sailed north towards Bering Strait, finding a large, previously unmapped sound on the American side, which he named Norton Sound. But it shoaled dramatically nearer to shore and was clearly not the passage Cook sought. Cook sailed into Bering Strait and on

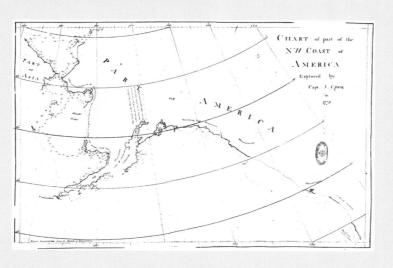

9 August passed the northwestern extremity of the continent, which he named Cape Prince of Wales despite the fact that it was shown on one of the maps he had with him—that of Gerhard Müller—as having been previously found by Mikhail Gvozdev (MAP 140, page 104).

Farther north still Cook's ship was stopped by the Arctic ice pack. After some time sailing along the ice to determine if there was any opening, Cook decided to return to Hawaii to refit. It was there, early the following year, that he was killed by natives. The captain of the *Discovery,* Charles Clerke, took over the expedition and tried to sail north again, but with the same result; he died of tuberculosis and it was another officer, John Gore, who took the ships back to England. The possibility of an easy or ice-free, north continental shore Northwest Passage had gone, but this was the right track. This *was* the true Northwest Passage—when a way through the ice could be found.

Map 172 (*right*).
Part of a map by German mapmaker Conrad Lotter that was published in Augsburg in 1781, three years before Cook's book was published. Compiled using unauthorized information from Cook's crew, it shows the track of the ships in the North Pacific and into Bering Strait.

Map 173 (*below*).
One of Cook's long-serving officers, Henry Roberts, was charged with the construction of a world map that showed all the new geographical information Cook had amassed on his three voyages. This is the North American part of the map, published in 1784. This edition, published separately from the book, shows the interior lakes and rivers from Samuel Hearne's 1771 map (**Map 152**, page 113), but because Hearne's longitudes were wrong and Cook's correct, they are placed too near to the Pacific coast. It was this apparent proximity that would induce Alexander Mackenzie to strike out for the Pacific in 1793. This map is the first to show North America correct in its basic outline and, in particular, the first to show it at its correct width.

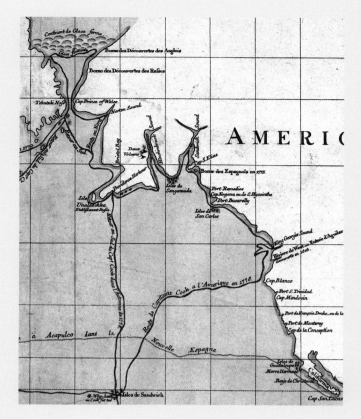

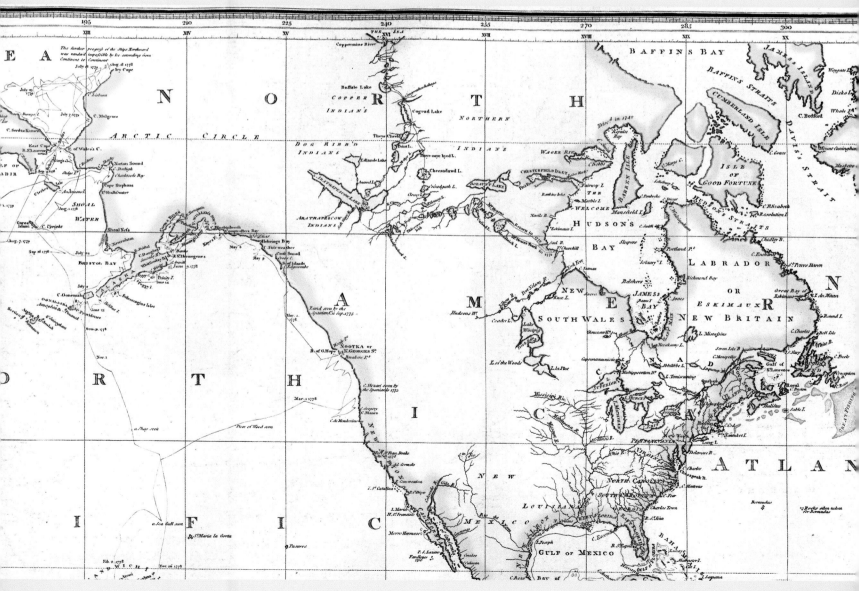

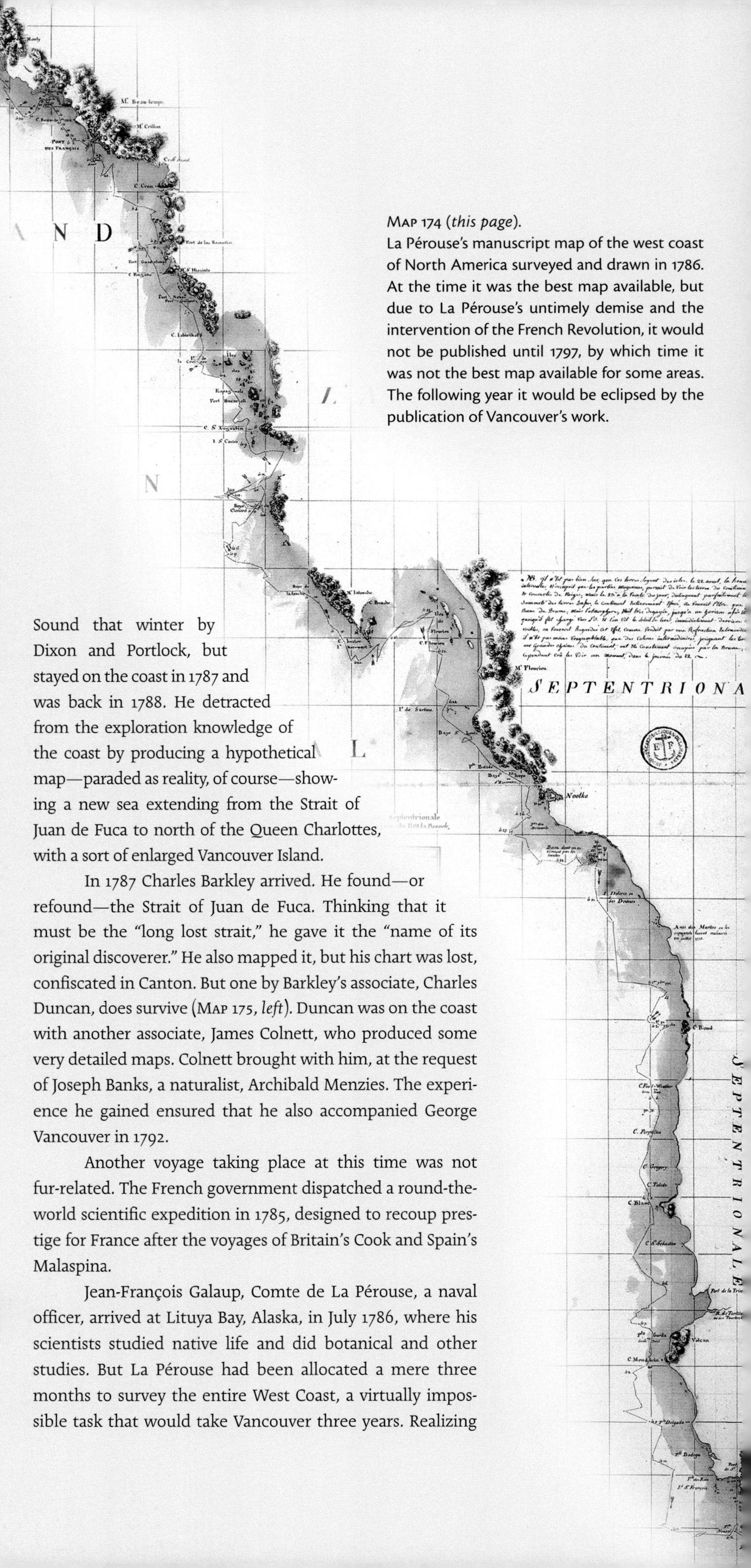

While Cook and his men were on the Northwest Coast they had traded with the natives for some particularly fine furs, which came from the sea otter. When the ships reached Canton, these were sold at outrageous prices. Perhaps a different sort of gold was to be found on this coast? So began a rush of traders hoping to cash in on the new discovery. Although the men who followed were traders rather than explorers, they needed to know where to go and how to get back there, and thus did a great deal of inadvertent exploration and mapping of the intricacies of the coast.

James Hanna was first, arriving on the coast in 1785 on the appropriately named ship *Sea Otter* from Macao. He explored the northern part of Vancouver Island. Two ships under the overall control of James Strange came the following year, again charting part of northern Vancouver Island and the coast farther north. The same year Nathaniel Portlock and George Dixon arrived, and over a period of two years traded and explored the Queen Charlotte Islands and ranged north to Alaska. The islands were named by Dixon, and his name is enshrined as Dixon Entrance, between the Queen Charlottes and the Alaska Panhandle.

Also in 1786, John Meares came to the coast. He was rescued in Prince William

Sound that winter by Dixon and Portlock, but stayed on the coast in 1787 and was back in 1788. He detracted from the exploration knowledge of the coast by producing a hypothetical map—paraded as reality, of course—showing a new sea extending from the Strait of Juan de Fuca to north of the Queen Charlottes, with a sort of enlarged Vancouver Island.

In 1787 Charles Barkley arrived. He found—or refound—the Strait of Juan de Fuca. Thinking that it must be the "long lost strait," he gave it the "name of its original discoverer." He also mapped it, but his chart was lost, confiscated in Canton. But one by Barkley's associate, Charles Duncan, does survive (MAP 175, *left*). Duncan was on the coast with another associate, James Colnett, who produced some very detailed maps. Colnett brought with him, at the request of Joseph Banks, a naturalist, Archibald Menzies. The experience he gained ensured that he also accompanied George Vancouver in 1792.

Another voyage taking place at this time was not fur-related. The French government dispatched a round-the-world scientific expedition in 1785, designed to recoup prestige for France after the voyages of Britain's Cook and Spain's Malaspina.

Jean-François Galaup, Comte de La Pérouse, a naval officer, arrived at Lituya Bay, Alaska, in July 1786, where his scientists studied native life and did botanical and other studies. But La Pérouse had been allocated a mere three months to survey the entire West Coast, a virtually impossible task that would take Vancouver three years. Realizing

MAP 174 (*this page*).
La Pérouse's manuscript map of the west coast of North America surveyed and drawn in 1786. At the time it was the best map available, but due to La Pérouse's untimely demise and the intervention of the French Revolution, it would not be published until 1797, by which time it was not the best map available for some areas. The following year it would be eclipsed by the publication of Vancouver's work.

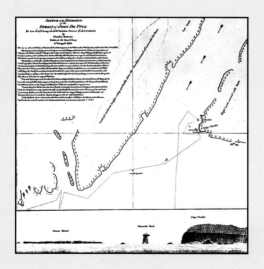

MAP 175.
Charles Duncan's map of the western entrance to the Strait of Juan de Fuca, drawn in 1788.

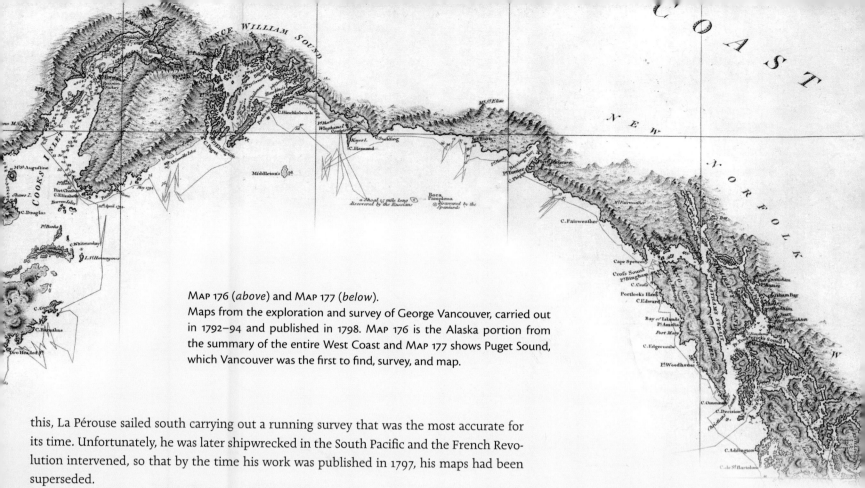

MAP 176 (*above*) and MAP 177 (*below*).
Maps from the exploration and survey of George Vancouver, carried out in 1792–94 and published in 1798. MAP 176 is the Alaska portion from the summary of the entire West Coast and MAP 177 shows Puget Sound, which Vancouver was the first to find, survey, and map.

this, La Pérouse sailed south carrying out a running survey that was the most accurate for its time. Unfortunately, he was later shipwrecked in the South Pacific and the French Revolution intervened, so that by the time his work was published in 1797, his maps had been superseded.

It was the work of British explorer-surveyor George Vancouver that produced the definitive map of the West Coast, which would last at least fifty years, longer in some places. The British had decided to make one last effort to determine whether or not a Northwest Passage existed. To achieve this, Vancouver was to survey the mainland coast—what he termed the "continental shore"—in enough detail to be certain that a Northwest Passage had not been overlooked around the next bend. Of course, the coast north of Cape Flattery is such that there are lots of bends, lots of long fiords, and many islands, so such an exhaustive survey was an immense task.

Vancouver arrived on the coast 175 miles north of San Francisco on 18 April 1792. He had two ships, *Discovery* and *Chatham*. In May and June he became the first to find and map Puget Sound, which is named after one of his officers. He met and cooperated with Galiano and Valdes, the Spanish officers on a similar but less thorough mission, and many of both the Spanish maps and Vancouver's maps acknowledge the other in their construction. One of Vancouver's boat parties found the way out of the Strait of Georgia back to the Pacific; today the passage is Johnstone Strait, named for another officer, James Johnstone. In October, William Broughton, commanding the smaller *Chatham*, surveyed the Columbia River for a hundred miles inland to a place he named Point Vancouver, close to today's Portland, Oregon. The river had first been entered earlier that year by Robert Gray, in his ship *Columbia Rediviva*.

Vancouver spent the 1792 season surveying as far north as 52° 20´, and then retreated to Hawaii for the winter. The following year he took up where he had left off and surveyed north to 56° in four months of painstaking work in small open boats. The 1794 season was spent surveying the coast south from Cook Inlet—and Vancouver changed the name of Cook's River to Inlet, having explored it past today's city of Anchorage to the end. By 31 July 1794 he had arrived at the point, near Juneau, Alaska, where he had left off the previous season, at a place he named Port Conclusion.

Vancouver was now able to write that he hoped the precision of his survey would "remove every doubt, and set aside every opinion of a north-west passage, or any water communication navigable for shipping, existing between the North Pacific, and the interior of the American continent, within the limits of our researches." The old dream of a temperate latitude Northwest Passage was finally dead and buried.

North West Explorations

After the fall of Québec in 1763, the French fur trade was taken over by the British. Around 1775, a group of these English and Scottish fur traders based in Montréal formed an informal alliance called the North West Company. Intent on beating the rival Hudson's Bay Company at their own game, they headed far inland to open regions with new fur sources first and to shut off the supplies to their rival on the bay. The farther they went, the more investment was required to finance longer periods between initial buying of trade goods and shipping of furs to customers. By 1784 the informal alliance had developed into a more formal partnership of the smaller groups and had better access to the resources required to open half a continent. The men of the North West Company explored vast areas of the North and West and even for the first time reached the Pacific.

The goal was the Athabasca region, that vast land drained by rivers flowing into the Arctic Ocean, technically outside the Rupert's Land (the drainage basin of Hudson Bay rivers) of their rival and, because of the colder climate, a producer of thicker and more valuable furs. Samuel Hearne had visited the region, and Great Slave Lake, in 1771 and noted the abundance of beaver (see page 112) but the Hudson's Bay Company had made no use of the information he brought back.

One of the preliminary partnerships was that of the American trader Alexander Henry (called "the elder" to distinguish him from his son who was also a fur trader). By 1776 Henry had likely traveled as far west as Lac Île-à-la-Crosse, on the Churchill River system. During this time he met Chipewyan at his base on Amisk Lake who gave him significant information about the land yet farther west. He learned of Lake Athabasca and noted in his journal what he was told.

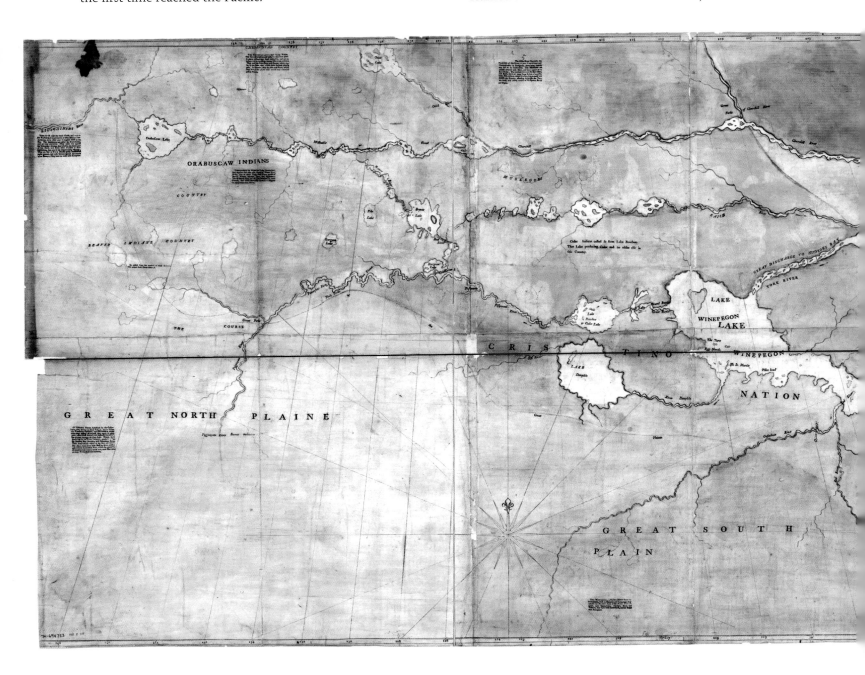

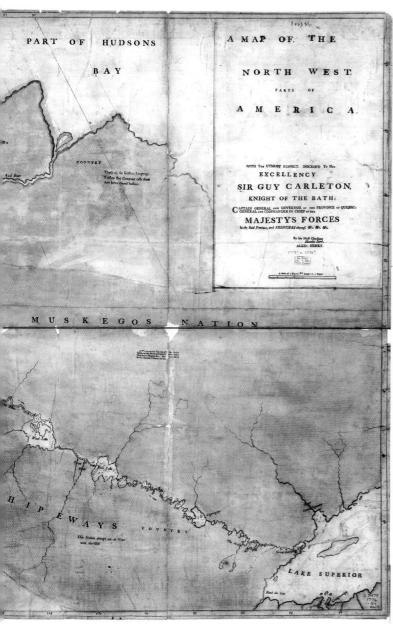

Map 178 (*left*).
In an attempt to gain a monopoly on the fur trade of the Athabasca region, which was outside of the Hudson's Bay Company charter area, in late 1776 Alexander Henry and his partners drew up a memorial, with this map by Henry himself, and presented it to Guy Carleton, the governor of Québec. They did not get their monopoly, but history got the map. It is very large, seven feet wide, and although it is hand-drawn the names have been printed, perhaps to impress Carleton. Lake Superior is at right, Lake Winnipeg (*Lake Winepegon*) at center. The Hudson's Bay Company farthest west post at *Cumberland* (House) is shown at the intersection of the *Posquyaw* (Saskatchewan) *River* and *Sturgeon Lake* (Cumberland Lake). Henry's *Beaver Lake* (Amisk Lake) just to the north, with a connection to the *Missinabie* River, is a compressed composite of the Churchill River with all its lakes, one of which, unnamed, is Lac Île-à-la-Crosse. Farther west is *Orabuscow Lake*, Lake Athabasca, with the *Kiutchinini River* flowing into or out of it. This could be the Peace, Slave, or even the Mackenzie River. All information west of Lac Île-à-la-Crosse was derived from native reports.

Map 179 (*above*).
This 1817 map by John Thomson shows the trade route from Lake Superior and Grand Portage (at right) to Lake Winnipeg (at top left).

There was, they said, "at the further end of that lake, a river, called Peace River, which descended from the Stony or Rocky Mountains, and from which mountains the distance to the salt lake, meaning the Pacific Ocean, was not great; that the lake emptied itself by a river, which ran to the northward, which they called Kiratchinini Sibi or Slave River [still the Slave today], and which flows into another lake, called by the same name [Great Slave Lake]; but whether this lake was or was not the sea, or whether it emptied itself or not into the sea, they were unable to say." Here, then, was an accurate description of the Athabasca region as far north as Great Slave Lake.

During the 1776 season, Henry traded about twelve thousand high-quality beaver pelts from natives coming from the Athabasca. Here clearly was a fur bonanza worth seeking out.

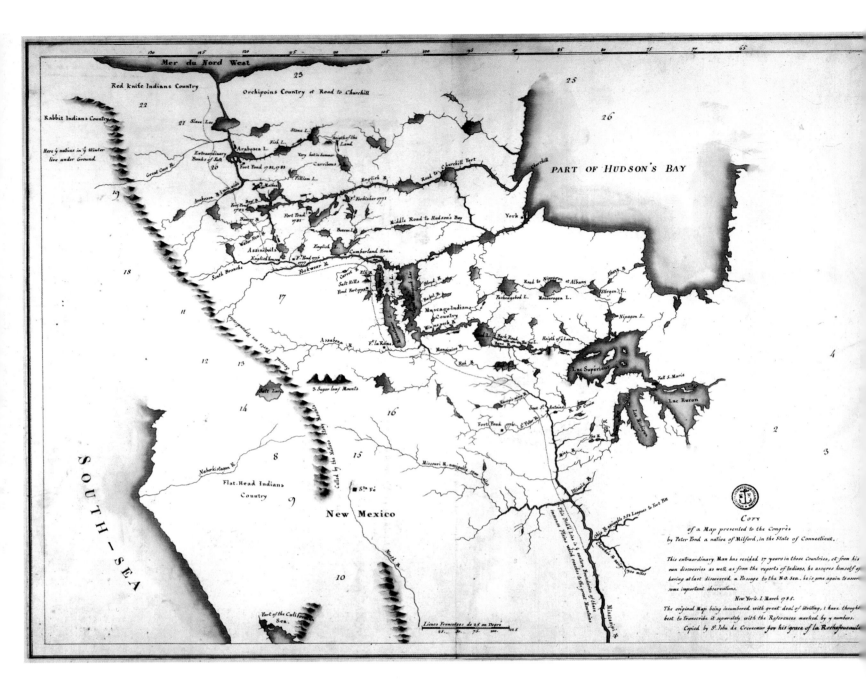

The map contains the following visible labels:

Mer du Nord West

Red knife Indians Country

Orchipoins Country et Road to Churchill

Rabbit Indians Country

Here ÿ natives in ÿ Winter live under Ground

Arabasca L.

Fort Pond 1781, 82, 83

PART OF HUDSON'S BAY

York

Middle Road to Hudson's Bay

Road to Churchill Fort

Cumberland House

Assinibols

Mascago Indians Country

Lac Supérieur

Fall S. Marie

Lac Huron

Lac Michigan

S. Sugar loaf Mounts

SOUTH-SEA

Flat-Head Indians Country

Missouri R. navigable 800

New Mexico

Sta Fé

North R.

Part of the California Sea

Lieues Françoises de 25 au Degré

Mississippi R.

COPY of a Map presented to the Congrès by Peter Pond a native of Milford, in the State of Connecticut.

This extraordinary Man has resided 17 years in those Countries, et from his own discoveries as well as from the reports of Indians, he assures himself of having at last discovered a Passage to the N.O. Sea, he is gone again to accert some important observations.

New York 1 March 1785.

The original Map being incumbered with great deal of Writing, I have thought best to transcribe it separately, with the References marked by ÿ numbers.

Copied by St. John de Crevecœur for his grace of la Rochefoucault.

The man chosen to be first into the new region was Peter Pond, an enigmatic Connecticut trader who had a particular knack for communicating with native peoples and who had been immensely successful at obtaining large quantities of furs. But he was, it seems, not a very nice person, with at least two murders of rivals attributed to him. Pond crossed into the Arctic watershed in 1778 and spent the next ten years gathering not only furs but information about the geography beyond his personal knowledge.

Alas, Pond, like most fur traders, was unskilled in the art of fixing his position longitudinally, and although he mapped the river and lake system with considerable accuracy, he did not know where it was in relation to the rest of the continent. And he misinterpreted native information. In 1784 he made a map of his conception of the region (MAP 180, *above*), which was presented to the new United States Congress with the suggestion that they annex the Northwest. But Congress was too busy getting their infant nation on its feet to be interested in a remote region such as Athabasca.

When information from James Cook's accurate fixing of the position of the west coast at Nootka reached Pond's hands, he was quick to incorporate it into his own maps. But combining the accurate map of Cook with his inaccurately positioned map of the river and lake system produced a map that showed the interior lakes far too close to the Pacific Ocean (MAP 181, *right, top*). There was also a suggestion on this map that there was a huge river (the Mackenzie River) that flowed west out of Great Slave Lake to the Pacific Ocean at Cook's River, the inlet which (as Cook's River) Cook had not mapped to its end (see page 126).

By 1788 Pond had reached the Athabasca River and had built a trading post just south of Lake Athabasca. At this point the partners of the North West Company came to consider him too much of a liability—he had just engineered the demise of another rival trader—and forced his retirement. But this occurred only after he had spent his final winter on the Athabasca with the young trader sent to replace him—Alexander Mackenzie.

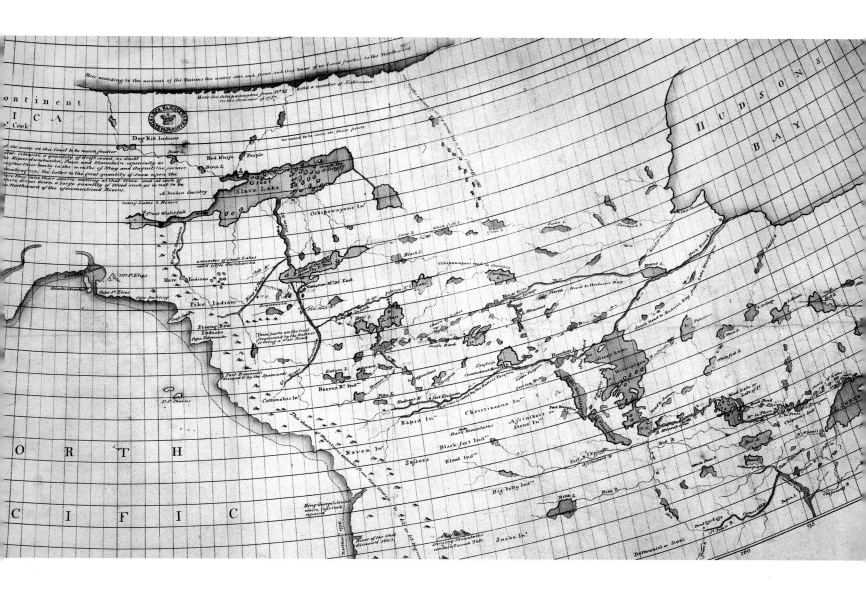

Map 180 (*left*).

A copy of the map Peter Pond presented to the Congress of the United States in 1784. *Arabosca Lake* (Lake Athabasca) leads north to Slave Lake and thence to the *Mer du Nord West* (the Arctic Ocean). A little of the Pacific coast is shown, but there is no suggestion of an easy pathway west, although the distance to the coast is apparently remarkably small. The river flowing south is the Missouri.

Map 181 (*above*).

By 1788 Pond had merged his information with that of the West Coast mapped by James Cook and produced this map, which shows the river and lake system of the interior amazingly close to the Pacific Ocean. Now the Mackenzie flows not to the Arctic Ocean but distinctly in the direction of Cook Inlet, on the Pacific coast. *Lake of the Hills discov*d *by P. Pond* is Lake Athabasca. Notably the *River of Peace* is shown correctly flowing from the west into *Slave R.* just north of Lake Athabasca. This is the route Alexander Mackenzie would use to reach the Pacific in 1793.

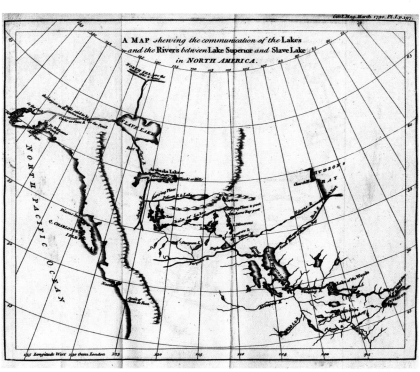

Map 182 (*right*).

Peter Pond's final map shows an overt river connection between Great Slave Lake and Cook Inlet, and a connection to the Arctic Ocean. As before, the rivers and lakes are far too close to the Pacific.

By now, Pond's final ideas about the nature of the Northwest had emerged. A map published two years later in Britain shows that he now considered the Mackenzie to flow to Cook Inlet in Alaska (Map 182, *previous page*), and the idea that it was a very short distance to the Pacific Ocean from Lake Athabasca encouraged Mackenzie to attempt to reach the Western Sea in 1789.

The North West Company had always been at a disadvantage to the Hudson's Bay Company in that they had to ship their furs out through Montréal, a considerable distance from their ever-farther-west fur sources. If an outlet could be found on the Pacific, furs could be shipped directly to markets such as China and the company would gain an enormous competitive advantage over their rival.

In 1788 Alexander Mackenzie took over the Athabasca operations of the North West Company and built Fort Chipewyan on Lake Athabasca itself. Determined to test Pond's ideas, he set out on 3 June 1789, following the Slave River to Great Slave Lake and then the large river that flowed out of its western end. For three days the river flowed to the northwest, the direction Mackenzie expected to go to reach Cook Inlet, but then, at a great curve now called the Camsell Bend, the river turned northwards, and after a short while Mackenzie realized that he was not going to end up at the Pacific. But he kept going anyway and on 12 July entered another ocean, the Arctic, which he at first thought to be another large lake. Paddling out to an island, he named it Whale Island. The presence of whales had led him to decide that it was indeed the sea. The island was Garry Island, and Mackenzie had become the second European to reach the Arctic Ocean overland.

But he had not reached his objective, and after a sojourn in London learning to use instruments, and more inquiry of native sources, he set off again in the fall of 1792, this time turning up the Peace River instead of continuing north to Great Slave Lake. He overwintered at a hastily built post at the junction of the Smoky and Peace Rivers, which he called Fort Fork.

Over the winter he obtained from the natives more information about the possible route to the Pacific, although the entire path was beyond their knowledge. Then on 9 May 1793, Mackenzie set off from Fort Fork with ten men and a dog up the Peace River.

It was an easy paddle until he reached the Peace River Canyon. This obstacle took many days to surmount, with much portaging, towing, and scrambling. At the end of the month they reached the point where the Peace becomes two: the Finlay River, flowing from the north, and the Parsnip, flowing from the south. Basing his decision on the native information he had received at Fort Fork, Mackenzie took the "south branch." Had he gone north it is unlikely he would have reached the Pacific.

The Peace River uniquely traverses the main ridge of the Rocky Mountains, but the Parsnip leads only to a difficult ridge farther west. Mackenzie missed a tributary,

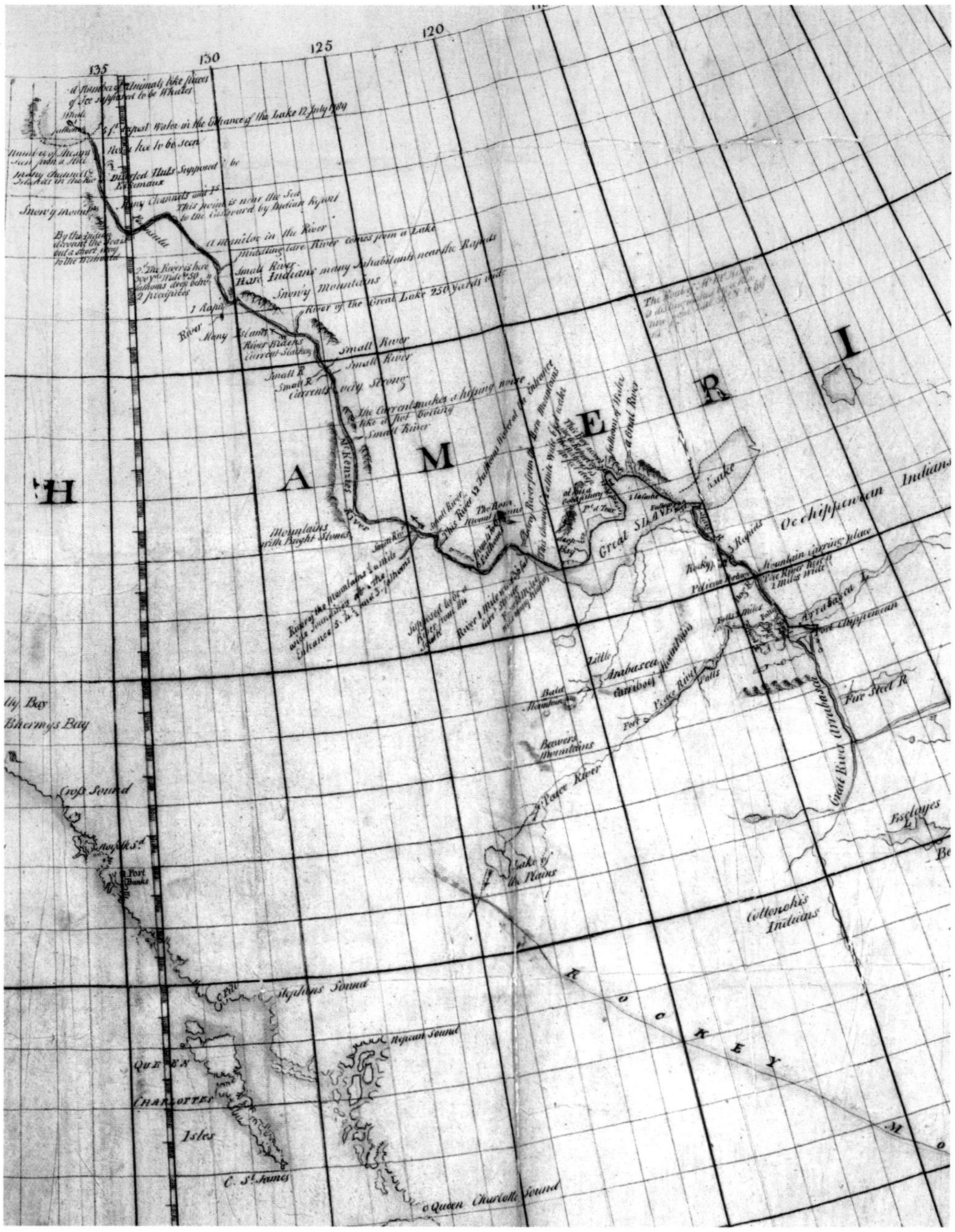

Map 183 (*left*).
This is the "Chart called Mackenzie's Map," the only known cartographic record of Alexander Mackenzie's first expedition, which reached the Arctic Ocean in 1789. It seems to be a direct copy of an original Mackenzie map made in the field, because it refers to the Arctic as a lake, his first impression. Note the Peace River shown in more or less the correct position, but too far west. This was the route Mackenzie would take in 1792–93 when he finally reached the Pacific.

the Pack River, which would have given him a much easier route across the watershed. It would be found in 1806 by another Nor' Wester, Simon Fraser.

The Continental Divide was crossed, but then came a descent down a river Mackenzie called the Bad River, a rushing torrent of rocks and debris that took them a week to descend, almost sinking their canoe in the process. But this water flowed to the Pacific, and on 17 June they emerged onto the relatively placid waters of Herrick Creek, which lead to the McGregor River, and that to the Fraser. However, the apparently easy way to the Pacific was barred by more almost impassable rapids, and indeed, farther down than Mackenzie

the first European crossing of the continent of North America north of Cabeza de Vaca's 1535–36 route in Mexico.

Mackenzie wanted to be able to properly fix his position and so continued out to sea in another canoe, this time a seagoing one. He was looking for the clear view of the horizon his sextant required. But, hounded by natives from the more warlike Heiltsuk tribe, he landed at a rock in Dean Channel, and it was here that he wrote his famous inscription on a rock: "Alexander Mackenzie, from Canada, by land, 22 July, 1793." Another landing a little later gave him the longitudinal position he needed, before he beat a hasty retreat. Finally, after others had tried for centuries, an explorer had reached the real Western Sea.

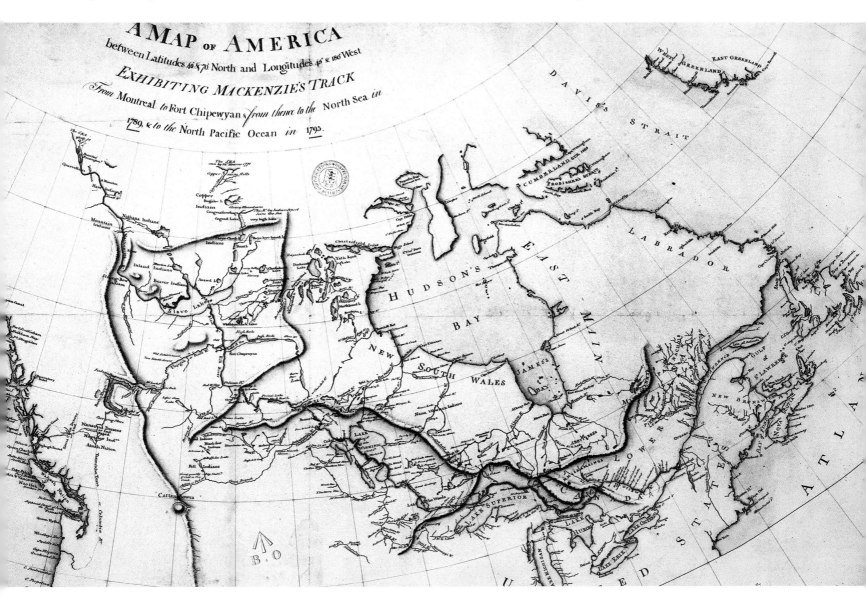

MAP 184.
A hand-drawn version of the summary map of Mackenzie's two expeditions, to the Arctic and the Pacific in 1789 and 1793. The engraved version appeared in his book *Voyages from Montreal,* published in 1801. This was likely the map drawn for the engraver.

reached, the Fraser flows in a canyon through which he would have been lucky to pass.

Taking native advice, he struck out overland along the valley of the West Road River on a native "grease trail" (a trading route for oolichan fish oil) and emerged into the valley of the Bella Coola River, where he was able to borrow a canoe from the Nuxalk to continue his journey to the sea. On 20 July he reached the village of Bella Coola and recorded: "We got out of the river, which discharges itself by various channels into an arm of the sea." He had completed

The Hudson's Bay Company Responds

Increasingly squeezed by the independent fur traders from Montréal, the Hudson's Bay Company hired for the first time a competent surveyor who would be required to draw accurate maps of the new country being opened up, into which they could fit traders' reports and use them to plot strategy.

The man they hired was Philip Turnor, who arrived at York Fort on the supply ship in 1778. For ten years Turnor traveled the rivers and lakes of the interior surveying and mapping, producing many accurate maps of previously only tenuously mapped areas. He also collected native information whenever he came by it, but did not incorporate it into his own maps, which contained only those parts that he had personally surveyed. In 1789 Turnor acquired an assistant to help him map the Athabasca country, Peter Fidler, chosen over David Thompson, who was recovering from a broken leg. Fidler also collected native maps, and he drew more copies of them into his journal than any other North American explorer. The result

is a fine collection of maps that show the way Native Americans perceived the land around them.

Peter Fidler took over Philip Turnor's job when the latter left North America for good in 1792. Even before that, Fidler had lived among the natives during the winter in order to learn their language, disappearing for months on end accompanied by no other Europeans. In the fall of 1792, Fidler decided to accompany a small band of Piegan who were returning to their wintering grounds, intending to once again learn a language. On 20 November he crossed the Red Deer River, recording his first sight of the Rocky Mountains. He wrote that they "looked awfully grand . . . very much similar to dark rain like clouds rising up above the Horizon in a fine summer evening." Fidler was recording his position all the time and now became the first to correctly locate the Rockies on a map. This information was passed on to Aaron Arrowsmith, and through his map (MAP 188, *right, bottom*) to Lewis and Clark.

Fidler was the first European to cross the Battle, Red Deer, Bow, and Highwood Rivers, all of which he mapped. He described the vast buffalo herds of the plains and the jumps over which they were herded to their deaths by the natives. Fidler found coal at Kneehills Creek, later mined as the Drumheller Coalfield. And he wrote the first description of the prairie cactus, opuntia.

In 1800 Fidler built Chesterfield House at the junction of the Red Deer River and the South Saskatchewan. Here he collected a number of native-derived maps, drawing on paper and thus preserving maps that would have otherwise lasted only a very short time, being drawn on bark with charcoal or, even more ephemeral, scratched with a stick in the bare earth. Perhaps the most significant of these was Ac ko mok ki's map (MAP 187, *right, top*) showing the entire drainage basin of the Upper Missouri and demonstrating more clearly than ever before the considerable extent of geographical knowledge of many natives.

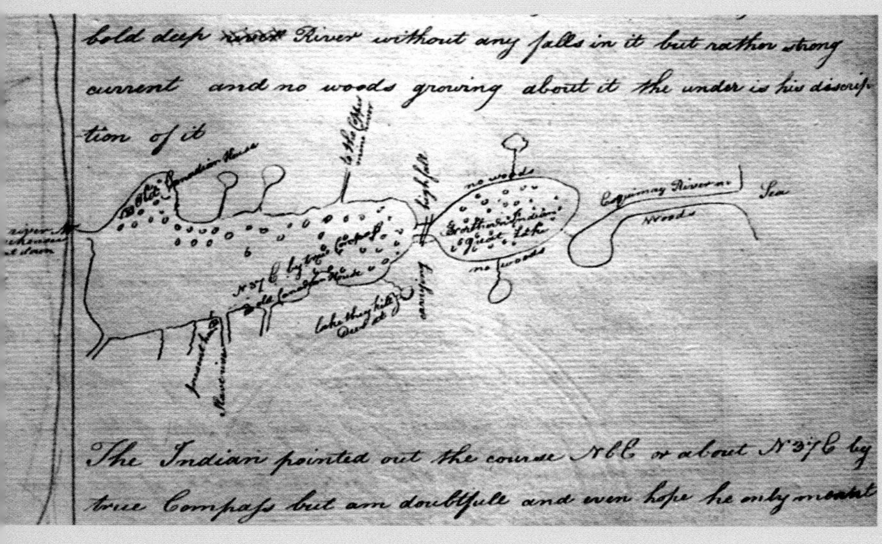

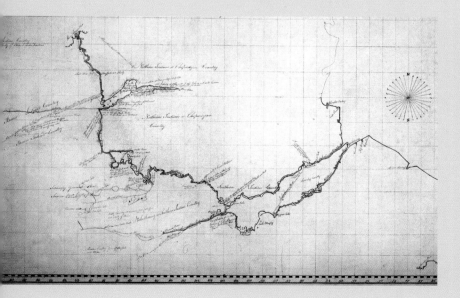

MAP 185 (*left, top*).
A map copied by Philip Turnor from Shew-dith-da, a Chipewyan, in 1791. It shows Great Slave Lake, at left, east to an inlet or river flowing into Hudson Bay, on the right. The vast maze of lakes on the Barren Lands between Great Slave Lake and Hudson Bay has been shown as a single lake, with the words *no woods* on its perimeter. It could also represent Dubawnt Lake, the largest in that region. At the west end of Great Slave Lake (partly off the part of the map shown) is *The river Mr Mackenzie went down* in 1789 on his way to the Arctic Ocean.

MAP 186 (*left, bottom*).
The first map Philip Turnor drew for his employer when he returned to London in 1792 was this one, which shows the route from Hudson Bay, on the right, to Great Slave Lake, at top left. The other large lake is Lake Athabasca. Now the company had a map its traders could use to get to this rich fur country themselves.

Map 188 (below).

Aaron Arrowsmith, a London commercial mapmaker, had a special relationship with the Hudson's Bay Company and received information from them long before other firms obtained it. He also updated his maps regularly, so that they have become a unique record of the expansion of European geographical knowledge in North America. His *Map Exhibiting all the New Discoveries in the Interior Parts of North America*, first published in 1795, went through many editions. This is from the 1802 edition and shows the results of Peter Fidler's expedition towards the Rocky Mountains in 1792–93. The map was used by Meriwether Lewis and William Clark for their 1804–06 expedition to the Pacific (see next page). The *Askow or Bad River* is the Oldman–South Saskatchewan, and *Chesterfield Ho*[ouse] is the post Fidler built at the confluence of the Red Deer and South Saskatchewan Rivers. Beyond the Rockies, from native reports, is a river tentatively connected to the Columbia, and which it must be: *The Indians say they sleep 8 Nights in descending this River to the sea.*

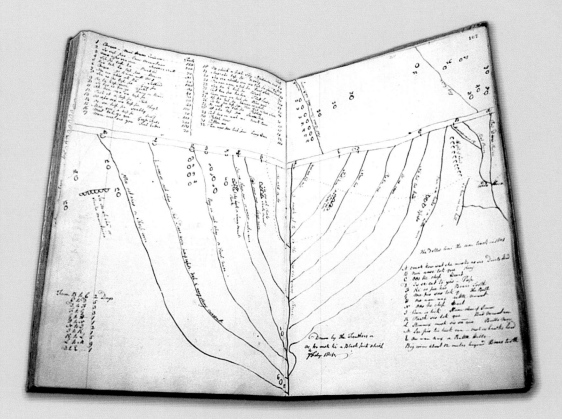

Map 187 (above).

The famous copy in Peter Fidler's journal of the map by Ac ko mok ki, a Blackfoot chief, showing the headwaters of the Missouri River system. It was drawn in February 1801. North is to the right. The double line is the Rocky Mountains, and the Pacific coast is the top edge of the journal. The two rivers west of the Rockies have been variously interpreted as the Columbia, Snake, or Fraser Rivers.

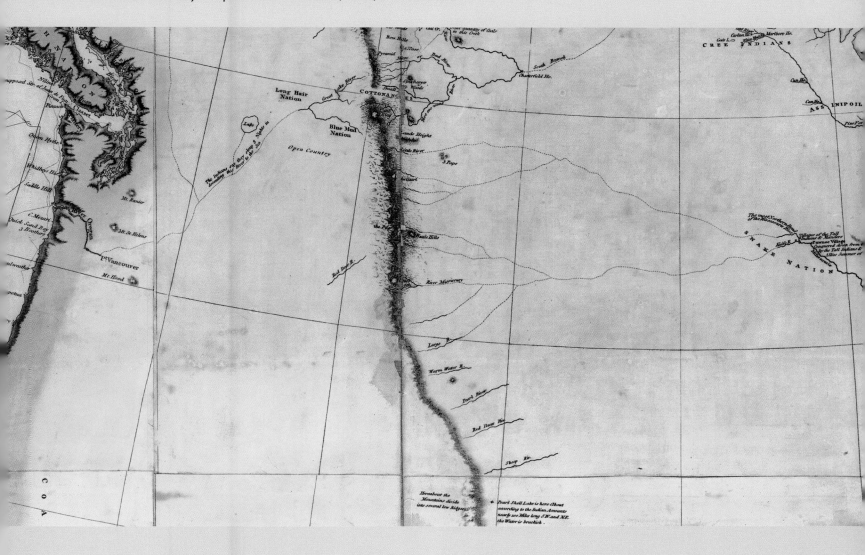

No Passage to India

The story of Meriwether Lewis and William Clark's exploration to the Pacific in 1804 to 1806 is so well known that it has entered the American psyche and become, as one historian put it, the American national epic poem. Many people think Lewis and Clark were the first to reach the Pacific overland, when in fact they were second,

after Alexander Mackenzie. But their journey had a tremendous political impact as well, their effect on American legend contributing to the incorporation of Oregon and the Pacific Northwest into the United States. They were forerunners of Manifest Destiny before the term had even been coined.

Ever since Louis Jolliet and Jacques Marquette found the mouth of the *Pekittan8i*, the Missouri, in 1673, European knowledge had been slowly ascending the river, hampered by some of the native groups who wanted to prevent incursions of outside traders. Bourgmont had reached the Platte by 1714, La Vérendrye seems to have found the Mandan villages (near Bismarck, North Dakota) by 1738, the Mallet brothers reached the Niobrara River (west of Sioux City) in 1739, and the La Vérendrye sons reached the vicinity of Pierre, North Dakota, in 1742. By 1787 traders from the North West Company had visited the Mandan villages, and in the

1790s traders from St. Louis began to travel up the river, but were often stopped by Indians.

In 1793 Jacques Clamorgan gathered together a group of St. Louis merchants, obtained a monopoly from the Spanish government, and formed the Company of Explorers of the Upper Missouri, usually known as the Missouri Company. It was welcomed by the Spanish as a foil to possible incursions into their territory by the North West Company or the Hudson's Bay Company.

The Missouri Company dispatched a major trading venture in 1794, led by Jean Baptiste Truteau (sometimes Trudeau), but this group got only to the villages of the Arikara Indians at the Grand River, near the present North Dakota–South Dakota boundary. The following year Clamorgan enlisted the services of James Mackay and John Thomas Evans. Mackay was an ex-Nor'Wester who had already visited the Mandans and now thought he could do better in St. Louis, while Evans was a seeker of a supposed lost tribe of Welsh Indians he now thought might be the Mandans. The pair led a group of traders to establish Fort Charles among the Omaha Indians, near today's Sioux City. Evans tried to go farther up the Missouri but was soon stopped by the Teton Sioux, who wanted to protect their own trade with native groups to the northwest.

Over the winter of 1795–96, Mackay and Evans worked out a new plan for the Missouri Company: they would find a passage to

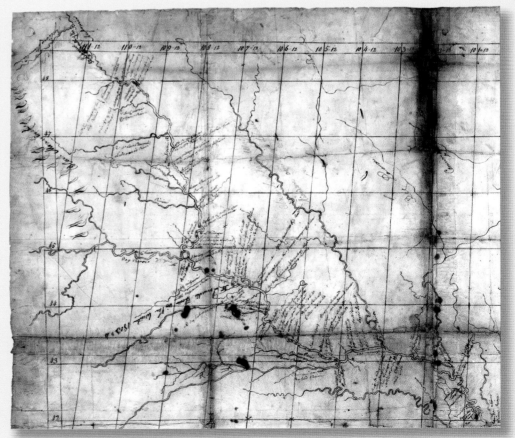

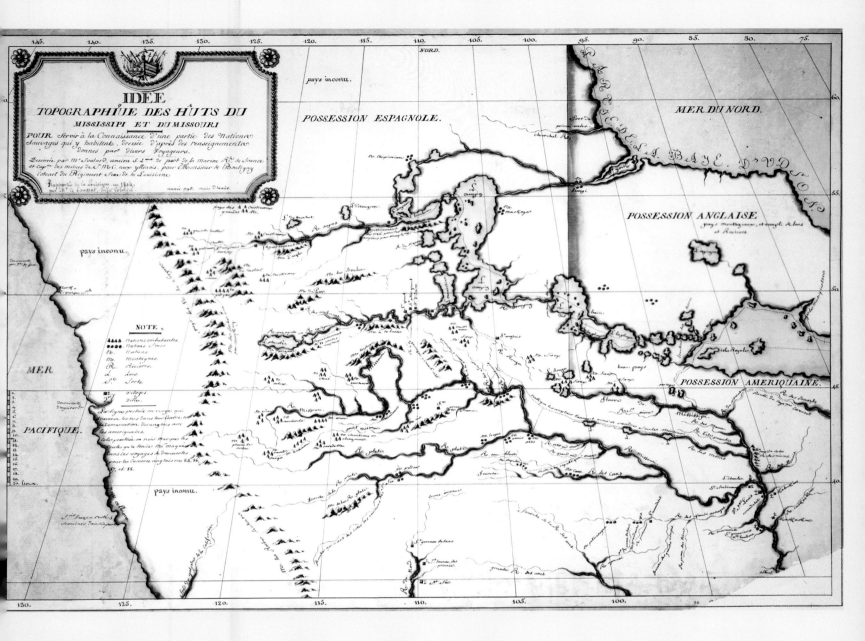

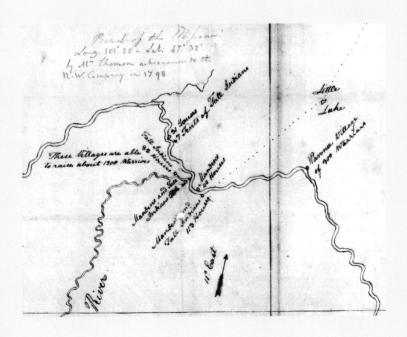

Map 189 (*left, top*).
William Faden's 1785 map of the new United States of America showed the Missouri as far as it was known at that time, with the notation *Missouri R. its source unknown*.

Map 190 (*left, bottom*).
Drawn by Spanish engineer Nicolas de Finiels, this map shows the Missouri and its tributaries between Fort St. Charles and the Mandan villages. It was derived from the Missouri Company, from information gained by James Mackay. Also known as the Indian Office map, it was used by Lewis and Clark during their expedition in 1804.

Map 191 (*above*).
A French copy of a Spanish map by Antoine Soulard, the surveyor general of Spanish Louisiana, which shows the West, and in particular the Missouri River system, as it was perceived in 1795. The headwaters of the river reach to a single ridge of mountains, which are shown very near to the Pacific coast.

Map 192 (*right*).
North West Company surveyor David Thompson made this map in 1798 of the Great Bend of the Missouri just upstream from the Mandan villages. Meriwether Lewis traced this map and carried the tracing with him on his expedition. Today this entire section of the river is submerged under the artificial Lake Sakakawea.

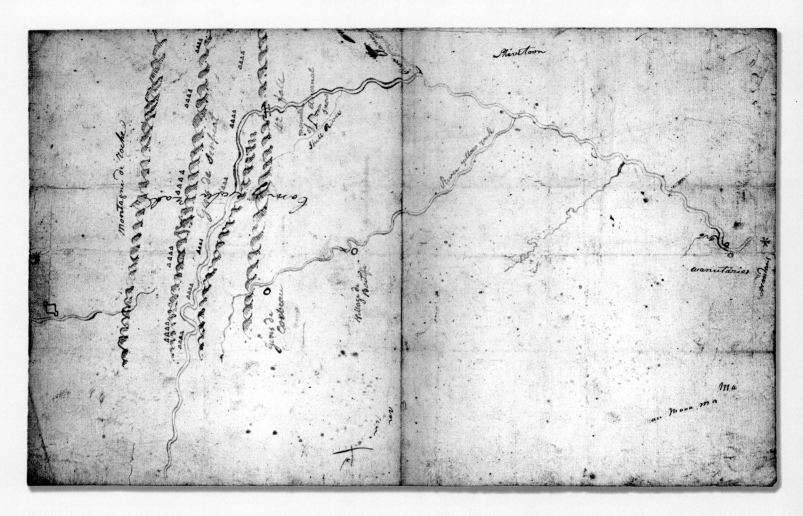

Map 193 (*above*).
John Evans's map of the country upstream from the Mandan villages, completely derived from native information during 1796–97. As a result of this information, Evans decided not to attempt to reach the Pacific; it was clearly a lot farther off than he had thought. The Yellowstone River (*River yellow rock*) is prominent. Note that there are now multiple mountain ranges, as in reality. The westernmost range is the *montagne de roche*—"rocky mountain."

Map 194 (*below*).
Part of a map drawn by Nicholas King in 1803, partly copied from Aaron Arrowsmith's 1802 map (**Map 187**, page 137), and taken by Meriwether Lewis on his expedition, when he added other information. It shows the territory from the Mandan villages, at right, to the Pacific. Note the "conjectural" river tentatively flowing through or around the Rockies to join the *River Oregan,* the hundred miles of so of the Columbia surveyed by Broughton (see page 129). Where this information came from is not known, but it suggests that someone, perhaps Thomas Jefferson, still thought it possible that an easy through passage existed. To the north, the *South Branch* is the South Saskatchewan, from Peter Fidler (see pages 136–37).

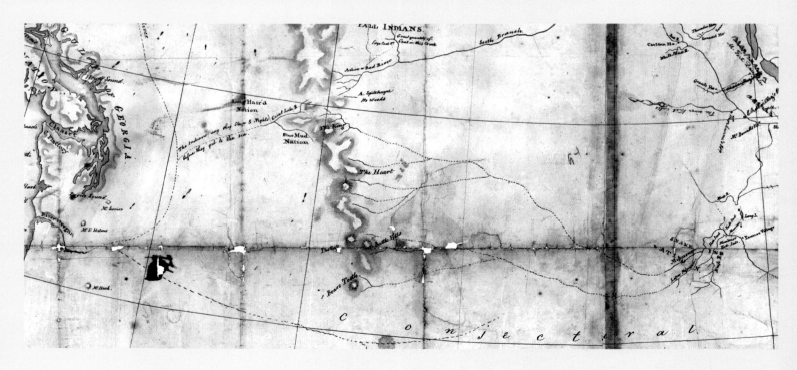

India by following the Missouri to its source, cross the easy portage they expected there, and find a river flowing to the Pacific. A chain of forts was to be built to guard the route. Unfortunately, these grand dreams came to nought when Evans again ascended the Missouri in 1796. Although he made it to the Mandan villages this time, he came into conflict with North West Company traders and this, together with information obtained from the Indians about the distance to the Pacific, induced him to abandon his grandiose plans. Evans's map of the territory west of the Mandans is shown as MAP 193 (*left*); significantly, there are now multiple mountain ridges,

MAP 195 (*right*).
Louisiana, by Philadelphia commercial mapmaker Samuel Lewis (no relation to Meriwether), published in his *New and Elegant General Atlas* in 1804. It represents the optimistic view of what was to be expected in the West. A single ridge of mountains is broken in several places by gaps, one of which is convenient to the Upper Missouri; and the Pacific coast is close by.

MAP 196 (*below*).
Nicholas King's composite copy, made in 1805, of various maps by William Clark. This map represents the sum total of the geographical knowledge of the expedition before starting up the Missouri. Although there are multiple mountain ranges, the map shows easy paths through them.

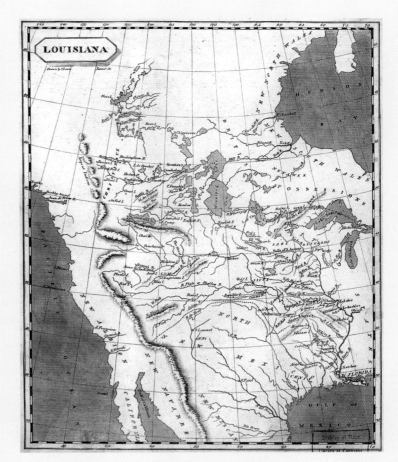

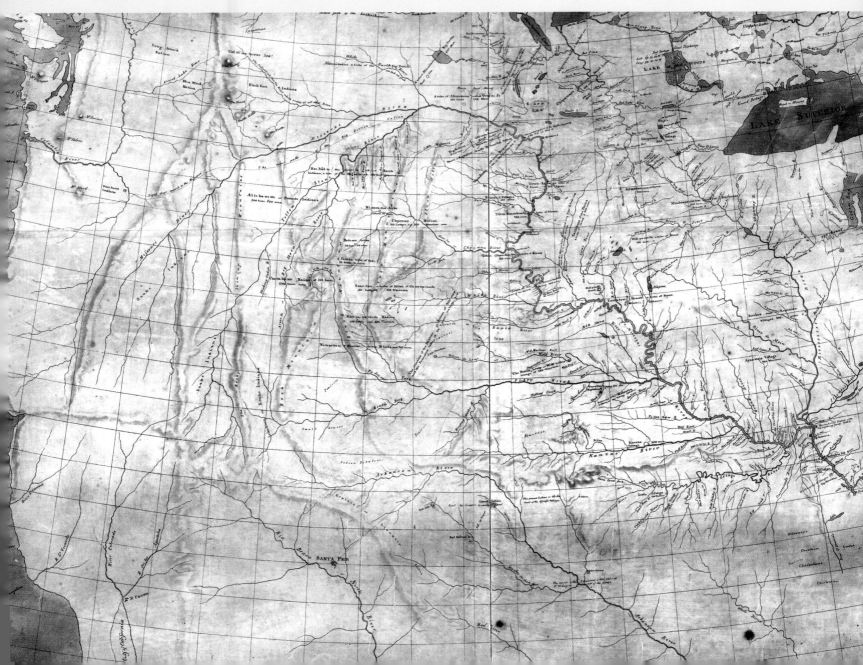

rather than the hoped-for single ridge. The Missouri from Fort St. Charles to the Mandan villages drawn from Mackay's information is shown on MAP 190, page 138. All available geographical knowledge was pulled together for the use of Lewis and Clark, and Nicholas King, a Philadelphia mapmaker, made composite maps for the expedition's use.

Thomas Jefferson, son of Peter (see MAP 150, pages 110–11), and principal author of the American Declaration of Independence, had always been fascinated by what might be found in the West and harbored dreams of a pan-continental United States. As early as 1783 he had tried to interest George Rogers Clark to undertake an expedition, to no avail. While in Paris in 1786 he supported the attempt by John Ledyard, who had been with James Cook, to travel to Siberia, cross the Pacific on a Russian ship, and find a route east by ascending the Columbia. Ledyard had in fact traveled to within two hundred miles of Kamchatka before being turned back by the Russians.

Then in 1793 the American Philosophical Society approved an expedition up the Missouri by a French botanist, Andre Michaux, and Jefferson drew up his instructions; his objective, he wrote, was "to find the shortest and most convenient route of communication between the U.S. & the Pacific Ocean," up the Missouri. The expedition never went anywhere, however, because Michaux became suspected as a spy, but Jefferson's instructions to him were virtually identical to those he would provide to Lewis and Clark ten years later.

Even before the Louisiana Purchase, Jefferson had laid plans for a renewed attempt to find a land route to the Pacific. As president, he was now in a position to realize such plans. He read Alexander Mackenzie's book in 1802 and was concerned about the advocacy of North West Company—that is, British—commercial establishments on the West Coast. Perhaps more than anything else, it was Mackenzie's book that prompted the Lewis and Clark expedition. Plans were well under way when Louisiana was acquired in 1803, and a commercial imperative became an national one.

Jefferson's choice to lead the expedition was his personal secretary, Meriwether Lewis. To share command Lewis attracted William Clark, whose brother George Rogers Clark had turned down the opportunity in 1783. Jefferson instructed Lewis to "explore the Missouri River, and such principal streams of it, as, by its course and communications with the waters of the Pacific ocean, whether the Columbia, Oregon, Colorado, or any other river, may offer the most direct and practicable water communications across the continent, for the purposes of commerce." Lewis was also to make enough astronomical observations to construct an accurate map.

The expedition was now styled the Corps of Discovery, a military unit charged with an objective, as it were. Clark left St. Louis on 14 May 1804, with a 55-foot-long keelboat and two pirogues (large dugout canoes with sails), twenty-five men, and five tons of food and other supplies. He was joined by Lewis, traveling overland, at St. Charles six days later. After a great deal of labor—the keelboat had to be rowed or towed—they reached the Mandan and Arikara villages near the Great Bend of the Missouri, and a thousand miles from St. Charles, by late October. Here they wintered. In the spring, once the ice was out of the river, the keelboat was sent back to St. Louis with the first reports of the expedition, and on 7 April Lewis and Clark continued upriver with six canoes and the two pirogues.

On 25 April they passed the Yellowstone River, and on 26 May Lewis climbed the bank out of the river and had his first view of the Rocky Mountains, getting an inkling of the problems this "snowey barrier" would cause his expedition. In the middle of June, as they were approaching the foothills of the Rocky Mountains, they came to a fork in the river that had not been anticipated in the native information they had acquired. The choice of which branch to follow, like the one Mackenzie had had to make at the fork of the Peace River twelve years before, would be critical. Lewis, determined to make the right choice, ascended the right branch for forty miles before he was convinced that it (which they named the Marias River) led north rather than west towards the Pacific. And so they took the left branch, which they were soon relieved to find was the correct decision, for they came to a large waterfall, the Great Falls of the Missouri (MAP 197, *left*), which they had expected from their native information. (It is marked as *the fall* on the map John Evans copied, MAP 193, page 140.) It took them a month to portage the falls and its upstream cascade of rapids, going back and forth four times. Their route bypassed what is now the city of Great Falls, Montana. By the time they could get going again it was 15 July.

Now in canoes, the expedition closed in on the Rockies, and on 9 August Lewis and some of the men left Clark with the canoes, which would soon become useless, to try to find Shoshone Indians, from whom they hoped to buy horses. The Shoshone, who had recently been chased from the plains by enemies who had acquired guns from European traders, were wary and difficult to contact. A deal was finally made with the intervention of Sacagwea, the Shoshone wife of Toussaint Charbonneau, a trader who had accompanied the expedition from the Mandan villages. Sacagwea recognized Cameahwait, the Shoshone chief, as her brother. The Corps got all the horses they needed.

Even with horses and a Shoshone guide, the route through the mountains was difficult. When Lewis finally reached the Continental Divide he expected to see the Columbia, or some other mighty river,

MAP 197 (*left*).
William Clark's map of the portage around the Great Falls of the Missouri, drawn in his journal on 4 July 1805. All the features have now been erased by a power project.

MAP 198 (*above*).
Clark's sketch map of the mouth of the Columbia River and the Pacific coast south of it, drawn in early 1806. Cape Disappointment is at top left, the location of modern Cannon Beach at the bottom.

flowing away from him to the Pacific in the distance. Instead, all he saw were more ranges of snow-capped mountains. They crossed Lemhi Pass, in the Bitterroot Range on the Continental Divide and today the boundary between Montana and Idaho. Snow fell and hunger descended, fended off only by eating a horse. "The difficu[lt]y of passing [these] emence mountains [has] dampened the Spirits of the party," wrote Clark. But they persevered, and after eleven days they reached a friendly Nez Percé Indian village on the Weippe Prairie, near the Clearwater River, in today's Idaho. Finally, here was what they had been looking for—a river that drained westwards.

Now the going became much easier and much faster. They borrowed canoes and floated down the Clearwater, then the Snake, and then the Columbia, which they reached on 16 October. Beacon Rock, at the beginning of Pacific tidewater, was passed on 3 November, and four days later Clark recorded in his field book his famous line: "Ocian in view! O! The joy." They were still twenty miles from the coast, but no matter, they were going to achieve their objective. After exploration of the huge Columbia estuary, on 3 December both Lewis and Clark found themselves suitable trees and carved

inscriptions on them. Clark, in emulation of Mackenzie, carved the words "Capt. William Clark December 3rd 1805. By Land. U. States in 1804–1805."

Just south of what is now Astoria, Oregon, the expedition built a camp from logs and settled in for the winter. This was Fort Clatsop, their home from December 1805 to March 1806. Clark used the time to convert his daily courses and distances into a larger, smaller-scale map. To it he added information he had been given by natives. On 14 February 1806 he was finished, writing in his diary: "I compleated a map of the Countrey through which we had been passing . . . We now discover that we have found the most practicable and navigable passage across the Continent of North America."

But not quite. On their way back the expedition was able to follow easier routes across the difficult Continental Divide—Lewis and Clark each followed different routes—adding yet more to the map. Clark kept the map in his office in St. Louis until 1810, adding information that was given to him. Meriwether Lewis died in 1809 either from suicide or murder, it is not clear which, leaving Clark alone the task of overseeing the creation of a final map. It was

copied and engraved by Samuel Lewis for inclusion in the 1814 book *History of the Expedition under the Command of Captains Lewis and Clark*. For the first time, here was a printed and thus widely disseminated, reasonably accurate map of the region west of the Mississippi.

The Corps of Discovery split up when they crossed the Rocky Mountains on their return trip, with as many as five separate parties at times exploring as much territory as possible along the Marias and Yellowstone Rivers. They met up again at the mouth of the Yellowstone and made a fast downstream journey to St. Louis, where they arrived—to much jubilation for they had been given up as dead—on 23 September 1806.

The dream of an overland Northwest Passage—the Passage to India—was finally laid to rest by Lewis and Clark, but they did find several routes through the Rocky Mountains that would prove useful to those coming after them. Now, indisputably, the Rocky Mountains had been demonstrated to be much wider in extent than had previously been shown on maps—except, perhaps, the native-derived one drawn by John Evans in 1796–97 (MAP 193, page 140). Clark had calculated that the distance from St. Louis to the Mandans was 1,500 miles, and this is quite accurate. From the Mandans to the Pacific, however, Clark's estimated 1,350 miles was almost half the real distance of 2,550 miles. The error was due to the incorrect positioning of the Mandan villages and the Rocky Mountains on previous maps rather than a misjudgment of the total width of North America, which was known after Cook's visit to the West Coast in 1778 and correctly known to Lewis and Clark, as other of their maps demonstrate.

MAP 199 (*left*).
William Clark's map of the West, which he kept in his office in St. Louis and updated until 1810. Clark was then superintendent of Indian affairs. Because of the additions, not all the details are correct, but all the information Lewis and Clark provided was reasonably accurate.

MAP 200 (*below*).
The engraved final summary map of the Lewis and Clark expedition, copied from William Clark and engraved by Samuel Lewis, the Philadelphia mapmaker. He was not related to Meriwether. The map was published in 1814 in the two-volume definitive book about the expedition edited by Nicholas Biddle. Here at last was a widely available and reasonably correct map of the West.

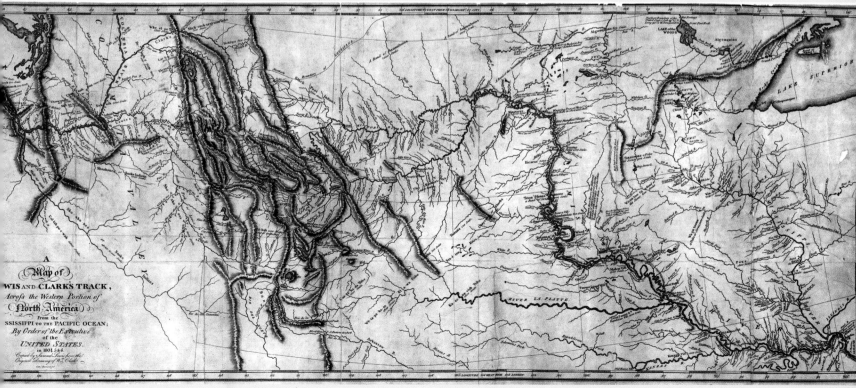

Internal Parts of Louisiana

With the transfer of the vast but ill-defined territory of Louisiana to the United States in 1803, Spain lost a huge buffer region that was protecting the frontiers of New Spain. American president Thomas Jefferson saw the new acquisition as including all the west bank tributaries of the Mississippi. The Spanish disagreed. Nevertheless, it was not long before American explorers and traders moved into this promising new land.

The Lewis and Clark expedition is of course the most famous, but there are others. Jefferson himself organized two other expeditions, the main purpose of which was to determine where the western boundary of Louisiana lay and improve on the maps available. The first was that of William Dunbar, a surveyor who was a member of the American Philosophical Society, which is how Jefferson knew of him. Early in 1804 Dunbar explored the Ouachita River, between the Mississippi and Red Rivers, and in the winter of 1804–05 for four months traversed the Ozark Plateau near what is now Hot Springs National Park. Accompanying Dunbar was a naturalist, George Hunter. With the Lewis and Clark expedition, it was the first of what would be a long line of government-sponsored scientific explorations of the West, and the first to be led by a civilian scientist. The expedition had originally been intended to ascend the Red River, since this was considered to be the southern boundary of Louisiana and needed to be defined, but the explorers soon found that the principal enemy in these parts was not the Spanish at all but hostile Indians, in this case the Osage.

In 1806 a second attempt at exploring the Red River was made, again at Jefferson's behest. Organized again by Dunbar, the new expedition was led by Thomas Freeman, another surveyor who had recently surveyed the new site of Washington, D.C.; he was accompanied by naturalist Peter Custis. They set out from Natchez in April 1806 and by the time they left Natchitoches, the westernmost American post, in June, they had thirty or more soldiers with them. This prevented Indian attacks, but this time they were stopped by a Spanish force under Francisco Viana after ascending the Red River for 615 miles. Freeman was back at Natchitoches by August. He was appointed by Jefferson to head another expedition, this time up the Arkansas River, the following year, but this was cancelled when Congress did not approve the funding.

In 1806 another expedition set out to find the source of the Red River, that of Zebulon Montgomery Pike. He was not sent by Jefferson but by General James Wilkinson, a double agent both for the Spanish and for himself, since it seems he intended to assist in the setting up of an independent republic between the United States and the Spanish territories in cahoots with Aaron Burr, Jefferson's vice president during his first term (an interesting parallel with what

MAP 201 (*below, bottom*).
This map of the Red River by Nicholas King is based on the exploration of Thomas Freeman in 1806.

MAP 202 (*below*).
Part of the large map of New Spain published by the scientist Alexander von Humboldt in 1804 showing the Red River (*R. Rojo de Natchitoches*) as it was then known.

MAP 203 (*right*).
The map of the west bank tributaries of the Mississippi from Pike's book, published in 1810. The lower reaches of these rivers are quite well-delineated by this time.

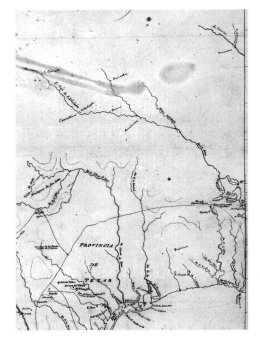

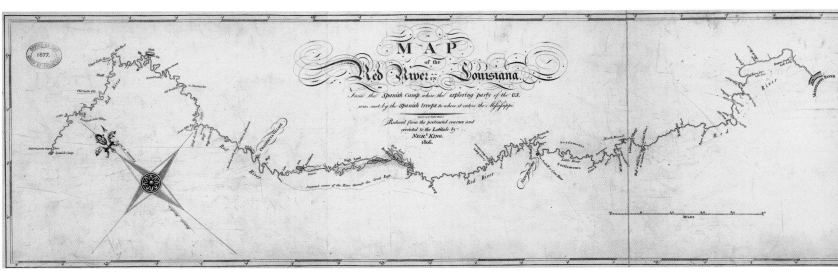

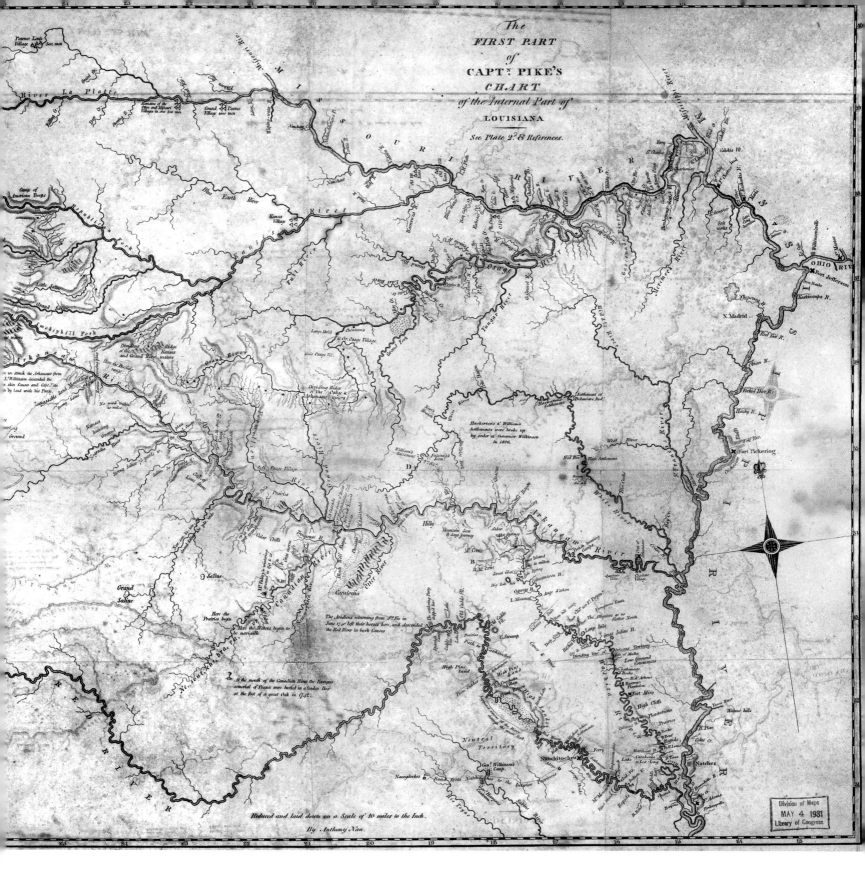

happened in Texas in 1836). Wilkinson had been made governor of Louisiana in 1805, which put him in a position to create an incident that might lead to war between the United States and Spain, which, he hoped, would allow a pretext for Burr's private troops to take over New Orleans and create the new republic. This did not happen, of course, but Pike's expedition was unwittingly part of the intrigue.

Pike had already explored the headwaters of the Mississippi and ousted British fur traders in 1805 when Wilkinson dispatched him west from St. Louis the following year. Wilkinson then in-

formed the Spanish that he was coming, and they sent out Facundo Malgares to capture him. Pike followed part of the Kansas River, then the Arkansas River, coming within sight of the Rocky Mountains on 15 November. Hoping to gain a good view of the surrounding territory, Pike and his men tried to climb what is now Pike's Peak, and although they failed they did climb nearby Cheyenne Peak, an excellent viewpoint of the southern Rockies.

In mid-January 1806 Pike marched to the Rio Grande, which he maintained was the Red River, though he undoubtedly knew where he

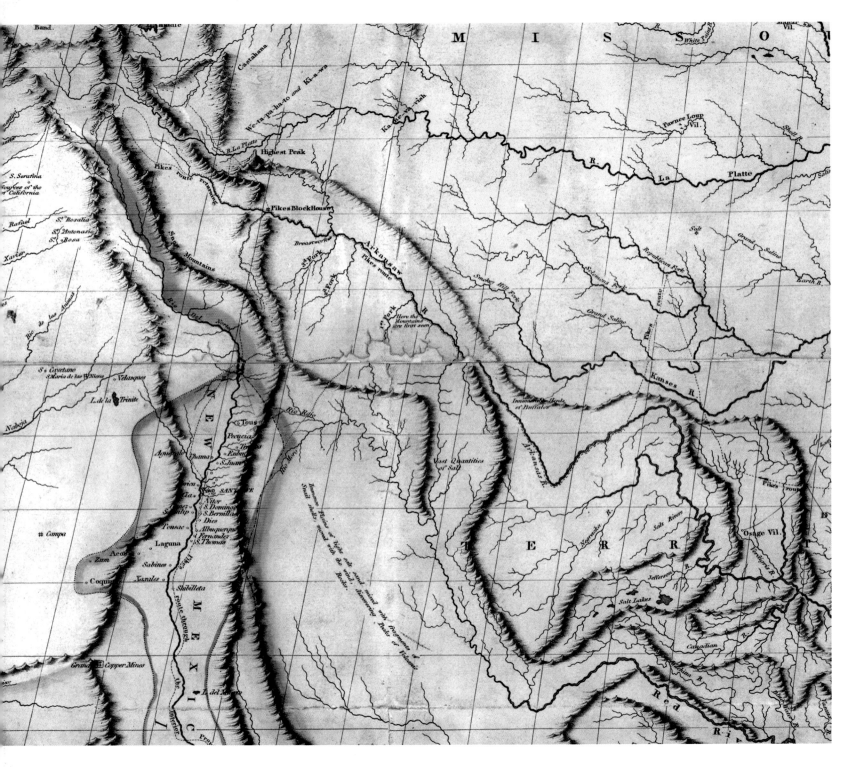

was. Here he built a small log structure and it was here that he was found by Spanish cavalry on 26 February. "What, is not this the Red River?" he was reputed to have exclaimed. The Spanish, not at all taken in, arrested him and sent him to Chihuahua, the New Mexican capital. But he was treated well and later released, gaining a great deal of information as he returned to the United States across Texas. His mission as a spy, if that is what it was, also succeeded; he arrived back with all sorts of military details of forts and numbers of men defending them.

Pike published an account of his adventures in 1810. In it he stated that the Great Plains were sandy deserts, "tracts of many leagues . . . on which not a speck of vegetable matter existed." This was the origin of the myth of the Great American Desert. Pike thought this beneficial, in that it would confine Americans to their

MAP 204.
Part of the map of the United States published by American commercial mapmaker John Melish in 1816, incorporating the work of Zebulon Pike. Santa Fe and the valley of the Rio Grande (*Rio Del Norte*) is within the red area, representing Spanish territory, at bottom left. The green-colored area is Louisiana, the northern part of which had become Missouri Territory in 1812.

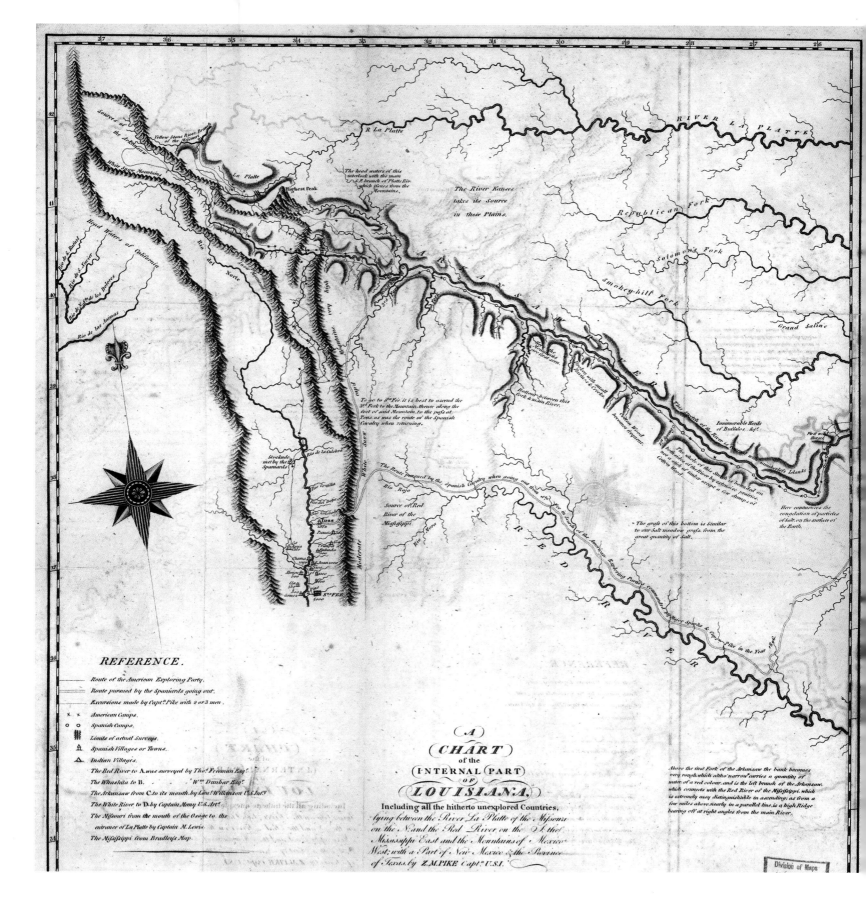

MAP 205.

Pike's map of the *Internal Part of Louisiana*, published in 1810. Aside from the parts Pike had mapped himself, he copied from a map by the scientist Alexander Humboldt. Yet Humboldt had never traveled in the region, and Pike had. Note the *Head Waters of California* on the left edge. Pike subscribed to the view that rivers draining directly into the Pacific flowed west from here. His route along the Arkansas River (at center) is marked; the Rio Grande, which he deliberately misconstrued as the Red River, is in the hachured valley at left, with the *Stockade met by the Spaniards* at the place Pike built his "fort." The Red River is shown at right, bottom, together with *The Route pursued by the Spanish Cavalry.*

own country and make them less likely to wander west. He also thought that the Arkansas and the Colorado Rivers would together provide a "Southwest Passage" though this desert. His map (MAP 205, *previous page*) shows the *Head Waters of California* peeking out from the left margin. Pike's view of the Southwest would shape the popular vision of the lands west of the Mississippi for fifty years.

The concept of this Great American Desert was further reinforced by the explorations of Stephen Harriman Long in 1820. Long was one of the first members of the Corps of Topographical Engineers, a division of the United States Army formed in 1818 to carry out military engineering surveys and explore routes for troop movements. The organization was to have far-reaching influence in the later exploration of the West.

Long had gained experience in 1817 with a survey of frontier defenses, during which he had traveled up the Mississippi as far as the Falls of St. Anthony (now the site of Minneapolis) in a six-oared skiff. The same year he had been the first to advocate the use of steamboats to explore the West. In 1819 he found himself appointed leader of an expedition that was to explore the Platte River and the Great Plains as far as the Arkansas and Red Rivers. A new secretary of war, John C. Calhoun, wanted to establish a military post on the Missouri at the Yellowstone River to counter the threat from British fur traders and to bring firmer American control to the region after the founding of the Red River Colony by Lord Selkirk just to the north. The colony had been granted to Selkirk by the Hudson's Bay Company in 1811 but was just getting established in 1817. Calhoun's concerns were partly assuaged by the signing of the 1818 Convention establishing the United States–British territories boundary on the forty-ninth parallel west to the Rocky Mountains, but the expedition went ahead anyhow.

The main expedition was a complete disaster. A thousand men in six steamboats—one carrying Long and his scientific contingent—ascended the Missouri to the Platte in 1819. Here they overwintered, and most of the men became too ill to continue. Long, recalled to Washington over the winter, had his mandate for the expedition radically changed; now he was to explore southwest towards the boundary with Spanish territories, up the Platte to the Arkansas and Red Rivers.

The motley group of engineers, soldiers, naturalists, a geologist, and a painter left Council Bluffs, on the Missouri, on 6 June 1820, and headed up the Platte. Following the South Platte, by the end of June they had reached within sight of the Rocky Mountains. Passing the place where the South Platte leaves the Rockies just south of Denver, they found Pike's Peak, which they were the first to climb. They attempted to ascend the Arkansas through the Royal Gorge, but failed. Long then split his party and sent one group, under Captain John Bell, down the Arkansas. Long continued south, looking for the headwaters of the Red River. Consulting Pike's map, he found a river he thought was the Red, but which he soon came to realize was the Canadian, a tributary of the Arkansas. The Canadian had originally been found by French traders seeking a route to Santa Fe, but its course was imprecisely known, and its upper part had been confused with the Red. Bell's group, intimidated by Cheyenne, Arapaho and Kiowa, suffered desertions, and with them all the scientific papers of the expedition disappeared.

Long's expedition was for many years considered a failure, largely owing to the loss of those scientific papers, although the map Long produced was very accurate for its time (MAP 207, *right,* is the first, manuscript version). He is also derided for the myth of the Great American Desert, which he is often considered to have originated, rather than Pike. Yet it is true that with 1820 technology the southwestern plains were unsuitable for agriculture, and since there was no wood for building or for fuel, settlement would have been all but impossible. For now, it would be a region to pass through.

Almost immediately the region became more important as a route west with the Mexican Revolution of 1821. William Becknell, who led an expedition to Santa Fe that year, was one of the first to find a new welcome, and two other expeditions made it there the same year. Suddenly, in the words of emissaries, the "mackeson provence" was "desirous of a traid." No more would traveling to Santa Fe be illegal; only the Indians would now sometimes threaten travelers. American president James Monroe ordered a road surveyed between Fort Osage, on the Missouri, and Santa Fe, and the survey was carried out in 1825. The trail crossed the headwaters of the Canadian River (MAP 206, *below*).

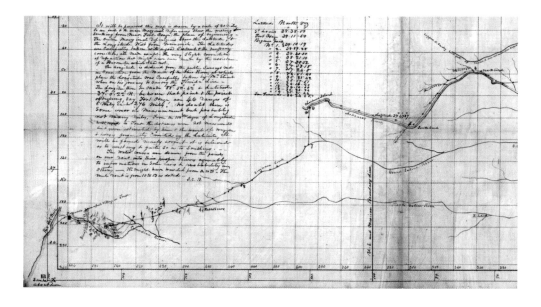

MAP 206 (*left*).
Drawn by surveyor Joseph Brown, this is the western part of the survey of the Santa Fe Trail commissioned in March 1825 by President Monroe. In the extreme bottom left corner is the *Rio del Norte* (the Rio Grande) and the words *Santa Fe about here.* The headwaters of the Canadian River are shown. The river at top right is the Arkansas.

MAP 207 (*right*).
The left part of Stephen Long's map of the drainage basin of the Mississippi, drawn in 1820 or 1821. The words *Great Desert* are emblazoned across the southwestern plains. On the printed version of this map this reads *Great American Desert.* At the time, Long's map was easily the finest map of the Trans-Mississippi West.

A Quest for Fur

In the wake of Lewis and Clark, a horde of traders and trappers moved into the Northwest, intent on exploiting the commercial potential of the newly available lands. Since the country beyond the Rockies was not officially American territory, British and American traders would compete with one another for the rich bounty of the mountains. The Oregon Country, as it was known, was by the 1818 Convention left as a region of "joint occupancy." It covered approximately the area now British Columbia, Washington, Oregon, and Idaho, west of the Rockies, but the entire Rocky Mountains region was also exploited. And the freewheeling fur traders did not stop at any boundaries, making many a foray into what was technically Spanish, and after 1821 Mexican, territory south of 42° N. In the process, not only was knowledge of this vast region considerably increased but new routes to it across the Rockies were discovered.

Before Lewis and Clark even returned, fur traders were making their way up the Missouri, and indeed they even met them

on the way. The traders had been sent by Manuel Lisa, a St. Louis merchant, guiding light of the Missouri Fur Company. Lisa himself ascended the river in 1807 and built a fort at the forks of the Yellowstone and Bighorn Rivers, called Fort Raymond. From here Lisa's men carried out a number of explorations to find sources of furs.

John Colter, who had been with Lewis and Clark, set out by himself that year to attempt to persuade Indians to trade. Colter's journal or maps have not survived—though he did pass on information to William Clark—so we do not know his exact route. But we do know that friendly Crow Indians led him to the Shoshone River with its sulfurous geysers and tar pits, the area other traders soon dubbed "Colter's Hell." He then entered the geyser region of what is now Yellowstone National Park, becoming the first Euro-American to see its wonders.

The following year Colter set out again, reaching the Three Forks, source of the Missouri. In 1809 he was attacked by Blackfoot

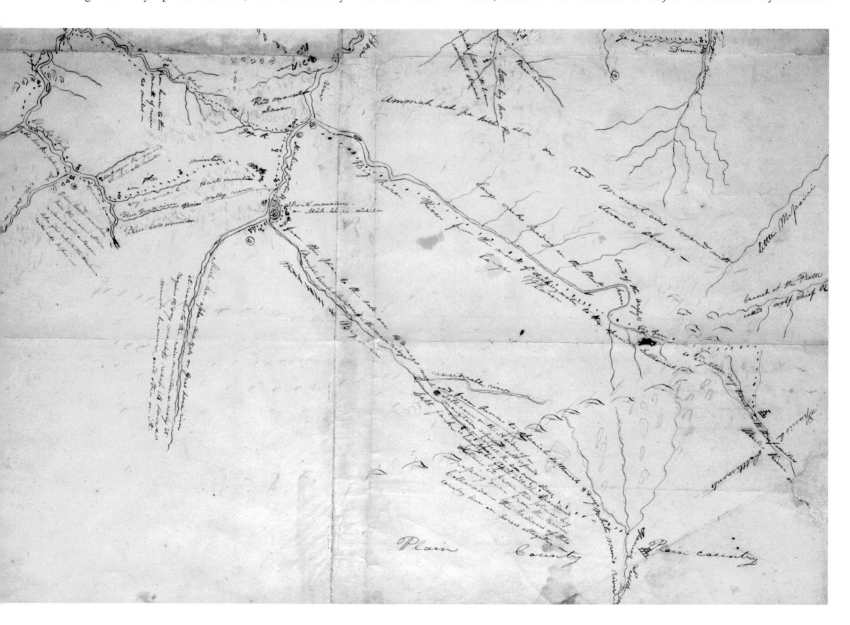

Map 208 (*left*).

William Clark's copy of George Drouillard's map of the supposed route from the Bighorn River to the rivers draining into the Rio Grande. This piece of fictitious geography was incorporated into Clark's master map of 1810 (Map 199, pages 144–45). The line of mountains at center bottom separates the two systems. The south branch of the Shoshone, a Bighorn tributary, leads to a *salt cave*, from which is noted *from hence to Spanish settlements 8 days*. Drouillard orginally referred to the "Spanish" river as the *river Collarado*, and it was Clark who changed it to *Rio del Norte* (the Rio Grande). The nearest tributary of the Colorado is the Green River, which, rising in the north part of the Wind River Range, is only about 35 miles from the headwaters of the South Shoshone. It may be that it was Clark's preconceptions as much as Drouillard's map that created the fiction on Clark's master map.

Map 209 (*above*).

The proximity of the south branch of the Shoshone to the Rio Grande is shown perhaps more clearly in this commercial map published in 1816 by John Melish. South of the *Yellowstone R.* is the *Stinking Water R.*—the Shoshone—the southern branch of which is not far from *Colter's River* to the south, which is shown draining into the Rio Grande (Rio del Norte), the river, unnamed on the part shown, that has its valley marked with a dark green swath. This map is the northern part of Map 204, page 148, which it overlaps. Drouillard's fiction removed from the map of North America the entire region that is now Colorado and part of Wyoming. *Pike's Route returning* is on the upper Arkansas River, and *L. Eustis* is Yellowstone Lake. *South Fork or Lewiss R.* is the Snake.

in the same area; his companion was killed and he was stripped and forced to flee in a sort of manhunt game the Indians played. He turned on a pursuer and killed him with his own spear, and then, with only the Indian's blanket, managed to hide and then flee back to the safety of Lisa's fort. It was a narrow escape.

Another of Lisa's men, George Drouillard, who had also been with Lewis and Clark, had less luck; he was killed in the same area by Blackfoot in 1810. Drouillard set off in 1808 to try to find a route to the Rio Grande—another route to that Holy Grail, Santa Fe. He ascended the Bighorn and produced a map which, unfortunately, superimposed onto reality his own convictions that the rivers draining into the Rio Grande to the south were only a few days away from the headwaters of the Bighorn and Yellowstone (Map 208, *left*). Clark included this information on his own master map (Map 199, pages 144–45), but, interpreted with Colter's information and seen through his own conviction that this region was a "pyramidal height of land" with the major rivers of the continent draining away in all directions, it led to a patch of fiction on an otherwise remarkable map. The supposed proximity of the Yellowstone and Shoshone Rivers (the Shoshone is a tributary of the Bighorn) to the Rio Grande is well shown in the commercial map dated 1816 published by John Melish (Map 209, *above*).

This continued illusion should have been dispelled by an expedition the following year. Twenty trappers, led by Jean Baptiste Champlain, left Fort Raymond and headed south. Men of their own minds, they soon split into three separate parties. One group was killed by Indians; another, led by Ezekial Williams, traveled south along the Front Range of the Rockies near today's Denver, then turned east, trapping down the Arkansas River. The other group appears to have continued south and reached Santa Fe, and eventually California; they were not heard from again. One member of the original twenty returned: Ezekial Williams. He must have known that Drouillard's map was wrong and that the entire central Rockies stood between the Yellowstone and Santa Fe, but no correction to the map was made.

Another of Manuel Lisa's men, Andrew Henry, went west, across the Continental Divide, and in 1810 briefly established what was the first American trading post west of the Rockies, on Henrys Fork, a tributary of the Snake.

By 1808, other American entrepreneurs were thinking that there might be money to be made in the fur trade of the far west. That year John Jacob Astor formed his American Fur Company and began to plan his strategy. He would establish a fort at the mouth of the Columbia to gather furs from a wide area of the Northwest and ship them to China or round Cape Horn to New York. This was exactly the plan first suggested by Alexander Mackenzie, and it was attractive because the cost of shipping furs back east and to export markets would be reduced. A ship, the *Tonquin,* left New York in 1810 to sail around Cape Horn, with a group led by Alexander Mackay, who had visited the Pacific coast before as Alexander Mackenzie's second-in-command in 1793. A land expedition, led by an inexperienced Wilson Price Hunt with recruited Canadian Donald Mackenzie, left St. Louis in the spring of 1811.

The *Tonquin* arrived at the mouth of the Columbia in March 1811, and after a harrowing experience trying to cross the Columbia bar, Fort Astoria was built. Hunt's expedition, the fifth to reach the Pacific overland (after Mackenzie, Lewis and Clark, Simon Fraser, and David Thompson), nearly didn't make it. Although he had a map drawn by William Clark, he decided to take a shortcut, and in so doing discovered Union Pass, at the north end of the Wind River Range. But when he reached the Snake, he decided to abandon his horses and float down that river, which is nearly impassable in the Hell's Canyon of the Snake. Near starvation, the expedition split into smaller groups. One, led by Mackenzie, made it to Fort Astoria in January 1812, and it was mid-February before Hunt arrived. Another group, led by Ramsay Crook, were only saved by a trapping party from the fort.

Astor's fort did not long remain in his company's hands, being handed over to the North West Company in 1813, during the War of 1812, but not before a return expedition had been organized. On 29 June 1812 Robert Stuart and six others set out from Fort Astoria to return to New York. This was the most significant of the expeditions by the Astorians, for Stuart followed a route up the Snake and then, hearing from an Indian informant about a "shorter trace," found his way around the *southern* end of the Wind River Range. This was the great South Pass, which would prove to be the major pathway through the Rockies for thousands of emigrant settlers following Stuart's route, the Oregon Trail. It was the major low pass that would allow transit by wagons.

Even before Astor established his American Fur Company, the British North West Company was pushing into the northern part of the Oregon Country. The effort was led by Simon Fraser, one of the company partners. He was also looking for the mouth of the Columbia,

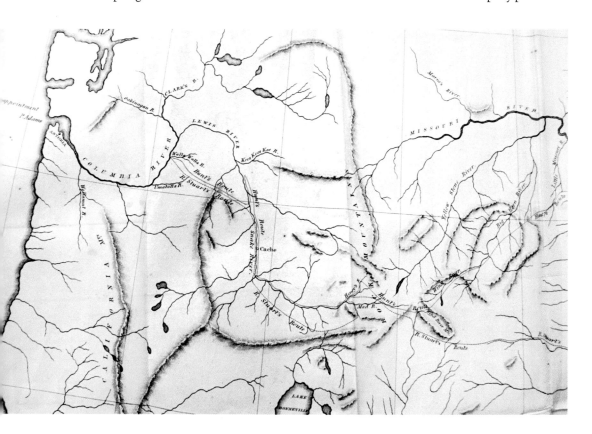

MAP 210 (*left*).
Part of a map of the routes of Wilson Price Hunt, going west, and Robert Stuart, going east, in 1811–12 and 1813, respectively. The discoveries of the American Fur Company traders, and in particular the critically important South Pass, remained known only to John Jacob Astor until 1836. In that year a book commissioned by Astor, who finally decided to protect his historical legacy, was published, detailing the exploits and discoveries of the Astorians. The book, *Astoria,* by Washington Irving, was an immensely popular success. This map comes from the book. Hunt's route north of the Wind River Range and Stuart's route south—South Pass (but not named on the map)—are shown at bottom right.

but found the wrong river. He followed Alexander Mackenzie's route up the Peace River in the fall of 1805 and crossed the Continental Divide. On McLeod Lake he built Trout Lake Post, the first permanent European settlement west of the Rockies. Fort St. James was built the following year on Stuart Lake. One of his men determined from the natives that the lake was connected to the Tacouche Tesse, the river he thought was the Columbia but which was in fact the Fraser. Thus the Pack River, which connected McLeod Lake with the Parsnip, could be used as a much easier route across the Divide.

After establishing another trading post at Fort George (now Prince George) in 1807, Fraser determined to follow his Columbia River to the sea. Twenty-four men in four canoes embarked on 28 May 1808. Although merely following a river to the sea, the expedition turned out to be quite a trial, for the rapids and gorges that Alexander Mackenzie had been warned about were nearly impassable. The Fraser Canyon has its own Hell's Gate, not inappropriately named. "We had to pass where no human being should venture," wrote Fraser. But they made it. On 2 July, after a journey of thirty-six days and five hundred miles, Fraser stood on the shores of the Pacific, actually the Strait of Georgia. He wanted to reach the "main ocean" but, harassed by

Musqueam Indians, he had to be content with what he had achieved. He managed to take an all-important positional fix, writing "the latitude is 49° nearly, while that of the Columbia is 46° 20´. This River, therefore, is not the Columbia."

While Fraser was establishing a northern fur trade network, David Thompson was to set up one farther south. In 1807 and 1808 Thompson established a number of trading posts on the headwaters of the Columbia as far south as Spokane.

At this time the North West Company thought it was unchallenged in the West, but in 1810 the news of Astor's efforts reached their ears. Thompson, who had been at Rainy Lake, "going down on rotation" for some leave, rushed back west. He was not, it seems, instructed to reach the mouth of the Columbia before the Astorians, because he carried trade goods with him; his journal for this period has been lost so we cannot be sure. Thompson crossed the Rockies through the Athabasca Pass at today's Jasper, Alberta, in the winter of 1810–11. In early spring, from the upper reaches of the Columbia, he followed a route he knew, up the Columbia, across Canal Flats to the Kootenay River, to the Pend Oreille River, and across to Spokane House on the Spokane River. The latter river

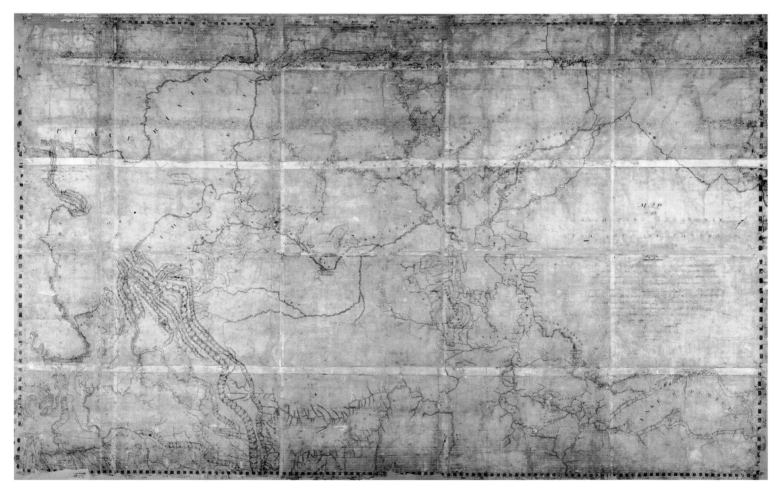

MAP 211.
David Thompson's great map of the West, which now hangs behind a curtain at the Archives of Ontario in Toronto. It is 16½ feet wide and 10 feet high, and has so suffered the ravages of age and light that it is now difficult to read. It was originally drawn with apple gall ink that has browned, and its glued overlaps have discolored. The result of the astronomical fixing of thousands of points across the West, the map was easily the most accurate of its day. Lake Superior is at bottom right. At the left edge, the Fraser hooks to the sea, with the words (illegible here) *Mr Fraser and party returned from the Sortie of the River* at the mouth of the river. Thompson named the Fraser after his friend; Fraser returned the compliment by naming its major tributary the Thompson.

being unnavigable below Spokane, Thompson then went north to the Colville River and emerged at the confluence of that river with the Columbia on 19 June. From here all he had to do was follow the Columbia to the sea, which he did, leisurely, stopping to "smoke with the natives," as he put it, to ensure friendly relations and good trade, not to mention a friendly reception when he came back upriver.

Thompson finally arrived at the mouth of the Columbia on 15 July 1811, only to find Fort Astoria built, and where, he wrote, he was "received . . . in the most polite manner." He had arrived well before Wilson Price Hunt's overland expedition, but had been beaten by sea. Despite his lack of priority, he had found what Alexander Mackenzie had not—a usable route through the Rockies to the Pacific.

The Americans soon lost Fort Astoria. In September 1813, during the War of 1812, John McTavish of the North West Company arrived at the fort with eight canoes. He bore a letter confirming that their supply ship *Isaac Todd* was en route with a British frigate, the *Phoebe,* which had orders to seize the fort. In light of this information, the Astorians, many of whom were British subjects in any case, accepted an offer to purchase the fort and all its supplies. Astorian Gabriel Franchère recorded in his diary: "Situated as we were, expecting from day to day the arrival of an English man-of-war to seize all we possessed, we listened to their proposition," and on 23 October the purchase papers were signed.

As it happened, it was the British corvette *Racoon* that arrived, and its captain, William Black, insisted in ceremonially seizing the fort. It was this supposed *seizure* rather than *purchase* that was used in the American case for sovereignty over the region, achieved in 1846.

Now the British fur traders had seeming control over the northwestern trade, at least for a while. And they would pursue their advantage. When the company merged with the Hudson's Bay Company in 1821, there began a concerted effort to create a "fur desert" in

MAP 212.
One of the Canadians recruited for Astor's American Fur Company was Alexander Ross. When the North West Company took over Fort Astoria in 1813, he, like many others, elected to join the North West Company and continue as if nothing had happened. Ross made many journeys up the Columbia and Snake in the course of his new employment, first as Donald Mackenzie's second-in-command and then on his own account. This large map of the drainage basin of the Columbia was drawn by him in two pieces; the western part is dated 1821, and the eastern part, drawn when he had retired to the Red River Colony, is from 1849. The map is annotated with historical details too numerous to enumerate. On the headwaters of the Snake, *Lewis's River or the Great South Branch* in the bottom right corner, for example, are the notations *Iroquois desert in 1819, six men killed in 1822,* and *Iroquois Robbed in 1824.* The Iroquois, in this case, were hunters with the fur brigades. On the Columbia at the mouth of the short Walla Walla River, close to the Columbia-Snake confluence, is *Establishment in 1806.* This is Fort Nez Percé or Walla Walla. At the mouth of the Columbia (at left) is *Fort Astoria in 1811,* the site of the first fort established by the Astorians. Surprisingly, Fort Vancouver is not marked; it is opposite the mouth of the *Wallamitte* (Willamette River), but *Pt. Vancouver,* the farthest point reached by William Broughton in 1792 (see page 129), is shown nearby.

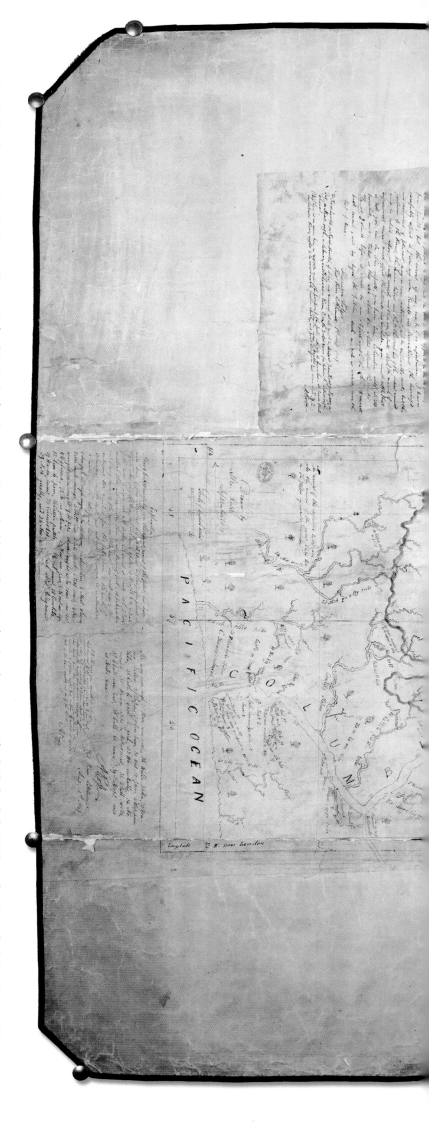

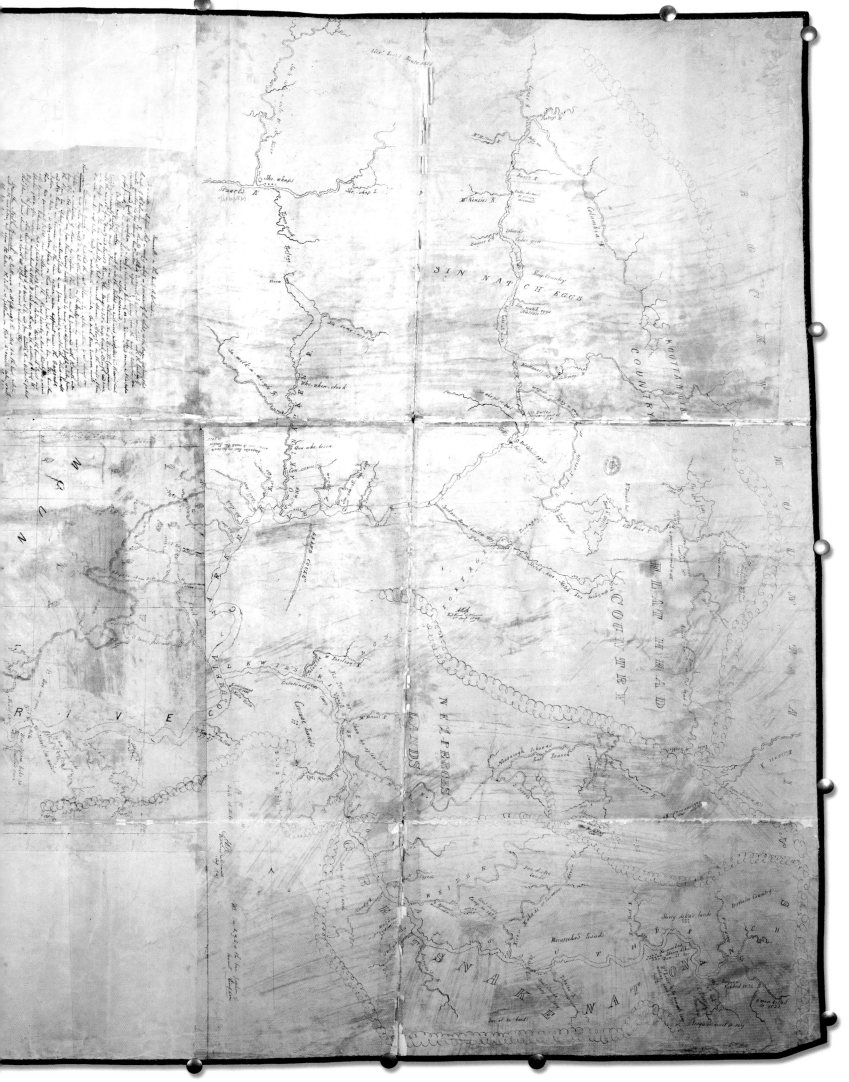

the Rocky Mountains in a vain attempt to keep out American traders by making it not worth their while to impinge on company territory.

Fort Astoria was renamed Fort George. The North West Company men initially found it difficult to go exploring and trapping because of hostile Indians. In July 1814 when Alexander Ross tried to find a more direct route from Fort Okanagan, established in 1811 where the Okanagan River meets the Columbia, to Puget Sound, he was forced to turn back for fear of Indian attack.

The arrival of company partner Donald Mackenzie in 1816 changed this somewhat. Mackenzie won over many of the Indian tribes by his kindness. He saw better than most the potential of the Snake River country and set about organizing things differently. The Indians of this region did not like to trap and the returns were poor, so Mackenzie began a system of "fur brigades" to trap the furs themselves. In the process, the brigades would explore considerably greater areas than they would have if they sat in trading posts waiting for the Indians to come to them. And since the rivers were often not passable, horses would be used. As an advance post, Fort Walla Walla, or Nez Percé, was built in 1818 by Mackenzie and Ross on the Columbia at the Walla Walla River, near the mouth of the Snake. Mackenzie made several expeditions into the Snake country, even going through the Hell's Gate of the Snake. His trapping parties penetrated as far east as Bear Lake, on the Idaho-Utah boundary.

After the North West Company merged with the Hudson's Bay Company in 1821, Snake country brigades operated from Flathead Post at today's Noxon, Montana. One brigade, led by Alexander Ross in 1824, came into contact with a group of American trappers led by Jedediah Smith, and they accompanied them back to the Flathead Post. Of course, Smith noted everything he could about the British operation. For this, Ross was soon retired. It was the opening event in a sequence that would eventually lead to the American takeover of the Pacific Northwest.

The Hudson's Bay Company had a tremendously energetic field governor at this time. George Simpson arrived on the scene in 1821, and it was he who formulated the plan to create a "fur desert" by overtrapping, to keep the Americans at bay. To do this he appointed

MAP 213 (*below*).

The complexity of the interlinked river systems is illustrated well by this map, drawn in 1825 by William Kittson, Peter Skene Ogden's second-in-command on his 1824 first expedition. Ogden left *Fort Flathead* at top left, just right of the compass rose, and went south, crisscrossing the mountain ranges of the Idaho-Montana boundary south nearly to the Great Salt Lake of Utah. Then he returned north, then west up the Snake (left, middle) to *Nez Perces Fort*, on the Columbia, a small section of which is shown. The junction of the Snake and Columbia is not shown because the route left the Snake to take a shortcut up the *Walla River* (Walla Walla River), shown to the immediate southeast of the fort. Kittson's map was the first detailed map of the Snake River system and the Bear River and the first representation of the Great Salt Lake since that of Miera y Pacheco, with Escalante in 1776 (see page 118). In the spring of 1825 Ogden became one of the first to find the Great Salt Lake.

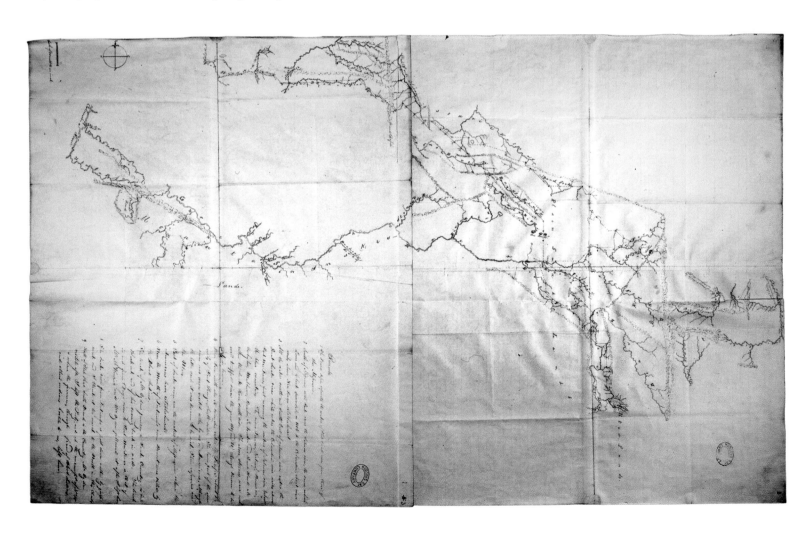

a man with a reputation of brutality and meanness who might otherwise have lost his job permanently when the 1821 merger took place. He was Peter Skene Ogden, by far the greatest of the British fur trade explorers. On no less than six expeditions he explored a large area of the West, and on the final one traveled far from the Snake country, south to the Gulf of California.

Many of Ogden's maps have been lost; on his return in 1830 from his final and most far-ranging expedition all his journals and maps were lost along with nine of his men, drowned in a whirlpool on the Columbia River just before he reached company headquarters at Fort Vancouver (moved from Fort George in 1825–26). Other maps have simply disappeared, but two that have survived, from his first and fifth expeditions, are shown on these pages (Maps 213 and 214). During his fifth expedition, in 1828–29, Ogden found the Humboldt River—he called it the Unknown River—which flows from a point west of the Great Salt Lake west to Humboldt Lake, in the Carson Sinks. This important valley would in 1866 become the route of the first railroad to cross the United States, the Union Pacific. The Humboldt was the nearest an explorer would ever come to finding the mysterious Buenaventura River, originally thought to flow from the Great Salt Lake to the Pacific at San Francisco Bay.

On his sixth and final expedition, in 1829–30, Ogden went much farther south. Again finding the Humboldt, he continued south across the arid Great Basin of Nevada to the Colorado River. There, near today's Lake Havasu City, Arizona, he was attacked by Mojave Indians, repelled by sheer firepower with the death of twenty-six of the attackers. Then Ogden descended the Colorado to the Gulf of California before returning north, entering the San Joaquin Valley over either Tehachapi or Walker's Pass. Near San Francisco Bay he met American fur trader Ewing Young, and they trapped together for some time. Despite the loss of many of his maps and journals, much of Ogden's knowledge of the West did find its way via London to the commercial maps of the day, especially those of Arrowsmith in London and Brué in Paris.

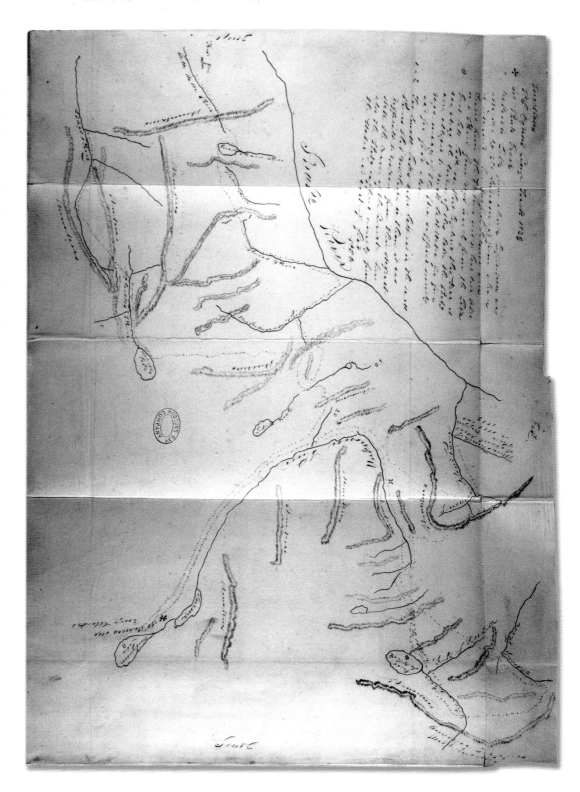

Map 214.

Peter Skene Ogden's map from his journal illustrating his fifth expedition, in 1828–29. For easier interpretation, the map has been oriented here with north (more or less) at the top. Starting from *Fort*, Fort Nez Percé or Walla Walla, at top, Ogden made his way south to *Sylvailles Lake,* Malheur Lake (at left center), and then to the Humboldt River (center), which he has labeled here with the name he gave it, the *Unknown River.* It led to Humboldt Lake in Carson Sink (bottom left), in Nevada just east of today's Reno, and then to the Bear River valley just north of the *Great Salt Lake* (bottom right). Ogden met with hostile natives at Humboldt Lake, where there is the notation (here upside down) *280 Indians seen Camp attacked.* The Salt Lake area is for some reason mistakenly rotated 90°. Relative positions are a little off: correctly Humboldt Lake is about 450 miles south of Walla Walla whereas the Great Salt Lake is about 375 miles south. Ogden's grand sweep of the West in 1828–29 and again in 1829–30 represented the acme of the Hudson's Bay Company's geographical coverage to the south, well beyond that part of the continent ultimately retained by the British. The Ogden River and the city of Ogden, Utah, are named after Peter Skene Ogden.

MAP 215 (*above*).
The imaginary *R. Buenaventura* is shown flowing to the Pacific at San Francisco Bay from *L. Salado* (the dry Sevier Lake) on this commercial map dated 1826. Escalante's Lake *Timpanogos* (the Great Salt Lake) is shown close by, just over a ridge from *Lewis's R. South Branch*, the Snake River.

The British supremacy in the fur trade of the Northwest lasted until the mid-1830s, but ultimately lost out to the incessant erosion of their territory by American traders and trappers. Many of these first came west at the behest of a newspaper advertisement placed in 1822 by General William Henry Ashley, together with his partner, Andrew Henry. Recruiting "enterprising young men," Ashley intended to exploit the fur resources of the Upper Missouri, but found that the various Indian tribes along the river had become so hostile—fourteen men were killed in one battle—that instead he sent his men out overland to the central Rockies. Ashley's recruits included a number who would achieve fame as mountain men: James Clyman, William Sublette, Edward Rose, David Jackson, Hugh Glass, Jim Bridger, and, perhaps the most famous of all, Jedediah Strong Smith, who early on had his scalp and an ear ripped from him by a bear, and who made his men sew them back on. Such was the toughness of the enterprise.

One trapping party was sent south from Fort Henry in 1823, led by John Weber and Jim Bridger, and they met with Smith's group in the valley of the Wind River, hunting buffalo with the Crow Indians. They failed to cross the Divide north of the Wind River Range because of deep snow in early 1824, but with the aid of a map on a deerskin using piles of sand for mountains, the Crow told them of the pass to the south of the range. This was South Pass, first found, again with Indian help, by Astorian Robert Stuart in 1813 (see page 154). Henceforth its existence would become better known, and it would become the principal pass used by settlers pouring in to the Northwest on the Oregon Trail.

Smith went on to trap on the Green River, known to the natives as Seeds-Kee-Dee, returning east later that year, but not before accompanying Alexander Ross back to Flathead Post to the north (see page 158). In another trapping party, in the late fall of 1824 or early spring of 1825, Jim Bridger floated down the Bear River into the Great Salt Lake, becoming one of the first to find it. Bridger thought it an arm of the Pacific because it was salty. Either he or Ogden (see page 158) or Étienne Provost, a trapper coming north from Taos at the same time, seems to have been the first Euro-American to discover the Great Salt Lake (see page 188). As a result of the trapping efforts of these mountain men, the central Rockies became much better known.

Jedediah Smith was back in the Rockies by 1826 and began a series of reconnaissances that were unequaled even by Ogden. In June he explored just west of the Great Salt Lake, looking for the Buenaventura River rumored to flow from the lake to the Pacific. In July Ashley sold his interest in the Rocky Mountain Fur Company to Smith, Sublette, and Jackson, and in August Smith set out south with eighteen men to find new fur trade sources. He marched to the Sevier River of central Utah, then to the Virgin River, which flows into the Colorado near today's Las Vegas (and into the artificial Lake Mead). He then continued south down the Colorado, trading with Mojave Indians before setting out west across the Mojave Desert. Then he traveled north, searching for the Buenaventura, to the San Joaquin Valley, finding an abundance of beaver there. In May 1827 Smith failed in a first attempt to cross the Sierras, going east, due to heavy snow. Leaving his men camped on the Stanislaus River, Smith and only two others struck out east once more, over Ebbetts Pass and down into the Great Basin.

In an epic of exploration history, Smith crossed the arid desert lands in thirty-two days, thirsty and starving, surprising his compatriots at their annual rendezvous on the Bear River of Utah. As if this triumph of survival was not enough, only ten days later he set out again, retracing his route south to the Colorado. This time the Mojave, smarting from recent violence by Taos trappers, attacked Smith's party, killing ten of them.

When he reached California, Smith was arrested by the governor as a spy, but he escaped by ship to San Francisco. Jailed again, he escaped once more and headed north, out of the hands of the Mexicans. Still hoping to find a Buenaventura River, and with it an easy route to the Rockies, he went up the Sacramento River, then to the coast, and north to the Umpqua River. It was 13 July 1828. He learned that the Multnomah, or Willamette, was a short distance farther north. But, camped that day, his men were suddenly attacked by Indians, and fourteen were brutally killed. Smith and three others escaped, stumbling into Fort Vancouver, the Hudson's Bay Company post on the Lower Columbia, in August. At great cost, he had circumnavigated the West, proved, to himself at least, that there was no Buenaventura, and added many details to the map.

At Fort Vancouver Smith drew a map of his travels for John McLoughlin, the chief factor (unfortunately now lost), and in the spring of 1829 met governor George Simpson, whom he managed to convince that the Northwest was unsuitable for American settlement, an opinion diametrically opposed to the one he conveyed to the American government, and which would ultimately encourage American colonization and expulsion of the British.

Smith's maps passed to William Ashley but have all been lost. Nevertheless, much information did find its way onto maps by Arrowsmith and Brué, and one by David Burr, who got the information from Ashley. Perhaps it was Burr who did not return the originals.

Other explorations were made into the Southwest as part of the fur trade by trappers from Taos, including Étienne Provost, who may have been the first to find the Great Salt Lake in the fall of 1824, just before Ogden and Bridger. The most far-ranging of the Taos men

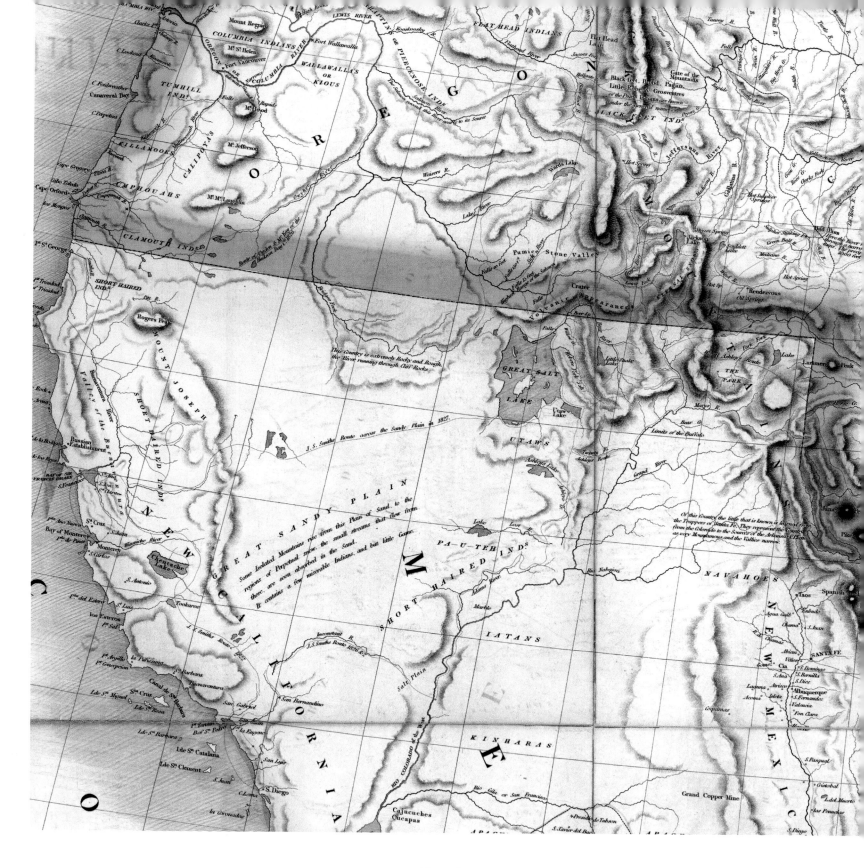

was James Ohio Pattie. With Ewing Young and others he reached the Colorado via the Gila River in 1826, returning up the Colorado and finding the Grand Canyon. In 1830, on another expedition, he reached the Gulf of California.

But from wherever the fur-seekers came, the halcyon days of the western fur trade were all but over by about 1835. Fur had for many decades provided the impetus for the exploration and opening up of large swaths of the West to Euro-American knowledge, but henceforth, exploration would largely be to find routes for settlers coming west, for the military, and then for railroads.

MAP 216.
Part of a map of the United States published by David Burr, official cartographer of the House of Representatives, in 1839. It uses information from now lost maps by Jedediah Smith, whose routes are marked all over the West. In many cases, the exact routes are not known, and Burr's map is all that we have left to go on. *Inconstant R.* marks Smith's route, twice traveled, across the Mojave Desert. *J. S. Smith's Route across the Sandy Plain in 1827* shows his epic trek across the Great Basin with only two other men. His route north to Fort Vancouver is also marked by a dashed line but not annotated. The Sacramento is named the *Buenaventura*, flowing from the north, not the east. Note the *Russian Establishment* near San Francisco; this is Fort Ross, built by the Russians in 1812. It lasted until 1842.

Explorations in Russian Alaska

In the late eighteenth century Russian fur traders and explorers had slowly advanced east along the Aleutian chain. The traders were independents, but in 1799 one group, led by Grigorii Shelikov, emerged as the strongest and was granted a monopoly by the tsar. Thus was born the Russian-American Company, Russia's answer to the Hudson's Bay Company of Britain. The company's influence would spread, and explorations would be commissioned by it, up to the 1840s. After that, as official Russian interest in Alaska declined, so did the enthusiasm of the company for new projects, including exploration. At its peak the Russian-American Company had posts as far south as San Francisco and Hawaii. Its headquarters in North America were at Novo Archangel'sk, today's Sitka.

The coast was of most interest to the Russians. Between 1787 and 1793, the expedition of Joseph Billings, one of Cook's men engaged by the Russians, and Gavriil Sarychev, a naval officer, had mapped the North Pacific and Bering Strait, reducing the number of supposed islands previously thought to exist in these seas. Then in 1804 Urei Lisianskii arrived in Alaska, on a leg of a circumnavigation intended to belatedly rival those of Cook, Malaspina, and La Pérouse. He explored the coast in detail and produced maps of his surveys.

Lisianskii's voyage was the first of a long line of such voyages to Alaska. Some explored a lot, some not at all. One that did was that of Otto Kotzebue in 1816. On 1 August, just north of Bering Strait, he found the entrance to a large inlet, which he took to be the Northwest Passage. But it was not; it was but a huge bay, now named Kotzebue Sound (Map 218, *right, top*), the last great inlet to be found on the west coast of North America.

Another expedition of note is that of Fedor Lütke in 1826. He explored and mapped details of the west coast of Alaska , but his was also a scientific expedition. His scientists produced more than 1,250 drawings and sketches, took meteorological observations, and collected thousands of animal specimens—amphibians, crustaceans, insects, and birds—plus 2,500 plants and 330 rock samples.

Inland exploration was less extensive. Russian-American Company men Andrei Glazunov and Semyon Lukin found the mouth of the Yukon River in 1833, the year a post was established on St. Michael Island close by, but an attempt to reach Cook Inlet the following year failed. In 1838 Petr Malakov ascended the Yukon as far as the Koyukuk River, building a post at Nulato the next year.

Map 217 (*below*).
Russian Alaska as drawn by Vasili Berkh, one of Urei Lisianskii's officers. The coastal part was surveyed in 1804, but the map was not published until 1821. Russian territory is shown as extending to Hudson Bay, which is depicted too far west.

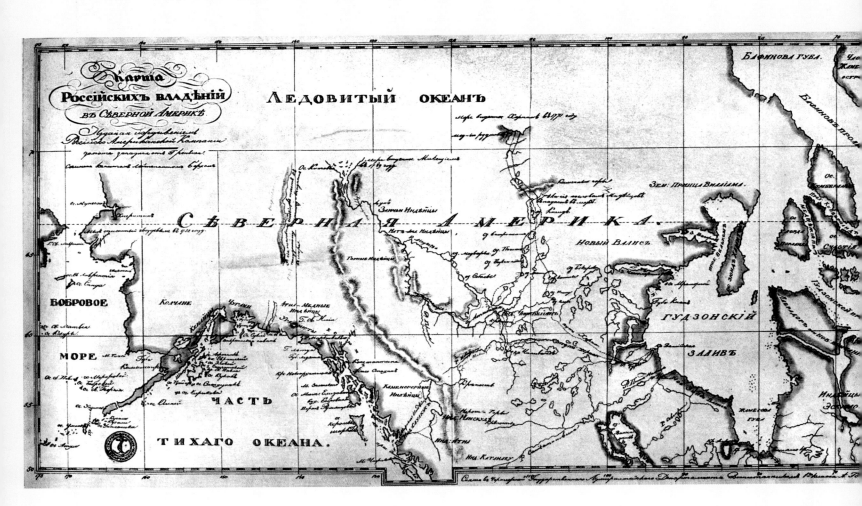

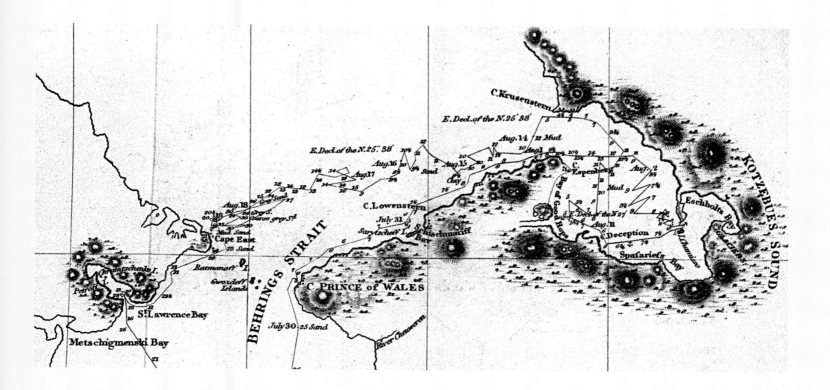

In 1842–43 Lavrentiy Alekseyevich Zagoskin was commissioned to trace the whole course of the Yukon River, the headwaters of which were reported by the natives to lie west of the Rockies. The river's difficult course, so far to the north and west of the coast it was initially so near, would eventually be traced by Hudson's Bay Company men in 1851 (see page 172). Zagoskin set out from Fort Saint Michael at the end of 1842, wintered at Nulato, then followed the river east in June 1843. Unfortunately for him, Zagoskin used a skin-clad umiak, and it proved difficult to handle and leaky. Although he intended to trace the Yukon to its source, he only got as far as today's Ruby, Alaska, still a thousand miles from the river's source.

Only much later, in 1863, did Lukin reach the Porcupine River, but then found that the rival Hudson's Bay Company had already built Fort Yukon there.

MAP 218 (*top*).
Otto Kotzebue's map of his sound, which he found just north of Bering Strait in 1816.

MAP 219 (*right*).
Lavrentiy Zagoskin's map of the lower part of the Yukon River, from his exploration of 1843. Zagoskin explored as far as today's Ruby, Alaska. The Yukon is the northern of the two long rivers shown; the southern one is the Kuskokwim. The Koyukuk River is shown at the top.

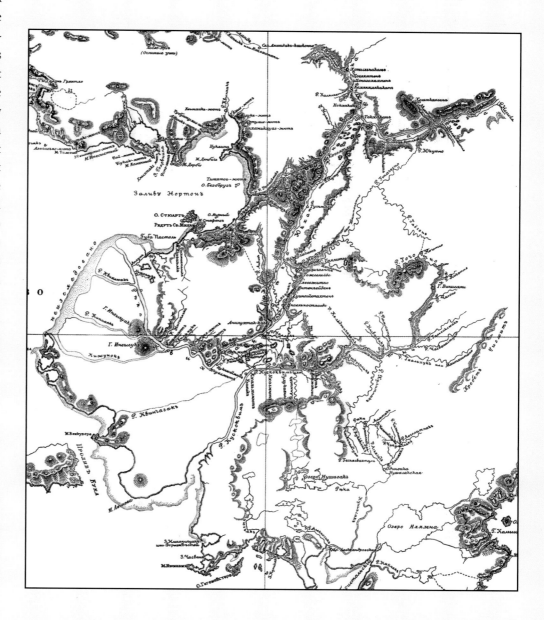

The Revealing of Arctic America

The dream of a navigable Northwest Passage across the top of North America was resurrected by the British in 1817. Numerous reasons were behind this resurgence of interest. Reports of unusually ice-free Arctic seas had come in from whalers, the result of the varying nature of the ice pack. Theories of ice-free seas once away from land still persisted. A £20,000 reward for the finding of a Northwest Passage, first offered in 1745, was extended to naval vessels, and applied to any passage north of 52° N. There were reports of Russian attempts to find a passage from the west (Otto Kotzebue in 1816, see *previous page*). And with the end of the Napoleonic Wars, a huge body of underemployed naval officers were living on half-pay, all anxious for sea service—any service. What better pursuit could there be, thought John Barrow, second secretary to the Admiralty, than the finding of a the long-sought passage for the glory of England? It was he who orchestrated the British effort to find and conquer the Northwest Passage. In the process many of the myriad islands of the Arctic Archipelago were found. Today, because of their British discovery, they are part of Canada.

In 1818 John Ross and William Edward Parry sailed into Davis Strait and began probing for outlets to the west. They found the possible passages originally discovered by William Baffin and reached

78° N, but could not enter Smith Sound because of ice. The ships then turned south along the Ellesmere Island shore, finding Jones Sound, then Lancaster Sound. It was here that Ross made a mistake that was to haunt him for the rest of his life. He believed that he saw a range of mountains at the head of the inlet and marked this on his

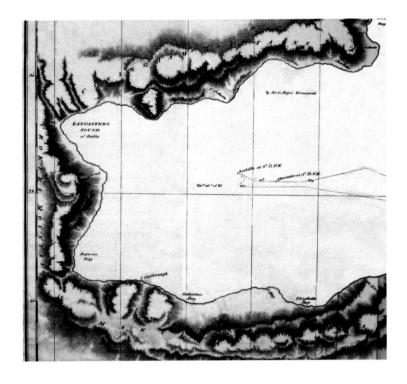

MAP 221 (*above*).
One of the most famous mistakes of exploration history is shown in John Ross's map of Lancaster Sound as a bay, complete with *Crokers Mountains* right across the inlet, the true eastern entrance to the Northwest Passage.

MAP 220 (*below*).
The northern part of Aaron Arrowsmith's great map of North America, 1802 edition, shows the extent of knowledge at the beginning of the nineteenth century, on the eve of the British expeditions beginning in 1818. Samuel Hearne's Coppermine River and Alexander Mackenzie's eponymous river are shown, establishing that there is an ocean or at least some salt water to the north of America, but the maze of channels and islands, ice-filled all, is not yet even hinted at.

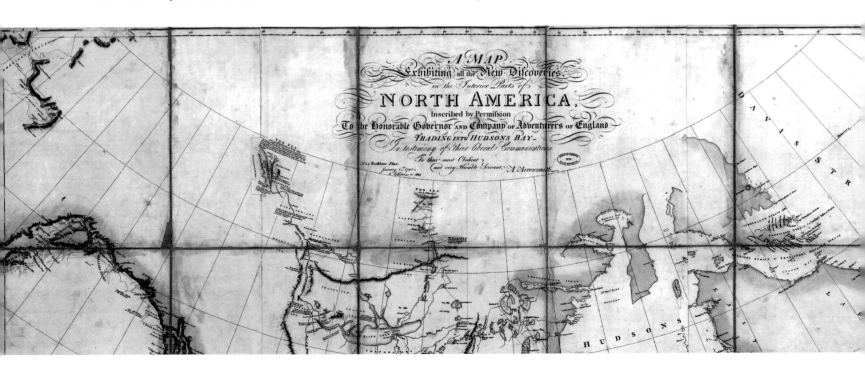

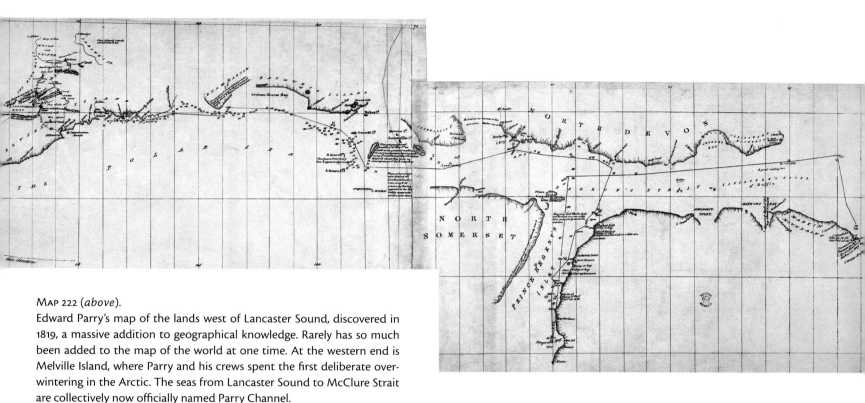

map (MAP 221, *left*). But it was in fact open at the western end, for Lancaster Sound is the true eastern entrance to the Northwest Passage. A mirage cost him fame and glory, and, de facto, his job.

The Admiralty, and even some of Ross's officers, were unconvinced, and Parry was ordered back the next year, without Ross, to investigate. Sailing with two ships directly to Lancaster Sound, he turned west to find not mountains but an open sea, a wide channel Parry named Barrow Strait. The compasses stopped working, for they were too near to the Magnetic North Pole, so they had to resort to unorthodox methods of navigation, such as keeping each ship directly ahead and directly astern in order to sail in a straight line.

The ships got as far west as Melville Island before the short summer ended and encroaching ice forced them into a bay Parry called Winter Harbour. Here they set about surviving the winter. The ships were covered and the gloom of the Arctic night made more bearable by putting on theater, publishing a newspaper, running a school, and promoting physical exercise. A supply of canned food, a new invention, ensured the continued health of the men. In June an exploration inland was undertaken.

It was 1 August before the ships escaped the ice. Parry attempted to sail west once more—he had been instructed to make for Bering Strait—but was stopped by the ice. They escaped back to Lancaster Sound in only six days and returned to England, satisfied with the fact that although they had not passed through the Northwest Passage, they had revealed to the world a vast swath of previously unknown land.

At the same time that Parry had sailed, John Franklin, already the veteran of an Arctic voyage, was given the task of traveling overland to the Arctic coast of North America, with the aim of linking Samuel Hearne's Coppermine River with Christopher Middleton's Repulse Bay, thus to "amend the very defective geography of the northern part of North America." Franklin, who sailed on a Hudson's Bay Company ship in 1819, was accompanied by John Richardson, a naval surgeon, and two midshipmen, George Back and Robert Hood. By the winter of 1820–21 they had a base established north of Great Slave Lake, which they called Fort Enterprise. On 18 July 1821, they reached the mouth of the Coppermine River and proceeded to map the coastline east to the Kent Peninsula, at a place Franklin named Point Turnagain.

In a bizarre sequence of events, Franklin gained fame as an Arctic explorer. Their supplies ran low. Hood was murdered by one of their voyageurs, and when they made it back to Fort Enterprise they were reduced to eating anything remotely edible, including moccasins. They were saved only by the opportune arrival of natives, fetched after an intrepid solo trek by George Back.

On his arrival back in Britain, Franklin was feted as "the man who ate his shoes," and the Gothic tales of hardship were lapped up by an admiring public. His book, published in 1824, was an immediate best-seller.

The next foray into Arctic America was again by Edward Parry. Between 1821 and 1823 he explored to the north of Hudson Bay and found a channel which in theory could be followed west, but which in reality is so ice-choked even at summer's peak that only a modern powered icebreaker would be able to get through. Another possible channel just north of Repulse Bay, Lyon Inlet, was explored and found to be a dead end by Parry's second-in-command, George Lyon. This was Fury and Hecla Strait, named by Parry after his two ships. His second expedition did not produce the spectacular results of his first, but nevertheless mapped considerable areas of territory previously unknown to Europeans.

In 1824, the Admiralty decided to throw four simultaneous expeditions into the effort to find a Northwest Passage. George Lyon

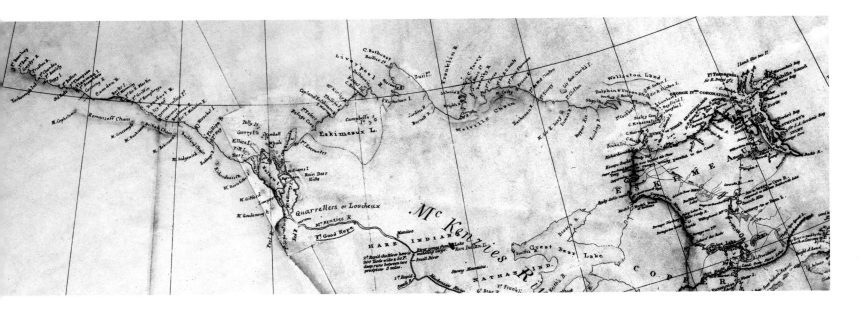

MAP 223 (*above*).
The Hudson's Bay Company copy of an 1824 map by Aaron Arrowsmith, showing the Arctic coast of North America. It has been updated to show information from John Franklin's second overland expedition in 1826, newly explored coastline east and west of the Mackenzie Delta.

was to sail into Repulse Bay and then strike out overland to connect with Franklin's Point Turnagain. But, his ship damaged in a storm, he did not reach Repulse Bay.

Edward Parry was to investigate any westward-leading channels from Prince Regent Inlet, south of Barrow Strait. He spent two years trying to get in and then out of the inlet, such were the ice conditions. One of his ships, the *Fury*, was wrecked at the southeast corner of Somerset Island, at a place still called Fury Beach. Her supplies were unloaded onto the beach and would become a lifesaver for a later expedition. This, Parry's third and last expedition, achieved less than either of his first two.

The third expedition was another overland effort by John Franklin. Again with Richardson and Back, plus Edward Kendall, Franklin left England early in 1825. He was much more careful to ensure his supplies were adequate this time, not relishing the thought of dining on his shoes once more. In 1826 he mapped the Arctic coastline both east to the Coppermine River, thus connecting with his previous survey, and also west, well into the northern coast of Alaska. The latter foray was supposed to connect with the fourth expedition, a ship, the *Blossom*, sent through Bering Strait and along the shoreline from the west. Led by Frederick Beechey, this expedition explored and mapped 140 miles of the northern Alaska coast, leaving only 185 miles of coast unmapped, the section between Franklin's farthest west and his own farthest east.

While all this exploration was going on, John Ross was smarting from his 1818 mistake and the refusal of the Admiralty to give him further employment. In 1829, having persuaded the gin merchant Felix Booth to finance him, Ross outfitted a shallow-draft paddle steamer, the *Victory*, and sailed (for steaming was to be reserved for special circumstances, to conserve coal) for the southern

part of Prince Regent Inlet, where he thought the Northwest Passage was sure to lie. He took with him his nephew James Clark Ross, who would become the foremost Arctic and Antarctic explorer of his day.

Ross intended to sail from Cresswell Bay, the last point mapped by Parry in 1825, to Franklin's Point Turnagain, a plan which overlooked the fact that there was land in the way. As it was, *Victory* became trapped in the ice at the narrow part of the Boothia Peninsula—named after the gin—and was never released. The steam engine, which was constantly giving Ross trouble, was taken out and left on the beach. Making the best of the situation, in 1830 James Clark Ross crossed the peninsula and found King William Island, and the following year he searched for the Magnetic North Pole, finding it on the other side of the peninsula. But by the third year, still trapped, the Rosses realized that desperate measures were needed; they abandoned the ship and trekked north to Fury Beach, finding Parry's abandoned supplies and repairable boats. The ice would not let them leave even Fury Beach that August, and so a building was constructed from wood and canvas insulated with ice, and they hunkered down for a fourth winter in the Arctic. Not until the following summer did they manage to get away, and after an epic effort of rowing and sailing in open boats, reached the entrance to Lancaster Sound, where they hailed a whaling ship. In a final ironic twist of coincidence, the ship turned out to be that which Ross was commanding when he mistook Lancaster Sound for a bay in 1818.

In 1833 George Back mounted a rescue mission for the missing John Ross, descending the Back River to Chantrey Inlet. He did not find Ross, but added more knowledge to the map. It was Back who in 1836 was sent to Repulse Bay with instructions to carry boats through Fury and Hecla Strait and map the coast from there to Point Turnagain. But his ship was caught in the ice north of Southampton Island and was released after a year of drifting, badly damaged. Back struggled across the Atlantic, beaching his ship in Ireland.

Most of the gap in the mapped coastline was filled between 1837 and 1838 by two traders from the Hudson's Bay Company, Peter Warren Dease and Thomas Simpson (MAP 225, *right*). Largely due to

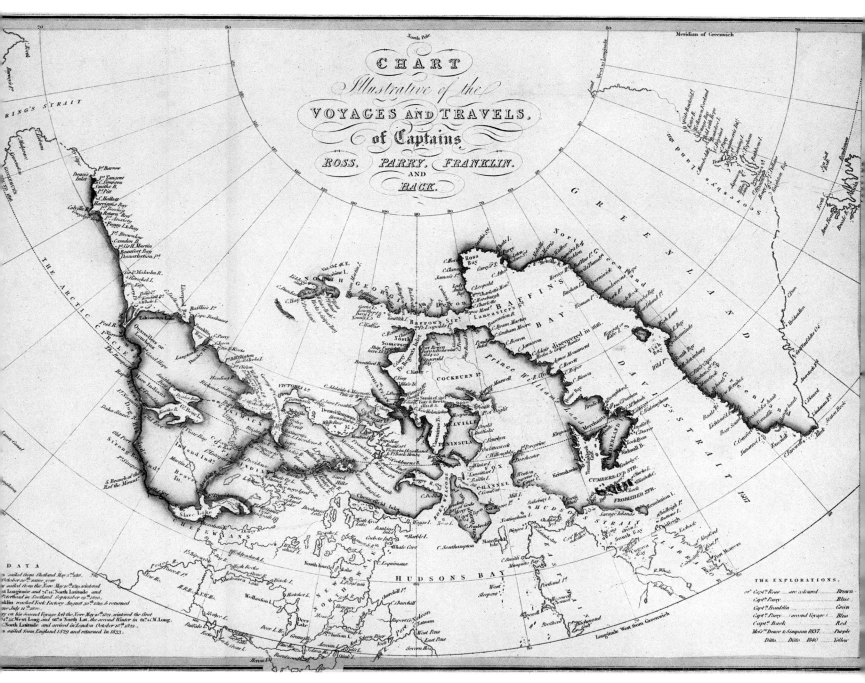

Map 224 (*above*).

A summary map published by John Arrowsmith in 1848, showing discoveries to 1847. John Rae is ignored, although his Committee Bay is shown. The discovery of much of the east coast of Somerset Island and the Boothia Peninsula is attributed to John Ross instead of Edward Parry, from his third voyage. Frederick Beechey's discoveries are not shown as attributed to him. The color key is at bottom right.

Map 225 (*right*).

This Hudson's Bay Company map shows the discoveries of Peter Warren Dease and Thomas Simpson in 1838 and 1839, when they filled in the gap between Franklin's Point Turnagain and the coast mapped by James Clark Ross and George Back.

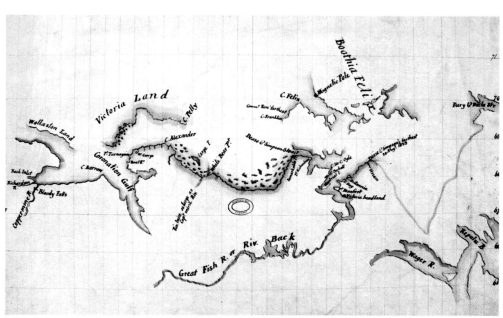

Simpson's energy, they showed that there was a strait between King William Island and the mainland.

Apart from a tiny twenty-mile gap, exploration of the coast eastwards was completed by another Hudson's Bay Company man, John Rae, in 1847; his Committee Bay forms the southern end of the Gulf of Boothia and proved conclusively that this was not the way through the Northwest Passage.

By this time John Franklin had left on what proved to be his final voyage. In 1845, sufficient coast had been mapped, it was thought, that all Franklin had to do was follow it west. But his two ships became trapped in the ice north of King William Island, and everybody aboard perished.

John Franklin holds the dubious distinction of causing a spectacular run of geographical discovery as a result of the failure of his own expedition. After he disappeared in 1845, for more than fifteen years over fifty expeditions were sent into the Arctic to look for him, resulting in a filling in of the map at a speed never to be equaled again. Exploration was not the main object, most of the time, but how could you search in an unknown land without exploring it?

John Richardson, now sixty, and John Rae were first to leave. They searched the coast between the Mackenzie and the Coppermine in 1848, and Rae was back in 1851, searching and mapping for the first time over 600 miles of the southwest and southeast coasts of Victoria Island. In 1848–49 James Clark Ross searched as far as Somerset Island and sent sledge parties down Prince Regent Inlet. Thomas Moore and Henry Kellett, in two ships, entered Arctic waters through Bering Strait, searching to the east and to the west, into Siberia. Two of their men, William Pullen and William Hooper, searched the coast east to Cape Bathurst in small boats over two seasons.

Then in 1850 came the first of two massive efforts by the Admiralty. A virtual armada of ships invaded the Arctic that year, led by Horatio Austin in the *Resolute,* with Erasmus Ommanney in *Assistance,* and two steamers, *Intrepid,* with John Bertie Cator, and *Pioneer,* with Sherard Osborn. They were joined by two private vessels fi-

nanced by public subscription organized by Lady Jane, Franklin's wife, and under the command of William Penny, an experienced whaling captain. Lady Jane also sent out another vessel on her own. The Hudson's Bay Company and Felix Booth helped finance John Ross, with another ship. And the Americans pitched in, sending two ships under Edwin Jesse de Haven and Samuel Griffin. At the same time two ships were dispatched by the Admiralty to enter Bering Strait and search eastwards: the *Enterprise,* under Richard Collinson, and the *Investigator,* under Robert M'Clure, both of which disappeared for three years.

This concentration of resources explored and mapped a large area, but did not find Franklin. Ommanney did find Franklin's 1845–46

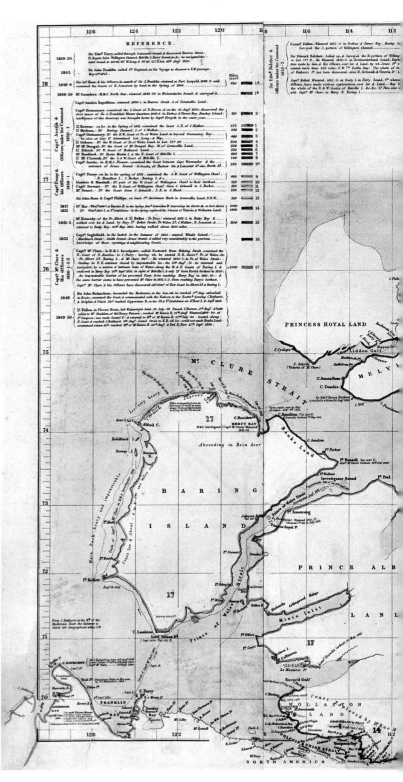

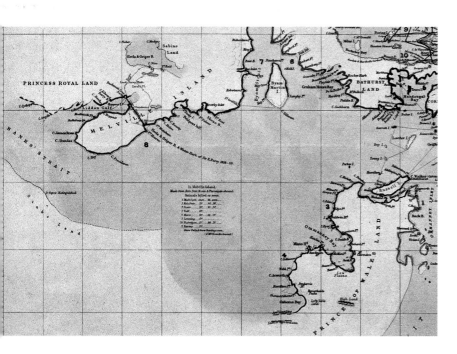

wintering place, on Beechey Island, at the southwest tip of Devon Island, but no clue as to where he had headed afterwards. Elisha Kent Kane, De Haven's surgeon, called it "an incomprehensible omission."

In 1851–52 another private expedition searched the east coast of Somerset Island, and the tiny Bellot Strait, which makes it an island, was found by William Kennedy and French naval volunteer Joseph-René Bellot.

In 1852, a final massive effort was made to find Franklin, with a fleet under Edward Belcher, who proved to be a remarkably inept commander. A huge sledge search that covered an immense area was mounted from four ships: *Assistance,* under Belcher himself; *Pioneer,*

MAP 226 (*below, left*) and MAP 227 (*below*).

John Arrowsmith rushed maps into print to illustrate the new discoveries by those searching for Franklin. MAP 226, published in April 1852, records the work of the Austin armada in 1850–51, and MAP 227, published in November 1853, records that of Belcher's soon to be abandoned fleet in 1852–53, using information brought home by Samuel Gurney Cresswell and others on the supply ship *Phoenix.* The discoveries of Robert M'Clure, in particular, have added much detail to the western archipelago. Most of Belcher's men, plus most of those with M'Clure, would not return until 1854. Now the Arctic Archipelago has mostly emerged onto the map, although many details remain to be filled in and the area farther north is not yet discovered. Note that the date on MAP 227 (at bottom right) is incorrect, the result of too much haste in making the map available to a hungry public.

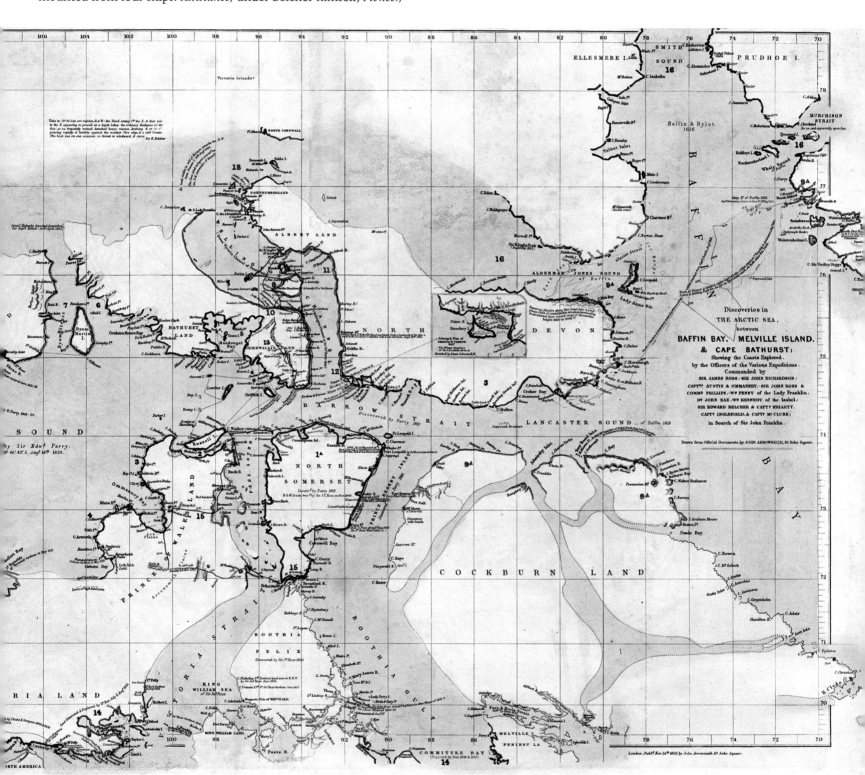

under Sherard Osborn, *Resolute,* under Henry Kellett; and *Intrepid,* under Leopold M'Clintock; plus the supply ship *North Star* under William Pullen. Their explorations are well summarized by John Arrowsmith's 1853 map (MAP 227, *previous page*).

Long trips were made by man-hauled sledge. George Mecham explored Eglinton and Prince Patrick Islands, at the western end of the archipelago, in the spring of 1853, covering an astonishing 1,100 miles, and a similar journey was made by Leopold M'Clintock.

Perhaps the major event of the searches for Franklin was the first transiting of the Northwest Passage, by Robert M'Clure and his men. His ship, *Investigator,* however, did not finish the journey with them, remaining stuck in the ice at Mercy Bay on Banks Island.

M'Clure had entered Bering Strait in 1850 and made stunning progress. After becoming the first to navigate in the Beaufort Sea he had progressed to the northern end of Prince of Wales Strait, between Banks and Victoria Islands. Here the ice stopped him, and a safe haven was found for the winter in the tiny Princess Royal Islands in the strait. The following year he sailed right around the western edge of Banks Island, against the normal eastward-flowing crush of the ice pack, to Mercy Bay, on the north side of the island. Here his ship was trapped.

For two years they waited for summer to release the ship, without success. Sledge parties explored extensively in all directions during this time, leaving a note at Parry's Winter Harbour north across what is now McClure Strait. It was this note that was found late in 1852 by George Mecham, sledging from *Resolute,* anchored at Dealy Island, east along the south coast of Melville Island. The following spring, M'Clure and his men were rescued by a sledge commanded by Bedford Pim, sent by the *Resolute*'s captain, Henry Kellett.

M'Clure wanted to stay with the *Investigator* over another winter, with a volunteer crew, to give the ship one more season's chance at extrication from the ice. Kellett, as the senior officer, at first concurred, but when on 2 May he saw the poor state of some of the crew, "felt that his responsibility would be great if he allowed the zeal of Captain M'Clure or his followers, in fulfilling the requirements of professional honour, to jeopardize the lives of those who had so gallantly done their duty." Kellett arranged for William Domville, the ship's doctor, to examine those who wished to stay aboard *Investigator,* but M'Clure's hopes were dashed when Domville found only four men that he felt were medically able to withstand the

MAP 228.
Robert M'Clure's map of Banks and Victoria Islands, likely drawn towards the end of 1851. *Barings Island* is the name he gave to the region already given the name Banks Land by Parry in 1819–20, being the land he saw to the southwest from Winter Harbour; it is at the top of the island on this map. The track of the *Investigator* is shown, up Prince of Wales Strait to the barrier of ice at its northern end, then right around the west coast of Banks Island to Mercy Bay, on the north coast, where the ship was trapped. The map was brought back to England in late 1853 by Samuel Gurney Cresswell.

rigors of another winter. At this, all the men were transferred to *Resolute* and *Intrepid.* Samuel Gurney Cresswell, one of M'Clure's officers, sledged east to Beechey Island, where he met the supply ship *Phoenix* and sailed to England, arriving with the information including MAP 228 (*above*). He thus became the first person to transit the Northwest Passage. *Resolute* and *Intrepid,* meanwhile, were trapped in the ice, and M'Clure and his men had to wait until 1854 before they could sail for England, not in those ships, however, for the incompetent Belcher ordered them abandoned, over Kellett's protestations. *Resolute,* in an epic all her own, later floated free of the ice and into Baffin Bay, where she was found by an American whaling ship. The American government bought her and presented her as a gift to Queen Victoria.

When M'Clure entered Bering Strait in 1850, he was followed by Richard Collinson in the *Enterprise*. In another Arctic odyssey lasting until 1854, Collinson penetrated the Arctic coast of North America as far east as the east coast of Victoria Island. There he found a note left by the Hudson's Bay Company's John Rae in 1851. Collinson's voyage was highly significant, however, in that he sailed close to the coast along what would become the real Northwest Passage, and the route first transited by Roald Amundsen, in 1903–06 (see page 206).

It was John Rae who found the first evidence of Franklin's demise. Sent to complete the map of the north coast along the southwest base of the Boothia Peninsula, he found articles belonging to the Franklin expedition; even as they fought for their very survival, it seems Franklin's men were lugging his silver plate across the ice.

The final major voyage of the Franklin search era was that of Leopold M'Clintock in the *Fox* in 1857–59. Financed by a persistent Lady Franklin he sledged all the way around King William Island, finding the only written evidence of what had happened, skeletons, and relics.

Another, rather unlikely expedition was undertaken by Charles Hall, a Cincinnati newspaper proprietor, just before M'Clintock returned. He had a false start at Frobisher Bay; in 1861 he determined that it was a bay after all, not a strait, and found relics not of Franklin but of Frobisher. Detained from further exploring efforts by the Civil War, Hall was back in the Arctic in 1869, and this time he trekked to King William Island, finding all manner of Franklin relics, a crest, pieces of a mahogany desk, and, most famously, sawed-off arms and legs that strongly suggested cannibalism. Such, it seems, were the last desperate days of Franklin's men.

Finally, in 1878 an American Geographical Society expedition led by a U.S. Army officer, Frederick Schwatka, journeyed to King William Island to search for journals or other records that might have been placed in cairns by Franklin's men. He found nothing written, but more relics and skeletons showed that the last of Franklin's men reached the American mainland on the Adelaide Peninsula, at Starvation Cove. The probable track of the survivors is indicated on MAP 230 (*right*).

Thus it was that John Franklin, who had already explored a large area of the Arctic while alive, was responsible for the exploration of even more when he was dead. Many details, and the northern archipelago, still lay undiscovered, but the general shape of the northernmost part of the continent was now revealed.

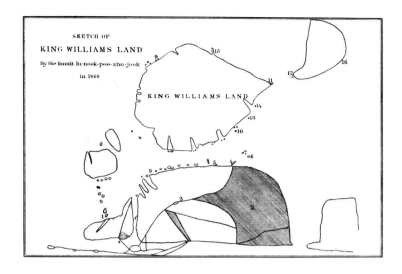

MAP 229 (*above*).
This map was drawn by an Inuit, In-nook-poo-zhee-jook, for Charles Hall in 1869. It was he who had first shown Hall a silver spoon belonging to Franklin. The map shows King William Island and the adjacent mainland coast.

MAP 230 (*below*).
A summary map of all the evidence collected by M'Clintock, Hall, and Schwatka with the likely track of Franklin's men, published by Britain's Royal Geographical Society in 1880. The probable position of Franklin's ships *Erebus & Terror Best Septr. 1846* is shown, together with the drift of the ships in the ice, and *Erebus & Terror Abandoned April 1848*. South of this, the solid red line is the likely track of Franklin's men, while the dashed line is the probable drift of the abandoned ships.

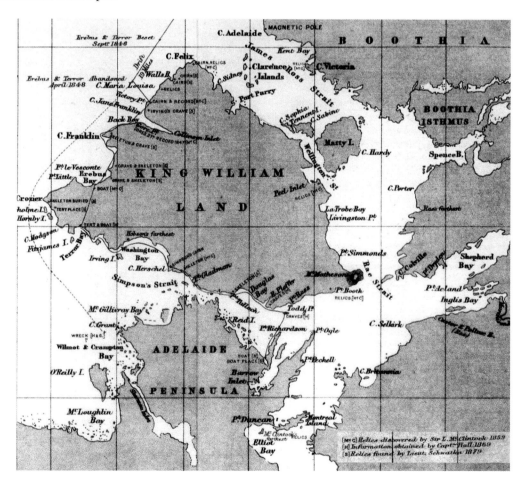

The Flanks of the British Northland

Remaining as blanks on the map until relatively late were the interiors of Labrador and Yukon, at the farthest northeast and northwest of the North American territories claimed by Britain. Both were explored by men from the Hudson's Bay Company.

In Labrador, there appeared little motivation to move inland, and the first tentative explorations, up the Eastmain River from the company's fort of the same name on Hudson Bay, were the result of one man's enthusiasm for adventure as much as anything. James Clouston reached Lake Mistassini by 1816, the lake on the French route up the Saguenay River, and by 1820 had reached the Koksoak River, which flows into Ungava Bay. This was the river later selected by governor George Simpson for a trading post. William Henry reached Ungava Bay in 1828, and in 1830 Fort Chimo was established there. The Little and Great Whale Rivers were explored by George Atkinson in 1816 and 1818, and in 1834 a route between Hamilton Inlet, on the Atlantic coast, and Fort Chimo was found by Erland Erlandson traveling south from Fort Chimo, while looking for a route to the St. Lawrence. In 1839 John McLean, again traveling south, followed the Grand River, which flows into Hamilton Inlet, until he came to a "stupendous fall" higher than Niagara. It was Churchill Falls, site of the modern hydro megaproject.

Labrador was not a profitable region for the Hudson's Bay Company, for the Indians were reluctant to trade and the routes were more difficult than they were worth. Fort Chimo was even shut down from 1843 until 1866, when it could be supplied by steamer.

Yukon, on the other hand, was a rich fur region worthy of company attention—but trading would be facilitated if the river system could be figured out. Expansion into the far Northwest was part of governor George Simpson's plan to increase fur production. Furs from the North would be of a better quality and command higher prices.

In 1823 John McLeod went up the South Nahanni River, which flows into the Liard west of Fort Simpson, on the Mackenzie. He established a trade with the natives of the region and found Virginia Falls, a waterfall higher than Niagara. The following year Murdoch McPherson ascended the Liard itself, finding the upper reaches to be rich beaver country.

About this time, Samuel Black ascended the Finlay River, the northern of the two branches that form the Peace—and the one Alexander Mackenzie had chosen not to follow in 1793. He discovered Thutade Lake, the source of the Finlay–Peace–Slave–Mackenzie River system, 2,360 miles from its mouth. George Simpson thought there might be another river a short portage from the head of the Finlay, paralleling the Mackenzie and flowing to the Arctic Ocean. He was right in a way, but the Yukon River is certainly not a portage away. Instead Black found a westward-flowing river that he called the Schadzue. It was the Stikine River, one of the major rivers of the coastal Northwest. It would have been useful to the company, but Black did not follow it as he had strict orders to look for a north-flowing river. Continuing north, Black came to another river, but it ran eastwards. Black gave up, naming the river the Turnagain. Still called by this name, it is a tributary of the Kechika, which in turn flows into the Liard. Black's difficulties were the first inkling that the rivers of the far Northwest were going to be hard to figure out.

John McLeod explored the headwaters of the Liard in 1831, finding Simpson Lake, on the Frances River, a tributary he thought the main stream. On his return journey down the ferocious upper Liard, his canoe was dashed to pieces and several of his men drowned. Three years later McLeod tried another branch of the river, the Dease, and found Dease Lake and then westward-flowing waters—the Stikine again. This time, however, the company realized its significance, and in 1838 Robert Campbell was sent to establish a communication between the interior and coastal trading posts.

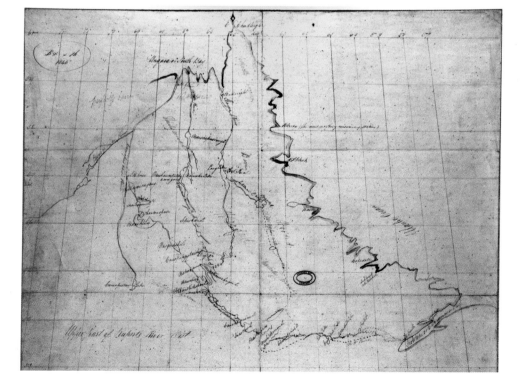

MAP 231 (*left*).
John McLean's map of the eastern half of the Labrador peninsula, drawn in 1840, the year after his expedition down the Grand River to Churchill Falls. The course of the river is drawn flowing into Hamilton Inlet, at bottom right. Fort Chimo is shown, on Ungava Bay at the top of the map.

Map 232 (*right, top*).
Robert Campbell's map showing his discovery of the Pelly River in 1840, later found to be a tributary of the Yukon. The westward-flowing Pelly is on the left third of the map. The Liard flows east from Frances Lake at center right, past the Dease River flowing in from the south.

Map 233 (*right, bottom*).
This 1857 edition of the Arrowsmith map of North America shows the puzzle solved: The *Yukon or Pelly R.*, the Yukon, flows from the Pelly, that unnamed part of its headwaters southeast of *Ft. Selkirk*. The *Lewes R.* is the upper part of the Yukon. *Porcupine R.* flows into the Yukon at Fort Yukon (not shown).

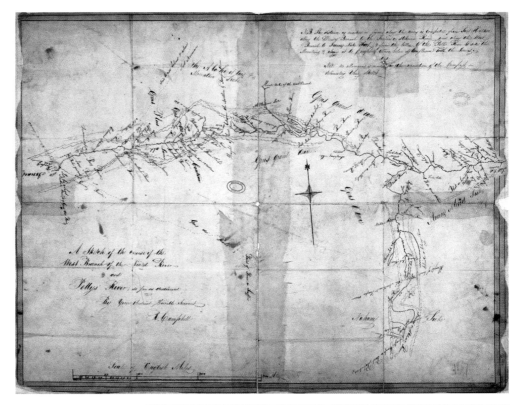

Campbell followed McLeod up the Liard in 1840, finding Simpson Lake, which he renamed Frances Lake after the governor's wife. Just north of the lake he found a short portage that led—at last—to a north-flowing stream, the Pelly River. Campbell did not realize it at the time, but the Pelly flows into the Yukon. Map 232 (*right, top*) shows Campbell's discovery of the Pelly.

In 1842, far to the north, John Bell, at Peel River Post, later Fort McPherson, near the Mackenzie Delta, was looking for a way over the mountains to the west. He found what he was looking for in a river that led to the Porcupine River of northern Yukon and northeast Alaska. In 1844 he followed it to its junction with an even larger west-flowing river, where, in 1847, his senior clerk Alexander Murray founded Fort Yukon. The fort was in Russian territory, a fact that mattered little until the American purchase of Alaska in 1867; in 1869 U.S. Army captain Charles Raymond determined its position and ordered the British out.

Perceptions of the possible river system in the region were confused yet more at this time by the notion that both Bell's Yukon and Campbell's Pelly might be the Colville, which flows to the north coast of Alaska and originates in the northwest corner of Alaska; its mouth had been found by Peter Warren Dease and Thomas Simpson in 1837. It is in reality but a short and relatively insignificant river. Murray was one of those who thought the Yukon must be the Colville, but was surprised to learn from natives at Fort Yukon that it was not. In a sand patch he kept for the purpose, the Indians traced a map of the course of the Yukon to its mouth well west of Fort Yukon.

Robert Campbell built Fort Selkirk on the Pelly where it meets the Yukon. Then in June 1851 he set off down the Yukon—which he did not know was that river—determined to find out once and for all where it led. He likely expected to end up at the mouth of the Colville. But after a short time Campbell came to Murray's Fort Yukon, at the mouth of the Porcupine. Thus it was proven that the river John Bell had discovered in 1844 and Campbell's Pelly River were one and the same; the puzzle of the river pattern in the far Northwest had been solved.

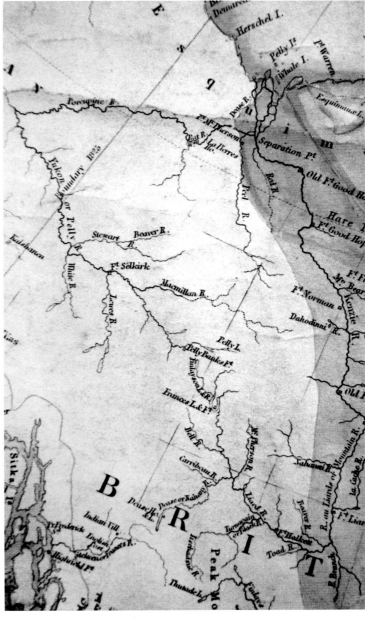

Sources of the Mississippi

Finding the sources of rivers has always held a fascination for explorers, the search for the Nile's perhaps being the most famous, and finding the source of a mighty river such as the Mississippi was clearly going to become someone's goal before long.

The task fell to a geologist, Henry Rowe Schoolcraft, in 1820. In 1818–19 he had been involved in a survey of Missouri as that region approached statehood and the following year explored the area that is now northern Minnesota. He found what he thought was the source of the Mississippi in a lake he named Lake Itasca, a name derived in a rather labored fashion from the Latin *veritas caput*—"true ending." As in turned out, Lake Itasca was not the ultimate source of the river as there was another small stream draining into the lake, but Schoolcraft was very close.

The person who thoroughly explored the Upper Mississippi Basin was a French scientist, Joseph Nicolas Nicollet. He had come to the United States in 1830 following a revolution in his homeland. In 1835 and 1836 Nicollet accompanied Pierre Chouteau of the American Fur Company on a trip up the Mississippi to map its upper reaches. Nicollet was a meticulous observer, and he not only mapped every turn and tributary but also noted the geology and more. He was the first to use fossils to date and correlate geological strata in the exploration of the West, and the first to use a barometer to measure altitudes. (Stephen Long had intended to use barometers but they were broken before they could be used.) Nicollet discovered the true source of the Mississippi.

Nicollet's work came to the attention of the secretary of war, Joel Poinsett, who asked him to work with the new Corps of Topographical Engineers. His second expedition, under the auspices of that organization in 1838, was from Fort Snelling—at the junction of the Mississippi and the Minnesota Rivers and the site of today's Minneapolis—west to the Red Pipestone Quarry near the present-day South Dakota–Minnesota border. Nicollet's assistant on this expedition was the young protegé of Poinsett, Lieutenant John C. Frémont (see page 178). Once again, Nicollet recorded many observations that he could add to his database documenting the hydrography of the Upper Mississippi Basin.

The following year Nicollet led another more wide-ranging expedition, up the Missouri to Fort Pierre (Pierre, South Dakota) and thence to Devil's Lake (now in northeastern North Dakota), across the headwaters of the James River, a tributary of the Missouri, and the Sheyenne River, which flows into the Red River (of the North) near present-day Fargo, North Dakota, and is thus in the Hudson Bay watershed.

On his return from this expedition, Nicollet began work on a monumental map, intended to correlate all his observations with other reliable geographical knowledge. He succeeded in creating a definitive map of the entire Upper Mississippi Basin. By 1842 Nicollet was becoming ill and was passed over for his assistant, Frémont, as leader of a new expedition that year, although Frémont had by this time enlisted the powerful help of Senator Thomas Hart Benton, largely by marrying his daughter. Nicollet had barely finished his map when he died, in 1843. His memorial is his map, a reduced-scale version of which is shown here (MAP 235). Gouverneur Warren (see page 192) called it "one of the most important contributions ever made to American Geography," high praise indeed from one who made a map of the West of which the same could be said. Joseph Nicollet's map was based on almost 2,000 astronomical and barometric observations and showed, he wrote, "more than 300 rivers and new lakes with their relations, the routes of winter and summer, opening all parts of the region to civilization which will soon be knocking at the door." And that was the real reason the government of the time was interested in his map.

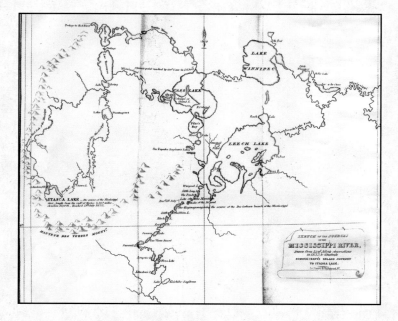

MAP 234.
Henry Rowe Schoolcraft's map of the sources of the Mississippi, published in his book in 1834.

MAP 235 (*right*).
Joseph Nicollet's landmark 1843 map of the Upper Mississippi Basin. This is the reduced-scale version of a two-sheet map published the year before, but still shows the tremendous detail of his work. The reduction was carried out by Lieutenant William H. Emory, who would go on to produce his own detailed maps of regions farther west (see page 182). The headwaters of the Mississippi are in the area of dense lakes to the west of Lake Superior, and the watershed between the Mississippi and Hudson Bay systems is marked just south of Lake Itasca. Devil's Lake is the large lake in the northwest corner of the map. *Fort Snelling*, today's Minneapolis, is shown at the confluence of the Mississippi and the *Peter R. Minisotah* (Minnesota River).

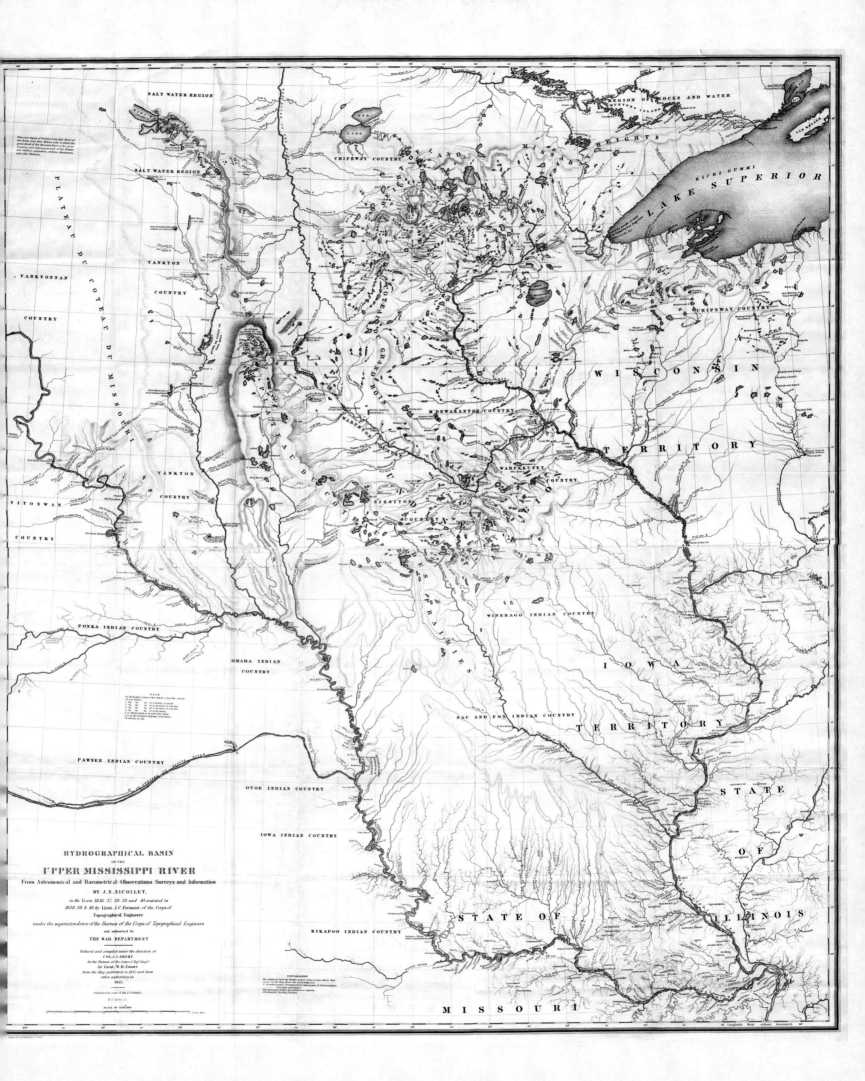

Exploring the Emigrant Trails

The Oregon Trail, that route to Oregon via South Pass traveled by thousands of settlers after the mid-1840s, was discovered by Robert Stuart in 1812 (see page 154) and rediscovered by Jedediah Smith in 1824 (see page 160). In 1832–35 the route was further defined by Captain Benjamin Louis Eulalie de Bonneville of the U.S. Army. No one knows for sure why in 1831 he asked for leave from his army position, but the most likely reason was a combination of a desire for adventure and a desire to make his fortune. Certainly he interested fur traders in New York into financing his scheme and indeed ended up taking no less than 110 men with him, most of whom were to trap for furs. But this may well have been simply his means to an end.

At any rate, when he left Fort Osage, on the Missouri near today's Kansas City, on 1 May 1832, he had with him a range of scientific instruments for fixing his position, so that he could draw accurate maps—except for barometers. The latter, he wrote, "are so clumbsy and so easily broken, that I do not contemplate taking any."

Following what would become the Oregon Trail, Bonneville crossed the Continental Divide at South Pass and reached the Green River, where he built a fort. He was the first to take loaded wagons across South Pass, proving that the route would be suitable for later emigrant wagons. From his Green River base Bonneville dispatched fur-trapping parties—presumably the bills had to be paid—but Bonneville devoted his time to planning, mapping, and exploring. Twice he went down the Snake River himself, but was not allowed to proceed past Fort Walla Walla by the British Hudson's Bay Company men, who either did not appreciate his apparent intent to trap furs on their territory or thought that he was spying on them.

In 1833 Bonneville sent one of his men, Joseph Reddeford Walker, to find the mythical Rio Buenaventura that he thought flowed out of the western side of the Great Salt Lake all the way to the Pacific. Of course, Walker did not find it. Instead he descended the Humboldt River (found by Ogden in 1828–29 and named later by Frémont), which drains much of central and western Nevada to Lake Humboldt and the Carson Sinks. Having run out of river, Walker then searched for a route across the Sierra Nevada. It is thought that he ended up in the Yosemite Valley, becoming the first explorer to see the impressive canyon, with its equally impressive giant redwoods.

On 20 November 1833 the "broad Pacific burst into view"—they had made it to the coast. But Walker realized that the route he had taken to the Pacific was not a practical one for emigrants, and so after resting on the coast he went south looking for an easier way across the Sierras. He found what he was looking for farther down the San Joaquin Valley, a crossing that was both low and easy. Today it is Walker Pass. The route back, across the barren Great Basin, was difficult because of the lack of water. Nevertheless, Walker had found one of the routes that would soon come to be used by immigrants to California.

Walker finally met up with Bonneville again in July 1834, but it was not until the following year that Bonneville returned east, only to find that he was in disgrace for overrunning his allotted leave time. He had added valuable information to the map that would help the United States claim its territory to the Pacific, yet was in trouble for taking too long about it. He did, however, survive a court-martial and was reinstated, eventually becoming a general.

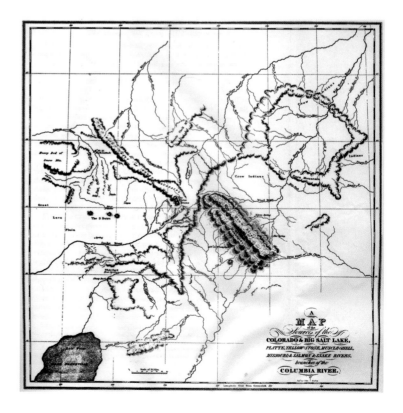

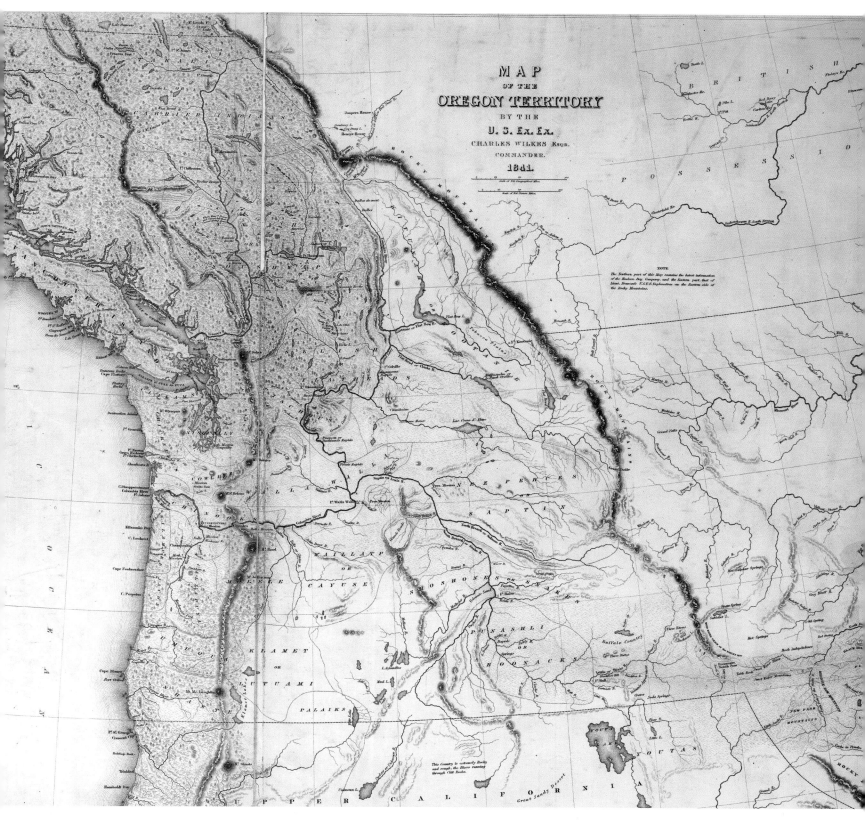

MAP 236 (*far left*).
Bonneville's *Map of the Territory West of the Rocky Mountains.* The Humboldt River is shown as *Mary or Ogden's River,* and the notation *Killed 25 Indians* refers to a battle Walker had with the Paiute. The Great Salt Lake is *Lake Bonneville*, a name that would come to be applied to an ancient and now disappeared lake that once occupied the Great Basin.

MAP 237 (*left*).
Another map by Bonneville, this of the critical region from the Sweetwater River to the Snake, including South Pass at the southern end of the *Wind River Mountains* (Wind River Range, in the middle of the map), and *Salt Water Lake Bonneville* (the Great Salt Lake, at the bottom of the map).

MAP 238 (*above*).
Charles Wilkes's 1841 map of the Oregon Territory, published in 1844. Oregon includes the territory of today's states of Oregon, Washington, and much of the Canadian province of British Columbia. It is the region west of the Rocky Mountains from 54° 40´ N to 42° N. The boundary line between the United States and British territories on the forty-ninth parallel (except for Vancouver Island) would not be agreed upon until 1846.

The first settlers traveled to Oregon along the Oregon Trail in 1836, a missionary group led by Marcus Whitman. The first settlers other than missionaries came over the trail in 1840, and the first wagon train in 1842.

In 1841, the round-the-world United States Exploring Expedition, a naval scientific exploration in the tradition of Cook, Malaspina, La Pérouse, and Lisianski, arrived to study the Oregon Country. Led by Charles Wilkes, the U.S. Ex. Ex., as it was universally known, had found new land in Antarctica—Wilkes Land—before coming to the Northwest.

Wilkes was charged with assessing the country in terms of its use to the United States, and he produced many maps (Map 238, *previous page*, was the summary map) and a multivolume report that included the individual reports of the various scientists of the expedition. The specimens that the expedition brought home from Oregon and the rest of the world formed the basis of the vast collections of the Smithsonian Institution, founded in 1846.

He noted that the Willamette Valley had many "advantages for raising crops, pasturage of stock, and the facilities of settlers becoming rich," but noted "one objection to its ever becoming a large settlement, in consequence of the interruption of the navigation of its rivers in the dry season." He also noted that "the salmon-fishery may be classed as one of the great sources of wealth, for it affords

a large amount of food at a very low price." Wilkes particularly emphasized the excellent harbor of Puget Sound, for one of his ships, the *Peacock,* foundered on the Columbia Bar while trying to enter the treacherous river's mouth. It was this observation that made the United States keen to draw the international boundary, decided in 1846, north of Puget Sound.

The final delineator of the Oregon Trail was John Charles Frémont, an officer in the Corps of Topographical Engineers, and his surveyor-cartographer Charles Preuss. Frémont was the protegé of Thomas Hart Benton, a senator who considered himself the moral successor to Thomas Jefferson as far as the promotion of western expansionism was concerned. It did not hinder Frémont's career when he married the senator's daughter.

In 1842 Frémont was instructed to map the Oregon Trail, determine where to build forts, and locate passes through the Rockies. Between 1842 and 1848 Frémont led a number of expeditions west.

Frémont hired mountain man Kit Carson in 1842 and set off to South Pass, where, with a good sense of the dramatic, he unfurled the American flag on the highest point he could find. His report, published the following year, established his reputation as "The Pathfinder."

That year he was ordered to connect the surveys of Charles Wilkes with his own reconnaissance of 1842, "so as to give a connected survey of the interior" of the continent. And connect he did. Not only did Frémont cross the Rockies at South Pass, he explored the Great Salt Lake region and continued north and west to the Columbia River, which he descended to The Dalles. With winter closing in he turned south down the eastern edge of the Cascades, then down the eastern flanks of the Sierra Nevada and traversed the Great Basin along its western edge, all in a last effort to make sure there was no Buenaventura River flowing to the Pacific. In a monthlong epic march through deep snow, they passed over Truckee Pass and into the Sacramento Valley, to Sutter's Fort. The route is shown on Map 240.

Here Frémont stayed until late March, when he traveled south down the San Joaquin Valley, crossed the Sierra Nevada at Tehachapi Pass (which Frémont thought was Walker Pass), and trekked north-

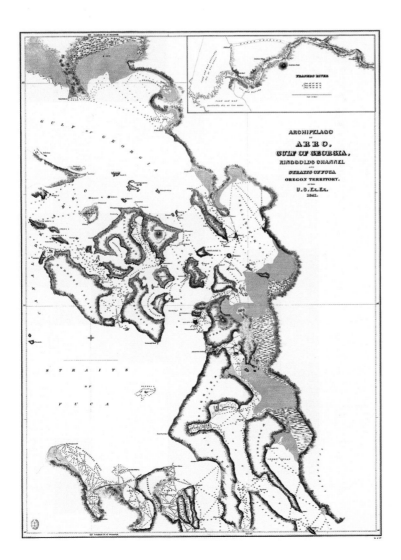

Map 239 (*left*).
The U.S. Ex. Ex. map of the eastern end of the Strait of Juan de Fuca, the San Juan Islands (the *Archipelago of Arro*), and Admiralty Inlet, the entrance to Puget Sound. Wilkes considered it critical that Puget Sound become part of the United States given the hazards of the Columbia and changed many of George Vancouver's place-names to American ones.

Map 240 (*right*).
This remarkably accurate map of the West, drawn and surveyed by Charles Preuss, appeared in Frémont's 1845 published report on his expedition of 1843–44. It was the first complete map of the West with scientific accuracy, and Preuss mapped only those parts that he had actually surveyed, with one notable exception: Utah Lake was assumed to be part of the Great Salt Lake. A cartographic landmark, it guided thousands of settlers west and fathered a number of commercial map copies that furthered its influence.

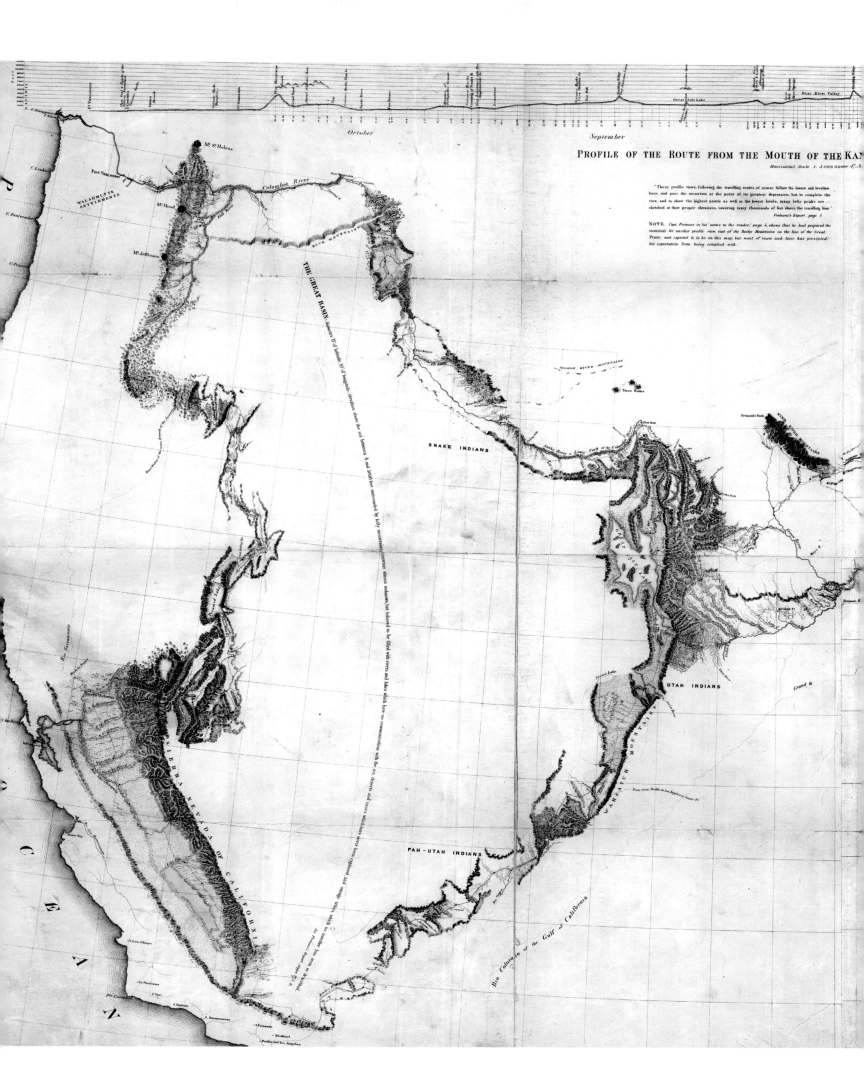

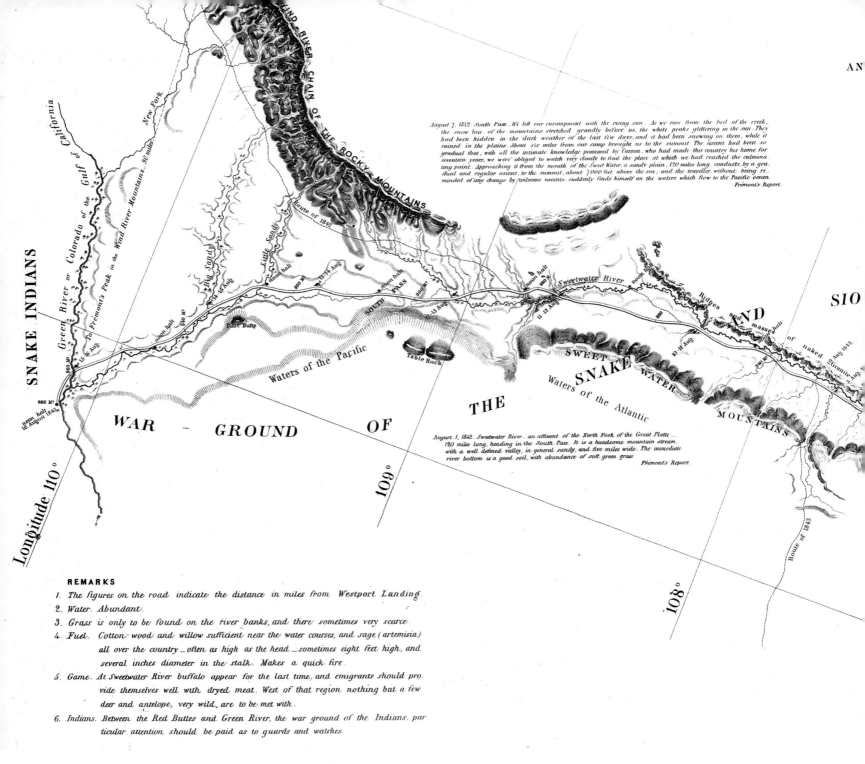

August 7, 1842. South Pass. We left our encampment with the rising sun. As we rose from the bed of the creek, the snow line of the mountains stretched grandly before us, the white peaks glittering in the sun. They had been hidden in the dark weather of the last few days, and it had been snowing on them, while it rained in the plains. About six miles from our camp brought us to the summit. The ascent had been so gradual that, with all the intimate knowledge possessed by Carson, who had made this country his home for seventeen years, we were obliged to watch very closely to find the place at which we had reached the culminating point. Approaching it from the mouth of the Sweet Water, a sandy plain, 120 miles long, conducts, by a gradual and regular ascent, to the summit, about 7000 feet above the sea; and the traveller, without being reminded of any change by toilsome ascents, suddenly finds himself on the waters which flow to the Pacific ocean.
Frémont's Report.

August 1, 1842. Sweetwater River. an affluent of the North Fork of the Great Platte. 120 miles long, heading in the South Pass. It is a handsome mountain stream, with a well defined valley, in general sandy, and five miles wide. The immediate river bottom is a good soil, with abundance of soft green grass.
Frémont's Report.

REMARKS

1. The figures on the road indicate the distance in miles from Westport Landing.
2. Water. Abundant.
3. Grass is only to be found on the river banks, and there sometimes very scarce.
4. Fuel. Cotton-wood and willow sufficient near the water courses, and sage (artemisia) all over the country — often as high as the head — sometimes eight feet high, and several inches diameter in the stalk. Makes a quick fire.
5. Game. At Sweetwater River buffalo appear for the last time, and emigrants should provide themselves well with dried meat. West of that region nothing but a few deer and antelope, very wild, are to be met with.
6. Indians. Between the Red Buttes and Green River, the war ground of the Indians. particular attention should be paid as to guards and watches.

eastward, paralleling the Colorado, to Utah Lake, which he thought the southern part of the Great Salt Lake. After a wide sweep through what is now northwestern Colorado, he found the headwaters of the Arkansas River, arriving at Bent's Fort on that river on 1 July.

The following year Frémont received orders to explore the Red River, but he chose to ignore them, heading instead to California, where he became leader of a group of American settlers in a revolt against the Mexican government, which led to the declaration of the California Republic and then to annexation by the United States. Despite his crucial role, Frémont was court-martialed for disobeying his orders. Disgusted, he resigned from the army. Map 242 (right) was the result of his 1845 travels, and it combines Frémont's information with that of others, notably Charles Wilkes. The result is another landmark map of the West, perhaps the first to look more like a modern map.

MAP 241 (above).
Part of one of the seven sectional maps produced by Charles Preuss in 1846 to delineate the Oregon Trail in some detail. This part shows *South Pass* and the Continental Divide with its *Waters of the Atlantic* on the east and *Waters of the Pacific* on the west. The Wind River Range is to the north. Each part of the trail map contained remarks intended to help emigrants, such as the ones here that note the abundant water, availability of grass for the horses and cattle, and the cottonwoods, willows, and sagebrush, which *makes a quick fire.* An amazing ten thousand copies of Preuss's map were ordered by Congress to facilitate migration to Oregon.

Map 242 (right).
Frémont's important comprehensive map of the West, published in 1848, reflects his travels and surveys from 1842 to 1845 and incorporates information from other sources, especially the Charles Wilkes U.S. Exploring Expedition to Oregon in 1841. New north and south boundaries of the United States are shown on this map.

In 1848 Frémont led the first of two private expeditions intended to locate and survey a route for a railroad, but both were disasters. In the first, after ascending the Arkansas, he became lost in the San Juan Mountains of southwest Colorado and, in deep snow, ten of his men perished. Despite this, and charges of cannibalism among his men, Frémont, ever the optimist, branded the expedition "entirely satisfactory." But there is no doubt that privately, he failed to achieve a fraction of that which he had achieved while under army command. Considered in his time one of the greatest American explorers, Frémont ran unsuccessfully for president, and made and lost millions investing in railroads. For a time, the public loved him, but after the Civil War he was largely forgotten. Nevertheless his pioneering maps, aided by the meticulous work of Charles Preuss, his surveyor on his first expeditions, live on as his legacy.

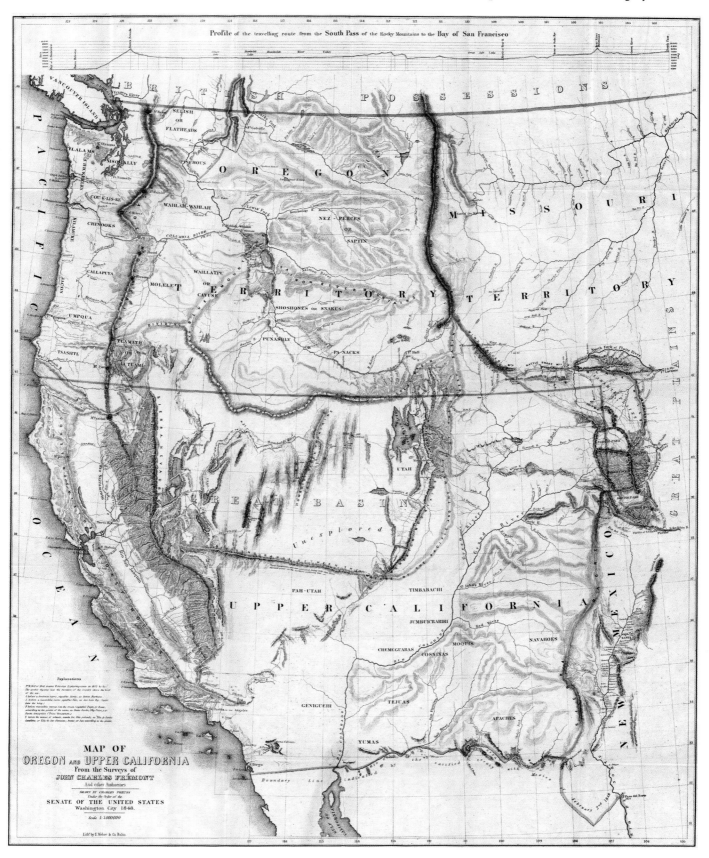

Southwest Military Surveys

With the Mexican War of 1846–48 came a considerable increase in army exploration in the Southwest, activity that continued after the war as the availability of accurate maps became more critical. Army surveying would soon expand to include railroad surveys for a number of possible routes west. In 1846, most of the invading armies had complements of Topographical Engineers with them. The Army of the West—actually but three hundred men—led by General Stephen Watts Kearny, was accompanied by Lieutenant William Hemsley Emory, a man destined to carry out the most accurate mapping of much of the Southwest performed to that time.

Although Emory had been instructed to act as a normal soldier when necessary, he determined that whenever "more immediate military demands" were not interfered with, he and his men "should be employed in collecting data which would give the government some idea of the regions traversed." And this they did, very well.

Kearny's army, initially about 1,600 men, set out from Bent's Fort on the Arkansas on 2 August 1846, took Sante Fe, and then with just three hundred marched southwards along the Rio Grande. Here it was learned from Kit Carson that California had fallen, and so Kearny continued west with only one hundred men. Emory's contingent was now only fourteen, and twelve of them were civilians.

During the journey down the Gila River, Emory discovered and carried out archeological investigations of ancient Indian villages. His book would bring the ancient civilizations of the Southwest to the attention of the American public for the first time. Emory astronomically fixed a number of locations along the route, including that of the junction of the Gila with the Colorado. But most of all he produced a map that was the most accurate to date (MAP 243), engraved and published by Congress in 1847, a map to the newly acquired Southwest, the spoils of the Mexican War.

The "more immediate military demands" referred to in Emory's instructions came into play more than once, notably when, having reached California, Kearny's force attacked Mexican Californios at the Battle of San Pascual, near San Diego, on 6 December. Emory came to the rescue of a beleaguered Kearny, saving him from certain death. It was probably the last time an explorer or surveyor of the West came into armed conflict with Mexicans. The battle's location is shown on the map, but the exact site is not now known.

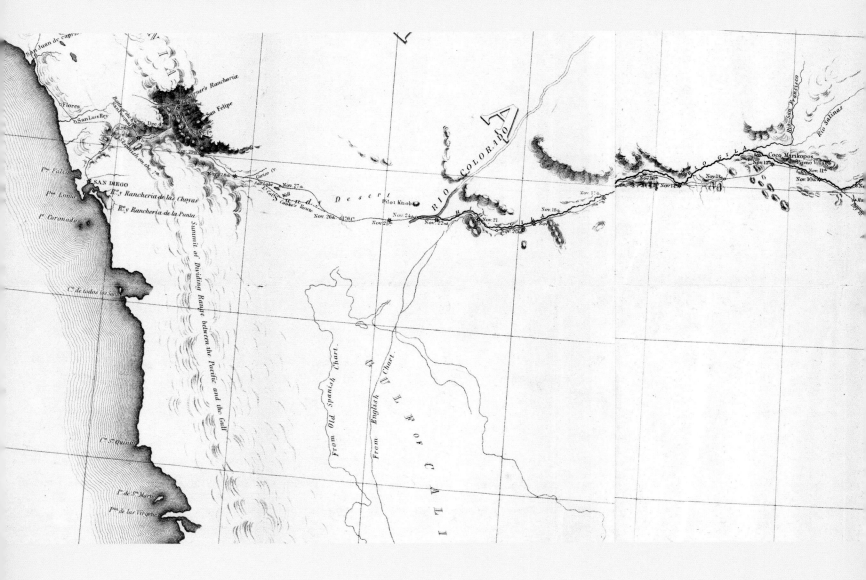

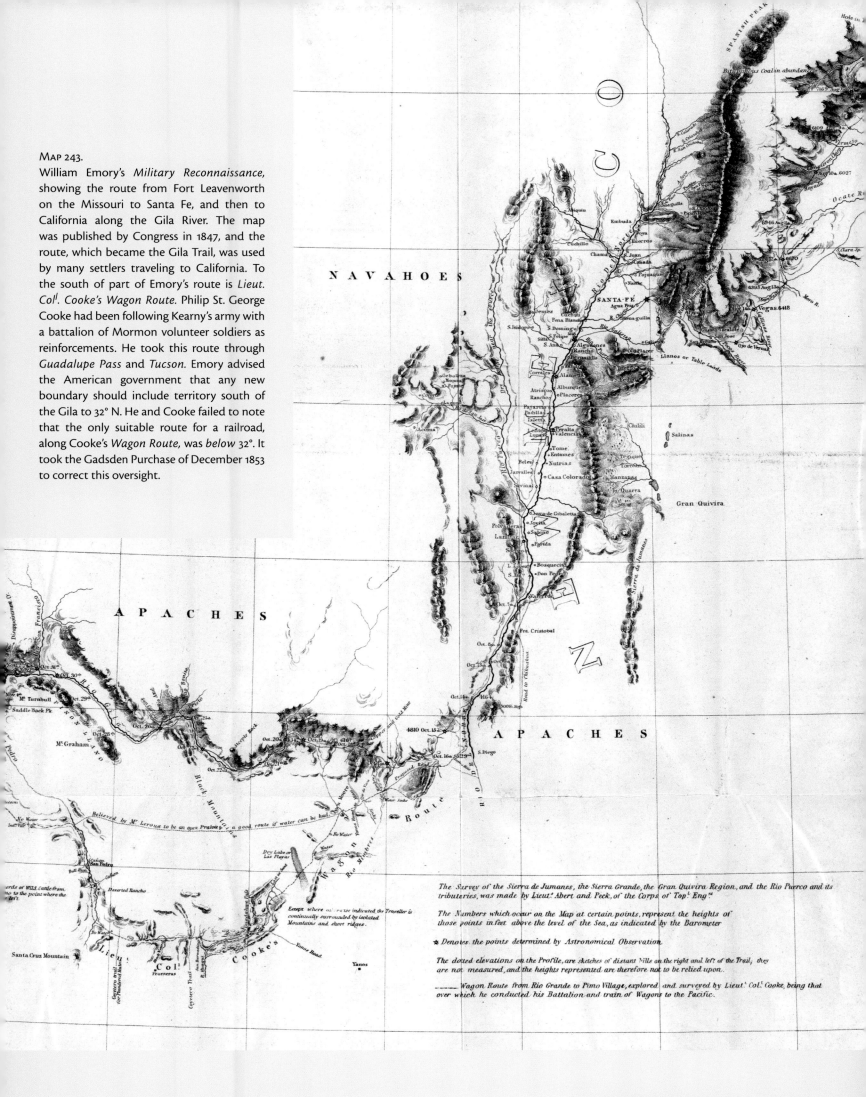

Map 243.

William Emory's *Military Reconnaissance*, showing the route from Fort Leavenworth on the Missouri to Santa Fe, and then to California along the Gila River. The map was published by Congress in 1847, and the route, which became the Gila Trail, was used by many settlers traveling to California. To the south of part of Emory's route is *Lieut. Col!. Cooke's Wagon Route.* Philip St. George Cooke had been following Kearny's army with a battalion of Mormon volunteer soldiers as reinforcements. He took this route through *Guadalupe Pass* and *Tucson.* Emory advised the American government that any new boundary should include territory south of the Gila to 32° N. He and Cooke failed to note that the only suitable route for a railroad, along Cooke's *Wagon Route,* was *below* 32°. It took the Gadsden Purchase of December 1853 to correct this oversight.

The Survey of the Sierra de Jumanes, the Sierra Grande, the Gran Quivira Region, and the Rio Puerco and its tributaries, was made by Lieut! Abert and Peck, of the Corps of Top! Eng!

The Numbers which occur on the Map at certain points, represent the heights of those points in feet above the level of the Sea, as indicated by the Barometer

★ *Denotes the points determined by Astronomical Observation*

The dotted elevations on the Profile, are sketches of distant hills on the right and left of the Trail, they are not measured, and the heights represented are therefore not to be relied upon.

—————— *Wagon Route from Rio Grande to Pimo Village, explored and surveyed by Lieut! Col! Cooke, being that over which he conducted his Battalion and train of Wagons to the Pacific.*

Emory's book on his survey is considered one of the gems of exploration literature for, like Frémont, he was a good writer. While in the Peloncillo Mountains along the Gila, for example, he wrote that "the high, black peaks, the deep, dark ravines, and the unearthly looking cacti, which stuck out from the rocks like the ears of Mephistopheles, all favored the idea that we were now treading on the verge of the regions below." Emory drew attention to the aridity of the region, pointing out that agriculture would be impossible without irrigation. He also noted that the environment would not allow slavery to be profitable.

Emory went on to command the Mexican Boundary Survey of 1850–57, where, for obvious reasons, accuracy was even more important. Disagreements over the definition of the boundary led to the Gadsden Purchase in December 1853 of the area south of the Gila River, giving the United States the southern boundary it has today.

The government realized that at least a road, and ultimately a railroad, was necessary to connect with California and hold in check the deprivations of the Comanches and Apaches, which had become an American responsibility in the treaty with Mexico. The chief of the Topographical Engineers, Colonel John J. Abert, thought the "integrity of the Union" was at stake, and he was probably right. Thus Abert ordered surveys to find suitable routes.

In August 1849, Lieutenant Colonel John M. Washington left Santa Fe on a punitive expedition against the Navajo, who had been raiding settlements. With him went Topographical Engineer James Hervey Simpson, newly arrived in Santa Fe accompanying

Randolph Barnes Marcy, exploring for and surveying a wagon road from Fort Smith, Arkansas, to Santa Fe.

In Chaco Canyon of what is now central Colorado, Simpson and his two assistants found ten ancient pueblos of the Anasazi, the largest group of Indian pueblos in North America. Farther west, and after a

MAP 244 (*left*).
Part of the map by Lorenzo Sitgreaves showing the middle Colorado River, explored and surveyed in 1851. It was published in his report the following year.

Above is Richard Kern's drawing of the spectacular pueblos in the Canyon de Chelly, in Colorado. It is a lithograph based on a drawing he made in September 1849, while under armed guard to ensure his safety from the Navajo.

MAP 245 (*right, top*).
Map of the route of John Washington's troops with Topographical Engineer James Simpson in 1849. They discovered ancient pueblos of the Anasazi.

At *right* is a painting entitled *The Needles* by J. J. Young from a sketch by geologist John Strong Newberry, who accompanied the expedition of John Macomb in 1859.

skirmish with the Navajo, they were in the Canyon de Chelly, home of outstanding prehistoric pueblos. Simpson examined them accompanied by a guard of sixty soldiers. Expedition artist Richard Kern was able to record some of them (*left*). Kept from Euro-American eyes by the fierce Navajo, these treasures were only revealed by force.

The return to Santa Fe was by a route down the Zuñi River to Albuquerque, and Simpson thought that this route might connect with the Colorado River well enough to provide a path for a railroad. This suggestion was followed up in 1851 by an expedition led by Captain Lorenzo Sitgreaves. With fifty men including a naturalist, Sitgreaves pushed west from Albuquerque up the Zuñi, then the Little Colorado, before cutting across to the Colorado, which they descended to Fort Yuma, then crossed the desert to San Diego.

Although they reached California, the route was not promising for a railroad, and Sitgreaves was continually ambushed by Indians. Even fifty men, it seems, were not enough to ensure safety. Sitgreaves also found more ancient Indian ruins, those of the Wupatki in Arizona.

By 1853 Congress had recognized that Abert was right and authorized a blitz of railroad surveys, designed once and for all to determine a suitable route west (see page 190).

Several other notable explorations were carried out by army men in the Southwest before the Civil War. They were prompted by a brief clash in 1857 between the United States and those who wanted to establish an independent Mormon state, Deseret, in the West.

Late that year, another Topographical Engineer, Joseph Christmas Ives, was sent up the Colorado to search for a water supply route to the Great Basin. With him went a geologist, John Strong Newberry; a topographer, Frederick von Egloffstein; and an artist, Heinrich Balduin von Möllhausen, who together

Another exploration, for a wagon road supply route to the Mormon region, was that by James Simpson in 1859. He explored from Camp Floyd in Utah across the Great Basin to Carson City, on the eastern flank of the Sierra Nevada (Map 247, *right*). His route shortened the distance from the East to San Francisco by 250 miles and, as Simpson wrote, it "was at once adopted by the overland mail, the pony-express, and the telegraph." Simpson's 1859 work was not published until 1876, due to the intervention of the Civil War.

Map 246 (*below*).
Frederick von Egloffstein's innovative map of the Colorado, including the Grand Canyon. The relief and shadow method of depicting topography is still popular today, but Egloffstein was the one who invented it. "This method of representing topography," wrote Ives in his book, is "truer to nature . . . an approximation to a bird's eye view, and is intelligible to every eye."

At *top left* is the uss *Explorer,* the prefabricated steam paddleboat used by Ives for his exploration up the Colorado in 1857 to determine if the river could be used as a water supply route for the fight against the Mormons.

would be responsible for the first popular lithographs of the spectacular Grand Canyon.

Ives arrived in the Gulf of California by ship and assembled a 54-foot paddle steamer, dubbed the uss *Explorer* (*above*). In this vessel they steamed up to Black Canyon, at the beginning of the Grand Canyon, and on hitting a rock, Ives declared that the head of navigation had been reached. Ives and some others paddled farther up the river in a skiff, but they could see that the river was not going to provide the supply route they were seeking. Ives struck out overland after sending half his men back downstream on the *Explorer.* Trailed by hostile Navajo they made it to Fort Defiance, near the head of the Zuñi River, by May 1858.

Newberry was the first geologist to see the vast Grand Canyon, and his enlightened study of the rock strata threw valuable light on the formation of the entire continent. Egloffstein, faced with mapping a difficult country, invented a new method of depicting it, a shadow-relief technique that gives a very good impression of the topography (Map 246, *right*).

Following Ives, another expedition of Topographical Engineers was sent to explore farther up the Colorado, setting out west from Santa Fe in 1859. The expedition, led by John N. Macomb, included the geologist Newberry. They were the first to reach the confluence of the Green and Colorado Rivers in eastern Utah, and the first Euro-Americans to see the Hovenweap Anasazi ruins of the San Juan Valley. Newberry was the first to view the spectacular cliff dwellings of Mesa Verde. Macomb and Newberry were also the first to find dinosaur bones in the West.

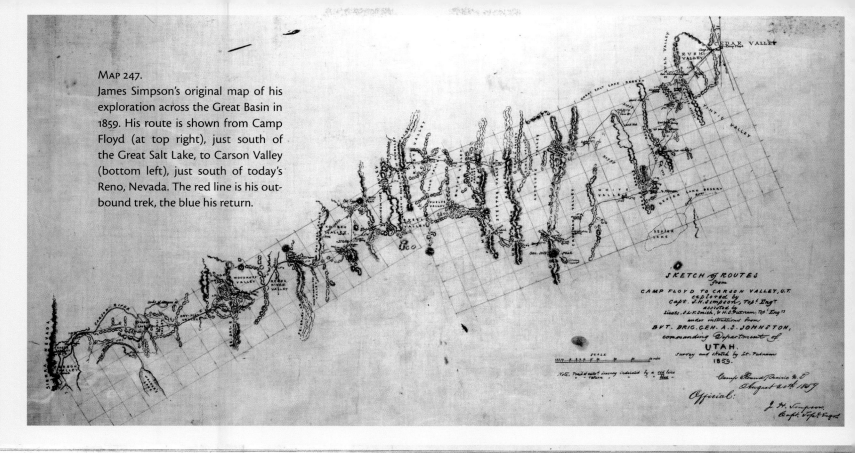

MAP 247.

James Simpson's original map of his exploration across the Great Basin in 1859. His route is shown from Camp Floyd (at top right), just south of the Great Salt Lake, to Carson Valley (bottom left), just south of today's Reno, Nevada. The red line is his outbound trek, the blue his return.

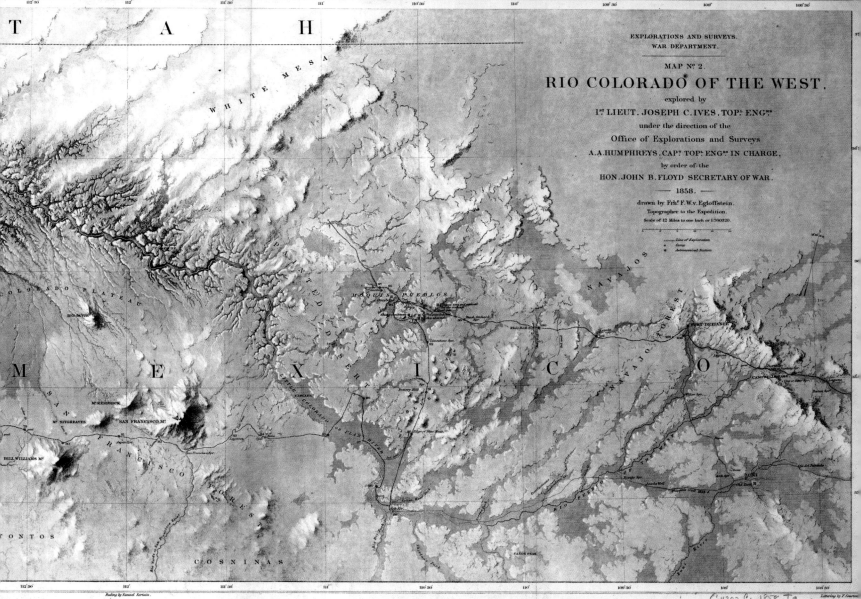

The Great Salt Lake

John J. Abert, chief of the Topographical Engineers, would probably have concentrated all his efforts on finding a good route to California in the Southwest had he been allowed to, but as a national government organization, he had to listen to demands that more northerly routes be surveyed as well. As a result, Captain Howard Stansbury was ordered in 1849 to reconnoiter a trail along the Platte River, then across the Wasatch Range to Salt Lake City, which had been established by the Mormons two years earlier. He was to survey the Salt Lake region in some detail, as it was recognized that it provided a resting place for settlers on their journey west.

The lake had been known to Euro-Americans at this point for more than twenty years. In late 1824 or early 1825, the lake was found by three explorers independently: Peter Skene Ogden of the Hudson's Bay Company; Étienne Provost, a trapper from Taos; and Jim Bridger of the Rocky Mountain Fur Company. Who saw it first is difficult to ascertain. Bridger, so the story goes, found the lake on a bet concerning the location of the mouth of the Bear River. He rode down the river on a raft and emerged into the lake. Because of its saltiness, Bridger was at first convinced it was an arm of the sea.

Stansbury, with Lieutenant John Gunnison, was ordered to map the lake, report on the Mormon settlements, and explore north to Fort Hall—and then return via a *southern* route to Santa Fe. With him went the experienced Jim Bridger, and together they attempted to find possible railroad passes over the Wasatch Mountains, but nothing suitable was found.

Stansbury then proceeded to circumnavigate and survey the Great Salt Lake and the surrounding region in considerable detail. It was the detail on his maps that had originally brought him to the

attention of Abert, and detail is what he now produced. His map, published in 1852 (MAP 249, *right*) was the first complete and accurate map of the lake. Gunnison surveyed Utah Lake, which is also shown on his map. Stansbury's exploration of the little-known west side of the lake, which was mainly desert, led him to the recognition that the Great Basin had once been the bed of a huge ancient lake, later named Lake Bonneville by geologists.

The survey of the lake took until the spring of 1850, and then Stansbury again tried to find a route through the mountains east of the lake region, ignoring Abert's orders to travel south. He found Cheyenne Pass through the Laramie Mountains, which might have been a suitable route for a railroad. After first intending to use Cheyenne Pass, the Union Pacific chose another pass about twelve miles to the south, at the site of modern Cheyenne, Wyoming. Nevertheless, most of the railroad was built along the trail Stansbury had taken east from the Great Salt Lake, and before the railroad it became the route of the Overland Stage.

Unfortunately, Stansbury was severely injured in a fall from his horse just after he found Cheyenne Pass. He was unable to promote the potential railroad route he had found, and so his discovery was not publicized very well.

At the same time as Stansbury was surveying the Great Salt Lake, another Topographical Engineer, William H. Warner, had been ordered to find a railroad route from the Upper Sacramento Valley east to link up with him. Warner, accompanied by Lieutenant Robert S. Williamson, did not get very far. Pressing on ahead of Williamson in September 1849, Warner discovered a pass he called Madeline Pass in northern California that might have been suitable for a railroad, but then he was attacked by Pit River Indians and killed. Such were the dangers of western exploration. Small parties were always susceptible to such deprivations, despite their military nature.

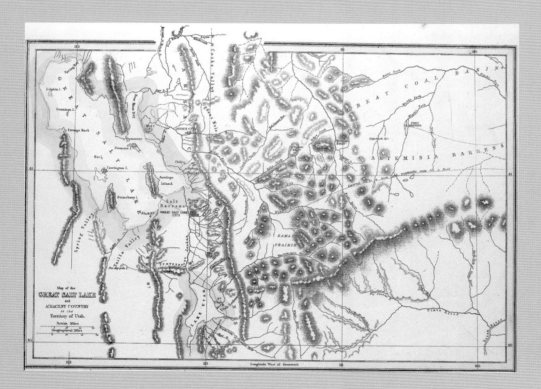

MAP 248 (*left*).
A commercial map of the Great Salt Lake published in 1863 and based in part on Stansbury's survey.

MAP 249 (*right*).
Howard Stansbury's *Map of the Great Salt Lake and Adjacent Country*, published with his report in 1852. Lieutenant John Gunnison published his own report that year, a study of the Mormons, with whom he had become fascinated.

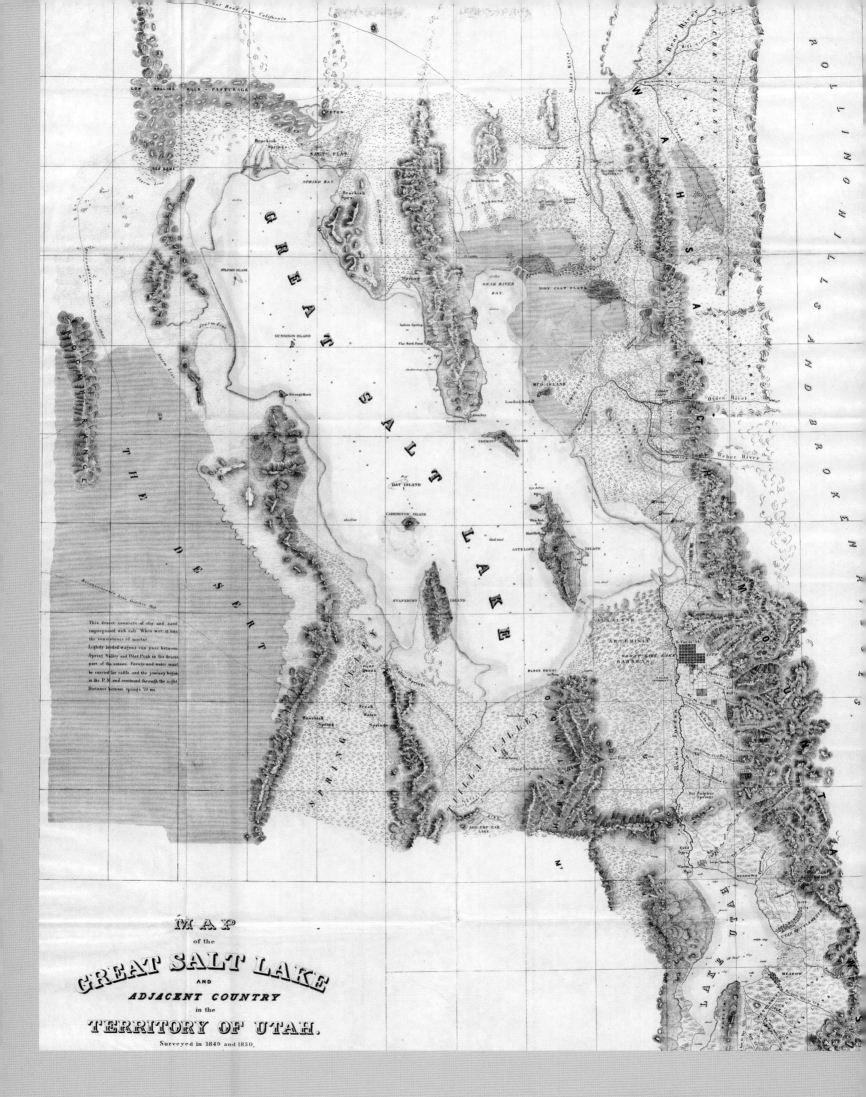

MAP
of the
GREAT SALT LAKE
AND
ADJACENT COUNTRY
in the
TERRITORY OF UTAH.
Surveyed in 1849 and 1850,

The Pacific Railroad Surveys

Explorations and surveys for a potential route for a railroad to connect California with the rest of the United States had begun even before it joined the Union. The first was that by John C. Frémont in 1848–49, and it ended in disaster (see page 181). But by that time railroads covered much of the eastern United States and it was obvious to anyone that a transcontinental railroad would soon become essential to the nation.

On 2 March 1853 Congress authorized a large-scale survey of possible railroad routes to the Pacific. Since it was a series of reconnaissances rather than detailed surveys, what might otherwise have proved impossible was completed within three years. The surveys were under the general direction of the secretary of war, Jefferson Davis, destined to become the first—and only—president of the Confederate States during the Civil War. Davis created a new de-

partment, the Bureau of Explorations and Surveys, and put William Emory in charge, succeeded a year later by Captain Andrew A. Humphreys. Nevertheless, it was the Corps of Topographical Engineers who were to carry out the actual survey.

The routes surveyed were all initially chosen as much for political reasons as practical; each was supported by some sectional interest. The use of supposedly unbiased Topographical Engineers to find the "most economical and practical" route was intended to resolve the issue. It did not, for the simple reason that there was not an obvious best single route; several would have filled the bill. So sectional interests continued their bickering until the Civil War led to the departure of Southern interests from Congress, and it was then that the middle route of the Union Pacific Railroad was given the go-ahead.

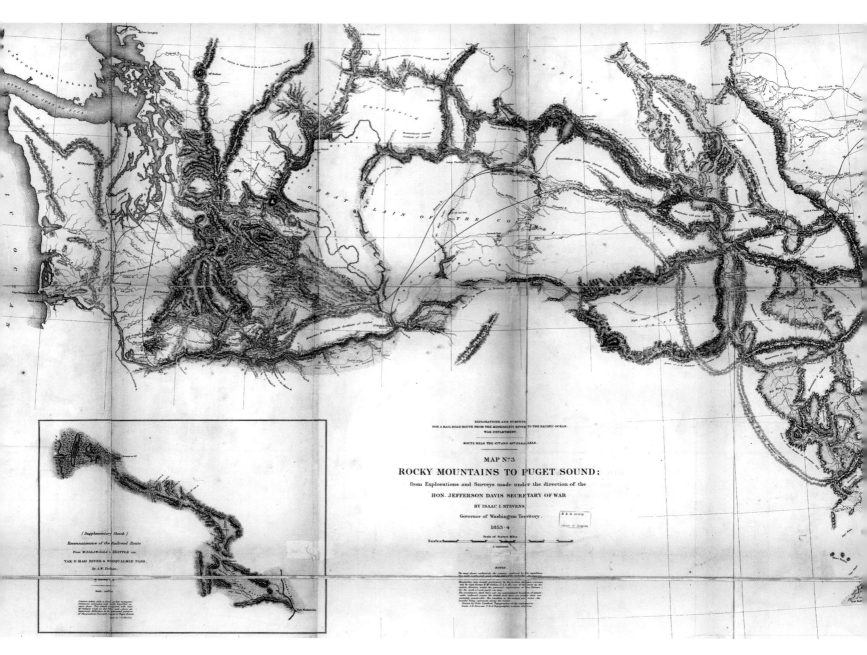

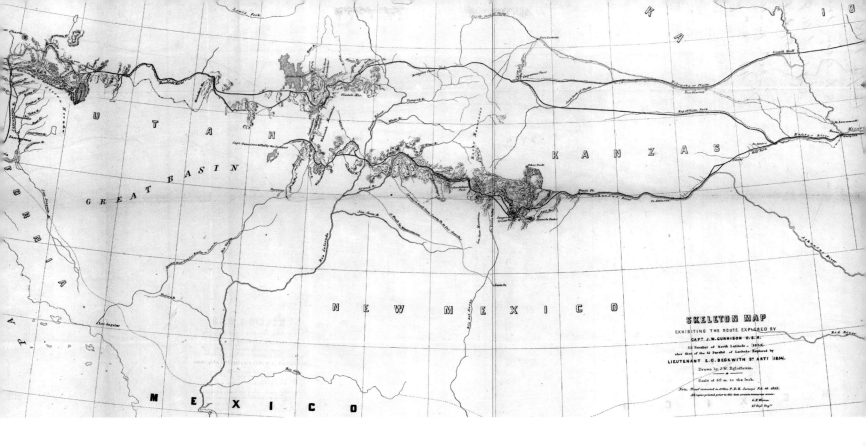

Three main routes were surveyed. The first, the northern, was overseen by the new governor of Washington Territory, Isaac I. Stevens. First into the field in June 1853, the expedition was split into two. Stevens led one party west from St. Paul, while another, led by Captain George B. McClellan, was detailed to find and survey passes through the Cascade Mountains. Stevens produced a glowing report, having found five passes across the Continental Divide, but McClellan, who would become known for overcautiousness during the Civil War, did not bother to test the snow depths in Snoqualmie Pass over the Cascades, the one pass that was acceptable for a rail-road; the snows were not as deep as McClellan thought. Stevens's possible routes (MAP 250, *left*) were considered dubious even by some of his own men, and the Washington Territory legislature commissioned Frederick West Lander, a civilian engineer, to survey another route through South Pass to Puget Sound, a route which was included in the final edition of the *Pacific Railroad Reports.*

In late June 1853 Captain John W. Gunnison began his expedition to survey the 38th parallel, or middle route. The route at about 42° N, recently surveyed by Howard Stansbury and before that by Frémont, was not resurveyed. After surveying across Cochetopa Pass

MAP 250 (*left*).
The westernmost sheet of the map of the northern route surveyed by George McClellan and Isaac I. Stevens.

MAP 251 (*above*).
An initial summary map showing the survey of John W. Gunnison along the 38th parallel and, after his death in October 1853, that of E. G. Beckwith along the 41st parallel. Near Sevier Lake in Utah is the notation *Capt Gunnison killed by the Indians.*

MAP 252 (*right*).
Part of Amiel W. Whipple and Joseph C. Ives's survey along the 35th parallel. This section covers the present-day site of Phoenix, Arizona.

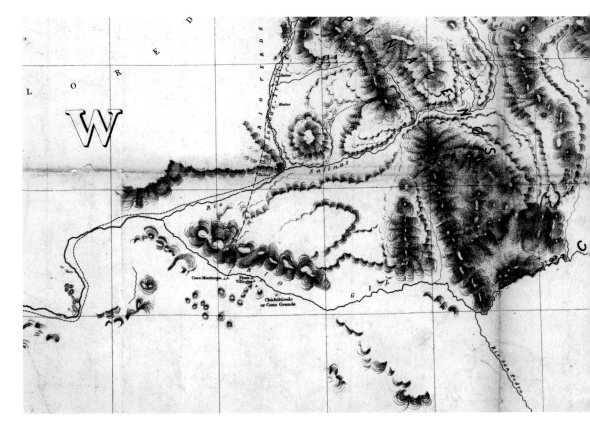

in southern Colorado, Gunnison got as far as Sevier Lake in Utah before falling victim to an attack by Paiute Indians in late October. His work was taken over by Lieutenant E. G. Beckwith, an artillery officer. After wintering at Salt Lake City he found routes across the Wasatch suitable for a railroad that Stansbury had not found. Then he turned west, successfully locating a route across the Great Basin and over passes into the Sacramento Valley. Unfortunately, despite his finding this viable route, he did not provide cost estimates for it—he was not an engineer—and his report was virtually ignored because of this.

Lieutenant Amiel Weeks Whipple was commissioned to survey the 35th parallel route. He left Fort Smith, Arkansas, in July 1853, following more or less the route surveyed by Marcy and Simpson four years before (see Map 245, page 185), and then approximately that surveyed by Sitgreaves in 1851 (see page 185) up the Zuñi and west to the Colorado. Here, however, he turned north, and then turned west across the Mojave Desert to San Bernardino. This route, he reported, was not only practicable but in many respects eminently advantageous. Whipple included costs but got them wrong, stating they were almost twice what they should have been.

Congress did not think Whipple's survey really a southern one, and one even farther south, along the 32nd parallel, was undertaken in 1854, in two sections. Lieutenant John G. Parke explored a route from San Diego to the Rio Grande, finding the Chiricahua Pass in southeastern Arizona, and Lieutenant John Pope surveyed a route from Fort Washita, on the Red River, over Guadalupe Pass to the Rio Grande, connecting with Parke's survey.

Finally, Lieutenant Robert S. Williamson, with Parke in 1853, tried to locate passes over the southern Sierra Nevada. He concluded that there were none and recommended a route from Fort Yuma to Los Angeles rather than San Diego. In 1855 Williamson, now accompanied by Lieutenant Henry L. Abbott, extensively explored coastal northern California and Oregon to the Columbia to locate possible routes to connect whatever Pacific terminal won the railroad race with those that did not.

The surveys were all analyzed by Humphreys, now in charge of the Bureau, together with his assistant, Lieutenant Gouverneur Kemble Warren. They were predisposed to the most southerly route, as was Davis, being a senator from Mississippi, and they concluded that "the route of the thirty-second parallel is, of those surveyed, the most practicable and economical route for a railroad from the Mississippi River to the Pacific Ocean." However, no consensus could be reached in Congress regarding what seemed a partisan decision, and no route at all was approved.

The Pacific Railroad Surveys did, nevertheless, produce a vast new library of information about the West, and Warren's summary maps, an early edition of which is shown here (Map 254, *right*), were a monumental achievement in their own right. The survey reports filled thirteen large volumes and included an entire volume of maps, panoramas, paintings, and drawings. They included three pioneering geological maps and hundreds of scientific illustrations of geological, botanical, zoological, and ethnological interest. The West was revealed as never before; the surveys had not been all in vain.

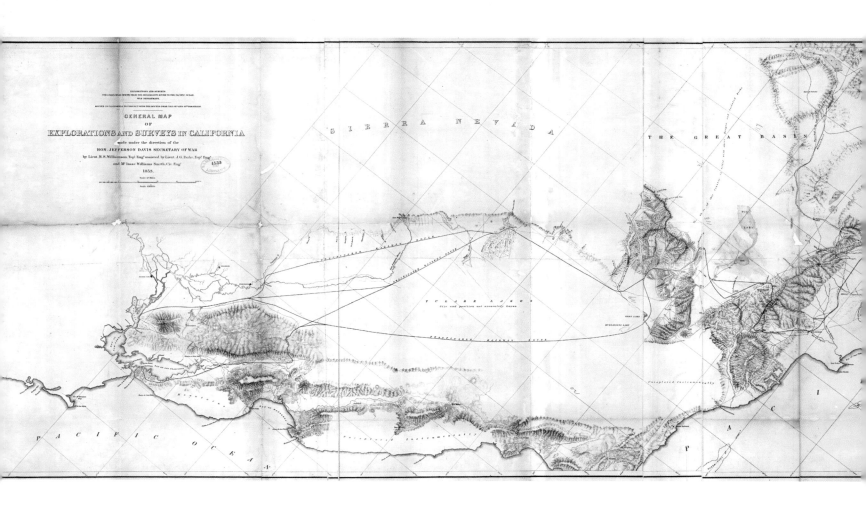

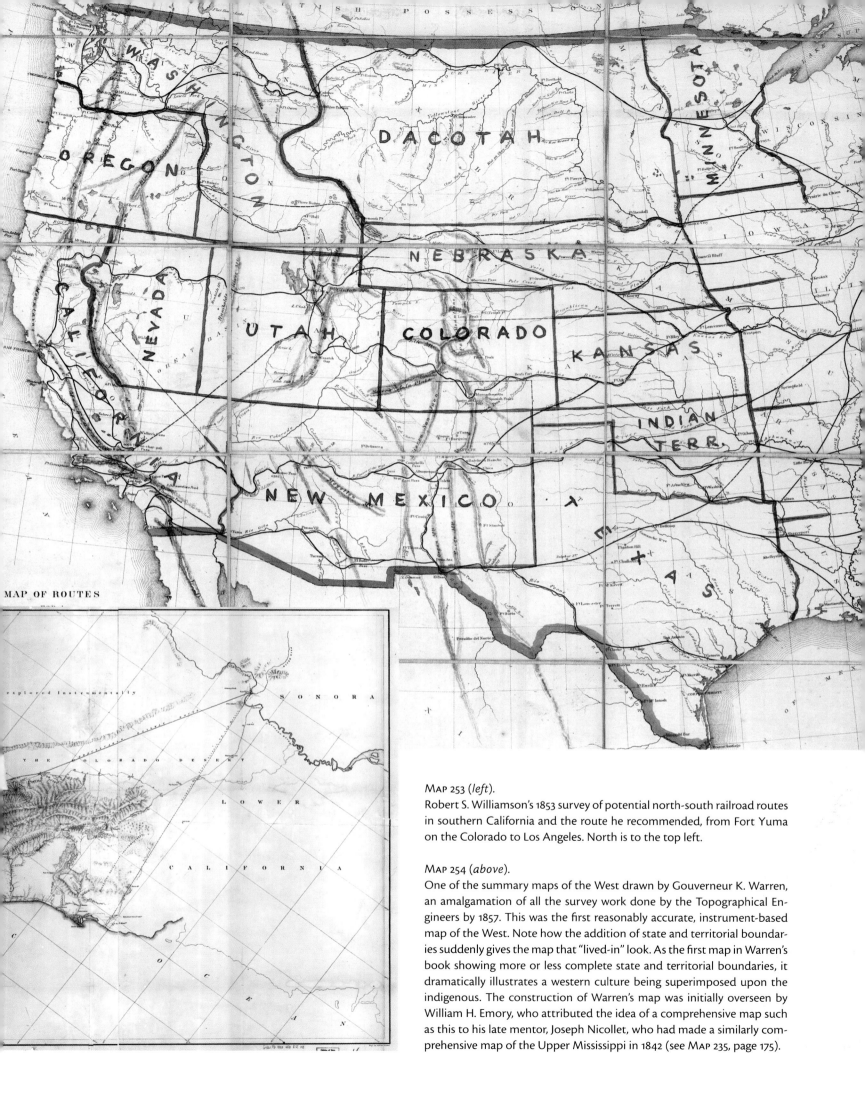

MAP OF ROUTES

MAP 253 (*left*).
Robert S. Williamson's 1853 survey of potential north-south railroad routes in southern California and the route he recommended, from Fort Yuma on the Colorado to Los Angeles. North is to the top left.

MAP 254 (*above*).
One of the summary maps of the West drawn by Gouverneur K. Warren, an amalgamation of all the survey work done by the Topographical Engineers by 1857. This was the first reasonably accurate, instrument-based map of the West. Note how the addition of state and territorial boundaries suddenly gives the map that "lived-in" look. As the first map in Warren's book showing more or less complete state and territorial boundaries, it dramatically illustrates a western culture being superimposed upon the indigenous. The construction of Warren's map was initially overseen by William H. Emory, who attributed the idea of a comprehensive map such as this to his late mentor, Joseph Nicollet, who had made a similarly comprehensive map of the Upper Mississippi in 1842 (see MAP 235, page 175).

Exploring a Prairie

As the Pacific Railroad Surveys were winding down, the lands to the north controlled by the Hudson's Bay Company were coming under pressure from would-be colonists. The British government was also wondering what to do about this vast Northwest, still unorganized except for Vancouver Island, which was created as a separate British colony in 1849. Its main concern was to avoid attracting American settlers to the Northwest, for, having seen what happened in the Oregon Country, the British realized that occupation was nine-tenths of sovereignty.

Several scientific expeditions were organized at this time whose primary purpose was to assess the prairie lands for their agricultural suitability. The first, led by George Gladman and termed the Canadian Red River Exploring Expedition, in 1857 traced a route from Lake Superior to the Red River Settlement (around today's Winnipeg, Manitoba) that would be suitable for use by immigrants to the West. The second, the following year, called the Assinniboine [sic] and Saskatchewan Exploring Expedition, was led by Henry Hind, who had been the principal scientist on Gladman's expedition.

Hind's report, published in 1860, defined a so-called fertile belt across the northern prairie, with a large part of the southern prairie being deemed too dry to sustain agriculture (Map 255, below). The southern part was thought to be an extension of the Great American Desert, the concept originated by Pike and Long and by now embedded in popular thinking.

In 1857 a pioneering book on the climatology of the United States by Lorin Blodget had confirmed a zone of low rainfall through the Great Plains, but nothing was known of conditions

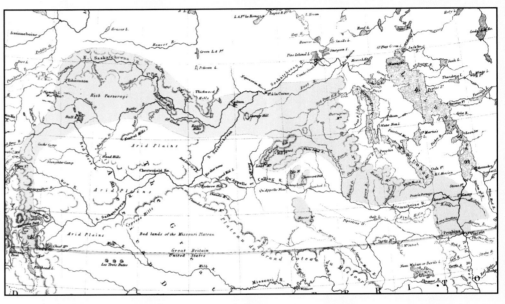

farther north—although Blodget's map suggested a continued belt of dryness—until Hind's book three years later.

The conditions for agriculture were also addressed by another expedition organized at this time by Britain's Royal Geographical Society and backed by the British government. This was the expedition of John Palliser, who crisscrossed the Canadian Prairies between 1857 and 1860 with a bevy of eminent scientists, which included geologist James Hector and French botanist Eugène Bourgeau.

It was easily the most comprehensive survey of the Prairies in the nineteenth century; Palliser's scientists "did not let a flower or a fly escape their spectacles or their nets." The botanist Bourgeau collected 10,000 dried specimens of an astonishing 819 species belonging to 349 genera for the collections of the Royal Botanical Gardens at Kew. Hector collected hundreds of fossils

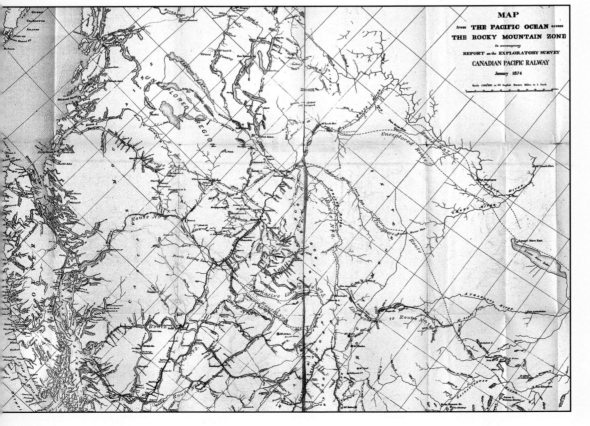

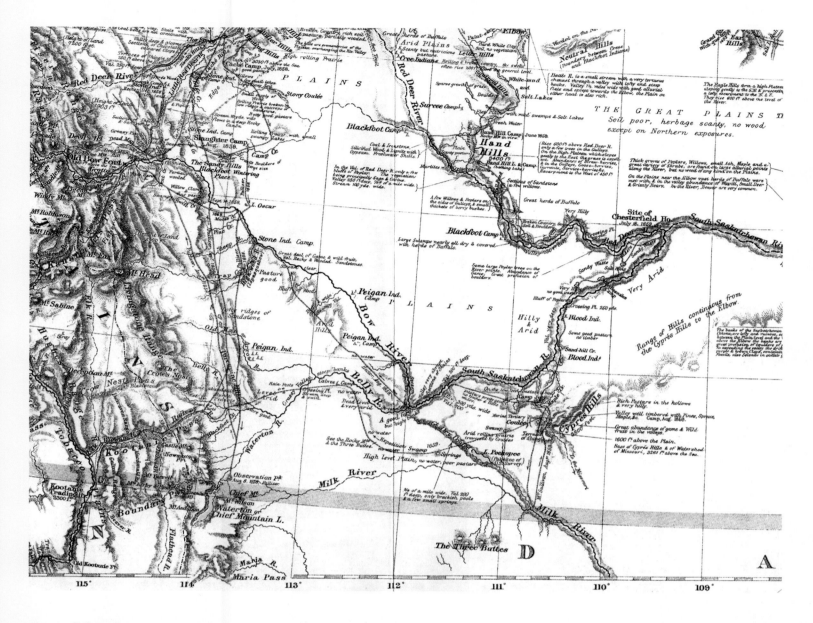

MAP 255 (*left, top*).
Henry Hind's map of the "fertile belt" (yellow) across the northern part of the Canadian Prairies, with *Arid Plains* to its south.

MAP 256 (*left, bottom*).
Sandford Fleming's summary map of potential railroad routes through the Rockies to the Pacific. Vancouver, the line's eventual terminus, is at bottom left.

MAP 257 (*above*).
Part of the detailed map of western Canada produced by John Palliser and published in a report in 1865. The red lines are routes of expedition members. The region shown is that of the Red Deer, Bow, and South Saskatchewan Rivers, approximately the area south from today's Red Deer, Alberta, to the forty-ninth parallel, shown as a red band. This was the arid region that later became known as Palliser's Triangle; the word *Arid* is repeated in many locations.

and rock samples and drew up the first reasonably accurate geological map of the Prairies and the Rockies.

Palliser delineated what has become known as "Palliser's Triangle," a triangular-shaped zone south of the fertile belt that Palliser considered to be an arid or semi-arid desert "forever to be compara-

tively worthless." Indeed, this part of the prairie is only viable even today because of irrigation, but it is good grazing land. The triangle is approximately that region shown on the section of Palliser's detailed summary map (*above*).

It was this delineation of the southern prairie as a virtual desert that caused the Canadian transcontinental railway to be routed across the north in the original proposals for such a line, and it was this route that was explored and surveyed by the Canadian Pacific Railway's engineer Sandford Fleming in the first half of the 1870s. Only as a result of more detailed investigation by botanist John Macoun in 1882 were the rails rerouted to the more direct route across the southern prairie when the rail line was finally built in 1882–85.

In a similar fashion to the American railroad surveys, Fleming was responsible for finding a route for the Canadian Pacific through the Rockies to Pacific tidewater. The several routes he surveyed are shown in his summary map (MAP 256, *left, bottom*). As part of his experiences planning long-distance railroads, Fleming devised the concept of standard time, with time changing only when defined zone boundaries were crossed, the system still in use today.

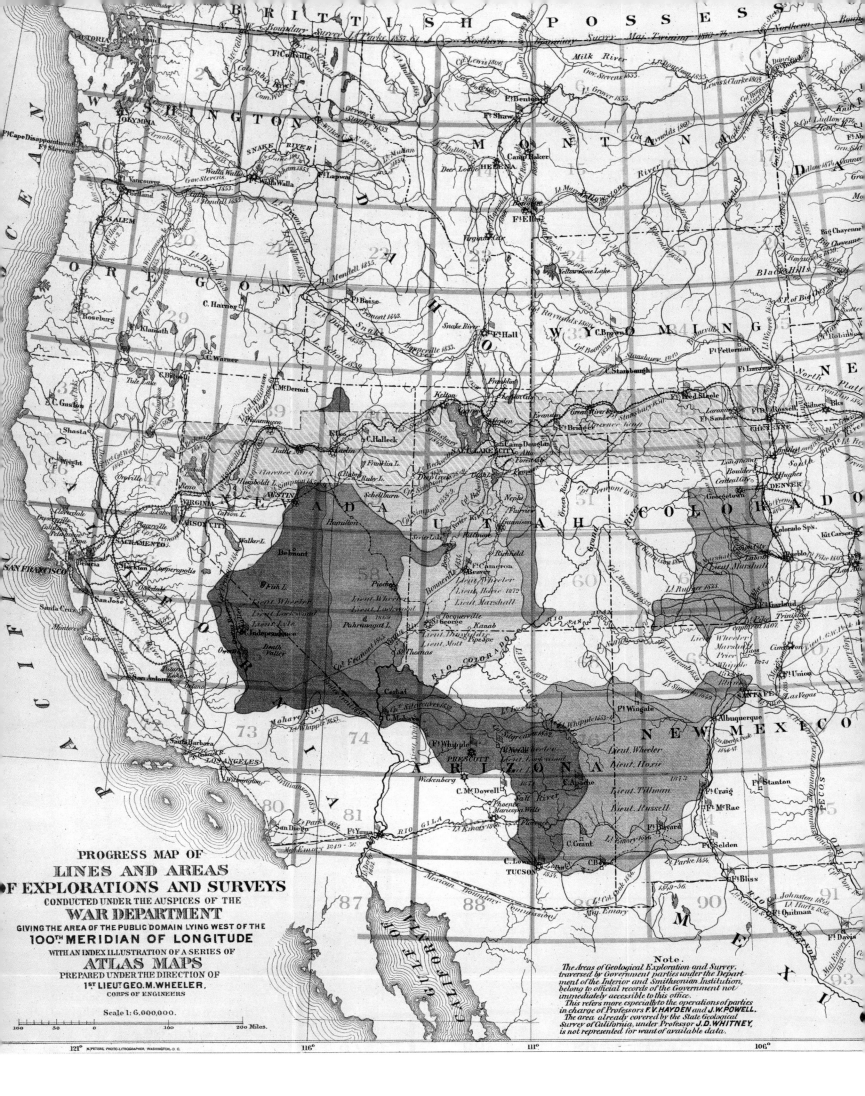

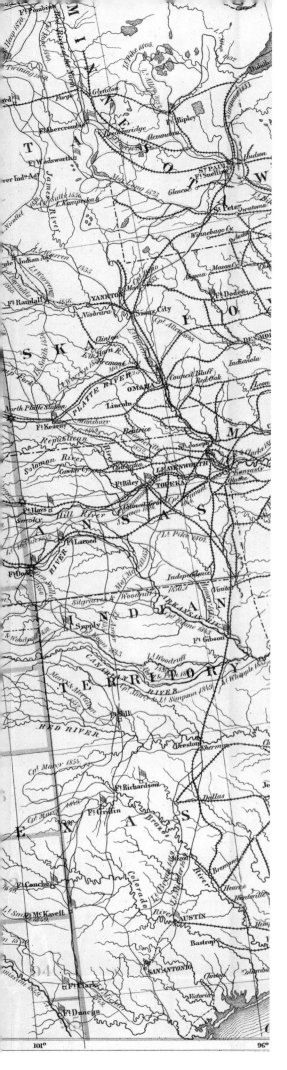

The Great Western Surveys

Up to the Civil War, sectional bickering between North and South also affected the West, with each side concerned at a possible upset of the balance between slave and free states if new western states were admitted to the Union. After the war, more emphasis was placed on the idea of turning the West into a resource reservoir for an industrial East. And to find these resources, much more detailed exploration would be required.

The first result of the cessation of the South was the approval by Congress of incentives to encourage the building of a railroad to the Pacific. Huge land grants were awarded to the Union Pacific and Central Pacific to build the line, which was completed in 1869.

After the completion of the railroad surveys of the 1850s and the compilation of Warren's great summary map (MAP 254, page 193), it could fairly be said that all that was now required to complete the map of the West was a filling in of details. Many of these details were geological and mineralogical, to find the raw materials to feed the factories of the industrial East, but also agricultural, to direct settlement to where it might succeed, which, in turn, would provide wheat and beef to feed the mouths of a growing industrial workforce in the East. And so the idea was born to conduct comprehensive surveys of huge swaths of the country—no longer a specific path to the Pacific, but an inventory of the resources that could be exploited. The first to come up with this idea was a young geologist named Clarence King.

King had cut his teeth as a member of the first California Geological Survey, directed by Josiah Whitney in 1860–64. King had assisted in the exploration of the High Sierra, adding to the map a huge area "as high as Switzerland." A survey was made of Yosemite, which led directly to its induction as America's first national park (although it was officially a state park until 1890). Whitney's development of triangulation as a survey method allowed accurate surveys of very large areas in a reasonable time, and his methods were applied to all the large surveys after that. From a measured baseline, the rest of the survey could be done instrumentally using careful measurements of angles to landmarks and the application of trigonometry. MAP 264, page 202, showing Ferdinand Hayden's triangulation of Colorado, gives a good idea of how it was done.

King was appointed head of a new Geological and Geographical Exploration of the Fortieth Parallel, created for him but still under the War Department, and in 1867 began his

MAP 258.
George Wheeler's tremendously detailed map of the West showing the progress of army explorations to 1873 (in red), the area covered by his own survey of 1869–73 (by year; see key below), and Clarence King's survey of the zone around the fortieth parallel. The route of the new transcontinental railroad is also shown.

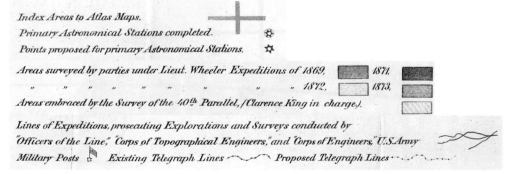

angles, was struck by lightning, with nearly fatal results for him. In 1872 he exposed a fraud attempt by revealing a supposed diamond field as salted, adding to public acclamation, which, like John C. Frémont, he manipulated, basking in its glory.

Many scientific reports brought the expedition's work to the notice of the scientific community and the public. Fellow geologist James Gardner was responsible for a large *Atlas of the Fortieth Parallel Survey*; James D. Hague wrote a classic book called *The Mining Industry,* based on his work in the silver mines of Colorado; and King himself produced a significant volume called *Systematic Geology.* Such was his renown that in 1879 King was appointed as the first chief of the new United States Geological Survey.

The army's last gasp at western exploration came with Lieutenant George Montague Wheeler, who in 1867 was ordered to carry out a complementary survey to that of King, covering an even larger area that amounted to most of the Southwest. The coverage of his survey is shown on his summary map, MAP 258 (*previous page*). The army would create another organization, the even more grandiosely named Geographical Surveys of the Territories of the United States West of the 100th Meridian. Wheeler's work has tended to be overshadowed by that of King. He was not as flamboyant as the latter, yet he produced much that was equally valuable. Wheeler was prepared to put his heart and soul into work in a remote and dangerous region shunned by many of his fellow officers, and he reaped its rewards.

MAP 259.
The meticulous detail of the new western surveys is embodied in this small section of just one map, published in 1882 by George Wheeler but also incorporating surveys of Clarence King. This portion shows *Lake Tahoe,* on the boundary of Nevada and California. The line of the Central Pacific now crosses the map through the railroad town of *Reno,* but other rail lines have connected to it from the south. Donner Pass, the pass finally used for the trancontinental railroad, is just west of *Truckee.*

monumental survey, backed up not by soldiers, except as an escort, but a team of scientists. Notably he did not take along an ethnologist, on the grounds that under the new reality, Indians were soon to be wiped from the West by the advance of "civilization." He did hire a photographer, however, Timothy O' Sullivan, whose excellent photographs documented the expedition's work and the wonders of the West. King spent six years crisscrossing the vast region shown on MAP 258 (*previous page*). Members of the expedition studied the deserts and the mountains, mines and glaciers—the first glacier to be found in the United States was discovered by King on Mount Shasta—and the geology of the Great Basin. King determined that the latter was the remnant of two ancient lakes, Lake Bonneville and Lake Lahontan, both named after explorers. At one point, high on a mountain peak, King's theodolite, used for measuring the critical

Wheeler's survey was more essentially military than King's, for as well as all things geographical and geological, on his 1871 exploration he was ordered to report on the "numbers, habits, and disposition of the Indians who may live in this section [eastern Nevada and Arizona], the selection of such sites as may be of use for future military operations or occupation." Wheeler even took along a newspaper reporter, Frederick Loring, figuring that he would gain much publicity from him. He did not last long. Poor Loring was killed by Apache in November 1871. Earlier the same year he had succumbed to sunstroke while accompanying the expedition through the furnace of Death Valley with its "stifling heat, great radiation, and constant glare from the sand."

By 1873, so much surveying was going on in the West that one of Wheeler's parties, sent to survey much of Colorado, encountered a similar party belonging to Ferdinand Hayden's expedition (see page 201 and MAP 264, page 202). Such was inter-organizational rivalry (Hayden's expedition was under the Interior Department) that neither would yield to the other, and both surveyed together but separately from peak to peak. Needless to say, Congress was not amused, and in 1874 began a process that would ultimately lead to the demise of army exploratory surveying in favor of civilian and the formation of a single body responsible for exploration and survey, the U.S. Geological Survey, in 1879.

One of the great western surveys started off as the personal ambition of one man, John Wesley Powell. After losing an arm in the Civil War, Powell had taught himself enough geology to teach it at a university. On a western field trip with his students in 1868 he looked down at the mighty Colorado River and decided to do what no one had—explore it by water.

The following year, after intensive preparation, he was back with nine others, boats, and equipment. They set off from Green River Station, where the Union Pacific crossed the Green River, on 24 May 1869, down, as Powell later termed it farther downstream, the "Great Unknown." Of course, by this time the course of the river was not unknown, but the cascades and rapids, rocks and twists and turns of the river were unmapped. Powell and his men would be continually shooting off precipices of water without knowing how far they might fall.

Canyon after canyon they descended, with adventure after adventure. Yet they were not necessarily the first, it seems, for on a rock in midstream on one difficult cascade (Red Canyon), "Ashley 1825" was scratched, an unrecorded journey by fur trader William Ashley (see page 160). Powell, climbing the canyon side, found himself trapped on a ledge, hanging on with his single arm. He was rescued by one of his men, who, thinking quickly and using the only materials to hand, took off his long johns and lowered them to the hapless Powell.

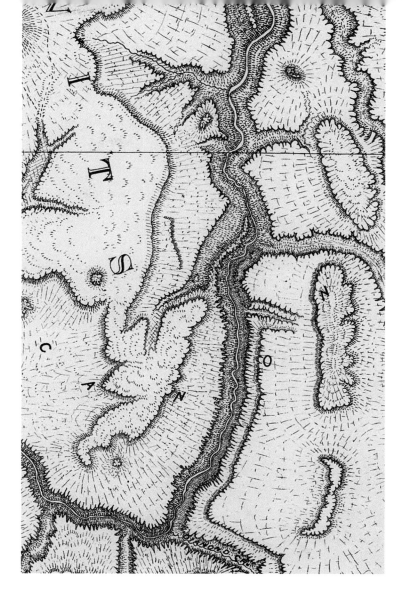

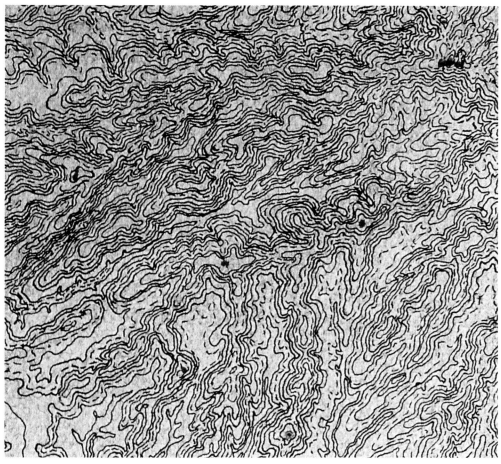

MAP 260 (*right, top*).
An early Powell map of the Grand Canyon, prepared in 1873.

MAP 261 (*right, bottom*).
The intricate detail of mapmaking in the canyon country is shown in this small part of an original manuscript map drawn by Powell's expedition of the "Eastern Tavaputo [Tavaputs] Plateau," now the Roan Plateau, between the Green and Upper Colorado (earlier called the Grand) Rivers in Utah. It was drawn about 1877 for Powell's *Report on the Arid Regions of the United States*, published the following year.

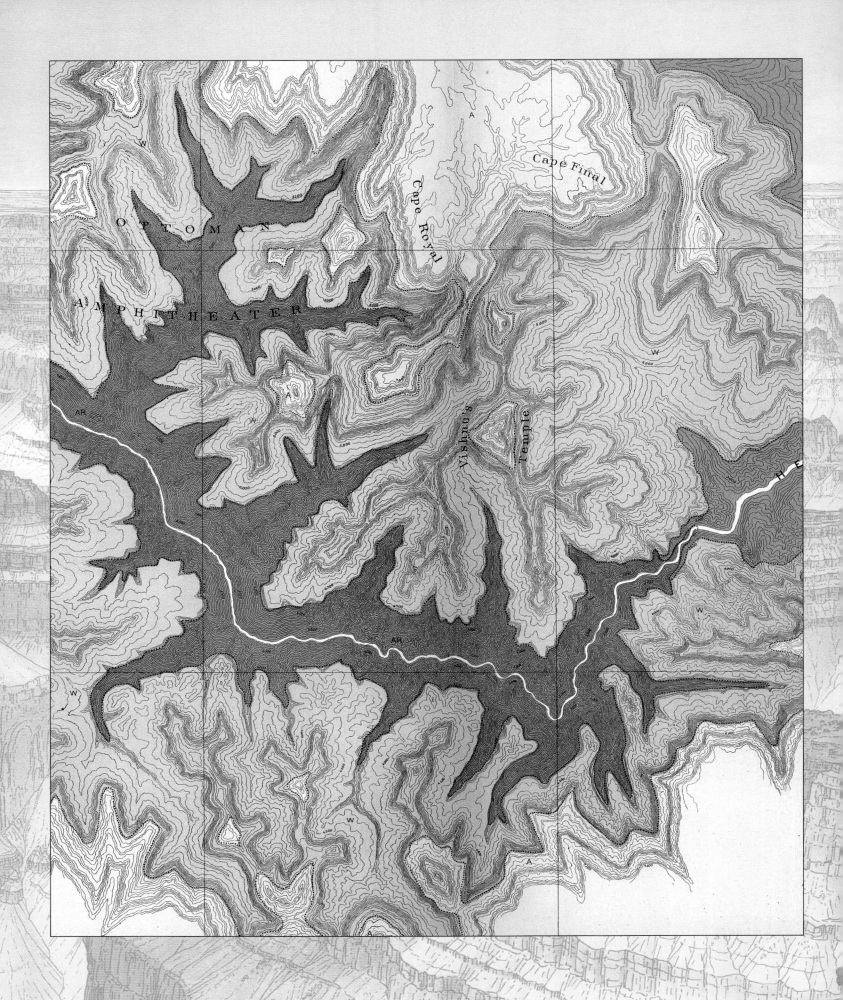

By the time they reached the Grand Canyon, three of his men had had enough of the dangerous bump and grind, and, facing yet another dangerous section, climbed out of the canyon to make for Mormon settlements; they were killed on the plateau by Indians. Shortly afterwards, at the end of August, Powell arrived at Callville Bay, Nevada, and the end of his epic journey of more than a thousand miles.

Powell was now a hero, idolized in the press, and received an appropriation from Congress to create a Geographical and Topographical Survey of the Colorado River similar, in prestige at least, to the other great surveys with which it was concurrent. Another downriver expedition was planned on a grander scale, with more support and with scientists and a photographer; it took two years but collected much valuable information. In May and June 1872 Powell's brother-in-law, Almon H. Thompson, discovered the Escalante River, which today flows into Lake Powell in the Glen Canyon, the last river to be discovered in the area now covered by the contiguous United States.

Powell became interested in native languages and was appointed special Indian commissioner in 1873 by the federal government, making proposals for a workable reservation system. In 1879 Powell established the Bureau of Ethnology to study Indian culture. The year before that he published his *Report on the Arid Regions of the United States*, which advocated cooperative irrigation and the regulation of grazing and farming.

Clarence Dutton, a geologist, joined Powell's staff in 1874, and another geologist, William Holmes, joined in 1879. Together with Powell, they produced several definitive volumes on American geological history, the most famous of which, and certainly the most spectacular, was *The Tertiary History of the Grand Cañon District*, written by Dutton and containing superb panoramas drawn by Holmes. (The background to this page is one example.) The panoramas were created by Holmes with the help of a camera lucida, a camera obscura with a prism that projected the outside image onto paper, enabling it to be traced. The results, much more than mere tracings, have become classic western images. The interpretation of the vast strata exposed by the canyons led to considerable advancements in the knowledge of geological history of the continent.

Another area that received special attention in the 1870s was Yellowstone. Although known since John Colter found it in 1808 (see page 152), few had penetrated the region since. Civilians from Helena, Montana, David Folsom and C.W. Cook, found the geysers again in 1869, and the next year Nathaniel P. Langford and Henry D. Washburn, Montana's surveyor general, explored the area. It was they who named one of the more regular and most spectacular geysers "Old Faithful."

In 1871, a more exhaustive survey, including scientists, a photographer, and an artist, was undertaken under Ferdinand V. Hayden. It is a measure of the duplication that was beginning to occur that simultaneously an army expedition under Captain J. W. Barlow also explored the region. Hayden had in 1869 been appointed head of another survey, the "United States Geological and Geographical Survey of the Territories," under the Interior Department. On his return from Yellowstone he lobbied for the establishment of a national park, and in 1872 President Ulysses Grant set the region aside as a "public park or pleasuring ground"; it was the first official national park. Hayden's detailed geological map of the Yellowstone area is shown as MAP 266, page 203.

Hayden went on to direct a survey of Colorado in the same detail as the surveys of King, Powell, and Wheeler in other areas. The considerable triangulation network used is shown in MAP 264 (*next page*). The survey lasted four years, 1873–76, and, as we have seen, at one point ran into Wheeler's overlapping survey.

The 1874 inquiry into duplication of western surveys was fought tooth and nail by Hayden, who mustered support from others for civilian surveys. The influence of the army was diminishing, however, and the writing was on the wall. Surveying continued, but in a much more coordinated fashion, after the surveys were all folded into the new United States Geological Survey in 1879. Clarence King was its first director, and he was succeeded in 1881 by John Wesley Powell.

With the coming of the railroad, the flood of settlers to the West increased, and for the first time significant settlement in the region east of the Rockies began. With settlement came demands for detailed surveys for landholdings, and although there were still many details to be filled in, the days of western exploration as such were over.

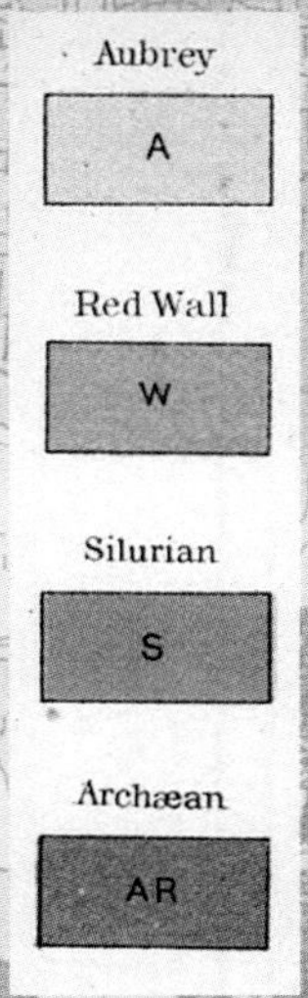

Aubrey

A

Red Wall

W

Silurian

S

Archæan

AR

MAP 262.
There can hardly be any exploration left to do if one can map an area in the detail shown in this map. It is a geological map of the southern Kaibab Plateau with the Grand Canyon and the Colorado River (the white line). The key to the four rock types indicated is also shown. The map was produced by Clarence Dutton in 1882. The background engraving of the canyon country also comes from Dutton's book but was drawn by William Holmes, aided by a camera lucida.

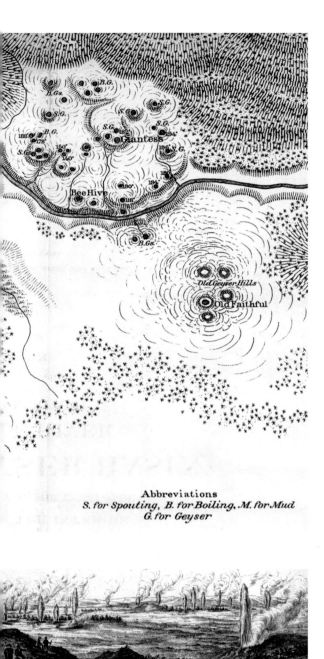

Abbreviations
S. for Spouting, B. for Boiling, M. for Mud
G. for Geyser

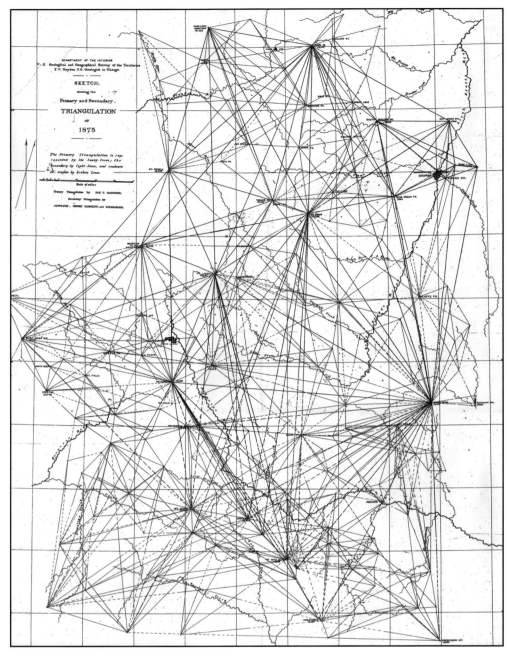

Map 263 (*above*).
Part of Ferdinand Hayden's map of the Yellowstone geyser region, showing *Old Faithful.* Under it is a contemporary illustration of a geyser field (with all the geysers spouting at once, it seems), engraved in 1871, by the German geographer Augustus Petermann.

Map 264 (*above, right*).
Ferdinand Hayden's 1873 triangulation of Colorado. The development of the triangulation method by Josiah Whitney of the California Geological Survey is credited with allowing the large-scale accurate mapping of the West. The measured baseline is shown near Denver, at top right.

Map 265 (*right*).
The geology is stunningly illustrated in this bird's-eye map of the Black Hills of Dakota published in 1880 by the new U.S. Geological Survey. It is from the *Geographical and Geological Survey of the Rocky Mountain Region* by Henry Newton and Walter P. Jenny.

Map 266 (*far right*).
Hayden's geological map of the Yellowstone area, published in 1878.

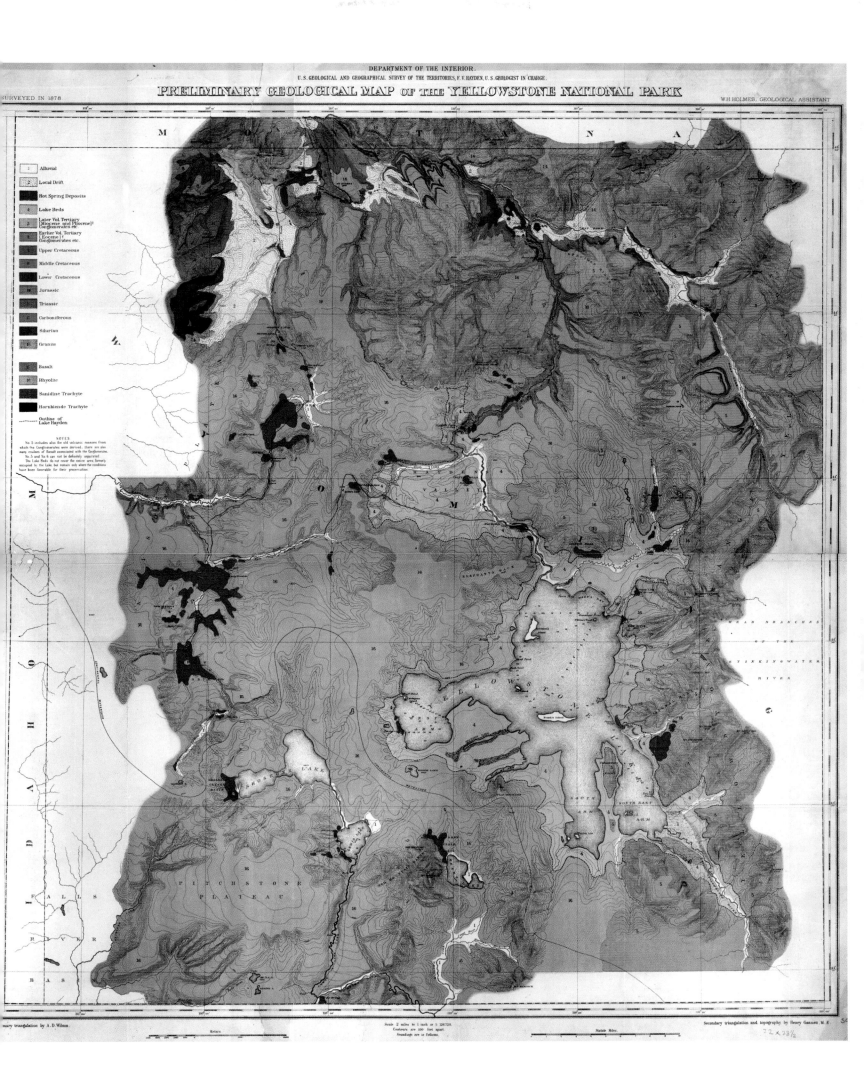

The Final Frontier — The North

The last frontiers of North American exploration were, not surprisingly, in the North. After the purchase of Alaska by the United States in 1867, there was no rush to "Seward's Icebox," as it was popularly known, after William Seward, the American secretary of state responsible for the deal.

Even as the agreement of sale was reached, an American exploring party was in Alaska, surveying a route for an overland telegraph. The Western Union Telegraph Expedition, led by William Dall, was cheered by the sale, which they learned of in July 1867, but then had all their hopes dashed at the same time when they learned of the completion of the transatlantic telegraph cable. One of its members, Frank Ketchum, ascended the Yukon as far as Fort Yukon in 1866.

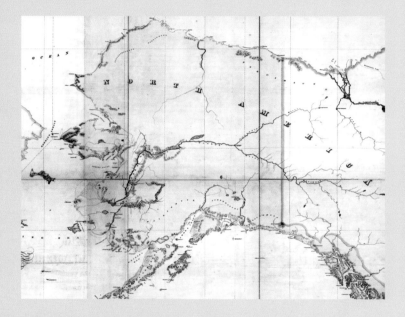

MAP 267 (*above*).
A map of Alaska produced by the Western Union Telegraph Expedition in 1867. The course of the Yukon River is known by this time, but there are still vast blanks on the map away from the coasts. The only river shown flowing into the Arctic Ocean is the Colville. It is a measure of ongoing confusion that the river has been incorrectly named the Pelly, the same river, actually a headwater of the Yukon, found by Robert Campbell in 1840 (see page 173).

The U.S. Coast Survey, after 1878 the U.S. Coast and Geodetic Survey, explored and mapped much of the Alaskan coast in the 1870s and 1880s; William Dall was also involved in this, commanding the schooner *Yukon,* which also carried out hydrographic surveys.

The army had one last exploring hurrah in Alaska, first by the Signal Service and then by the Department of Columbia. First there was Captain Charles Raymond's expedition up the Yukon in 1869, which resulted in the ousting of the Hudson's Bay Company from Fort Yukon (see page 173). In 1883 Lieutenant Frederick Schwatka, not long returned from his search for Franklin (see page 171), followed the Yukon from Chilkoot Pass, providing a survey of one of

the routes that would be followed by gold-seekers en route to the Klondike fourteen years later. Lieutenant Henry Allen made a significant exploration in 1885 up the Copper River, which flows to the Gulf of Alaska just east of Prince William Sound. He crossed from its watershed over to that of the Tanana, a tributary of the Yukon, and completed his journey down the Yukon to the sea.

But the new U.S. Geological Survey, under John Wesley Powell, eventually took over Alaskan exploration. The organization did not get involved in Alaska until the latter part of the 1890s, largely in response to mineral exploration and the 1897 Klondike gold rush and one at Nome a year or two later.

Another expedition of note was the private 1899 Harriman Alaska Expedition, in which railroad magnate Edward H. Harriman financed a shipload of scientists of every description who in relative comfort collected a vast number of natural history specimens, heightening public interest in this last remaining American frontier.

Attainment of the North Pole itself, rather than as a shortcut to the East, emerged as a goal of explorers only in the second half of the nineteenth century. Many of the pole-seekers used the Smith Sound to Robeson Channel route, the strait separating Greenland from Ellesmere Island, the northernmost large island of North America. As a result of these quests for the Pole, each expedition extended northwards the map of the Ellesmere coast.

Edward Inglefield, ostensibly searching for John Franklin, in 1852 reached 78° 28´, and parties from an 1854 expedition by American

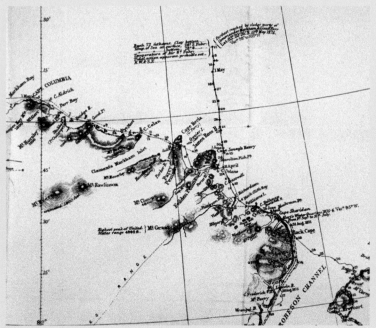

MAP 268.
This 1876 map from the Nares expedition shows the newly defined northeastern coast of Ellesmere Island as well as the tracks of the Pole attempt north over the ice and Pelham Aldrich's track west along the coast to Cape Columbia, the northernmost tip of the North American continent.

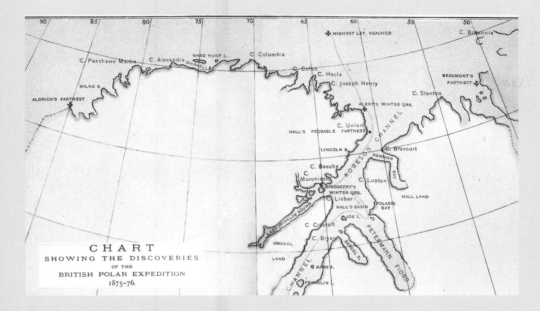

In one of the most harrowing of Arctic expeditions, an American scientific party led by Adolphus Washington Greely in 1881 set up an observatory at Fort Conger, on Discovery Bay, near the northeast tip of Ellesmere. While others sledged northwards, Greely explored the interior of the island, finding and naming the large Lake Hazen. The following year James Booth Lockwood, one of Greely's men, crossed Ellesmere and found a fiord on the west coast he named Greely Fiord. But the expedition's supply ship failed to arrive for the second season running, and in the summer of 1883 they

MAP 269 (*above*).
Map of the discoveries of the Nares expedition in 1876, from an 1877 book.

surgeon Elisha Kent Kane, the popular Victorian epitome of a dashing explorer, reached 80° 34´ and Kane became rich on the proceeds of his book. In turn his surgeon. Isaac Israel Hayes, attained about 80° in 1861. Charles Hall, who in 1861 had found evidence of Martin Frobisher and searched King William Island for evidence of Franklin in 1869 (see page 171), in 1871–73 made a considerable breakthrough due to relatively good ice conditions and reached Robeson Channel, at the entrance to the Arctic Ocean.

A British naval expedition in 1875–76, led by George Nares, reached the northern coast of Ellesmere Island—and the farthest north coast of North America—exploring and mapping it as well as making the first over-the-ice attempt on the Pole (MAP 268, *left*). As they had before, the British navy refused to use dogs to pull its sledges, and so teams of wretched sailors had to do the work instead. Despite sterling efforts, it was an inefficient way to travel and was too slow to be practical for a dash to the Pole. A sledge led by Lieutenant Pelham Aldrich slogged west along the north Ellesmere coast in 1876, achieving Cape Columbia, the northernmost point of North America, and continuing west again to Alert Point, the northwestern tip of the island. The Nares expedition may not have reached the Pole, but it defined the continent's northern edge.

MAP 270.
The discoveries of the Second Fram Expedition, led by Norwegian Otto Sverdrup in 1898–1902. *Axel Heiberg* [Is]*Land, Ellef Ringnes* [Is]*Land,* and *Amund Ringnes* [Is]*Land* were discovered by Sverdrup and all named after his sponsors. Ellesmere Island is the land at right. The map was drawn by Sverdrup's cartographer, Gunnerius Isachsen, and comes from the English edition of Sverdrup's book, published in 1904. The original map, sold to the Canadian government in 1930, is missing.

began an agonizing trek southwards. Seven of an original twenty-five men survived to be picked up by a relief ship; the rest succumbed to starvation or scurvy or, in one case, execution by the others for repeatedly stealing food.

In 1908–09 the Pole was claimed by both Frederick Cook and Robert Peary; there is, however, considerable doubt that either actually reached the Pole.

Over 100,000 square miles of new land were discovered by a Norwegian expedition that set out in 1898 and spent four years in the Arctic. This was the Second Fram Expedition of Otto Sverdrup, (the first being the famous drift of Fridtjof Nansen across the Arctic Ocean while stuck in the ice). The *Fram* ("Forward") was the ship and Sverdrup its captain. In 1898 he steamed into Jones Sound and found a harbor for his ship, and from this base he set out to the north and northwest. He explored and mapped the west coast of Ellesmere Island and found the huge Axel Heiberg Island and two other islands, Ellef Ringnes and Amund Ringnes Islands, all named after his financial backers, in the case of the Ringnes brothers, beer merchants; thus the names of brands of beer were added to those of gin (see page 166) in the North American Arctic.

Being its discoverer, Sverdrup naturally claimed the new territory for Norway, much to the chagrin of the British and Canadians; Canada had inherited British claims to the Arctic in 1880. Not until 1930 did the two countries work out an agreement: Norway

dropped its claims and in return Canada paid Sverdrup $67,000 for his "exploring services," as if he had been in the employ of the Canadian government at the time. By this fiction Canada reclaimed the North it thought it always had.

In response to Sverdrup's claims in 1903, the Canadian government immediately dispatched an Arctic patrol to ensure no further land was claimed. Geologist A. Peter Low led the first, and it was followed by a series of voyages beginning in 1906 by Joseph-Elzéar Bernier, who sailed around the Arctic Archipelago building cairns and conducting formal ceremonies of possession, just like in times of old.

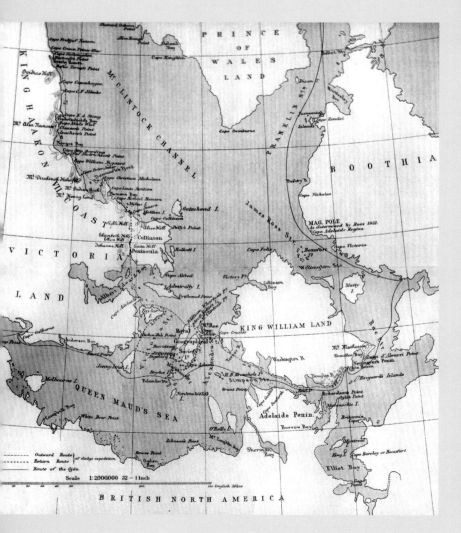

MAP 271 (*left*).
Roald Amundsen's map (English edition) showing the 1903 and 1905 routes of his ship *Gjøa* (solid red line) around the east and south of King William Island, the viable Northwest Passage that had eluded so many for so long. The dashed red line is the track of a sledge exploration of the northeast coast of *Victoria Land*, until that time unmapped and unexplored. *Gjøa Haven* is marked at the southeast corner of *King William* [Is]*Land*.

MAP 272 (*above*).
This map was originally produced in 1907, then reissued in 1909 with overprinting to show the supposed routes of Frederick Cook and Robert Peary to the North Pole. Yellow-colored coasts are those discovered by Otto Sverdrup.

In 1913, the Canadian government sponsored another, more elaborate Arctic expedition to carry out further exploration, mapping, and scientific studies. It was led by Vilhjalmur Stefansson. He left Victoria, British Columbia, in June on the *Karluk,* which by mid-August had become trapped in the ice north of Bering Strait. Stefansson left the ship and continued by sledge; the *Karluk* drifted and was crushed in the ice north of Siberia. Stefansson spent the next four years ranging far and wide by sledge and discovered more islands, this time for Canada (MAP 273, *right*).

Beginning in 1928, the Royal Canadian Mounted Police patrolled the Arctic, largely to protect Canadian sovereignty. In 1940, police officer Henry Larson took the *St. Roch* through the Northwest Passage from west to east, reaching Halifax in 1942. Two years later Larson returned west, and the *St. Roch* became the first ship to sail through the Northwest Passage in both directions. Later still, in 1950, after passing through the Panama Canal, the ship became the first to circumnavigate North America.

From the 1920s, aircraft started to become reliable enough to fly in the Arctic. They were, of course, the ideal exploration vehicle. Yet it was not until after the Second World War that the last land of significant size was found in the Arctic. On 28 July 1948 E. C. (Al) Kerslake, captain of a Royal Canadian Air Force Lancaster of 413 (Photo) Squadron, flying out of Frobisher Bay, found a large island in the Foxe Basin, comparatively far south. A few days later two more islands were found. The large island, twice the size of the state of Delaware, was named Prince Charles Island, after the British Queen's newborn son; Foley Island, after the plane's second navigator, who was killed in a plane crash shortly afterwards; and Air Force Island, after the plane's "sponsor." Some things hadn't changed! With the advent of aerial reconnaissance the age of geographical exploration in North America was essentially over.

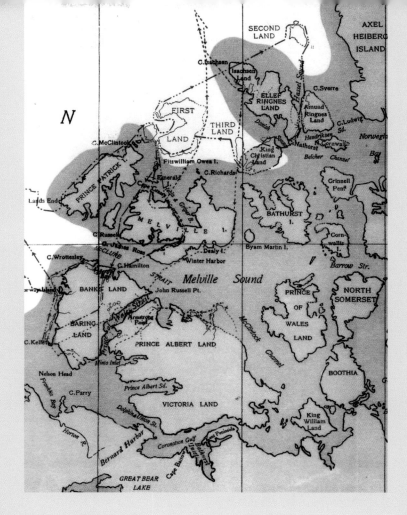

MAP 273 (*above*).
Part of a summary map showing the tracks (red lines) of Vilhjalmur Stefansson from 1914 to 1917. The long dashes with one dot represent 1914; those with two dots, 1915; and those with three, 1916, with short dashes only representing 1917. *First Land* is a combination of Borden Island and Mackenzie King Island, with Brock Island (unnamed) to their west. *Second Land* is Meighen Island, likely the land seen by Frederick Cook in 1908. *Third Land* is Lougheed Island, in reality an island rather than a peninsula.

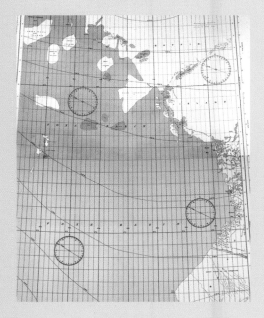

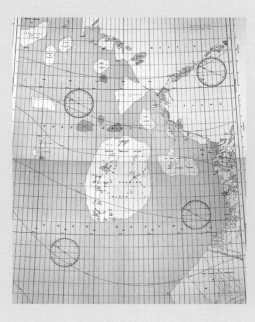

MAP 274 (*above, left*) and MAP 275 (*above, middle*).
The last major land to be discovered in North America, Prince Charles Island, with Foley Island and Air Force Island, are not on the 1946 map (MAP 274) of the Foxe Basin but appear on the 1949 one (MAP 275). The land to the right on both maps is southeast Baffin Island. The aerial photograph at *right* is a view of Gravell Point, the southern tip of Prince Charles Island, taken by a Canadian Air Force plane on 21 August 1949, the year after the discovery of the island.

An Ongoing Frontier

What is left to explore? In a purely geographical sense, not much after the advent of the satellite, but satellites can see in different wavelengths from the human eye and are thus able to detect details a mere mortal would miss. And the definition of North America itself expanded in the 1980s to include national claims to a zone two hundred miles from the coast, the 200-mile Exclusive Economic Zone. Here, in the twentieth century, was territory still unknown ready to be explored.

The United States, and to a lesser extent Canada, embarked on a program to map the new extension of their jurisdiction. They were aided by the development of a new technique called multibeam bathymetry. Sonar had first been used by the U.S. Navy in 1922 and was a tremendous jump in the ability to investigate the sea bottom, a quantum leap in speed over the sounding line used before. Then sonar was mounted on a sled towed behind a ship at some depth. This method, called side-scan sonar, scanned the seabed obliquely and enabled the production of detailed topographical maps. An extension of this arrangement uses multiple sonar devices that overlap and, just like stereoscopic photography, allows the creation of large-scale three-dimensional views of the seabed. And so, with the creation of the 200-mile Exclusive Economic Zone, the tools were in place to explore this new land under the sea. The computers and software used to analyze the wealth of new data grew, so that early maps of the seabed such as MAP 276, essentially a series of cross-sections considered state-of-the-art at the time, have been replaced by three-dimensional views either vertical or oblique (MAP 277 and MAP 278). From these, conventional contour maps of the seafloor can be generated (MAP 279).

Such seafloor mapping now utilizes the satellite-based Global Positioning System (GPS) to determine the exact location of every scan, and geo-referenced high-resolution bathymetric and side-scan data can be collected a high speeds, thus enabling coverage of a large area. What would our explorers of old have given for a handheld GPS!

But then, what trouble could so many of them have been saved if they had just had a satellite view of their terrain? The LANDSAT remote sensing satellites, of which there have been seven (the first was launched in 1972), fly over the same area of the Earth's surface every sixteen days, relaying their data to a ground station at Sioux Falls, South Dakota. This provides a valuable regular sequence of views that can be used to record changes over time, and has applications in geology, agriculture, forestry, regional planning, and even national security. Thus we have replaced the explorer's one-time experience with a regularly updated record. Yet still scientists are needed to interpret the onslaught of data such a system provides, and in a real sense they are now the explorers. It is just that their tools and their methods have changed.

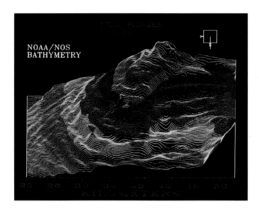

MAP 276 (*above*).
An early three-dimensional map of a section of the seabed, an undersea ridge near Pioneer Seamount, about fifty miles off the coast from San Francisco. The map was created in 1989 as part of the NOAA Exclusive Economic Zone Mapping Project. Turbidity currents pass out from nearby undersea Pioneer Canyon, strike this ridge, and are deflected; huge dune structures are formed, extending many miles to the south. Increased computer sophistication has now allowed better visualization of undersea topography.

MAP 277 (*below*).
A 1998 three-dimensional view, created using multibeam bathymetry, of the Pioneer Seamount. It rises about 6,300 ft from the 9,000 ft deep seafloor and is about 8 miles in diameter.

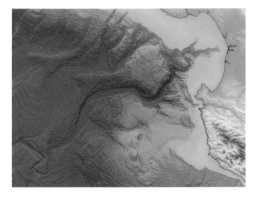

MAP 278 (*above, top*) and MAP 279 (*above*).
A multibeam image of the Monterey Canyon, which extends from Monterey Bay (top right on both images) out to sea, and a detailed contour map created from the data. The multibeam produces a stunningly detailed map of an area that may never have been explored personally by humans.

Map 280.

A stunning LandSat satellite image of the northeastern part of the United States and part of eastern Canada. It is a composite of six separate images that have been orthorectified, that is, adjusted to look as if the view was directly down to Earth at 90° to a tangent over every point on the surface, making it exactly like a modern map. More clearly than most maps, the image illustrates the pathways to the interior and the mountain barriers in the way. Prominent rivers penetrating far inland include, from north to south, the Hudson, Delaware, Susquehanna, Potomac, and Roanoke, while the St. Lawrence flows from Lake Ontario at top.

LandSat has been a succession of seven satellites, the first of which was launched in 1972 and the seventh in 1999. Purple areas are urbanized, pink have much bare rock, and vegetated areas are green. The image is artificially colored based on the specific wavelengths received by the satellite. The image was taken between 1989 and 1993.

Map Catalog

Common Map Source Codes

AGI	Archivo General des Indias, Seville, Spain
BL	British Library
BNF	Bibliothèque nationale de France, Paris
LAC	Library and Archives of Canada, Ottawa
LC	Library of Congress
NARA	National Archives, U.S.
NYPL	New York Public Library
SHM	Service historique de la marine, Vincennes, France
TNA	The National Archives (formerly the Public Record Office), U.K.

All other source names are not abbreviated. Maps with no source indicated are from private collections.

MAP 1 (title pages)
A Map Exhibiting all the New Discoveries in the Interior Parts of North America
Aaron Arrowsmith, 1802
LC: G3300 1802 A7 Vault Casetop

MAP 2 (page 4)
A New & Correct Map of the Whole World
Herman Moll, 1719
LC: G3200 1719 .M6 TIL Vault

MAP 3 (page 6)
America Sive Quartae Orbis Partis Nova et Exactissima Descriptio
Diego Gutierrez, 1564
LC: G3290 1562 .G7 Vault Oversize

MAP 4 (page 7)
Map of the United States showing Routes of the Principal Explorers from 1504 to 1844
Frank Bond, 1907
LC: G3701.S12 1907 .B58 TIL

MAP 5 (page 8)
Siurdi Stephanii terrarum hyperborearu delineatio Ano 1570
Sigurdur Stefánsson, 1670, copy of a 1590 map
Danish Royal Library: gl. kgl. saml. 2881 4° (10v)

MAP 6 (page 9)
Gronlandia Iona Gudmundi Islandi
Jón Gudmonson, c1640
Danish Royal Library: gl. kgl. saml. 2881 4° (11R)

MAP 7 (page 9)
Vinland Map, 1440 (claimed)
Beinecke Library, Yale University

MAP 8 (page 10)
Geographische Vorstelling eines Globi. welchen Anno 1492. Herr Martin Behaim
Johan Doppelmayr copy of Behaim globe, 1730
Nordenskiöld, *Facsimile Atlas*, 1889

MAP 9 (page 11)
[Part of a world map known as the Cantino planisphere]
Anon., 1502
Bibliotheca Estense, Modena, Italy
(Su concessione de Ministero per i Beni e le Attività Culturali)

MAP 10 (page 11)
[Part of a world map]
Bartolommeo Columbus, c.1503

MAP 11 (page 12)
[Part of a world map known as the Cantino planisphere]
Anon., 1502
Bibliotheca Estense, Modena, Italy
(Su concessione de Ministero per i Beni e le Attività Culturali)

MAP 12 (page 13)
Universalior Cogniti Orbis Tabula Ex Recentibus Confecta Observationibus
Johann Ruysch, c.1507
LAC: NMC 19268

MAP 13 (page 13)
[Northeastern coastal detail of world map]
Juan de la Cosa, c.1500
Museo Naval

MAP 14 (page 14)
[Map of the Gulf of Mexico]
Alonzo Alvarez de Pineda, 1519
AGI

MAP 15 (page 15)
[Ponce de León and part of Florida]
From: A. Herrera y Tordesillas, *Historia General*, 1728

MAP 16 (page 15)
[Map of the Gulf of Mexico]
Peter Martyr, 1511
Nordenskiöld, *Facsimile Atlas*, 1889

MAP 17 (page 15)
Tabula Oceani Occidentalis Seu Terræ Novæ
Nordenskiöld, *Facsimile Atlas*, 1889

MAP 18 (page 16)
[Part of a world map]
Juan Vespucci, 1526
Hispanic Society of America, New York

MAP 19 (page 17)
[Part of a map of North America and the Caribbean]
Jean Rotz, 1534 or 1535
From: *Boke of Idrography*
BL: Royal 20.E.IX, ff. 23 verso

MAP 20 (page 17)
[Part of a world map]
Diogo Ribiero, 1529
Bibliotheca Apostolica Vaticana, Vatican City

MAP 21 (page 19)
Illustri Viro, Domino Philippo Sidnaes Michael Lok Civis Londinensis Hanc Chartam Dedicabat: 1582
Michael Lok, 1582
From: *Divers Voyages touching the Discoverie of America*, Richard Hakluyt, London, 1582

MAP 22 (pages 18–19)
[Part of a world map]
Girolamo Verrazano, 1529
Bibliotheca Apostolica Vaticana, Vatican City

MAP 23 (pages 20–21)
[Southern North America, part of a page from an atlas]
Battista Agnese, 1544
LC: G1001 .A4 1544

MAP 24 (page 22)
[Mapa del Golfo y costa de la Nueva España desde el Rio de Panuco hasta el cabo de Santa Elena]
Alonzo de Santa Cruz, c.1544
LC: G3860 1572 .S3 Vault

MAP 25 (page 23)
[Map of California, Japan, and the Pacific]
Joan Martines, 1578
BL: Harley MS 3450, Map 10 in atlas

MAP 26 (page 23)
La Florida auctore Hieron. Chiaues.
Abraham Ortelius, 1584
From: *Theatrum Orbis Terrarum*
LC: G3290 1584 .O7 Vault

MAP 27 (page 24)
[Map of Baja California and adjacent coast of Mexico]
Hernan Cortés, 1535
AGI

MAP 28 (page 24)
Tartariae Sive Magni Chami Regni
Abraham Ortelius, 1570
From: *Theatrum Orbis Terrarum*
LC: G7270 1570 .O7 Vault

MAP 29 (page 25)
Universale Descrittione di tutta la terra conosciuta fin qui
Paolo Forlani, c.1562
LC: G3200 1565 .F6 Vault

MAP 30 (pages 26–27)
[Part of a map of North America and the Caribbean]
Jean Rotz, 1534 or 1535
From: *Boke of Idrography*,
BL: Royal 20.E.IX, ff. 23 verso

MAP 31 (page 27)
La Terra de Hochelaga Nella Nova Francia
Giacomo Gastaldi, 1556
LAC: NMC 116744

MAP 32 (pages 28–29)
[Map of part of eastern North America, known as the Vallard map]
Anon., for or by Nicolas Vallard, 1547
Huntington Library, San Marino, CA

MAP 33 (page 29)
[Map of the Gulf of St. Lawrence]
Jean Alfonce, c.1544
From: *La Cosmographie*
BNF: MS français No. 676

Map 34 (page 30)
The Promontory of Florida, at which the French touched, named by them the French Promontary
Drawing by Jacques Le Moyne,
engraved by Theodor De Bry
From: Theodor De Bry, *America*, Part 2, Plate 1, 1591

MAP 182 (page 133)
*A Map shewing the communication of the Lakes
and the Rivers between Lake Superior and Slave Lake
in North America*
From: *Gentleman's Magazine,* March 1790

MAP 183 (page 134)
"Chart called Mackenzie's Map, illustrative of his tract
from Athabasca Lake down Mackenzie River to the
North Sea"
Anon. (Alexander Mackenzie), c.1789
TNA: CO 700 America North and South 54

MAP 184 (page 135)
*A Map of America between Latitudes 40° & 70° North and
Longitudes 40° & 180° West Exhibiting Mackenzie's Track
From Montreal to Fort Chipewyan & from thence to the
North Sea in 1789, & to the North Pacific Ocean in 1793.*
Anon. (Aaron Arrowsmith [?]/David Thompson/
Alexander Mackenzie), c.1800
TNA: CO 700 Canada 59A

MAP 185 (page 136)
[Great Slave Lake to Hudson Bay]
Shew-ditha-da, copied by Philip Turnor, 1791
HBCA: B9/a/3, page 83

MAP 186 (page 136)
*Chart of Lakes and Rivers in North America
by Philip Turnor those Shaded are from Actual Survey's
the others from Canadian and Indian information*
Philip Turnor, 1792
HBCA: G2/13

MAP 187 (page 137)
[Map of western Canada and the United States, showing
the rivers draining from the Rocky Mountains]
*Drawn by the Feathers or ac ko mok ki a Blackfoot chief
7 Feby. 1801*
Ac ko mok ki, copied by Peter Fidler, 1801
HBCA: E3/2 folios 106 verso - 107

MAP 188 (page 137)
*A Map Exhibiting all the New Discoveries
in the Interior Parts of North America*
Aaron Arrowsmith, 1802
LC: G3300 1802 A7 Vault Casetop

MAP 189 (page 138)
*The United States of North America, with the British
& Spanish Territories According to the Treaty of 1784*
William Faden, 1785
LC: 3700 1784 .F21 Vault

MAP 190 (page 138)
[Map of the Missouri River from Saint Charles
to the Mandan villages of North Dakota]
Nicolas de Finiels, 1797 or 1798
LC: G4127 .M5 1798 .F5 Vault Oversize

MAP 191 (page 139)
Idée topographique de Hauts du Mississipi et de Missouri
Antoine Soulard, 1795 (French copy)
SHM: Recueil 69 No. 37

MAP 192 (page 139)
[Bend of the Missouri River]
David Thompson, 1798
LC: G4127.M5 1798 B4 TIL Vault

MAP 193 (page 140)
[Sketch map of the Missouri west of the Mandan villages,
derived from Indian sources]
John Evans, 1796–97
Beinecke Library, Yale University

MAP 194 (page 140)
[Map of the Missouri River, the Rocky Mountains,
and the Pacific Coast]
Nicholas King, c.1803
LC: 4126.S12 1803 .K5 TIL Vault

MAP 195 (page 141)
Louisiana
Samuel Lewis, 1804
From: *A New and Elegant General Atlas,* Samuel Lewis
and Aaron Arrowsmith, 1804

MAP 196 (page 141)
A Map of Part of the Continent of North America
(composite of several William Clark maps)
Nicholas King, 1805
LC: G3300 1805 .C5 Vault Oversize

MAP 197 (page 142)
Draught of the Falls and Portage [of the Missouri]
William Clark, 1805
American Philosophical Society,
Clark Journal, Codex E: 132–133

MAP 198 (page 143)
[Sketch map of the mouth of the Columbia River]
William Clark, 1806
Beinecke Library, Yale University

MAP 199 (page 144)
A Map of part of the Continent of North America
William Clark, 1810
Beinecke Library, Yale University

MAP 200 (page 145)
*A Map of Lewis & Clark's Track, Across the
Western Portion of North America from
the Mississippi to the Pacific Ocean*
William Clark, engraved by Samuel Lewis, 1814
From: *Meriwether Lewis, A History of the Expedition
under the Comands of Captains Lewis and Clark,* 1814

MAP 201 (page 146)
*Map of the Red River in Louisiana from the Spanish Camp
where the exploring party of the U.S. was met by the
Spanish troops to where it enters the Mississippi*
Nicholas King, 1806
LC: G3993.R4 1806 K5 Vault

MAP 202 (page 146)
General Chart of the Kingdom of New Spain
Alexander von Humboldt, 1804
LC: G4410 1804 .H8 Vault

MAP 203 (page 147)
*The First Part of Captn. Pike's Chart of the Internal
Part of Louisiana*
Zebulon Pike, 1810
From: *Atlas accompanying an Account of Expeditions
to the Sources of the Mississippi and through the Western
Parts of Louisiana to the Sources of the Arkansas, Kans,
La Platte, and Pierre Jaun Rivers,* 1810

MAP 204 (page 148)
*Map of the United States of America with the
Contiguous British and Spanish Possessions*
John Melish, 1816
LC: G3700 1816 M4f Mel

MAP 205 (page 149)
A Chart of the Internal Part of Louisiana
Zebulon Pike, 1810
From: *Atlas accompanying an Account of Expeditions
to the Sources of the Mississippi and through the Western
Parts of Louisiana to the Sources of the Arkansas, Kans,
La Platte, and Pierre Jaun Rivers,* 1810

MAP 206 (page 150)
[Map of the route to Santa Fe]
Joseph C. Brown, 1825
LC: G4052.S3 1825 .B7 TIL Vault

MAP 207 (page 151)
*Map of the Country Situated between the Meridian of
Washington City and the Rocky Mountains exhibiting
the route of the late Exploring Expedition commanded
by Maj. Long*
Stephen Long, 1820 or 1821
NARA: RG77, US Series CWMF, 1 of 2, 2 of 2 (in two parts)

MAP 208 (page 152)
[Map of the "Upper Yellowstone Country"]
George Drouillard, c.1808
LC: Lewis and Clark Collection "L",
Geography and Map Division

MAP 209 (page 153)
*Map of the United States of America with the
Contiguous British and Spanish Possessions*
John Melish, 1816
LC: G3700 1816 M4f Mel

MAP 210 (page 154)
Routes of Hunt and Stuart
From: Washington Irving, *Astoria,* 1836

MAP 211 (page 155)
*Map of the North-West Territory of the Province of
Canada from actual survey during the years 1782 to 1812*
David Thompson, 1814
Archives of Ontario: AO 1541

MAP 212 (pages 156–57)
[Map of the Columbia River Basin]
Alexander Ross, 1821 and 1849
BL: Add. MS 31,358 B

MAP 213 (page 158)
[Map of the Snake River country]
William Kittson, 1825
HBCA: B202/a/3b

MAP 214 (page 159)
P. S. Ogdens Camp Track 1829
Peter Skene Ogden, 1829
HBCA: B202/a/8, fo. 1

MAP 215 (page 160)
*Map of North America including all the recent
geographical discoveries*
D. H. Vance, 1826
From: A. Finlay, *A New American Atlas,* 1826

MAP 216 (page 161)
*Map of the United States of North America
with parts of the adjacent countries*
David H. Burr, 1839
From: J. Arrowsmith, *The American Atlas,* 1829

MAP 217 (page 162)
[Map of the northern part of North America]
Vasilli Berkh, 1821
A.V. Efimov, 1964

Select Bibliography

Adams, Alexander B.
The Disputed Lands: A History of the American West
G. P. Putnam's Sons, New York, 1981

Amundsen, Roald E. G.
*Roald Amundsen's "The North West Passage"; Being the Record
of a Voyage of Exploration of the Ship "Gjoa" 1903–1907*
A. Constable, London, 1908

Bray, Martha Coleman
Joseph Nicollet and His Map
The American Philosophical Society, Philadelphia, 1980

Carver, Jonathan,
Travels Through the Interior Parts of North-America in the Years 1766, 1767, and 1768
Printed for the author, London, 1778

Cumming, W. P., R. A. Skelton, and D. B. Quinn
The Discovery of North America
American Heritage Press, New York, 1972

Cumming, W. P., S. E. Hillier, D. B. Quinn, and G. Williams
The Exploration of North America, 1630–1776
G. P. Putnam's Sons, New York, 1974

DeVoto, Bernard
The Course of Empire
Mariner/Houghton Mifflin, New York, 1998 (original edition 1952)

Dolnick, Edward
*Down the Great Unknown: John Wesley Powell's 1869 Journey of Discovery
and Tragedy Through the Grand Canyon*
Harper Collins, New York, 2001

Dunbar, Moira, and Keith Greenaway
Arctic Canada from the Air
Canada Defence Research Board, Ottawa, 1956

Efimov, A. V. (ed.)
Atlas geograficheskikh v Sibiri i severo-zapadnoy Amerike XVII–XVIII vv.
[Atlas of geographical discoveries in Siberia and northwestern America
in the 17th–18th centuries]
Nauka, Moscow, 1964

Fairley, T. C.
Sverdrup's Arctic Adventures
Longmans, London, 1959

Foss, Michael
Undreamed Shores: England's Wasted Empire in America
Phoenix Press, London, 2000

Goetzmann, William H.
Army Exploration in the American West, 1803–1863
Yale University Press, New Haven, 1959

Goetzmann, William H.
*Exploration and Empire: The Explorer and the Scientist
in the Winning of the American West*
Texas State Historical Association, Austin, 2000 (original edition 1966)

Goetzmann, William H., and Glyndwr Williams
*The Atlas of North American Exploration:
From the Norse Voyages to the Race to the Pole*
Prentice Hall, New York, 1992

Golay, Michael, and John S. Bowman
North American Exploration
Wiley, Hoboken, NJ, 2003

Hayes, Derek
Historical Atlas of the Pacific Northwest
Sasquatch Books, Seattle, 1999

Hayes, Derek
*First Crossing: Alexander Mackenzie, His Expedition Across North America,
and the Opening of the Continent*
Douglas & McIntyre, Vancouver, BC, 2001

Hayes, Derek
Historical Atlas of the North Pacific Ocean
Douglas & McIntyre, Vancouver, BC, 2001

Hayes, Derek
Historical Atlas of Canada: Canada's History Illustrated with Original Maps
Douglas & McIntyre, Vancouver, BC/University of Washington Press, Seattle, 2002

Hayes, Derek
Historical Atlas of the Arctic
Douglas & McIntyre, Vancouver, BC/University of Washington Press, Seattle, 2003

Irving, Washington
The Adventures of Captain Bonneville in the Rocky Mountains and the Far West
Edgeley W. Todd (ed.), University of Oklahoma Press, Norman, 1961

Johnson, Adrian
America Explored
Viking, New York, 1974

Luebke, Frederick C., Frances W. Kaye, and Gary E. Moulton (eds.)
Mapping the North American Plains: Essays in the History of Cartography
University of Oklahoma Press, Norman, with the Center for Great Plains Studies,
University of Nebraska, Lincoln, 1987

Norall, Frank
Bourgmont, Explorer of the Missouri, 1698–1725
University of Nebraska Press, Lincoln, 1988

Rich, E. E.
The History of the Hudson's Bay Company, 1670–1870 (2 volumes)
Hudson's Bay Record Society, London, 1958

Rollins, Philip Ashton (ed.)
*The Discovery of the Oregon Trail: Robert Stuart's Narratives
of His Overland Trip Eastward from Astoria in 1812–13*
University of Nebraska Press, Lincoln, 1995 (original edition 1935)

Ronda, James P.
Astoria and Empire
University of Nebraska Press, Lincoln, 1990

Ronda, James P.
Revealing America: Image and Imagination in the Exploration of North America
D. C. Heath, Lexington, MA, 1996

Ronda, James P.
Beyond Lewis & Clark: The Army Explores the West
Washington State Historical Society, Tacoma, 2003

Sherwood, Morgan B.
Exploration of Alaska, 1865–1900
Yale University Press, New Haven, 1965

Sverdrup, Otto
New Land: Four Years in the Arctic Regions
Longmans Green, London, 1904

Williams, Glyndwr (ed.)
Peter Skene Ogden's Snake Country Journals, 1827–28 and 1828–29
Hudson's Bay Record Society, London, 1971

Index